Liberty, Equality, and Justice

Duke University Press   Durham & London 1997

Liberty, Equality, and Justice

Civil Rights, Women's Rights, and the Regulation
of Business 1865–1932

Ross Evans Paulson

© 1997 Duke University Press
All rights reserved
Printed in the United States of America
on acid-free paper ∞
Designed by Katy Giebenhain
Typeset in Aldus by Keystone Typesetting, Inc.
Library of Congress Cataloging-in-Publication Data appear
on the last printed page of this book.

Contents

Preface

In any project spanning a decade, one encounters many obligations to individuals and institutions. I began writing this book during a sabbatical leave in the spring term 1988–89. I am indebted to the Faculty Research Committee of Augustana College, to Thomas Tredway, president, and Harold Sundelius, dean of the college, and to Van Symons, chairman of the history department, for their support. Over the numerous versions and revisions of the manuscript, I am especially grateful to Stanley I. Kutler, University of Wisconsin-Madison; Nancy A. Hewitt, Duke University; Peter Kivisto, Nancy Huse, David Dehnel, and Bradley Levinson of Augustana College; Stacy A. Cordery of Monmouth College; and Paul Salstrom of St. Mary of the Woods College. Numerous individuals read a portion of the manuscript and made helpful comments: David Crowe, Tamara Felden, Demetrius Johnson, Ellie Beach, Richard Ballman, John Hildreth, Debra Hartley, Neeco McKinley, Angela Troy, and James Winship. For special assistance in research I wish to thank my protégée, Jane Tiedge, and Ron Tiedge, and the Augustana College library staff: Barbara Doyle-Wilch, John Pollitz, Loretta McKamey, Lesley Meier, Sherrie Herbst, Marian Miller, Carla Tracy, Sue William, Judith Belan and Carrie Ferm. Student assistants Martha Hanson, Paul Kieffer, Sean Heidgerken, Maria Curcuru, and Nate Roe labored valiantly to check quotations and secure library resources. For typing the numerous versions of the manuscript history should record the diligent efforts of Maria Diaz and Jane Tiedge. For editorial help by Duke University Press I am indebted to Rachel Toor, Valerie Millholland, Richard Morrison, and the anonymous reviewers of the various drafts. A special thanks to my daughters, Linnea Anderson and Lisa Paulson, for encouragement and comments on feminism and history and to my wife, Avis Paulson, for surfing the internet in search of sources and putting up with the project for ten years. I alone am responsible in the end for any inadvertent errors or shortcomings that may be found in the book.

Liberty, Equality, and Justice

Introduction

"Unlike many other peoples, Americans are not bound together by a common religion or a common ethnicity. Instead, our binding heritage is a democratic vision of liberty, equality, and justice. If Americans are to preserve that vision and bring it to daily practice, it is imperative that all citizens understand how it was shaped in the past, what events and forces either helped or obstructed it, and how it has evolved down to the circumstances and political discourse of our time."
—The Bradley Commission on History in Schools

This quotation, from a prestigious panel of experts, sets forth a compelling rationale for the study of American history in our schools and for public discussion of the basis of citizenship.[1] I have no disagreement with the goal of the commission's report; but, as I will show in this book, the attempt to create such a "binding heritage" based on "a democratic vision of liberty, equality, and justice" has been a more problematic endeavor than this quotation assumes. In particular, this book will argue that, during the period of 1865 to 1932, the history of the attempt to achieve civil rights, women's rights, and the regulation of business was, for the most part, a story of failure. Yes, there were victories and some notable achievements by the heroic pioneers of these three social movements: (1) the enactment of the Civil Rights Act of 1866 and the adoption of the Fourteenth and Fifteenth Amendments to the Constitution; (2) the creation of women's organizations, the achievement of woman suffrage, and the passage of protective welfare legislation for women and children; and (3) the enactment of the Granger laws to regulate railroads, the creation of the Interstate Commerce Commission and the Federal Trade Commission, and the passage of such laws as the Sherman Antitrust Act and the Clayton Act. The thesis of this book, however, is that the failures and disappointments of these three social movements stemmed primarily from the fact that so many Americans ranked liberty (for themselves) higher than equality (with others) and justice (for all).

As a success-oriented culture, we Americans have had a difficult time dealing with failure. Periodically, we have either ignored or conveniently forgotten crucial aspects of our collective shortcomings. Like the story of Prohibition, another of our historic failures, we have turned the memory of these events into a series of cultural icons and have isolated them from their historical contexts. It is necessary, therefore, to return to these controversies and long-forgotten incidents in our history for two main reasons. First, because they represent perennial problems in our society. Second, because they illustrate significant dimensions of the core values mentioned in the Bradley report—liberty, equality, and justice—and the complex interactions between them.

Why are these core values so unfamiliar in their historical meanings? Part of the burden of responsibility must fall on historians, political theorists, and social scientists. Some of the professionals who experienced the shock of the Great Depression ended up suspicious of the word "liberty." After all, it had been used by conservative courts in the "liberty of contract" doctrine to oppose New Deal legislation, it had been inculcated by Hoover in his attacks on the New Deal, and it had been institutionalized in the name of an anti-New Deal coalition, the Liberty League. During World War II and after, "liberty" became part of the wartime propaganda and Cold War rhetoric and an element in the litany of conservative anti-communism. At the same time, the civil rights protests in the 1940s, and court cases in the 1950s, seared the words "equality" and "justice" into public and professional consciousness. When historians and political scientists returned to the past to find answers for the questions and public policy concerns prompted by the events of the 1950s–60s, they tended to take this ranking of core values with them. They found plenty of references to equality and justice in the past record but tended to overlook or downplay references to liberty. The result was that they did not always find that past behavior, particularly political behavior, conformed to their expectations about the priority of certain core values. What was wrong? A younger generation of historians and political scientists espoused monocausal interpretations, radical explanations, or focused on hegemonic elites to claim that America was simply, or primarily, "racist," "sexist," or "statist." But these interpretations were not totally satisfactory.[2]

The participants in the civil rights, women's liberation, and consumers' rights movements in the 1950s–70s were largely unaware of the continuities and similarities between their efforts and those of the past. "Each generation of black dissenters," historian Steven F. Lawson has noted in summarizing a 1976 essay by August Meier and Elliot Rudwick, "acted in response to current situations without drawing on history for guidance." Betty Friedan's influential book that launched the modern women's liberation movement, *The Feminine Mystique* (1963), began as a survey of the experiences of her Smith College classmates fifteen years after their graduation. A chapter entitled "The Passionate Journey" summarized the available scholarship on women's history but projected the currently fashionable psychological concept of the "identity crisis" back onto the pioneers of the earlier women's movement. For the activists, writers, and anthology compilers who followed Friedan's lead, the past was seen primarily as a burden to be shed, not a legacy to be shared. If they did acknowledge a "useable past," it was as a warning against past mistakes that ought not to be repeated in the present.[3]

A parallel perceptual bias beset the consumers' rights movement of the 1960s. Whether dated from President Kennedy's special message on consumer affairs in 1962 or the publication of Ralph Nader's *Unsafe at Any Speed: The Designed-In Dangers of the American Automobile* in 1965, one thing was clear. The student interns, dubbed "Nader's Raiders," who spent a summer reading government documents and writing reports, and the young "legal eagles," who won precedent-setting product liability suits, tended to focus on current controversies and recent trends. Furthermore, Nader's creation of the Center for the Study of Responsible Law (1968), the Project on Corporate Responsibility (1969), the Center for Auto Safety (1970), and the Public Interest Research Group (1970) institutionalized these tendencies. Even the conservative counterattack on consumer regulations, ecological protection laws, and workplace safety standards shared the same present-oriented focus and preference for statistical data, trend analysis, and macroeconomic models.[4]

How, then, can we overcome our collective memory lapses as a society, compensate for the tendency of social activists or their followers to emphasize immediate experience, and challenge the reliance on present-oriented social science methods in dealing with our social conflicts? How can students of history avoid imposing current ideological terms on past controversies? We can begin by asking some basic questions about the past. What did the advocates *at the time* think that they were doing? What were their values? What roles did they seek to play in institutions and social movements? Did institutions help or hinder their efforts? How did language either reveal or conceal their values? What similarities exist between their past endeavors and our present dilemmas? What cultural differences shaped their sense of strategies and tactics compared to ours? This introduction will outline the historical methodology used in this he might have left Europe a socialist (or a social democrat) and became in America a capitalist of sorts.[7]

For a woman immigrant in the late nineteenth century the experience might have been even more complex, as participation in some of the "Americanizing" institutions—the political party or the corner saloon, for example—was closed to her. But, more subtle avenues might be open to her, such as work as a servant in a middle-class home, contact with a settlement house worker, longer enrollment in public education, or work in "sweat shops," mills, and retail establishments. In any case, the point is that the core values of a society are neither experienced identically by men and women nor are they unitary in the responses they elicit from people.[8]

A Four-Part Response Model

Individuals are not merely the passive recipients of the end-products of these cultural processes; rather, they are active participants in them.[9] To illustrate this generalization, consider the following situation. All your life you have been taught to believe that your nation or community embodies certain core values—liberty, equality, democracy, "fair play," or "justice for all." Suddenly a traumatic event, a sequence of seemingly inconsequential experiences, or a set of facts encountered in the media bring you up short. The facts (the *description* of what "is" the case) do not match up with the core values (the *prescriptions* of what "ought to be" the case). You search for further information or instances of similar experiences among friends or colleagues and in books, articles, videos, and films. You feel a growing sense of unease, frustration, and insecurity. You have come to the *perception* that there is something fundamentally wrong in the current situation: the *practices* of your society do not measure up to its *profession* of adherence to these core values. The gap between them seems intolerable not simply in *individual* terms ("I can't stand it anymore!") but also in *institutional* terms ("The constitutional system is in jeopardy!"). What should you do?

In such a situation, there are four logically possible (and socially prevalent) options: (1) you can *rationalize* the gap as inevitable, see the erosion of one value as tolerable for the sake of the preservation of others, and opt to *retain* the familiar status quo as preferable to any unfamiliar alternative; (2) you can attempt to *return* to some past situation (or an imagined variant of it) in order to temporarily *restore* the balance between the "is" and the "ought" by ritual activity; (3) you can attempt to *reform* the situation by an idea and a strategy of change and thus *realign* the balance between the "is" and the "ought," perhaps redefining or reordering the priority of the core values in the process; or, (4) you can *renounce* the current core values as hypocritical in light of the seemingly persistent gap between the "is" and the "ought," propose alternate core values (or under-standings of them), plan strategies of action, and envision new institu-tional arrangements to *replace* the current system (or put in a new foun-dation). We may, for brevity, call these four options by the following titles: (1) resignation, (2) ritual withdrawal and renewal, (3) reform, and (4) radicalism.[10]

Resignation: Life as Routine

This option calls to mind the famous aphorism of Henry David Thoreau: "The mass of men lead lives of quiet desperation." As long as historians were enthralled by "Great Men" or "Outstanding Women" frameworks for history and relied primarily on public documents or published letters of "eminent persons," they had difficulty keeping in focus the great mass of the people in any society who lead ordinary, routine, obedient lives. Their lives change slowly, if at all. Confronted with the gap between the practices and professed values of their society, they may shrug their shoulders, sigh a bit over the status of affairs, and quote some familiar folk saying to rationalize their acquiescence in the status quo. "That's just the way it is," they say. "You can't fight city hall."

Social historians have devised new techniques to use available histor-ical sources—tax rolls, census data, oral memories, genealogies, payroll records, everyday objects, diaries, letters, rituals, novels, newspapers, films, floor plans, and fashions—to recreate the collective lives of these "anonymous Americans." Studies of history seen "from the bottom up" show that such groups are far from passive and unimportant in the great dramas of history. Like the chorus in a Greek tragedy, they may embody the folk wisdom or "moral economy" of the community. Like the crowd at a fair, political rally, or circus, their attention must be wooed and won by the leading actors on the stage. Those who accept the status quo are, in some sense, the "grand jury" that reformers and radicals must cajole into accepting, or at least tolerating, the innovations carried out in the name of the society's institutional core values or a revolutionary set of alternative ones.[11]

Ritual: Life as Periodic Withdrawal and Renewal

Anthropologists describing the life of premodern, tribal societies have long noted the phenomena of "rites of passage." At set times in the life cycle the tribal member would be separated from the daily routine and social structure, initiated into a temporary group or cohort through rituals (in which normal roles are symbolically reversed), instructed in the core values appropriate to their new social roles, and then readmitted to the tribal society. Such temporary groups or cohorts are called "liminal." The rituals involved are seen as "creative" as well as "recreative"; that is, they do not simply inculcate the *current* core values of the society, they also forge new emotional bonds between members of the cohort that enhance *future* actions. As Mary Jo Deegan has observed in her study of such ritual dramas: "This experience of the self and the other as one in community is called 'communitas.'" Furthermore, such "rituals perform the function of uniting meaning, action, the abstract, and the real."[12]

In the transition from traditional tribal societies to modern societies, such rites of passage become increasingly diffuse and, in some sense, optional. The process of inculcating core values is assigned to institutions, particularly school systems, apprenticeship programs, military training, political parties, the media, and sporting events. The "liminal" permanent cohorts of tribal societies are replaced by temporary phenomena called "liminoid" groupings. They are particularly characteristic of arts and leisure activities. Rituals no longer simply represent what in the traditional society would be regarded as the sacred; rather, they become secularized and generalized. They are unable, therefore, to form the permanent bonds of "communitas" although they may form the temporary bonds of "community." The audience at a rock concert may experience an intensity of feeling, a temporary reversal of hierarchical roles and values, and a fleeting sense of community; but, once the concert is over and the audience disperses, there is no lasting "communitas" to bind the cohort together, although they may share the memory of the event. The repetition of a fleeting secular ritual, such as singing the national anthem at sporting events, may contribute to a sense of community that lasts beyond the event itself, but it does not create a true "communitas."[13]

Historians use these concepts borrowed from anthropology in several ways. They have studied, for example, men's fraternal orders of the nineteenth century, with their elaborate and popular secret rituals, and women's study clubs, sororities, missionary societies, fraternal "auxiliaries," and benevolent aid societies as equivalent to "liminal" cohorts. Ritual functioned as an indirect mode of clarifying and inculcating values by symbolic means rather than as a direct mode of communicating them by rhetorical means. The fraternal order initiate who symbolically enacted a search for wisdom by seeking patriarchical figures, a lengthy quest for a holy grail, or a journey among the "spirit voices" of the past learned important lessons for life in a rapidly changing society. Women, whether through formal rituals in a sorority or informal networks in a study club, also learned to symbolically encode values into their life styles.[14]

Utopian and communal societies, also prevalent in the nineteenth century, showed some of the characteristics of "liminal" experience. The participants did not reject the core values of the society (although they were critical of its current performance); they did, however, try to create alternate sets of institutions to achieve these core values. They tried to change their own lives (microstructures) rather than the whole society (macrostructure). They experienced "communitas" for awhile, but these efforts were usually short-lived and the commune disbanded. Historians have also become sensitive to the "liminoid" aspects of modern societies, particularly the creation of "social space" by women's rituals of mutual support, the creation of "symbolic space" by artists and writers in their celebration of a community, and the leisure and cultural activities by which individuals periodically withdrew from the daily routine to reaffirm traditional values and reduce the perceived tension between them and their lived experiences.[15]

Reform: Life as Response and Reordering of Values and Institutions
What is the historian to make of those individuals and groups that do not simply acquiesce in the status quo or withdraw into self-contained (albeit temporary) ritual renewal? What of those persons whose sense of frustration, impatience, or anger at society prompts them to propose partial remedies? Reform is this attempt to *renew* the values and behavior of the society. Rhetorically, the reformer's proposals can involve redefining the current meaning of core values or reordering their relative importance. Behaviorally, reform can involve rededication of individuals to the values, with appropriate changes in their life styles, and proposals for the restructuring of the institutional arrangements that articulate the values in everyday affairs.

Historians who deal with such a plethora of proposals categorize them as politicoeconomic when they deal with the exercise of power in the political and economic institutions, as civil rights and civil liberties when they deal with legal rights, civic responsibilities, and remedies for group-based grievances, and as social/moral/ethical when they deal with assumptions about permissible public and private behavior.[16] These categories are heuristic devices to help clarify complex situations. Some historians have argued that reform is simply periodic adaptation of institutions to social changes. This view of reform rests on the assumption that social changes are like *natural* processes: you cannot control them, you can only adapt to them. In this viewpoint, social changes are the "causes" and reform programs are the "effects" linked together in a causal sequence. However, *social* phenomena are not simply the products of determinate natural forces; they are primarily the products of indeterminate social actions. Reform, in this viewpoint, is a social activity that is interactive and partially goal-directed, but it is not simply reactive and adaptive to external situations. Acting together within institutions and within the conventions of public discourse, people can "affect" the social changes in their society, however gradually and minimally it may seem to the participants at the time.[17] The net effect of this perspective on the reformer's role is to emphasize that, in any period of history, the dedicated reformers are few in number, that they have to work long and hard, and that, however inadequate their proposals may seem to a later generation, they are essential players in the drama of history.

Radicalism: Life as Revolutionary Protest

The responses discussed so far—resignation, ritual withdrawal and renewal, reform—all share one thing in common: they believe that the professed core values of the society are real or appropriate. The radical option, on the other hand, holds that the professed core values are unreal or inappropriate. The current performance of the society is the "real," the true nature of the politicoeconomic or sociocultural system. Stripped of their illusory excuses, the current data reveal the operative values of the society, its implicit premises underlying its false promises. Furthermore, for the dedicated radical the only way to escape the situation is to reject these false, hypocritical public values and propose new ones. Frequently, the new values are rhetorical opposites of the current values (a strategy of debate that I have elsewhere called the "leap of negation"). Another rhetorical strategy is to retain the old terminology ("democracy") but give it entirely new meaning ("people's democracy"). This radical option also entails the proposal of alternate institutional arrangements. It is not enough in this radical option to simply change your *individual* values, ideas, or lifestyle. The old, false values are embodied in the current *institutions* and will continue to exercise their obfuscating spell over collective consciousness until they are replaced by a new system of institutions that will inculcate the new values.[18]

This traditional model of radicalism has recently been challenged by a group of political theorists, philosophers, and social critics in the aftermath of the collapse of communism in Eastern Europe and the dissolution of the Soviet Union. They base their criticism on a strict and literal adherence to liberal democratic ideals. Chantal Mouffe has expressed this attitude succinctly: "Because of the wide gap between those professed democratic ideals and their realization, the general tendency on the Left has been to denounce them as a sham and aim at the construction of a completely different society. This radical alternative is precisely what has been shown to be disastrous by the tragic experience of Soviet-style socialism, and it needs to be discarded."[19] In place of the old radicalism of going over to the opposite side, so to speak, Mouffe proposes a new radicalism of going beyond current understandings of core values and proposing alternate intellectual foundations for institutional arrangements in order to realize these core values. Alternate institutional arrangements need not constitute a *total* system. Whereas reform contemplates *correcting* abuses in the old or *current* institutions, this new radicalism contemplates putting current institutions on correct new intellectual foundations. For example, "in order to formulate a satisfactory concept of the political community," according to Mouffe, "we must go beyond liberal individualism to questions of justice, equality and community." Such an intellectual reformulation of the understanding of values may lead organically and gradually to radically new institutional arrangements.[20]

All advocates of change—whether reformer, radical, or ritualist—must face the distinction between goals and means. A goal tells *what* you want to do or accomplish; a means tells *how* you propose to accomplish it. Whether you propose to act gradually by persuasion and individual conversion, persistently by the democratic exercise of power, or suddenly by violence and revolutionary seizure of power is a matter primarily of means, not of goals. But any strategy can be both a practical means and a symbolic goal; for example, democracy can be both a way of exercising power and a symbol of the kind of society desired. Any single means (for example a legislative proposal) can be supported by a coalition of reformers, radicals, ritualists, even traditionalists, at any particular moment; however, the tension between their ultimate goals will force them apart. Those who want to *renew* their commitment to the current system, those who want to *repair* the system, and those who want to *replace* the system or *reformulate* its base are "going in different directions" and will eventually diverge. All advocates of change also face the formidable task of inspiring and organizing others to follow their agendas. However, the radical has the harder task. The reformers or the ritualists in their visions for society can rely on the emotional identification with past values or familiar rituals and can allay the fears of others by advocating partial solutions and compromise. The radical, on the other hand, must exploit more deep-seated emotions such as anger, outrage, or resentment in order to overcome the discomfort of confronting the unfamiliar and must articulate a vision of a new society or a new basis for society that will make the "impossible" seem possible. The radicals who persist in such a role are few in number; their moment in the spotlight of history may be brief, and it is frequently tragic as well.[21]

Language and the Use of Terms

In the quotation from William M. Reddy noted earlier in this introduction there was reference to a three-way cultural exchange that included "the struggle to clarify cognition [what does it mean?] and to order desires [what are the priorities?]." It is necessary, therefore, to indicate succinctly how this book approaches the task of elucidating the meaning and priority of core values in historical situations as opposed to current language use. I assume that core values are communicated within particular social languages, that they are embedded in their vocabularies, and that they are partially revealed by rhetorical strategies. By social languages I mean those sets of arguments and illustrations used to communicate perceptions about social, political, economic, and moral problems within a public discourse. They are to be distinguished from technical jargon or slang. As part of the *public* discourse on *common* problems, core values function within social languages not so much as descriptions of *what* we should do to solve a problem but more as prescriptions of *why* we should do it. Some examples of social languages encountered in this book include natural rights, equal rights, free labor, Victorian piety, antimonopoly, social bonds and human nature, and the "gospel of efficiency." Social languages may *supplement* more systematic ideologies—conservatism, liberalism, progressivism, socialism, feminism—or they may act as *substitutes* for them. But, every social language has its characteristic vocabulary, including certain key words.[22]

Mediating between the speaker and the audience in such public discourses are conventions or rhetorical strategies. Nineteenth-century editorials were bound by certain personalistic conventions and were highly partisan; public orators were expected to provide not only information but entertainment and moral "uplift." Women who spoke in public did so according to gender specific stereotypes or risked public censure. Women's autobiographies were bound by strict rules that defined the genre. Linguistic and literary critical studies have emphasized that the relationship between the speaker and the audience was not a "one way street" but a dialogical or interactive relationship. And language itself can both partly reveal and partly conceal the values of those who use it.[23] In order to extract the meaning and priority of core values from the social languages in which they are embedded and the rhetorical strategies in which they are communicated, this book follows this methodological rule: establish the context, scrutinize the text, listen attentively for any possible subtext, and be wary of rhetorical or ideological pretext.[24]

One final word of caution for the student of history: words change their meanings over time, and terms must be used carefully to distinguish historical description from current critical analysis. For example, in the 1830s to 1850s, the word used to describe someone who advocated extreme means to achieve a goal was ultra; it was applied particularly to abolitionists. The word radical meant going to the root cause of a condition, invoking a fundamental principle, or going to the etymological roots of a word. Gradually these two terms became synonymous. In the heated public discourse of the 1860s, radical replaced ultra as the term to be applied to political abolitionists and, eventually, was applied particularly to a faction of the Republican Party. The term radical will be used in this book, therefore, in two senses: (1) as a *descriptive* term for certain historical developments in the 1860s, and (2) as an *analytical* term according to the four-part response model explained earlier in this introduction.[25] Another example of the changing meanings of words has been emphasized by historian Nancy F. Cott. She has shown that the term *feminism* entered American public discourse during the 1910s. "People in the nineteenth century did not say *feminism*," she has noted. "They spoke of the advancement of woman or the cause of woman, woman's rights, and woman suffrage." Like the word radical, the word feminism will also be used in this book in two senses: (1) as a descriptive term for certain historical developments in the twentieth century; and (2) as an analytical term for evaluating women's history according to scholarly models.[26]

In summary, this book starts from the assumption that core values are not generalized abstractions with fixed meanings that are simply described by language. Rather, the attempt is made to see core values as *embedded* in the texture of daily life and its routines, in the rituals of organizations and institutions, and in the dynamics of social movements and political controversies as well as in the vocabulary of social languages. Furthermore, this book assumes that meaning *emerges* from human behavior in the actions, interactions, and temporary resolutions of these ongoing controversies. Care is taken to minimize imposing definitions and concepts inherent in current methodological or ideological positions on the past, and no attempt is made to "prove" that an individual or group "really meant" something other than what a fair assessment of the historical evidence will warrant. The insistence here is on distinguishing between the *historical actor's* use of terms *in the past* as presented in descriptive narrative and reconstruction of past public discourse and the *historian's* use of terms *in the present* for analysis and interpretive explanations. This methodological caution is necessary if we are to understand not only the *logical* meaning of core values but their *lived* meaning as well. In short, the approach of this book might be characterized as a combination of situational analysis, historical semantics, and methodological caution. Such an approach acknowledges the humanity of the historical actors, the integrity of the evidence, and the contingency of historical inquiry.

This book does not intend to be a comprehensive textbook for the time period it covers, 1865–1932, and does not include such topics as foreign policy or military events. Rather, this book was written for use in upper division history courses or graduate seminars as a supplement to standard textbooks or in conjunction with other specialized books. This book is primarily an interpretation of certain aspects of American history based on the methodology spelled out in this introduction. Given the complexity of the issues and the need to clearly identify the actors and various intellectual options, the issues of civil rights, women's rights, and the regulation of business are dealt with in separate chapters in the first part of the book. Then these issues are brought together in somewhat more integrated chapters in the second part to illustrate their interactions. In emphasizing the contested nature of core values, the variety of roles that individuals can play in institutions and social movements, the importance of social languages, and the factor of contingency in human affairs, this book sees history itself as an open, underdetermined, and humanistic endeavor.[27] Perhaps that is the truth behind the old saying that the cause of freedom must be won anew in each generation.

PART I

Old Languages and New Realities

On 18 April 1864 President Lincoln spoke in Baltimore, Maryland, at one of the innumerable "sanitary fairs" held to raise money for medical supplies and private relief efforts during the Civil War. He touched on one of the themes that has continued to intrigue students of history ever since: How could people who shared a common history and proclaimed allegiance to common values—such as liberty, equality, justice—engage in such a fierce and fratricidal war? Lincoln cut to the heart of the problem:

> The world has never had a good definition of the word liberty, and the American people, just now, are much in want of one. We all declare for liberty; but in using the same *word* we do not all mean the same *thing*. With some the word liberty may mean for each man to do as he pleases with himself, and the product of his labor; while with others the same word may mean for some men to do as they please with other men, and the product of other men's labor. Here are two, not only different, but incompatible things, called by the same name—liberty. And it follows that each of the things is, by the respective parties, called by two different and incompatible names—liberty and tyranny.[1]

A year later the terrible war was over, and Lincoln was dead. But the basic questions remained. What did liberty, equality, and justice mean to the reunited nation? Whose definitions would prevail? What was the relationship between power and public discourse, between individual aspiration and institutional restraint, or between private responses and public roles?

Three issues helped to define the contexts within which the postwar generation struggled to answer some basic questions about liberty, equality, and justice, to define these core values, and to institutionalize their legal and moral authority: (1) the need to determine the status and rights of the former slaves and former Confederates in the Reconstruction Era;

(2) the conflict between the demands for women's rights and the imperatives of social respectability that was made acute by the splintering of the prewar alliance of male abolitionists and female advocates of women's rights, and (3) the creation of the modern business corporation, attempts to regulate the terms of competition, and experiments in internal organizational control and coordination of such large-scale enterprises. And, as Lincoln had indicated, in such contests—where one person's liberty was perceived as another's tyranny—the results were accompanied as much by conflict, confusion, and tragedy as by compromise, clarity, and victory. In dealing with these three issues, the participants in the public discourse and political conflicts attempted to apply old social languages from the prewar political arena to the new realities of the postwar economic and social worlds. The results were not always predictable or easily explainable, but they were illustrative of underlying values in conflict and of continuity and change in American history.[2]

1

Presidential Reconstruction and the Meaning of Liberty, Equality, and Justice, 1865–1866

In April 1865 the war was over, but the suffering did not cease. In a culture saturated with an evangelical ethos and biblical language,[1] in which even the martyred president's second inaugural address had been a brief homily on divine justice and human mercy, people—black and white, North and South—could recall in the immediate postwar situation the words of the prophet Isaiah:

> The Spirit of the Lord God is upon me;
> because the Lord hath anointed me
> to preach good tidings unto the meek;
> he hath sent me to bind up the brokenhearted,
> to proclaim liberty to the captives,
> and the opening of the prison to them that are bound;
> to proclaim the acceptable year of the Lord,
> and the day of vengeance of our God;
> to comfort all that mourn.[2]

But how should one define liberty? What was the meaning of equality for the former slave and the former slaveholder, for the prewar abolitionists and their postwar antagonists, or for the temporarily unemployed workers—white as well as black—and the newly impoverished businessman? How should justice be administered? Who presumed to enact the vengeance of God? This chapter will answer these questions by exploring the range of meanings of the core values of liberty, equality, and justice as they were played out by various individuals and groups. Finally, this chapter will set the stage of presidential Reconstruction and the issue of civil rights as it became defined and institutionalized in 1865–66. This will set the context for the emergence of congressional Reconstruction and its subsequent judicial interpretation that will be examined in the next chapter.

Slavery had died a slow death by attrition, as slaves had escaped via "underground railroads" conducted with the help of free African Americans and abolitionists, by military action, by presidential proclamation, and, finally, by constitutional action in the Thirteenth Amendment, which was passed by Congress in January 1865 and sent to the states for ratification. But the response to the fact of freedom had been immediate. Former slaves took to the road to search for family members separated by sale or wartime impressment, to move beyond the physical barriers prescribed by the old slave codes and the white patrol and pass system, and to seek better economic and social conditions elsewhere. Former slave owners tried to convince, cajole, and ultimately to coerce the newly emancipated laborers into returning to work on the devastated plantations and farms under conditions that approximated the dependency of the old system. Union army officers and agents of the wartime Freedmen's Bureau, caught between conflicting governmental directives, political ideologies, and personal inclinations, sporadically intervened to draw up labor contracts for the freedmen, to dispense or to take back plantation land abandoned during the war, or to acquiesce in the "local customs" of the Southern white leadership. The good tidings to the meek were not uniformly good, and those who expected a day of vengeance were sometimes those who, in the end, had cause to mourn.[3]

The attempt to define the meaning of freedom rapidly became a contest of wills to determine who would exercise political as well as economic power. Given the divisions between Northern and Southern political leadership, and between black freedmen and white yeoman farmers, the events of 1865–66 also represented a clash of values. Contending factions sought economic preferment and political power, all the while viewing events, and each other, through suspicious eyes and reacting according to differing interpretations of common values. The task of reconciling these diverse claims, of defining the legal and constitutional meaning of freedom, and of shaping the political nature of reconstruction fell initially to the leaders and opinion makers of the dominant Republican Party, particularly to those in Congress. Contemporary commentators and hostile political opponents frequently used the political epithet "radical" as a secular substitute for the older religious term "ultra" to describe those abolitionists-turned-politicians who supported the rights of freedmen. Historians carefully distinguish among three groups. A small group, called the Radical Republicans, provided vision, incessant moral pressure, and specific legislative proposals. A broader group of moderate Republicans (including many prewar, antislavery Democrats) exercised considerable power within the party, the press, and key congressional committees. Another smaller, more amorphous, coterie of conservative Republicans sided with President Johnson on specific issues. The pattern of events over the ten years 1866–76 would constantly push the moderates, and occasionally a conservative Republican, into support of positions or programs that had previously been advocated only by the Radical Republicans.[4]

Although they divided frequently over tactics and the timing of their political actions, the Republicans, nevertheless, operated within a coherent intellectual tradition. Liberty in the sense of independence was the great desideratum; for the broadly conceived "producing classes" its dialogical opposite was dependence. As a legal term, liberty could refer to the specific status of being an independent citizen; its opposite was the permanent status of slavery. As a social term, liberty could refer to the general condition of living at will as opposed to the temporary status of being bound by law or the will of another. One could lose such freedom upon conviction for crime and be jailed, no longer "at liberty to come and go as you pleased." As an economic term, liberty could refer simultaneously to the *freedom to* pursue your own interest and the *freedom from* external restraint (by government, established church, or privileged institutions and classes). Such liberty was synonymous with economic individualism. As a psychological term, liberty also referred to a self-willed, consensual status, of being obligated or bound only by one's freely given word or pledge.[5]

Given the evangelical ethos, the abolitionist antecedents, and the middle-class aspirations of the former Whigs, antislavery Democrats, and Free-Soilers who constituted the Republican Party of the 1860s, it was both logically consistent and psychologically satisfying when they sifted out of this maze of potential meanings certain emphases. They created what historians call the free-labor ideology.[6] The free individual, subject to the self-control of disciplined work habits and deferred gratifications and free from the "unfair competition" of slave labor, could pursue his own self-interest bound only by conscience (self-willed obedience to community norms), by law (bearing equally on all) and by a decent respect for the esteem and opinions of others. Thus, the classical notion of virtue as the priority of the common good was wedded to the liberal concept of liberty as the pursuit of self-interest. In the Republican Party version of the free-labor ideology, government stood ready to help these aspiring entrepreneurs with free public education, readily available transportation systems, a reliable postal service, sound credit (via the national banking system), tariff protection, and a generous homestead or free land option.

While liberty as independence was presumed to be the goal of life for all men, most of these same political leaders and opinion makers assumed that dependence was the destined lot of most women.[7]

If liberty was an absolute goal in Republican thought in 1865–66, equality was, for most Republicans, a relative means to achieve it. Republican orators and editors spoke or wrote of the necessity of ensuring equality under the law; that is, they specified those minimal legal and procedural rights essential to make contracts, to use the courts to protect property and personal liberty, and to be treated publicly with the dignity inherent in the free status. A few of the Radical Republicans and some African American leaders, such as Frederick Douglass, pressed on to demand the right to vote. Much breath and ink were also expended on the question of whether equality existed between the triumphant Northern states and the rebellious Southern states. The question was also raised as to what would happen to the egalitarian premises of popular sovereignty and consensual democracy if significant numbers of former voters (i.e., Confederate office holders) or potential voters (i.e., the freedmen) were excluded from the political process.[8]

In economic terms, it was an unvoiced assumption of most participants in postwar debates that equality of opportunity would be accompanied by inequality or proportionality of financial rewards. One favorite metaphor was that of the foot race. The prize went to the swiftest. One person received the gold medal, one the silver, one the bronze. The rest "also ran" in the race of life. Such was simply the natural order, if unhindered by favoritism. Of the private realm, of equality between persons, the party leaders and opinion makers had little to say, except for ritual references to the need for education and mutual forbearance and for reassuring statements that the Radicals did *not advocate* "social equality." That is, they did not advocate forcing contact between persons or races beyond the limits of self-willed, consensual agreement. Behind this euphemism lay the white uneasiness about sexual interactions and intermarriage between racial groups. Thus Republicans distinguished equality in three aspects: with respect to civil rights, to social rights, and to political rights. As legal historian Mark Tushnet has noted: "The core of each conception was . . . well defined: The core civil rights included the rights to sue and testify; social rights included the right to select one's associates; voting was the central political right." Modern readers would do well to think of these rights not as separate spheres but as overlapping categories in the minds of Reconstruction Era lawmakers. While some aspects of equality adhered to the person as preemptory rights, others were granted by society as privileges or prudential benefits.[9]

Existing in uneasy tension with liberty and equality in Republican thought in 1865–66 was another multivalent concept—justice. Justice in the prewar era had been primarily a local matter, a rough reconciliation of contending personal and property rights to be decided as much by emotional, unwritten community norms as by logical, printed laws. Where the rudimentary reach of the courthouse and sheriff seemed inadequate, there had stretched the shadowy domain of *code duelo*, the vigilante mob, the frontier gunfight or ambush, and the spontaneous urban riot. Justice at any higher level, whether state or federal, was seen as a matter of strict constitutional limits, specified procedures, and infrequent appeals to higher courts. When, in the *Dred Scott* case, the Supreme Court had subordinated justice to political expediency in the eyes of Northern abolitionists and Free-Soil politicians by declaring that blacks were not citizens and had none of the rights of white citizens, the newly organized Republican Party had been prepared to curb the power of the courts.[10]

During the Civil War the Lincoln administration had presided over a nationalizing of the concept of justice. Lincoln had also suspended the right of habeas corpus, ignored local civil courts, utilized military courts, and suspended the freedom of the press. Jefferson Davis's Confederate administration was forced to take similar centralizing, nationalizing actions in reference to justice and constitutional rights, much to the disquiet and the occasional resistance of some stricter, states'-rights oriented Confederate governors. In short, by 1865 important segments of the political leadership, both North and South, had been willing to subordinate justice in order to protect liberty (at least for themselves or their region). Whether the Republicans would continue to uphold national norms for justice or whether the Supreme Court would reverse the wartime precedents was a matter of serious contention.[11]

To emphasize the understanding of the core values of liberty, equality, and justice held by the Republicans in 1865–66 does not imply that their Democratic Party opponents necessarily believed the opposite. It is, rather, to recognize that the Republicans were, at this moment in history, the agents of change, while the Democrats represented the forces of continuity. The Democrats shared core values from the country's past, but defined them in different ways or translated them into policies with different priorities. For example, an expert on post–Civil War newspapers has concluded: "Northern Democrats were willing to take the risks in a peace settlement that brought the country as close to a restoration as possible: 'The Union as it was and the Constitution as it is,' as they put it." For many Democrats, then, liberty meant *freedom from* dominance by Washington and *freedom to* do as they pleased at the state and local level.

Equality meant equal rights between the states and unfettered economic opportunity within the states. Justice meant the restoration of Southern white rights, property, and prerogatives as expeditiously as possible.[12]

There were, of course, other voices that attempted to be heard between the contending Republicans and Democrats. African American communities, North and South, which had long found their leadership among the ranks of the prewar free black population, continued to look to them to express their views through conventions and newspapers. Liberty as *freedom from* the bonds of slavery was now a dream come true, but liberty as *freedom to* do as one willed was not yet assured. Therefore they focused on the meaning of equality. Their concerns, as summarized by recent students of their rhetoric, ran the full spectrum of meaning: "Equality before the Law, Equal Chance, Equal Justice, Equal Footing, Equal Opportunity, and Equal Rights." Nor did they shrink from demanding immediate political equality. While Frederick Douglass could espouse the laissez-faire, no-government-assistance slogans of contemporary Northern liberalism, the Southern African American leaders recognized the necessity of some form of governmental protection in the face of Southern white resistance. Nor were the African American voices as timid as some of their white Unionist allies in articulating the dimension of social equality, which blacks understood as social recognition of their equal civic status rather than any form of coerced social interaction. Above all, the freedmen cried out for justice. They did not call for vengeance or retribution on their former masters and their yeoman allies. Rather, they called for recompense, either in the form of land from confiscated or abandoned plantations or at least an end to laws and traditions that prohibited the purchase of land and houses by freedmen who could afford them. Their motto in 1865–66 was thus simple and direct: "Freedom, justice and equality (that is equality before the law)."[13]

But who would make the law? Having mounted from the subordinate status of dependence to the superior status of independence by virtue of emancipation, what rights could the freedmen now expect to enjoy? Having violated the law by rebellion (at least in the eyes of the victorious Union forces) or, in some cases, having broken their solemn oaths to uphold the *federal* Constitution as prewar public officials, what did justice demand that the former Confederates must now forfeit in the way of rights or privileges? In short, what did it mean to be free and equal in law and constitutional theory? For the moment, the initiative lay in the hands of Andrew Johnson.

As the 1864 presidential election had approached, the Republican Party had been badly divided by Lincoln's pocket veto of the Wade-Davis Bill, which had set forth congressional terms for reconstruction and emancipation, and by tensions between its "radical" and "conservative" wings over war aims.[14] To attract the support of prowar Democrats, the Republicans had created a Union ticket of Lincoln for president and Johnson, a prowar Democrat, for vice president. Success in the election had relegated Johnson to the traditional anonymity of his office until Lincoln's death had thrust him into the center of political power as president. A careful student of Johnson's career has concluded that the Republicans had ignored much of Johnson's prewar background and heard only what they wanted to hear in his postwar oratory.[15]

But they were wrong. Johnson had his own values and agenda. Born in North Carolina in 1808, Johnson was the epitome of the nineteenth century's favorite cultural model—the self-made man. Apprenticed as a youth to a tailor, largely self-educated, and socially marginal in class, he had followed the route of opportunity westward to Tennessee in 1826. For the next three decades, he had risen through the ranks of politics within the Democratic party. He was known as a champion of working-class whites and a determined foe of the slave-owning planter aristocracy. He opposed secession, remained in his seat in the U.S. Senate when Tennessee joined the Confederacy, and was later appointed military governor of Tennessee by President Lincoln. Having once owned a few slaves, he was neither an abolitionist nor a friend of the free blacks. But, by February 1863 he had come to the conviction that slavery must go. "Is not this Government, the giant embodiment of the principles of human liberty, worth more than the institution of slavery?" he asked rhetorically. Emancipation, he believed, would destroy the economic base of power in the planter aristocracy and free the poor whites from their political domination.[16]

The initial advantage in defining the nature of postwar relations between the North and South rested with Johnson. Neither waiting for the newly elected Congress to convene at its regular time nor calling it into special session, Johnson issued his own proclamations on 29 May 1865. Johnson granted a general amnesty for "all persons who have, directly or indirectly, participated in the . . . rebellion," except for specified categories of former Confederate officeholders and wealthy landowners. He set up a system for presidential pardons and appointed provisional governors for the formerly rebellious states. Once the loyal voters, who had taken an oath to obey the Constitution and to uphold the Union, had reconstituted their state governments, recognized the emancipation of slaves, and repudiated secession and their war debts, their states would be readmitted. By December 1865 all the former Confederate states (except Texas) had complied, and on 6 December 1865 Johnson declared in a message to Congress that the Union had been restored.[17]

Why didn't the controversy over reconstruction end right there with the restoration of the *status quo antebellum* (except for the abolition of slavery by the Thirteenth Amendment)? Over the years historians have pointed to a number of factors in the immediate historical context. One was concern over the federal debt and its impact on the state of the economy. By maintaining the high wartime income taxes, tariff rates, and luxury taxes and by rigorously cutting government expenses after the end of hostilities, the secretary of the treasury could report a temporary surplus in the federal budget. He applied this surplus toward the federal debt. But this deflationary policy coincided with a decline in wholesale prices and helped to trigger a postwar recession. Returning war veterans, increased numbers of immigrants, and free blacks thus competed with each other in the labor market for the dwindling number of jobs. A number of Republicans voiced the fear that the resurgent Democrats, augmented by newly-elected representatives from Johnson's reconstructed Southern states, might repudiate the Union war debt or, worse yet, move to assume the Confederate debt and to compensate planters for the loss of their slaves.[18]

Allied with these economic fears was the political realization that the Thirteenth Amendment by abolishing slavery also abrogated the old constitutional three-fifths rule for apportioning seats in Congress. This rule held that only three-fifths of the slave population would be counted in apportioning seats in Congress. As Elizur Wright, a New England abolitionist, pointed out in a March 1865 letter to the Boston *Daily Advertiser:* "The effect of this, when passed, is to take away about $1/27$th of the power of the loyal States in the lower house of Congress, and give it to the reconstructed rebel States, provided all are restored." To forestall such an eventuality, some Republicans were willing to enfranchise freedman and to disenfranchise most former Confederate officeholders for as long as was necessary to reconstruct the South on a free-labor base and establish Unionist governments in the South. Not everyone in the Republican Party was willing to go this far—just yet.[19]

Northern psychological perceptions and emotional responses to events in the South complicated these economic and political considerations. Emancipation had become a symbol in Northern eyes of the moral meaning of the war and a religious justification for its sacrifices. But the news from the South seemed to be anything but reassuring: Black Codes were passed, which restricted the freedmen's legal rights; violence was directed against the freedmen in the form of racial riots; social ostracism was practiced against white Unionists and carpetbagging Northerners; and political power was being exercised by the old planter aristocracy and Confederate leadership. What particularly grated on Northern sensibilities, according to historian Daniel T. Carter, was "the lack of any sense of wrong doing, of sinfulness" on the part of the unrepentant white Southerners. While this situation "was not the most critical factor," Carter has concluded, nevertheless, "the absence of these 'outward signs of inner grace' . . . inevitably accentuated the divisions between North and South."[20]

There were differences, too, of perception and emotional response, of economic goals and political agendas, among the free blacks of the North and the freedman of the South. For example, Frederick Douglass had demanded as far back as December 1863 that emancipation be followed by full equality of rights, including the right to vote. In April 1865 he had reiterated this demand: "I am for the 'immediate, unconditional, and universal' enfranchisement of the black man, in every State in the Union. [Loud applause] Without this, his liberty is a mockery; without this, you might as well almost retain the old name of slavery for his condition; for in fact, if he is not the slave of the individual master, he is the slave of society, and holds his liberty as a privilege, not as a right. He is at the mercy of the mob, and has no means of protecting himself."[21] But, Douglass had also imbibed the ethos of the self-made man and had embraced the laissez-faire ideology of mid-nineteenth-century liberalism. In the same speech of April 1865, he remarked, "Everybody has asked the question, . . . 'What shall we do with the Negro?' I have had but one answer from the beginning. Do nothing with us!" As he put it succinctly a month later in a letter to the Reverend J. Miller McKim of the American Freedman's Aid Society, "The negro needs justice more than pity, liberty more than old clothes."[22]

On the other hand, to many destitute freedmen in the South, the aid and the protection provided by the Freedmen's Bureau and the philanthropy and education provided by the Northern volunteer aid societies were viewed in a different light. And there were numerous claimants in the South for the role of leader of the black communities, particularly ministers, women, skilled artisans, and some former Union soldiers. They had their own priorities and sense of the possible. Above all, according to historian Eric Foner, the "freedmen wished to take control of the conditions under which they labored, free themselves from subordination to white authority, and carve out the greatest measure of economic autonomy."[23]

Similar tensions and divisions existed among Southern whites but were less obvious to Northerners dependent on newspaper accounts of distant events. The Southern economy was shattered. The Southern banking system, never too vigorous even before the war, reeled under the double impact of the worthlessness of Confederate bonds and currency and the discriminatory federal tax on state bank notes. Credit was least available when it was needed the most, and planters, merchants, and entrepreneurs had to improvise as best as they could. In addition there were class tensions among white Southerners. Up-country yeomen farmers who had bitterly resented the unequal burdens of a "rich man's war and poor man's fight," former Whigs and Constitutional Unionists who had initially opposed the fire-brand secessionists, and merchants and advocates of railroads, industrialization, and urbanization who resented the prewar planter elites all jostled for leadership positions. Men who had tasted the rewards of command in the military were strategically placed to elbow aside some of the lawyers and gentlemen of leisure who had constituted much of the prewar political cadres. For all the social deference to the local aristocracy and the preponderant role of the planters in public office, power in the South ultimately flowed from ownership of property and not simply from the prescription of birth or class. And it was precisely the property base of the Old South (slave labor) that had just collapsed; ownership of the property base of the new Southern order (land) was what was at stake in the immediate political and economic situation.[24]

How were all these conflicting interests and values to be reconciled? How were the fruits of the victory by Union forces to be preserved in the eyes of Northern Republicans? Speaking through the Senate judiciary committee, congressional Republicans presented their answer in their proposed Civil Rights Act of 1866. First, they addressed the issue of the status of the former slaves in light of the 1857 *Dred Scott* case in which the Supreme Court had denied their status as citizens. Section 1 of the Civil Rights Act defined citizenship as applying to anyone who was native-born or naturalized. Senator Lyman Trumbull of Illinois clarified during the debate in the Senate that this definition included all native-born blacks, Indians who had left their treaty nation reservations and who paid taxes, and children born of Chinese parents who were resident in the United States. Section 1 declared that citizens "of every race" ought to have the same rights as those "enjoyed by white citizens." What were some of these rights that the authors of the bill believed were fundamental to citizenship? They included the right to make contracts, to sue and to give evidence in court, to own and sell real and personal property, to enjoy the security of person and property, and to be subject to the same punishment or penalty as anyone else convicted of a similar crime.[25]

Sections 2 and 3 of the Civil Rights Act dealt with further legal means to protect these equal rights. Starting with a presumption of federal judicial supremacy, Section 2 held that anyone who, under the color of law or custom, deprived another of the rights spelled out in the law because of color, race, previous condition of slavery or involuntary servitude would be guilty of a misdemeanor and, if convicted, subject to a $1,000 fine and/or one year in jail. Section 3 further authorized federal courts to have jurisdiction over such cases and suits brought in state courts upon motion by the defendant. Positively, the Civil Rights Act imposed upon the federal government and the states the obligation to protect the civil rights of *all* citizens as enumerated in Section 1; negatively, it warned the Southern states that if they failed to do so, the federal courts would. The Civil Rights Act of 1866 passed Congress with the support of all but three Republicans. President Johnson, citing states'-rights doctrines and fear of excessive federal power, vetoed the bill. He had earlier vetoed a revised Freedmen's Bureau Act on similar grounds. On 9 April 1866 the congressional Republicans rallied the necessary votes to override the presidential veto; shortly thereafter they overrode the veto of the Freedmen's Bureau Act.[26]

The president's vetoes, the tone of his messages, and his partisan political remarks to supporters convinced many Republicans that a constitutional amendment would be necessary to fully protect the rights of black freedmen and white Unionists in the South and to prevent a future Democratic-controlled Congress from repealing the Civil Rights Act or, perhaps, other crucial wartime legislation. The final product of such Republican efforts—the Fourteenth Amendment—was excessively complex, deliberately ambiguous in language, and disingenuous in its methods. Section 1 stipulated that all persons born or naturalized in the United States were citizens of both the national and state governments. It prohibited the states from abridging their "privileges or immunities," depriving any person of "life, liberty, or property without due process of law," or denying them "equal protection of the laws." The question of the number of Southern representatives in Congress was approached cautiously by the Republicans. Rather than requiring black suffrage in the South, Section 2 provided that if the right to vote was denied "to any of the male inhabitants" of the state (i.e. black freedmen), then its representation in Congress would be reduced proportionally. Section 3 disqualified from public office most former Confederate officeholders but provided a mechanism for congressional pardons. Section 4 invalidated the Confederate war debt, guaranteed the validity of the Union war debt, and barred any compensation for emancipated slaves. The amendment was a political document as well as a legal one. As Eric Foner has succinctly put it, "The Amendment supplied Republicans with a platform for the fall [1866] campaign, while leaving to the future the issue of black suffrage."[27]

The stage was thus set in June 1866 for that sequence of events that would be known as congressional Reconstruction. The economic situation added to the sense of political crisis. In April 1866, Congress had passed the Contraction Act, which authorized the secretary of the treasury to exchange short-term, high interest federal notes for longer term, lower interest bonds and to withdraw $10 million worth of paper currency, or "greenbacks," every month for six months (thereafter $4 million a month). The act was prompted by concern over the federal debt, but the net effect was deflationary. Banks were reluctant to extend credit. Therefore the postwar business recession would last until December 1867 and further exacerbate social and political tensions. A National Union convention in August 1866 failed to create a political party that would unite Democrats and pro-Johnson Republicans. Johnson's disapproval of the Fourteenth Amendment meant that moderate Republicans felt alienated from the president. In the fall congressional elections, Republicans gained enough seats in both houses of Congress to be able to override any presidential veto, provided they could stick together. And the news from the South pushed them toward each other. All the former Confederate states (except Tennessee) plus Delaware and Kentucky had rejected the proposed amendment. The Supreme Court joined the fray in *Ex Parte Milligan* by ruling unconstitutional the wartime use of military tribunals when the civil courts had been open.[28]

Psychological perceptions and emotional predispositions were as important as the realities of economic and political power. How should liberty, equality, and justice for the freedmen, the white Unionists, and the loyal Southerners be secured? Politically, President Johnson had acted out of conscientious, long-held constitutional scruples, and the Supreme Court had acted to protect traditional judicial rights from wartime excesses. However, Radical Republicans were not satisfied and moderate Republicans were uneasy. Radical Republican Thadeus Stevens staked out an advanced position: he linked the protection of Southern white Unionists with the extension of equal political rights to black freedmen. Frederick Douglass, writing in the *Atlantic Monthly,* asked rhetorically whether the war had been in vain or whether there was to be a "solid nation, entirely delivered from all contradictions and social antagonisms, based upon loyalty, liberty, and equality." The stage was set for a political and legal showdown.[29]

2

From Congressional Reconstruction to the Civil Rights Cases of 1883

What was the meaning of civil rights for the Republicans who controlled Congress in 1866? How did their actions relate to the core values of liberty, equality, and justice as they understood those terms? What roles did various groups play in the process by which the Republicans attempted to reconstruct the South? In order to answer these questions, this chapter will focus on the passage of the congressional Reconstruction acts and the adoption of the Fifteenth Amendment. Having done this, the chapter will trace out the fate of congressional Reconstruction over the next decade and the interpretation given to the legal aspects of these developments by the Supreme Court. The story that will be told starts in triumph but ends in tragedy. The story begins in 1867 with the Republican efforts to address the issues raised by presidential Reconstruction and the resurgence of the traditional white South. What was more important: reconciliation or reconstruction of Southern society?

The majority of the congressional Republicans brushed aside sentiments in favor of expedient actions. In effect, they declared the existing presidential Reconstruction governments in the South "null and void," placed them under military control, and directed the Union army to reconstitute the electoral process on a biracial basis. New test oaths excluded those who had actively participated in the support of the rebellion. When the duly elected conventions had rewritten their state constitutions so as to provide for equal voting rights, when the majority of voters and Congress had approved the state constitutions, and when the newly constituted state governments had endorsed the Fourteenth Amendment and it had been formally adopted, *then* the reconstructed states would be entitled to their representation in Congress. Concerned about Johnson's expected veto, and fearing his attempts to subvert the process by removing military officers with Republican sympathies, the Republican-dominated Congress passed some supplemental acts. These empowered military officers to act in the absence of civilian initiative to facilitate the political process and required the president to follow the chain of military command (which made General Grant the key actor in the drama of contending factions). When Johnson persisted in his obstructionist tactics, the Republican congressional leaders, in an inept and politically motivated action, tried to impeach him. They failed in their endeavor to convict him by one vote. When a divided Supreme Court, under the influence of its Democratic members, seemed obstreperous, congressional Republicans responded by changing the appellate jurisdiction of the Court. The legislative branch of the government, for the moment, appeared to assert its supremacy over the other two branches in the struggle for political power.[1]

The issues of equal political rights and legal-constitutional restructuring of the Southern states became entangled with economic issues in the 1868 presidential election. The Republican Party endorsed a hard-money position that promised to repay the federal debt in gold, a stance that favored national banks, railroad promoters, export-import businessmen, and certain classes of investors. The Democratic Party endorsed the "Ohio Idea" that proposed to repay the federal debt in "greenbacks," or U.S. Treasury notes, a stance that favored those who hoped to benefit from the resulting currency-induced inflation: some farmers, local-oriented entrepreneurs, capital-hungry manufacturers, and labor unions looking for higher wages. The Democratic Party also added a blatant appeal to racial inequality to counter the Republican's emphasis on equality of rights regardless of race. The Republican ticket of Ulysses S. Grant and Schuler Colfax, buttressed by black votes from the reconstructed states, won by approximately 300,000 votes over the Democratic ticket of Horatio Seymour and Francis P. Blair. The Republicans moved quickly to consolidate their gains. In February 1869 congressional Republicans introduced the Fifteenth Amendment: "The right of citizens of the United States to vote shall not be denied or abridged by the United States or by any State on account of race, color, or previous condition of servitude." It was approved, despite Democratic complaints that it was "revolutionary," and ratified by the requisite number of states within a year. In short order after Grant's inauguration, the Republicans also pushed through the Public Credit Act, which pledged to repay the national debt in gold. Thus, they had defined the political and economic issues of the ensuing decade.[2]

How should students of history regard this extraordinary series of events? It is instructive to note a speech by William Lloyd Garrison at the final meeting of the American Anti-Slavery Society in April 1870. He referred to a speech that he had given in 1830 in which he had said to a group of free blacks: "I believe . . . that the time is not far distant when you and the trampled slaves shall be free and enjoy the same rights in this country as other citizens. If you will hold on with a firm grasp, I assert that liberty, equality, every republican privilege, is yours." Looking back from the perspective of 1870, he conceded: "I wish you to remember that the party which has given you the ballot, which in Congress has done everything that could be done to give *liberty and justice and equality* throughout the land, is the Republican party." To abolitionists such as Garrison, congressional Reconstruction was simply a promise fulfilled. On the other hand, historian Eric Foner, in a magisterial synthesis, has concluded that congressional Reconstruction was a second American Revolution (albeit an unfinished one), "a stunning and unprecedented experiment in interracial democracy." Robert J. Kaczorowski, a legal historian, has argued that it was not the advocacy of equal voting rights that was most significant, but the "revolutionary theory of constitutionalism" that placed the authority to protect the civil rights of American citizens in the hands of Congress and the federal judiciary. In short, they see congressional Reconstruction as "a radical departure" (Foner) or a "revolutionary change in American constitutionalism" (Kaczorowski).[3]

If the focus of the analysis is shifted from the *means* used by the Republicans during congressional Reconstruction—military rule, black suffrage, federal judicial supremacy—to an examination of their *values* and their *priorities,* then the nature of congressional Reconstruction can be further clarified. Republican congressional leaders consistently appealed to the egalitarian principles of the Declaration of Independence (understood as equal rights to life, liberty, and security of property), to the premises of classic republicanism (equal civic status and political rights coupled with sufficient public virtue to seek not only one's own self-interest but also the common good), and to the judicially monitored aspects of citizenship in the Constitution and relevant amendments. In this sense, the leaders and advocates of congressional Reconstruction were fulfilling the role of reformers. They were trying to narrow the gap between the "ought" of their society's institutionalized core values (as they understood them) and the "is" of its current practices in an unprecedented situation. The values were old and familiar and were expressed in traditional language. If the means used to achieve them were, at times, unprecedented and dramatic, that was because of the new realities they confronted.[4]

What made some Republican opinion makers and congressional leaders seem "radical" to their opponents, on the other hand, was not their values per se but the *priority* a few of them placed on the concept of equality. Whereas most people were willing to claim equality for themselves, their class, or their race, there were former abolitionists among the Republicans who were willing to extend the same rights to others. In religious terms, belief in equality was an expression of one's love for the neighbor, although, admittedly, at times it was a paternalistic expression. In an era when racial hierarchy and inequality was a prevalent social assumption, when the reunited Democratic Party was committed to white supremacy, when state constitutional amendments for black male suffrage had periodically gone down in defeat in the North (prior to the Fifteenth Amendment), and when significant numbers of Republicans believed that self-interest operating through the market in a free-labor economy would be sufficient to protect the freedmen—in such a climate of opinion to fight for equality for African Americans, Native Americans, and resident Chinese was to play the public role of the radical (as defined by the four-part model in this book). These abolitionists turned politicians retained old terminology but read new meaning into the term equality. To do so took moral courage and political conviction. They shifted the basis of equality from self-interest to the interest of others, from self-love to other love.[5]

There were, of course, other ways to respond to the perceived gap between old and familiar values and current realities that seemed less dramatic than the reforms of congressional Reconstruction or less threatening than the egalitarian priorities of the abolitionists turned politicians who constituted Radical Republicanism. Historians of fraternal orders have pointed to an extraordinary growth in the membership and variety of such organizations in the immediate postwar period. While appealing primarily to males of the working class and middle class, newly established fraternal orders touched on a variety of interests such as veterans affairs, agriculture, and labor needs. Even the prewar fraternal orders, particularly American freemasonry and the Independent Order of Odd Fellows, flourished in the postwar ethos.[6] Black males, members of the minuscule, urban middle class, joined the Prince Hall masonic lodges that paralleled the white lodges from which they were excluded. As an historian of African American masonry, Loretta J. Williams has noted, "there was a phenomenal emergence of Prince Hall lodges in the three years following the cessation of the Civil War."[7]

What were the old and familiar values that the fraternalists tried to incorporate into their elaborate, esoteric, and immensely popular secret rituals? One example is found in the career of Albert Pike, the commissioner of Indian Affairs for the Confederacy. He devised a popular Scottish Rite freemasonry ritual while dodging Union troops during the final stages of the Civil War. He believed that the initiate should be "a lover of wisdom, and an apostle of liberty, equality, and fraternity." Indeed "fraternity" in its broadest sense was the primary value of all the ritualistic lodges; moreover, such organizations in reaffirming predominantly middle-class, masculine values "promised men both a sense of brotherhood and a badge of respectability." The lodge brothers were, symbolically at least, all equal. However, equality was attenuated within the lodge by an emphasis on hierarchy—of earned degrees, of honorific offices, and of symbolic titles and regalia—and equality was proscribed externally by the exclusion from the lodge of women, blacks, Chinese, some recent immigrants, and even the physically handicapped at times.[8]

What did all these postwar lodge members see in the elaborate rituals and inflated rhetoric of the orders? Most likely it was some momentary rekindling of small town or rural community in the anonymity of the expanding urban environments, some echo of the soldierly camaraderie around the Civil War campfire, some reaffirmation of racial solidarity in the face of interracial tensions, some remembrance of frontier revivalistic "masculine" religion in opposition to the increasingly "feminized" liberal Protestantism, some resistance to the entry of women into government employment and factories, some artisanal autonomy in the midst of the erosion of handicraft and proprietary status, and/or some hunger for public respect for the dignity of farming, or "husbandry," in the cross currents of a highly competitive commercial system. Individually, participation in fraternal orders could have been related to any one of these specific reasons for the appeal of ritualism. Collectively, it represented a temporary withdrawal into a liminal, brotherly "communitas" during a time when the civic, political polis and the socioeconomic society were both rapidly changing. Unlike the Radical Republicans who attempted to extend equality and justice to the freedmen or the moderate Republicans who were content to simply undergird the liberty of *all* loyal citizens with constitutional guarantees, the fraternal ritualists' values were directed mainly toward themselves.[9]

To what extent did the politically active public, both North and South, understand or sympathize with the moderate Republicans' notions of liberty and justice or the Radical Republicans' emphasis on equality? What was the relationship between the fraternal ritualists' symbolic inculcation of liberty and fraternity and their political behavior? The issues were complicated by cross-cutting tensions. Republicans had not only enfranchised the freedmen but they had also disenfranchised a portion of the former electorate. While in Radical Republican eyes those who were excluded had forfeited their rights by rebellion and continued resistance, the prevalence of presidential pardons and the promise of congressional pardons in the Fourteenth Amendment had implied that this status would be temporary. The use of "iron-clad" oaths in congressional Reconstruction, however, made such disabilities seem more permanent and raised, obliquely, another issue. To what extent did the reconstruction constitutions rest on the consent of the governed, popular sovereignty, or the "will of the people"? Resistance to congressional Reconstruction, then, could be justified in Southern whites' eyes by appeal to concepts of liberty going back to the colonial heritage of resistance to "tyranny," to the Jeffersonian suspicion that the powerful could corrupt government to serve their own ends, and to Jacksonian "laissez-faire" principles. This Southern tradition of "natural liberty" as *freedom from* external restraint thus complimented the notion of "constitutional liberty" as *freedom to* assent to the laws that were to be binding upon the community. Racial bias further complicated the response. As legal historian Michael Les Benedict has noted, "for most [white] southerners racism interacted with deeply held principles of constitutional liberty in a manner that convinced them that they were the oppressed, not the oppressors."[10]

By 1870 the legal, constitutional, political, economic, and cultural basis for the protection of civil rights of all citizens existed within the framework created by the congressional Reconstruction laws and constitutional amendments. Yet, within a few years the "experiment in biracial democracy" would be largely thwarted, the constitutional "revolution" of assertive federal judicial supremacy turned back, and the political and civil rights of black freedmen rendered increasingly tenuous. The promise of equality of opportunity under a "free-labor" regime was also blighted by the crop-lien credit system and various forms of sharecropping and tenant farming in the South and by the challenge of the newly created corporations in the North. What went wrong?

First, a wave of what was popularly known as Ku Klux Klan violence swept through the South directed against black voters and white supporters of congressional Reconstruction. The ritualism of some fraternal orders turned into a reign of fratricidal terror. So called "redeemer" governments overturned or undercut previous attempts to secure legal and political equality for freedmen and white Unionists. The Republican-dominated Congress responded reluctantly in 1870 and 1871 with enforcement acts to protect voting rights and, finally, in 1871 with the Ku Klux Klan Act. These acts were designed to punish conspiracies to deprive citizens of their civil rights, to promote federal judicial and military intervention if the states failed to uphold rights, and to designate certain acts as crimes that could be prosecuted under federal law. Senator Charles

Sumner, who had foreseen the need to protect civil rights from *private* acts as well as *public* actions, had introduced a new civil rights bill in 1870 to guarantee equal access to public transportation and accommodation, schools, cemeteries, and houses of worship. The bill had languished in the Senate and had become a political football only to be passed in a watered-downed version in May 1872 as part of the political maneuvering for the upcoming presidential election.[11]

Second, in the North the endemic corruption of the Grant administration divided the Republicans, promoted a Liberal Republican revolt in 1872, and brought the issue of civil service reform to the fore. The alienation of many Southern whites from the congressional Reconstruction governments because of their ambitious educational, welfare, and industrial programs (and the resulting tax burden) led them to support the concerted efforts to "redeem" these state governments by any means deemed necessary. Many Northern citizens grew tired of the continual alarms of Reconstruction issues, convinced themselves that the abolitionist movement had achieved its goal, believed that the concerns of the Civil War could be safely relegated to the halls of memory and the conventional pieties of oratory, or succumbed to the rationalizations of racial inequality found in the new Social Darwinist thought. Economically the prosperity of the railroad boom collapsed into a severe depression in 1873 that diverted public attention to other issues and raised again the cry for more currency or credit.[12]

The questions facing the nation in the 1870s, then, were deeply fundamental. What were the "privileges or immunities" of individual citizens, those civil rights that had supposedly been guaranteed by the adoption of the Fourteenth Amendment? And what was the national government's responsibility to act in defense of them? In 1873 the Supreme Court in the *Slaughter-House* cases had to confront the issue head on. The crux of the case, which involved a challenge by unemployed butchers against a grant of monopoly to a meat-processing corporation in New Orleans, turned on the question of whether the Fourteenth Amendment had "federalized" the rights of *all* citizens or had only extended to the African Americans the rights already enjoyed by white citizens. The majority of the Court in a five to four decision upheld the narrower interpretation that Congress had intended only to *extend* to blacks certain rights held by whites and not to *expand* the rights of all or to change traditional federal-state relations. In the process of deciding the case, the members of the Court listed twenty-two "privileges or immunities" of citizenship. Impressive as the list might have appeared to be, the message of the *Slaughter-House* cases was clear. According to the legal scholar David P.

Currie, "the Court arguably reduced the privileges or immunities clause to nothing more than authority for congressional enforcement of rights found elsewhere in federal law, hinted that equal protection might apply only to racial classifications, and dismissed a due process argument with little more than a bare conclusion."[13]

In the eyes of those congressional Republican leaders who were still anxious to protect civil rights, the Southern states were the crux of the problem. In 1875, to shore up what remained of the Reconstruction legacy, Republicans steered through a parliamentary maze additional enforcement acts. They also passed a revised civil rights act that outlawed racial discrimination in inns, theaters, and railroads. The burden of enforcement, however, fell primarily upon the individuals who had to sue in federal court to secure their rights. Few African Americans, moreover, could afford—financially, personally, or politically—to challenge the tightening ring of discrimination being perpetuated by private businessmen and state officials alike. The Supreme Court, meanwhile, in *United States v. Reese* (1876) and *United States v. Cruikshank* (1876) further extended the *Slaughter-House* cases doctrines. As Robert J. Kaczorowski, a careful student of the 1866–76 judicial proceedings, has concluded: "The Supreme Court preserved a modified theory of state sovereignty, resurrected a theory of American federalism based on states' rights, and recognized primary authority over citizenship and civil rights as residing in the states." Thus, a decade after the initial Civil Rights Act of 1866, the situation had returned to its starting point, with some modifications. Civil rights had been ensconced in the Constitution, interpreted by the courts, and experienced briefly in daily life by freedmen and others. But, primary responsibility for the protection of those rights now rested with the states, while the federal courts exercised a secondary role of protecting individuals who sought relief from violations of the numerous acts. Furthermore, court-supervised protection of the male citizen's right to vote was limited to cases of discrimination based solely upon "race, color, or previous condition of servitude."[14] (The question of the civil rights and voting rights of women will be dealt with in the next chapter.)

Events soon revealed many of the institutional weaknesses of these arrangements as well as the tenacity of courageous individuals and the persistence of communal hope. Congressional Reconstruction became one of the casualties of the political crisis attending the presidential election of 1876 because of disputed returns from three Reconstruction states. According to Eric Foner, in the backroom maneuvering that preceded the creation of an electoral commission to resolve the dispute, the Republican candidate Rutherford B. Hayes "at least gave tacit approval to a series of complex negotiations involving his close political associates, representatives of South Carolina and Louisiana Democrats, and a group of self-appointed maneuverers who hoped to promote their own vision of a New South." In the end, the electoral commission, along strict partisan lines, resolved the election in favor of Hayes over the Democrat Samuel J. Tilden. The newly inaugurated president and congressional leaders, also on partisan lines, confirmed some of the innumerable bargains, promises, and plans that had been made by others. Hayes would see to it that the federal troops in the South returned to their barracks and avoided political matters. Furthermore, he would allow the Reconstruction regimes in South Carolina and Louisiana to be overthrown and he would appoint a few former Confederates to patronage positions. Southern Democratic leaders promised to protect the rights of the freedmen and to uphold the recent constitutional amendments.[15]

For many African Americans in the South, however, the "Compromise of 1877" represented a final blow to hopes for equality and justice. A group left the South in 1877 to establish Nicodemus, Kansas, an all-black town. This migration seemed symbolic of an alternative way out of the situation in the South and received widespread publicity, as did a proposed African American expedition to Liberia in 1878. However, very few could actually migrate. "The total black influx into Kansas *throughout the 1870s*," historian William Cohen has noted, "can hardly have numbered much more than twenty-five thousand, and it appears that most of the blacks who made it to Kansas came from Kentucky, Tennessee, and Missouri, rather than from the Deep South." With a worsening political situation, deteriorating economic conditions, and realization that going to Liberia was not feasible, a mass hysterical, millennialist "Kansas Fever" seized some of the poorest of the blacks in the lower South. These "exodusters" may have believed rumors that the national government would help them, but a boycott by white steamboat captains of all black passengers and the failure of the federal government to act stemmed the tide by June 1879. Even attempts by northern Republicans to bring some black voters up from North Carolina to the politically important state of Indiana for the closely matched 1880 presidential election failed.[16]

Finally, the Supreme Court in *United States v. Harris* (1882) held that the sections of the Ku Klux Klan Act of 1871, designed to punish conspiracy to deprive someone of equal protection of the law under the Fourteenth Amendment, were unconstitutional because the equal protection clause regulated only *state* sanctioned actions, not individual ones. The next year, in the *Civil Rights* cases (1883), Justice Joseph P. Bradley of the Supreme Court held that the Civil Rights Act of 1875 was also unconstitutional. "Individual invasion of individual rights," Bradley said, "is not the subject matter of the [Fourteenth] Amendment." Justice John Marshall Harlan, in a classic dissent, concluded otherwise: "Constitutional provisions, adopted in the interest of liberty, and for the purpose of securing, through national legislation, if need be, rights inhering in a state of freedom, and belonging to American citizenship, have been so construed as to defeat the ends the people desired to accomplish by changes in the fundamental law." How is the student of history to account for the phenomenon of a Republican-dominated Supreme Court invalidating or narrowing the meaning of Republican-created congressional Reconstruction laws and constitutional amendments? Michael Kammen, an astute commentator on American constitutionalism, has proposed a convincing theory. "Republican sentiment on behalf of civil rights for freedmen was counterbalanced by a continuing commitment to federalism," he has argued. "Most Republicans accepted the notion that a protected sphere of state jurisdiction remained beyond the reach of national authority, and their acceptance required difficult decisions in response to perplexing alternatives."[17]

Why did "the people" (in Justice Harlan's phrase) not rise up in righteous indignation against the Supreme Court's decision as some of them had done a quarter of a century earlier over the *Dred Scott* case? Why did not the political landscape ring with denunciations and calls for new coalitions to redeem the promises of the past? Frederick Douglass, speaking on the twentieth anniversary of the Emancipation Proclamation, viewed the *Civil Rights* cases as an example of the failure of historical memory. Above all, he blamed the psychological and emotional reconciliation of white Northerners and Southerners, the pervasiveness of the myth of the Confederate "Lost Cause," and the ritualization of the war experience in veterans' fraternal organizations, reunions, and public nostalgia. The past, Douglass realized, was also a contested terrain, where parties struggled not just to preserve the memories of former times but to use these symbols as means to acquire power or to justify current policies.[18]

If neither presidents, Congress, courts, political parties, state legislatures, local editors, historical memory, reasonable rhetoric, nor fraternal organizations could, or would, protect the civil rights of the African Americans, then the burden fell, ultimately, upon the individual. If civil rights in the 1870s and 1880s meant essentially such activities as the right to enter into contracts, to acquire property, to bargain for the terms of labor, to travel or to change one's residence at will, then the extent of such liberty must finally be measured not only at the macrolevel in national politics, state legislation, or judicial interpretation but also at the micro-level as found in dusty court house records, fading photographs, and oral traditions handed down over generations. Even at this level, historians armed with the techniques of the new social history record a tale that is more negative than positive. In a predominantly agricultural society, ownership of land was still the key to maintaining one's independence. But the Southern white landowners, allied with the "credit furnishing" merchants, were determined to maintain their predominant position. The freedom they were determined to protect for themselves was their access to a dependable labor supply and some control of it on a day-by-day basis. The freedom, or autonomy, that the African Americans wanted to protect was control of their own family labor, some say in managerial decisions over crops, and rewards proportionate to effort. But the lack of credit, failure of communal alternatives, and the political structures of contract laws, antienticement enactments, and convict labor systems severely restricted them. Ironically, the Reconstruction-instituted "free-labor" system, as modified by the redeemer governments, left the freedman with little option except the freedom to labor for someone or to move on periodically. Tenant farming or sharecropping might preserve a measure of an African American family's control of its labor, but such relative autonomy was purchased at a terrible price in limited opportunities.[19]

If civil rights in the 1870s and 1880s also included the right to sue and to be sued, to testify in court, to serve on juries, to appeal cases to a higher federal court, to bear only the same punishments or penalties as others convicted of similar offenses, then justice was denied whenever an individual African American could not afford to sue, whenever his or her testimony was automatically discounted by those who heard it, whenever freedmen were barred from jury duty either by law or custom, whenever the convict lease system flourished, or whenever a lynch mob broke into a county jail and seized a terrified victim. If civil rights, broadly conceived, might also be said to encompass the right to vote as an expression of citizenship, then equality was or would be under attack whenever "redeemer" governments enacted poll taxes, literacy tests, or multiple ballot box systems, and controlled elections by fraudulent counts and physical intimidation.[20] Well might the former slaves and their political allies have recalled in this context the biblical words of the prophet Jeremiah:

The harvest is past, the summer is ended,
and we are not saved.
For the hurt of the daughter of my people
am I hurt; I am black;

astonishment hath taken hold on me.
Is there no balm in Gilead;
is there no physician there?[21]

That numerous individuals persisted in the defense of life and liberty and in the pursuit of happiness in these circumstances was indeed a testimony to the human spirit.

3

Which Way for Women's Rights? 1868–1888

Women in the mid-nineteenth century confronted deep ambiguities in the roles that filled their lives and the values that bound their behavior. Confronting them in the pre–Civil War period was the set of cultural conventions known to historians variously as the "cult of domesticity," "the Victorian mentality," or the "doctrine of the separate spheres." Men were supposed to occupy the public sphere of increasingly specialized economic activity in an emerging market economy, to participate in the democratized political system, and to exercise authority over all those subordinate to them or dependent upon them. Women were supposed to occupy the private sphere of domestic economy, child rearing, moral instruction, and primary health care, to participate in charitable and religious activities, and to embody the self-sacrificial values deemed necessary to the maintenance of "civilization." The boundaries of the separate spheres were never so rigid in practice as they might appear in theory, and the whole concept was oriented more toward the pretensions of white, middle- and upper-class, urban women than to the realities of slaves and free black working women, frontier farm wives, immigrant factory workers, or single women and widows trying to support themselves as teachers, professionals, or shopkeepers. Furthermore, the concepts had not been so restrictive as to preclude some women from acting collectively outside the home in creating a separate *public* sphere for women as charitable organizers, antislavery advocates, temperance lecturers, public school lobbyists, and managers of farms, plantations, or mercantile establishments (particularly if widowed). Separate spheres, then, were a set of cultural norms for "proper behavior," partly created by and for white women, which were continually inculcated, internalized, and justified by the daily routines and the periodic rituals of home, church, support networks, women's organizations, educational institutions, and community. They could restrict women, but they could also be manipulated by women to some extent to further their own goals.[1]

Within this system of cultural norms women struggled to define the meaning of their lives in terms of three concepts: dependence, independence, and interdependence. Dependence referred both to the legal status of women as being subordinate to their husbands or male relatives and to the economic situation of depending on another to furnish the money needed to purchase clothing, shelter, and medicine. For slaves dependence was total and lifelong. Independence could refer to a variety of situations. It could mean recognition in law of one's separate personhood (particularly if unmarried), control of one's own property, and the right to earn a living. It could encompass political rights as well. Interdependence was a more subtle concept. It referred to the social relationships in which women helped, supported, and nurtured each other in informal networks, rituals, and community activities. The term could also be used to describe the economic relationships *within* the family, particularly the working-class and farm families, and the relationships *between* families in kinship networks and neighborhoods. This chapter will explore the ways in which these three concepts interacted with the women's rights movement and influenced the creation of women's organizations during the period 1868–88 as they pursued liberty, equality, and justice.

Even rebels against these cultural norms felt the inner tensions and the pull of such assumptions on their pioneering public behavior. Lucy Stone, a pre–Civil War college graduate, teacher, antislavery orator, and women's rights advocate, only married after issuing a joint declaration with her husband denouncing the current laws and customs governing women's status in marriage and retained her own name after marriage (in spite of the legal difficulties it sometimes occasioned). In 1855 she had written to a friend:

Paulina Davis has written me, that she wants the marriage question to come up at the National [Woman's Rights] Convention. . . . It seems to me that we are not ready for it. . . . And yet it is clear to me, that question underlies, this whole movement and all our little skirmishing for better laws, and the right to vote, will yet be swallowed up in the real question, viz, has woman, as wife, a right to herself? It is very little to me to have the right to vote, to own property & c. if I may not keep my body, and its uses, in my absolute right. . . . This question will *force* itself upon us some day, but it seems to me it is *untimely* now.[2]

Lucy Stone was as culturally radical, then, as some of her more well-known contemporaries, such as Elizabeth Cady Stanton and Susan B.

Anthony. At the 1855 National Woman's Rights Convention, when a speaker criticized the woman's movement for appealing to women who were disappointed with their lot in life, Lucy Stone replied, "It shall be the business of my life to deepen that disappointment in every woman's heart until she bows down to it no longer."[3]

The changes wrought by the Civil War put great stress on the cultural norms that were binding upon women. When the men were called away to war, women on the plantations and farms were expected to shoulder the additional burdens of managing the complex cycles of planting and harvesting, to hire and supervise temporary laborers or to control the work of the slaves, and to deal with the economic realities of barter, credit, and home manufacturing. White women in the South had to bear the additional strains of a war-ravaged countryside, where foraging armies seized livestock and food and commandeered shelter and labor. In the slave quarters, African American women engaged in the subtle subversion of daily discipline, waited anxiously for freedom, or joined the tide of refugees flocking into the areas controlled by the Union army. In urban areas, North and South, the war had created new or expanded opportunities for women as clerks in government bureaucracies, as caregivers for the wounded, as unskilled or semiskilled "operatives" in the factories, mills, and shops, and as temporary replacements for men in the retail, transportation, and service industries. While women might experience some new responsibilities and experience briefly the rewards of independence, they were still bound in the systems of interdependence that marked their rural communities or working-class cultures. When the war ended and the men returned, the economy plunged into a recession. Most of the gains in women's economic opportunities disappeared. Only the newly emancipated slaves tasted the joy of freedom from total dependence but soon discovered that freedom to reshape their lives was severely limited. As African American women faced both discrimination because of their race and restrictions because of their gender, their survival strategies and priorities were more complicated than and frequently at odds with those of white women who were also pursuing civil rights and women's rights. A few white female abolitionists responded to the call for teachers to come to the South and help in the freedmen's schools. In some cases they unwittingly crowded out free black women who had pioneered in establishing schools for the children of the slaves and who desperately needed the income and expanded opportunity that teaching provided.[4]

If the small group of northern women's rights advocates and free black women believed that their activities during the war would engender grateful responses from the Republicans who were creating a new constitutional order, they were soon disappointed. Elizabeth Cady Stanton and Susan B. Anthony, in fact, were furious with the Republicans. By introducing the word "male" into the Constitution in the Fourteenth Amendment, they had raised new barriers to expanding women's rights as citizens, particularly the demand for the right to vote. The Republican leaders and male abolitionists admonished such women's rights advocates not to burden the drive to protect the rights and lives of the freedmen with another controversial issue. Undaunted, Stanton and Anthony helped to engineer the creation of an American Equal Rights Association in 1866 to work for the right to vote for *both* black freedmen and women. (And, as the black suffragist Sojourner Truth reminded them all, "women" included the black women, too.) Stanton and Anthony plunged into efforts to secure equal voting rights in the New York constitutional convention and Kansas constitutional amendments campaigns in 1867. Stanton and Anthony were deserted by many of their former allies among the abolitionists, opposed by most Republicans, and manipulated into an embarrassing alliance with an eccentric racist Democrat, George Francis Train. Their equal suffrage campaigns all ended in failure. Seizing upon Train's offer of financial assistance, Stanton and Anthony established a newspaper, the *Revolution,* in New York City as a vehicle for expressing their wide-ranging feminist ideas. The first issue, on 8 January 1868, was the opening shot in a war for control of the women's rights agitation in the postwar scene.[5]

This war did not go any better than their previous campaigns. By the end of May 1868 it was clear to Stanton and Anthony that the American Equal Rights Association was splitting apart. A moderate group of New England reformers formed the New England Woman Suffrage Association, with Julia Ward Howe as its president. They supported the Fourteenth Amendment, "universal" suffrage (i.e., black males as well as white males now, women as well as men eventually), and the Republican Reconstruction program. As a temporary expedient, Stanton and Anthony countered by publishing a call: "A National Woman's Suffrage Convention [is to] be held in . . . Washington, D.C. [January 1869]. . . . All associations friendly to Woman's Rights are invited to send delegates from every state. Friends of the cause are invited to attend and take part in the discussions." According to historian Kathleen Barry, Stanton and Anthony had drawn an important lesson from their experiences in 1866–67: "Men—as a group—in whatever party or movement they organize, cannot form a material alliance with women's rights—however supportive some individual men might be." In short, women as a gender group would have to go it alone to secure their rights. By May 1869, when they created a permanent organization, the National Woman Suffrage Association (NWSA), Anthony explained "that it was thought best to keep absolute control in the hands of women."[6]

By November 1869 the moderates, including Lucy Stone, Julia Ward Howe, and Henry Blackwell, responded by creating their own organization, the American Woman Suffrage Association (AWSA), which shared leadership among men and women. Lucy Stone might have been as culturally radical as Anthony and Stanton when it came to the question of liberty as freedom to control one's own body even in marriage, but she was much more cautious when it came to public agitation, particularly by women's organizations. She tried to explain this in a letter to Elizabeth Cady Stanton, 19 October 1869: "People will differ, as to what they consider the best methods & means. The true wisdom is not to ignore, but to provide for the fact." As a leader of the American Woman Suffrage Association and one of the editors of its newspaper, the *Woman's Journal*, Lucy Stone in the 1870s would try to steer clear of controversial issues such as divorce, "free love," working women's rights, or feminist attacks on institutional religion.[7]

Anthony and Stanton were radical in a deeper sense than simply being willing to use extreme means to achieve their goals. They had more comprehensive feminist philosophies than most of their contemporaries. Confronting their society's core cultural value of female *dependence,* they advocated the alternate value of female *independence.* As Lois W. Banner has noted in her biography of Elizabeth Cady Stanton: "Few feminists have gone beyond her vision of the amphiarchate: an androgynous society in which roles and responsibilities are assigned by ability and interest and not by sex, in which power is shared equally by men and women, and in which all sex stereotyping is eliminated in the raising of children." In this vision lay the unity of Stanton's seemingly contradictory statements: if women had the opportunity to achieve economic independence, they would not need to seek shelter in a dependent marriage, sell themselves in prostitution, or stay in a loveless marriage. If women were assured of social independence, they would not become "slaves" to fashion and denigrating social customs. If women were guaranteed legal independence, they would use the ballot wisely to protect their own interests and to promote society's well-being in keeping with their maternal instincts. Anthony and Stanton were radicals rather than reformers precisely because they did not want to simply *mitigate* (or minimize) the effects of dependence; they wanted to *eliminate* it.[8]

There was a nagging set of questions that arose when others heard the message that Anthony, Stanton, and other cultural radicals presented in their newspapers, speeches, and activities. Even if women achieved *independence* as freedom from *dependence* in marriage, the economy, and society, would they still be bound in the networks of *interdependence?* Did liberty mean a radical, isolating individualism, a freedom to pursue one's desire rather than to do one's racial, familial, or communal duty? And what did equality mean for women? Equality before the law might promise more secure control over wages, property, and personal possessions, but what of those extraordinary duties that contemporary rhetoric said adhered in the status of motherhood? Did equality apply within the family and its numerous roles? Did the mother as moral guardian and mentor have an equal claim in the home with the father as protector, provider, and disciplinarian? Equality of opportunity in the workplace and marketplace might expand the range of options for young, educated, single women, aspiring professionals, and widows, but what about the injustices of unequal pay for identical work, gender-based restrictions on professional training, or common law discriminations in the division of estates and joint property? How could women achieve justice? Was access to power in the public realm limited to possession of the vote as a means, or were there other goals to be achieved as well? Did the creation of a separate, female *public* sphere enhance or diminish woman's status in the interdependent, dual gender *private* sphere? How did race complicate the answers to all these questions?[9]

There was a deep irony, then, in Anthony and Stanton's seemingly single-minded pursuit of woman suffrage over the next two decades. Given their broad ranging and fundamental analysis of the problems of women's dependence, why did they seem to narrow their focus to the issue of the right to vote? According to Kathleen Barry, Anthony's biographer, Anthony realized that a new generation of women's rights advocates had come of age in the immediate postwar period. The inheritors and benefactors of the first generation's achievements, the new generation was more individualistic in its concerns and more piecemeal in its awareness of the particular problems faced by women rather than conscious of their *status* per se. While in awe of the charismatic dedication of the pioneers of the prewar era, they were less inclined to sacrifice *all* for the sake of the cause. And some African American activists were concerned that empowering the freedmen but not the freedwomen would simply create new "masters." Such diffuse anxieties and concerns had to be focused. Anthony, with her greater executive ability and sense of institutional dynamics, seized the moment and harnessed this energy for a realizable and symbolic goal—woman suffrage. The events of the day transfixed the attention of all parties. For the radical feminists, the trauma of rejection in the Fourteenth Amendment's definition of voter as male and the limiting of the Fifteenth Amendment protection of the vote to racial issues seared the issue with emotional connotations. Stanton could never quite forget that her society was willing to extend the right to vote to presumably "immoral" men—particularly "illiterate" blacks and "intemperate" Irishmen—while denying the same right to presumably "moral" white, middle- and upper-class, educated women. If women had been stamped with the seal of dependence and inferiority by constitutional amendments, then, Anthony and Stanton argued, only a constitutional amendment could undo the damage and bestow upon them the symbol of independence and equal citizenship, the right to vote.[10]

Woman suffrage was, nonetheless, a peculiarly multifaceted issue. Viewed symbolically as a goal, a sign of women's independent status, it was *culturally* a radical rejection of the society's cultural stereotype of female dependence; however, viewed narrowly and instrumentally as a means, a way to correct current legal disabilities, woman suffrage could be viewed *politically* as a reform, a way to enhance the society's core value of equality. These differences were evident in Anthony and Stanton's attempt in 1868 to form an alliance with working women in New York City and to work with labor unionists in the National Labor Union. Anthony attempted to form female trade unions, but her encouragement of women typesetters to seize whatever employment opportunities opened up to them, even if it meant acting as strikebreakers against male unions, did not endear her to the more traditional male trade unionists. While some labor leaders—black and white—supported the idea of woman suffrage, the bulk of the delegates at labor conventions were not willing to endorse the controversial idea. In 1869 Stanton and Anthony created another organization, the Working Women's Association, but it soon collapsed. Working women had immediate, job-related concerns that could not wait for the eventual achievement of the right to vote. The split between middle-class suffragists and working-class trade unionists became as wide as the division among the suffragists themselves between the NWSA and AWSA.[11]

The two decades after the split in the women's movement and the creation of rival suffrage organizations saw a subtle shift in arguments concerning women's rights. Even though women were discriminated against as a group, some of the leaders came to think about more individualistic solutions to their problems. Some suffragists argued that the Fourteenth and Fifteenth Amendments had nationalized the rights of citizenship. Because the right to vote was inherent in the nature of citizenship, and women were citizens, women as individual citizens had only to claim and exercise this right. The argument was ingenious in that it put the authorities on the defensive and opened the way for enforcement of the right to vote by congressional legislation and judicial interpretation rather than by further constitutional amendments. Thus, some men and women tried to invoke the "privileges or immunities" and "equal protection of the law" aspects of the Fourteenth Amendment to extend women's rights. However, neither the dominant factions in the Republican Party nor the federal courts ultimately accepted the argument. Expansion of rights by novel judicial interpretations seemed too anarchistic to men confronting economic chaos after the depression of 1873. In a series of legal cases—*Bradwell v. State of Illinois, United States v. Anthony,* and *Minor v. Happersett*—state and federal courts in 1873–75 applied to women's rights the newly announced *Slaughter-House* cases doctrine. They ruled that the Fourteenth Amendment did *not* establish *new* national rights of citizenship and that states exercised primary control over existing rights. Therefore, a state could refuse to admit women to the legal profession (*Bradwell* case) or to extend to women the "privilege" of voting (*Anthony* and *Minor* cases). Thus, at the same time that Reconstruction was collapsing in the South and the federal courts were beginning to narrow the interpretation of the Fourteenth Amendment, suffragists came to the realization that they would have to amend the Constitution (or state constitutions) in order to secure their right to vote.[12]

While Stanton and Anthony claimed to speak *for all* women in their feminist analysis, in fact they spoke *to* only small groups in their suffragist agitation. Lucy Stone, Julia Ward Howe, and Henry Blackwell claimed to reach a broader, more moderate group of women, but they, too, represented only one wing of the woman suffrage movement. While militant African American suffragists such as Sojourner Truth, Mary Ann Shadd Cary, Harriet Purvis and her daughter "Hattie" Purvis supported the National Woman Suffrage Association, a larger number of such African American women supported the more moderate American Woman Suffrage Association and its emphasis on local and state action. But none of the woman suffrage organizations were very successful in the early 1870s. In contrast to the failure of the woman suffragists was the apparent success of a parallel woman's movement. A spontaneous temperance movement in 1873–74 among women in the small towns and cities of the middle-western and mid-Atlantic states dramatized woman's role as "protector of the home," in the language of the doctrine of separate spheres. Such women were alarmed by the failure of existing prohibition laws, by the surge of liquor consumption during and after the Civil War, by the intrusion of the rootless, hard-drinking male camaraderie of the saloon culture into the small towns along the expanding railroads, and by the seeming inability or unwillingness of local authorities to enforce liquor license laws. They were also disturbed by public drunkenness and disorder, which threatened women in the home and on public streets. Some women decided to act. Bands of praying, singing, determined women, dubbed the Woman's Temperance Crusade by the press, descended on the saloons and drugstores that sold liquor to demand that they cease selling alcoholic beverages. With varying degrees of success, the groundswell of activity involved an estimated 54,000 to 57,000 women in over 850 crusades. They attracted the attention of leaders in more traditional temperance, benevolence, and Sunday school teachers organizations. In November 1874 these leaders created a new organization, the Woman's Christian Temperance Union (WCTU), and tried to harness some of the energy of the crusaders in support of their own more modest and traditional goals.[13]

The temperance crusade soon attracted the attention of Frances Willard, a skillful educational administrator who was adrift at that moment in her professional career. For five years, 1874–79, the local, state, and national activities of the WCTU provided a precarious base for Willard as she tried to find a new career in evangelism, public lecturing, and newspaper administration. Finally, in 1879 she was elected the national president of the WCTU and found her role for the rest of her life. She helped to make the WCTU into the largest and most active woman's organization in America. With her "do everything" philosophy, pragmatic political instincts, and skillful manipulation of public images of womanly virtue, she pushed and prodded the organization over the next decade into support of a wide range of issues: woman's right to vote, equal pay for equal work, early childhood education, "social purity" (antiprostitution), third party politics, prison reform, federal aid to education, cooperation with the labor unions, and freedom from "domestic drudgery." She carved out a public, political role for herself by pushing the strategy of a separate female public sphere to its logical limits. If women were entrusted with the care of the home and moral instruction of the young, they had to be empowered to protect the home by exercising the vote at a minimum in local option or liquor license issues and school board elections. They had to educate the public on the need for preventive or "protective" legislation. The rise of Frances Willard to power in the WCTU indicated that power and leadership in the area of women's rights was shifting from the radicals to the reformers. Willard's conversion to woman suffrage in

1875–76 did not change her dedication to reform goals and public respect for Victorian pieties.[14]

Increasingly in the 1870s the rhetoric of women's rights agitation shifted from the wrong of denying women their rights to the role of women in righting the wrongs of society. But this shift spurred a reaction. As part of a larger shift toward conservative social philosophies, anti-democratic political arguments, and a prevalent fear of social disorder, many middle- and upper-class women who opposed the right to vote for women began to organize. Largely under the leadership of urban, upper-class, native-born, Protestant women who were married to Republican political leaders and local spokesmen, these conservative women became vocal in defense of their understanding of cultural norms and current values. Thus, when women's rights advocates brought proposals before the state legislatures to allow women to control their own wages and earnings, they made more headway if they cast their pleas in the form of protecting working-class women from improvident, intemperate, or absent husbands. If they argued abstractly about the need to emancipate women from the semislavery of the marriage bond or to enhance their economic independence, they made less headway.[15]

In short, what was happening in the middle- and upper-class consciousness of Gilded Age Americans was a slow, subtle shift in the sense of what "ought" to be the case in reference to women, but not necessarily in ways that would be pleasing to feminists. Both private duties toward home, family, and religion and public roles of women as defenders and protectors of these institutions were slowly expanding. But Victorian ethical norms ranked doing one's duty higher than fulfilling one's personal desire. The popular Christian romances of the time, which were widely read by women, reinforced this belief. As the twentieth-century writer Joyce Carol Oates has observed: "The Christian romance demands the sacrifice of the self *as a liberation;* in this distant region of the soul, piety is not contrived but utterly natural." *Freedom from* selfish love (desire) was the prelude to *freedom to* love others (duty). Thus, many of the women who followed Frances Willard's "do everything" banner into the WCTU and other benevolent organizations operated within these social and political limits, and they found a sense of freedom in this way of doing their duty.[16]

Organizational efforts among women during this period would also take the form of a ritual withdrawal and renewal within a separate "female space" to strengthen adherence to traditional cultural stereotypes. Women's study clubs, educational endeavors, and the WCTU all paid deference to Victorian gender norms. However, these activities also slowly expanded the boundaries of women's public sphere, encouraged self-confidence among the participants, and enhanced their understanding of the meaning of core values. These developments were evident even in the women's auxiliaries created by the male fraternal orders. In the post–Civil War period of phenomenal growth among such fraternal organizations, the fostering of women's auxiliaries or the creation of separate orders for women was part of a complex response to changing gender roles. The creation of these liminal groups and the growth of their sense of community was fostered by the rituals in such organizations as the Order of the Eastern Star (Masonic), Daughters of Rebekah (Odd Fellows), the Pythian Sisters (Knights of Pythias) and the Royal Neighbors of America (Modern Woodman of America). The women's rituals seemed designed to ensconce women in their primary familial roles of daughter, sister, wife, mother, and widow and to underscore the familiar virtues of love, fidelity, purity, and self-sacrifice. Yet the history of the women's auxiliaries during this period was also characterized by a "struggle for power" between men and women. Women initiated incremental changes in the fraternal auxiliaries and reached out in cooperation to other women's organizations. "Women's fraternal auxiliaries," sociologist Mary Ann Clawson has concluded, "can thus be seen as part of a larger attack upon the inviolability of male social institutions, an attack that was implicit in the temperance movement as well."[17]

African American women felt this clash between the dominating male institutional environment and the changing meaning of womens' lives more acutely than did their white sisters because the pressures on black women were compounded by the factor of racial discrimination as well as by the factor of class status. Given the pressures on the African American community after the end of Reconstruction, women created liminal space for themselves in their churches and in the club movement by using their strategic roles as teachers and fund-raisers. According to historian Evelyn Brooks Higginbotham, "the first statewide convention of black Baptist women was organized in Kentucky in 1883 specifically around the issue of black higher education." The focus of their efforts was always two-fold: first, to earn respect for themselves as educated women who adhered to Victorian values, and, second, to raise the status of their race by education and culture. "The Baptist women's preoccupation with respectability reflected a bourgeois vision that vacillated between an attack on the failure of America to live up to its liberal ideals of equality and justice," Higginbotham has noted, "and an attack on the values and lifestyle of those blacks who transgressed white middle-class propriety." Their financial and educational activities could not avoid a certain paradox, however. The Victorian, middle-class values inculcated by these black women were the professed values of the very white society whose practices denied them both the respect and the status their efforts should have earned for them.[18]

Whoever wanted to challenge the social and political limits of American society had to find a language that would communicate with a potentially large but basically cautious and religiously oriented middle-class audience. The 1876 centennial of the American Revolution and the Declaration of Independence provided one such opportunity. Susan B. Anthony and some other members of the NWSA prepared a Women's Declaration of Rights. Although they were not part of the official proceedings, they did manage to make a presentation of the declaration and to hand out copies to the curious crowd. The declaration was a wide ranging summary of feminist criticism of the status and treatment of women in law and social custom couched in the legal language of a bill of impeachment against male power holders. It included veiled references to the *Anthony* and *Minor* cases (which involved denial of voting rights), used recent legislation "forbidding the importation of Chinese women on the Pacific coast for immoral purposes" as an attack on the double standard of morality, and recited suffragist, or at least NWSA, complaints against congressional attempts to restrict the right to vote in territories and new states to men. A final assertion—"that woman was made first for her own happiness, with the absolute right to herself"—was reminiscent of Lucy Stone's views on marriage and Elizabeth Cady Stanton's attack on current marriage laws. The Women's Declaration of Rights evoked the language of the 1776 Declaration of Independence and its natural rights philosophy of life, liberty, and the pursuit of happiness, but, curiously, the 1876 document did not specifically use the term liberty in its closing sentence: "We ask justice, we ask equality, we ask that all the civil and political rights that belong to citizens of the United States, be guaranteed to us and our daughters forever."[19]

In the context of the mid-1870s to mid-1880s, the traditional religious language of benevolence and duty seemed more effective in communicating with the audience of middle- and upper-class women than the older natural rights and legal language used by the suffragists, even though they were sensitive to new realities and assertive of the priority of desire over duty. Did the reluctance of conservative women to embrace the suffragists' views reflect not only their preference for religious language but also an unresolved intellectual tension between the issues of dependence/independence/interdependence? Did the feminists' reluctance to highlight the concept of liberty in the rhetorical strategy of the 1876 declaration represent a reaction against masculine misuse of the term to mask their privileged access to power? Which was the best way to talk about, let alone to achieve, women's rights?[20]

The Stanton and Anthony forces stuck doggedly to their strategy of seeking to amend the federal constitution. But, at the 1878 convention, the NWSA delegates approved a change in the wording of the proposed amendment. Gone was the statement that "the Right of Suffrage in the United States shall be based on citizenship" and the broader prohibition against "any distinction or discrimination whatever founded on sex." Instead, the language of the Fifteenth Amendment provided the model. The new version simply said that the right to vote "shall not be denied or abridged by the United States or by any State on account of sex." In spite of Stanton's vigorous defense of traditional natural rights for such constitutional action, the speeches of other delegates and the drift of suffrage rhetoric elsewhere showed that younger suffragists accepted the idea that women were forces of stability and morality in the home as well as in the state. The AWSA moderates continued to stress securing woman suffrage at the local and state level. Rebuffed in their own ranks, Stanton and Anthony tried over the next decade to enhance their prestige and power by working for the creation of an international woman suffrage association. Clearly, perceptions among upper- and middle-class women about what they "should do" or "ought to do" had changed since the traumatic events of 1867–68, but these changes did not always benefit the more single-minded militant suffragists.[21]

The gulf that had opened between middle-class advocates of woman suffrage and working-class trade unionists had also widened since 1869. Working-class culture emphasized different values from the independence so highly prized by middle-class suffragists and women's rights advocates. Working-class cultural values also differed from the condescendingly inculcated dependence advocated by upper-class matrons in their women's clubs, benevolent societies, and protective activities. The primary value of working-class culture was interdependence in the home, neighborhood, and class. The main organization for such working-class aspirations in the 1870s and 1880s was the Knights of Labor. Begun in 1869 by a small group of skilled male craftsmen, the order had been modeled on the secret, fraternal lodge pattern. Soon the Knights of Labor opened its ranks to skilled and unskilled, rural and urban, male and female, black and white. In 1881 the Knights formally admitted female locals and in 1886 decided to establish a woman's department to investigate the conditions of working women. In 1887 Leonora Barry, the head of the woman's department, estimated that there were about 65,000 women in the Knights. They constituted about 10 percent of the lodge's membership.[22]

By 1888 the advocates of women's rights had separated into three main streams related largely to racial category, class position, and cultural commitments. This separation did not mean that each group was totally isolated from the others, for there were some points of contact. In spite of their differences, the various women's rights groups did emphasize some common values, particularly equality and justice. Middle-class women might focus on equal rights under the law to protect their property rights, women members of the Knights of Labor might raise the cry for equal pay for equal work, and upper-class, college-educated women might discover the injustices of urban life and respond to the problem with individual acts of charity or by joining a benevolence group. African American women put community needs ahead of individual aspirations. Temporary coalitions might support married women's wage laws or restrictions on female and child labor in the name of justice and home protection, but racial stereotypes and elitist presuppositions hindered coalition building. African American women felt increasingly isolated in this context. In their public roles, women activists as social reformers thus appealed increasingly to class-oriented versions of common core values. It fell to cultural radicals, such as Susan B. Anthony, Elizabeth Cady Stanton, and Lucy Stone, for all their personal limitations, to try to remind women's organizations that these values must be universalized lest they become narrow appeals to self-interest. And equal rights *for all* would require an extensive realignment of institutions and a complete redrafting of laws. This was something that many of their colleagues were not willing to admit.[23]

The rhetoric and the strategies of the various women's rights groups in reference to the core value of liberty masked a fundamental ambiguity. Valiantly the suffragists tried to make possession of the right to vote stand as a symbol for liberty as independence, *freedom from* subordinate status, in much the same way that citizenship had served as a symbol for the freedmen's newly won liberty as *freedom from* slavery. But if women expanded their *public* roles, pursued liberty as *freedom to* develop themselves, to define the "pursuit of happiness" for themselves, to pursue their heart's desires, what would happen to their *private* duties? Was individual *independence* compatible with marital, familial, or racial *interdependence?* And what would happen to women's claim to private moral authority if they publicly pursued equality and justice and had to learn to compromise, bargain, and make deals in the political realm? Of all the barriers to women's advancement in the period 1868 to 1888—economic, legal, constitutional, and political—these cultural barriers were the hardest to overcome. Regardless of what social language women utilized to express their values—natural rights theory, Victorian mores, ethnic and communal norms, or religious benevolence—they were all old and familiar languages from the pre–Civil War Era; however, they increasingly confronted new realities as business, particularly in its many corporate forms, transformed America.[24]

4

Business and Labor from the Panic of 1873 to the Depression of 1893: Reorganization, Regulation, and Community Response

Since the Civil War, railroad promoters had overextended the sale of securities in order to raise capital for the construction of extensive, transcontinental systems. These securities had been particularly popular with European investors as well as with American banks, businesses, and insurance companies. A European banking crisis in May 1873, however, had led to the widespread withdrawal of European funds from the American securities market. The leading American broker in such sales to foreign investors, Jay Cooke and Company, was forced to close its doors in September 1873. This traumatic event contributed to a wave of bank failures, business bankruptcies, and falling prices that swept across the American economy. These events revealed dramatically the weakness of inherited ideas and values, the tenacity of old languages, and the growing strength of some new institutional forms in the American economy. This chapter will explore these issues in the period 1873 to 1893 by looking at the impact of changing forms of business structure and behavior; attempts to regulate some of these corporate forms, particularly the railroads; and the ensuing conflicts between workers and their communities and these evolving business enterprises.

Even before the panic of 1873, many Americans—workers, merchants, farmers, family-oriented entrepreneurs—had felt a sense of unease, a growing realization that their individual and community welfare depended not so much on their interpersonal efforts and personal character as on the impersonal machinations of distant institutional actors who interfered with "natural" market forces. The culprit seemed to be the limited-liability corporation. Unlike the individual entrepreneur who shouldered all the risks attendant upon his enterprise or who shared it equally with others in a partnership, the investor in a limited-liability corporation was responsible for its debts only to the limit of his personal investment in its stock or his capital investment in it. How, then, could there be equality of competition between the individual entrepreneur and the corporate investor? Furthermore, a partnership expired upon the death of one of the partners or was dissolved by mutual consent, whereas the corporation's existence was perpetual regardless of the life span of individual investors. How could there be justice between the various forms of business? How could the artisans or skilled workers maintain liberty and independent control of their labor and its product when reduced to the status of dependent wage earners?[1]

The issues were not new. They had been debated in the 1830s and had become part of the rhetoric of Jacksonian democracy. When state legislatures or Congress had granted limited-liability charters to groups of investors, they had freed them from certain forms of *personal* liability in order to accomplish definable *public* goals. Corporate charters had been granted to establish banks, to build canals, toll roads, or railroads, and to promote education. But such grants of "special privilege" to a few politically favored elite investors violated the canon of "equal rights" for all "producers" in the eyes of the Jacksonians. Jacksonian social language was ambiguous enough to encompass a variety of interests and comprehensive enough to create a powerful political tradition. Several attempts had been made in the 1830s–50s to restore the equality between the individual entrepreneurs and the corporations in order to ensure that they both had liberty to compete in the market place. One politically viable option was to regulate business behavior by law. State courts held that all corporations were subject to legislative regulation either because of specific clauses in their charters or because of common law principles that held that businesses engaged in certain public activities conducive to the common welfare were subject to communal control. Another option was to make the limited-liability corporate form available to anyone on minimal terms via "general incorporation" laws. What was available to all on equal terms was no longer seen as a "special privilege" but as an "equal right." Business, in short, had been democratized. Another option, particularly appealing to the urban labor unions, was to create an alternative to dependence on corporate employers by starting independent cooperatives or to form political coalitions to maintain communal norms.[2]

Corporations were in competition, then, not just with other forms of business, such as individual proprietorships, unlimited-liability partnerships, or family enterprises, but also with workers' traditional culture and community norms as expressed in common law doctrines and political alliances. Two developments in the 1850s–60s changed the balance of power between these contending actors. First, the emergence of the Re-

publican Party and the enactment of its Whig-oriented legislative programs during the Civil War had tipped the balance toward business in
general and corporations in particular. Business benefited from the creation of a national bank system, subsidies in the form of land grants
for homesteads and transcontinental railroads, high tariff protection for
manufacturers, government contracts for war supplies, and experiments
in "mixed enterprises," that had congressional charters and boards of directors with both public and private representatives. Second, as Alfred D.
Chandler Jr., has pointed out in his classic study, *The Visible Hand: The
Managerial Revolution in American Business,* "the rail and telegraph companies [of the 1850s–60s] were . . . the first modern business enterprises
to appear in the United States. They were the first to require a large
number of full-time managers to coordinate, control, and evaluate the
activities of a number of widely scattered operating units." In so doing,
the railroads changed the customary conditions of labor, the mechanisms
of control of the workplace, and the community's power over the corporation. The modern institutional form of business was created, Chandler
and others have argued, not simply by the application of technology to
manufacturing techniques or by the consolidation of large numbers of
workers under one roof, but by the systematic and periodic control and
evaluation of employees and their efforts.[3]

The pioneers of management on the railroads had been primarily
trained as civil engineers or gained their experience as military staff officers in the Civil War. They approached problems with a rational, analytical method of solving mechanical problems that put a premium on immediate control and medium-range institutional stability. With their
high fixed costs for tracks, trains, buildings and personnel, the railroad
managers intuitively manipulated rates and conditions of service in order
to ensure a sufficient volume of traffic that would generate an income that
equaled or exceeded minimal costs of operation. Their tactics violated the
traditional "logic of the market," which assumed that rates and conditions
of service would be set "impersonally" by supply-and-demand calculations operating freely in the marketplace. The growth of the railroad
systems also challenged the idea of a competitive environment that would
be maintained by a multitude of similarly sized units. The behavior of the
managers impinged, too, on the logic of the market when they tried to
regulate the terms of competition by such devices as long-haul/short-
haul rate discrimination, rebates or special refunds on rates for preferred
customers, drawbacks on competitor's rates for selected high volume customers, fluctuating rate schedules, and higher rate schedules on noncom-

petitive or "monopolistic" lines than on lines in more competitive situations. At the same time, the pioneers of railroad management were themselves challenged within the corporate structure by cautious investors who wanted long-term, stable rewards in the form of dividends on invested capital and by reckless speculators who wanted short-term personal profits. Speculators hoped to benefit from increases in stock prices, quick sales of overcapitalized or "watered" stock, and buyouts of overvalued competitive lines in which the speculators were sometimes also involved.[4]

As the largest and most modern corporations, the railroads faced the problems accompanying the 1873 panic and ensuing depression: how to maintain their extensive operations with high fixed costs, how to protect profits and dividends with declining volume of traffic, and how to prevent ruinous rate cutting with competitive pressure from all sides. From the point of view of the managers, then, the problem was how to keep the "logic of the market" (competition) from undermining the "logic of the system" (control/coordination) and how to keep the investors and speculators at bay. Yet, managers, investors, and speculators lacked a common vocabulary to translate the *private* values of the corporation—efficiency, stability, profitability, speculative margin—into the traditional terms of *public* debate. Therefore, they seized on one of the dominant public values of the time, liberty as self-control, independence, or autonomy, and tried to make it fit their situation.[5]

But the railroad managers, investors, and speculators were not the only voices in the debate. While the railroads set the model for the *new* forms of business organization, the debate over the behavior of the railroad corporations involved the vocabulary of earlier controversies, particularly the antimonopoly rhetoric of the Jacksonian Era. Attempts to regulate the railroads involved the courts and the legislatures as the focus of the debate. What appeared to railroad operators as a matter of liberty, as maintaining their independence by intrafirm control and interfirm cooperation, was viewed as a matter of equality by some commercial farmers, community-oriented merchants, and competitive-minded shippers. For example, the so-called Farmers' Declaration of 4 July 1873, had attacked "the present railway monopoly" and had pledged "to reduce all men claiming the protection of American laws to an equality before those laws, making the owner of a railroad as amenable thereto as the 'veriest beggar that walks the streets.'" Furthermore, they charged: "[Railroads] have combined together to destroy competition; contrary to the expressed provisions of our Constitution and the spirit of our laws." In sum, "monopolies" violated the norm of equality of competition; they used their special legal privileges and enormous concentrated power to reduce farmers, workers, merchants, and competitors to the status of dependents.[6]

Even before the onslaught of the depression, a number of midwestern states, responsive to antimonopoly rhetoric, had passed stringent laws to oversee railroads. To counter these attempts, and to get the issue out of partisan legislatures, some states had established railroad commissions to regulate rates. The Illinois Railroad and Warehouse Commission created in 1873 became a model for such moderate attempts at regulation. Known as "Granger laws" after the prominent agricultural organization that had supported the earlier law, these various attempts at regulation were largely the work of merchants, shippers, and railroad experts. In December 1873 Republican congressman McCrary of Iowa introduced legislation in the House of Representatives to establish a national railroad commission empowered to set "reasonable" rates. The bill passed the House but ultimately died in the Senate.[7] In the Senate, a report in 1874 (named the Windom report after Republican senator William Windom of Minnesota) rehearsed the litany of complaints against the railroads but noted somewhat blandly, and inaccurately, that: "The theory here has always been, as in England, that the transportation business, like other commercial affairs, would regulate itself on the principle of competition. . . . The General Government having never interfered, and, until recently, the States having made but little effort to control or direct it, the system has developed itself under the influence of the natural laws which govern that kind of business."[8] Nevertheless, the report was willing to countenance more drastic means to correct current abuses, regulate trunk lines, curb excessive combination and, thereby, lower costs of transportation.

As the depression deepened in 1874–75, political power in Congress shifted toward the Democrats. Casting a wary eye on these economic and political trends, the major railroads formed regional cartels or self-governing committees, such as the Western Railroad Bureau and the Southern Railway and Steamship Association. These cartels set rates, allocated traffic, and adjudicated internal complaints among the railroads. But competition from newer "trunk lines" and pressure from eastern seaport merchants for preferential treatment undercut the agreements. Eventually a new regional cartel, the Eastern Trunk Line Association, would be formed. But, clearly, self-governing agreements among railroads, informal pools, or regional cartels had their limits in the context of a long-term depression and growing political hostility. To the issues of liberty as independence or autonomy and equality of opportunity were thus added the issues of competitive fairness and interregional balance, that is, of justice and equity (or rewards proportionate to effort among competitors). While railroads engaged in *intrastate* commerce (within one state) had lived with state regulation for decades and even tolerated state railroad commissions, as long as they served the railroads' interests, those railroads engaged in *interstate* commerce (between several states) found state regulation to be a nuisance. Accordingly, a number of these inter-state, interregional railroads had decided to challenge state regulation in a series of court cases known collectively as the *Granger* cases.[9]

The state attorney generals who argued for the state railroad commis-sions and rate regulation laws in the *Granger* cases had the greater weight of judicial precedent and common law on their side. The attorneys for the railroads tried to stretch the language of private rights stemming from the debate over the Fourteenth Amendment, and the legal conflicts over local and state prohibition laws, to fit their situation. Thus, the legal experts for the interregional railroads appealed to general legal principles, such as due process of law, and to the concept of private property that endowed it with certain privileges or immunities. When such legal rea-soning proved inadequate, they made extravagant emotional appeals and played upon public fears stemming from recent communist uprisings in Europe. "It is the beginning of the operation of the commune in the legislation of this country," argued John Cary, a Milwaukee attorney, "and if not checked at the threshold, will ultimately overthrow not only the rights of property, but personal liberty and independence as well."[10]

The Supreme Court in its majority opinion in the key Granger law case, *Munn v. Illinois* (1 March 1877), took a "yes—but" stance: yes, corporate businesses had certain private rights that fell under judicial protection; but, railroads and warehouses, as quasi monopolies, were "clothed with a public interest." The community, through the legislature, had a right to regulate them and, until Congress acted to preempt inter-state commerce control, the states could act, subject to review by the federal courts. In the short run, the Supreme Court had simply upheld traditional doctrine; in the long run, it had acknowledged a line of reason-ing that could transcend the original meaning of the Fourteenth Amend-ment and elevate the "rights of economic liberty" as private property rights in the hierarchy of public core values.[11]

Whatever the long-term implications of the Supreme Court decision, the railroads were confronted with more immediate problems in the spring of 1877. Oil producers in Pennsylvania were pressing for anti-rebate and anti-rate discrimination laws; the Eastern Trunk Line Associa-tion pool was being renegotiated in the light of repeated failures. In June and July 1877 the main eastern railroads agreed to make wage cuts and began to implement them. From 17 to 19 July 1877 startling events on the Baltimore and Ohio Railroad and the Pennsylvania Railroad seemed to confirm John Cary's fearful rhetoric. Strikes, with widespread community support, spread along the main lines. When state troops were called in, they were harassed and had to fight with enraged mobs, who subsequently burned railway buildings, looted cars, and destroyed whole sections of the Pittsburgh warehouse district. The specter of anarchy and the Paris commune of 1871 haunted the imagination of railroad presidents and managers as they demanded, and received, federal troop protection. What startled the railroad operators was not simply the scale of violence and destruction but evidence of cooperation, coordination, and conviction among the strikers and the extent of community support in the railroad towns strung along the tracks and sidings. While public debate focused on images of class *conflict*, the private response of the railroad managers focused on the issues of internal *control*.[12]

During the next decade the railroads experienced a familiar but distressing pattern of expansion and collapse. As prosperity returned in 1879, the major railroads rushed to extend their lines across relatively underpopulated territory. With a temporary shortage of skilled workers in these new growth areas, the unions, called brotherhoods, could bid up wages, exert some control over work rules, and rely on the support of community leaders in the newly plotted "railroad towns" that blossomed as service centers for the expanding systems. The railway brotherhoods tended to be narrowly based along skill lines, highly suspicious of each other, and heavily involved with mutual aid and insurance schemes. When overbuilding of railroad systems triggered another economic decline after 1883, the situation for the workers rapidly deteriorated. Wage cuts, arbitrary changes in work rules, and the weaning of community leaders away from the "particular interest" of the railroad workers in favor of the "general interest" of future community growth (based on vague promises by the railroad corporations) undercut the position of the craft-oriented brotherhoods. When the Pennsylvania Railroad announced a relief scheme for its workers in 1886, Eugene V. Debs of the Brotherhood of Locomotive Firemen indignantly replied, "[The workers] do not require the guardianship of their employers. All they demand is justice, fair play, fair wages for a day's work, the control absolutely of the money they earn without question or qualification." When a series of railroad strikes failed in 1887, the workers were left confused, angry, and divided.[13]

Parallel to the rise and temporary decline of the railroad brotherhoods was the evolution of the Knights of Labor. Founded in 1869 by Philadelphia garment workers, the Knights began as a secret, oath-bound fraternal order with rituals and symbolism heavily influenced by the Masonic and Odd Fellow lore. In January 1878 the order established a general assembly to coordinate its growing membership and, in 1879, elected Terence V. Powderly as its leader or grand master workman. Under Powderly's leadership, the Knights stressed organization, cooperation, and education, downplayed strikes, and participated in local labor politics. In 1881 they dropped the secret oaths and also admitted an all-woman local. In general, the Knights became an open, expanding organization that tried to unite all "producers": railroad workers and industrial workers, skilled and unskilled laborers, male and female, white and black, wage earners and small-scale shopkeepers and manufacturers. The Knights represented an attempt to use the antimonopoly rhetoric and producer psychology of the past to preserve interpersonal communal norms in the face of both the impersonal imperatives of corporate managers and the pragmatic calculations of commercially oriented town "boomers." As railroad historian Shelton Stromquist has observed, "the distinction between class and community interest was blurred. Producerism masked sharpening class divisions." Nevertheless, for the moment, 1881–86, the Knights were the largest labor organization in the country. The exaggerated hopes of 1886 collapsed amidst the failure of some railroad strikes, the futile demand for an eight-hour limit on daily labor, and the public reaction to violent clashes between police and protestors that aroused fear of anarchism and triggered official repression of labor dissent. Using the rhetoric of labor republicanism, which was a variation of the 1830s emphasis on equal rights and civic virtue, some local Knights pushed the older language of mutualism to encompass a cooperative vision of society. Thus, the Knights, 1877–87, had represented primarily a ritual withdrawal and renewal option based on traditional values; however, for a few members it represented a culturally radical alternate to current economic reality.[14]

The Knights were not the only group to seek to regulate railroads in the name of community norms. Merchants, farmers, and competitive-minded shippers had attempted to expand state regulation. State regulation, however, was complex, confusing, and sometimes discriminatory, particularly for long-distance interstate lines. Furthermore, the Supreme Court in *Wabash v. Illinois* (1886) denied the right of Illinois to regulate *interstate* rates because that right was reserved for Congress under the commerce clause of the Constitution. Pushed by the economic depression, the resurgence of the Democratic Party in the election of Grover Cleveland as president in 1884, and by divisions among Republicans, Congress was forced to deal with the issue. Basically there were two conflicting approaches. The Reagan Plan, authored by Congressman John Reagan, a conservative Democrat of Texas, used a prohibitory approach against specific abuses. As historian Stephen Skowronek has observed, "Overall, Reagan claimed that by outlawing all forms of discrimination and prohibiting pools, his bill would secure the most noble standards of competition, end rate wars, and reestablish the natural harmony of the marketplace." Reagan's approach was in harmony with Democratic Party values of local autonomy, state sovereignty, limited executive power, negative government, and reliance on majority rule or popular opinion as expressed in frequent elections. The Cullom Plan, written by Senator Shelby Cullom, a moderate Republican of Illinois, used a commission approach. In Skowronek's words, "Cullom feared direct recourse to the courts in regulatory disputes almost as much as he feared a restrictive specification of controls by the legislature." Rival House and Senate versions were compromised, and Congress passed the Interstate Commerce Act in January 1887 after bitter debate. Political scientist Scott C. James has found the act "was written with an eye to the interests of groups in states that were central to the maintenance of the Democratic party's electoral college majority [particularly the 'swing' states of New York, New Jersey, Connecticut, and Indiana] and the goal of party victory in the 1888 presidential elections."[15]

The opponents of the Interstate Commerce Act need not have worried overly much about this attempt at federal regulation. The act outlawed pools and rate discrimination, rebates and drawbacks, and long-haul and short-haul discrimination. It required "reasonable and just" rates, regularly published rate schedules, and standardized accounting and annual reports. However, the Interstate Commerce Commission (ICC), appointed by President Cleveland, was cautious and internally divided. Nevertheless, according to Skowronek, "over the years, the agency proceeded to elaborate a constructive rather than a restrictive interpretation of the law, one as fully in line with the expert opinions expressed before the Cullom Committee [1885–86] as could be expected under the statute." But a disastrous strike in 1888 on the Burlington lines, an attempt in 1889 by financier J. P. Morgan to set up a self-policing interstate railway association, and a proposal in 1889 by railway expert Charles Francis Adams Jr. for rate and traffic agreements that would be approved *in advance* by the ICC all indicated that the ICC was losing initiative and was not totally in control of the situation.[16]

In short, with the politicians confused by rapid change and operating with outmoded vocabularies and contradictory approaches, with the ICC cautious and regulating on a case-by-case rather than industry-wide basis, with workers' strikes subject to state or federal militia intervention, and with railroad communities increasingly divided between "boomers," business leaders who wanted economic growth, and "boycotters," union leaders who wanted to maintain collective norms, the task of stabilization and regulation of the railroad industry fell *externally* to the courts and would ultimately reach the Supreme Court. Legal historian Herbert Hovenkamp has observed that the Supreme Court in the *Santa Clara* case (1886) "first suggested that a corporation is a 'person' within the meaning of the Fourteenth Amendment, noting only that it found the issue too plain for argument." Furthermore, the long-standing constitutional doctrine that a state could exclude or discriminate against an out-of-state "foreign corporation" created the legal anomaly that a corporation might be regarded as a "person" under the Fourteenth Amendment for certain purposes but not a "citizen" of a state under the "privileges or immunities" clause of the same amendment for other purposes. It would take some time for the courts to sort all this out.[17]

The railroad managers also experienced repeated failures in their attempts to secure either judicial sanctions for their private regulatory arrangements or favorable federal regulatory rate control through the Interstate Commerce Commission. To the managers, therefore, the solutions were clear: they had to create a self-contained, highly controlled system and undercut the appeal and power of unions by strict labor discipline. They used such means of labor control as blacklists, employee record systems, and promotion by "merit" (i.e., loyalty to the firm) or strict seniority. They received support from courts willing to use injunctions to curb unions and strikes. Some railroads also engaged in modest experiments in paternalism: pensions and accident insurance, savings and mortgage loan programs, and support for temperance, YMCA, and "self-improvement" programs. The railroad managers in the 1880s thus shifted from reliance on regional strategies and embraced interregional, self-sustained systems. The dominant imperative of their corporate behavior was the logic of the system, and they were beginning to find some support for it among regulators and, eventually, among the courts.[18]

In summary, the railroads had created a model for the modern corporation during the 1850s–60s. They combined the freedom of the limited-liability corporate form with the functions of control, command, and coordination in hierarchical systems much like those of the military. By the 1870s they had experimented with a variety of rate structures and rules to ensure sufficient volume of traffic to pay their fixed costs and, by implication, their dividends on stocks. But they lacked a public language to explain their private motives and the values of the logic of the system in a way that would advance their interests in public discourse. Instead railroad leaders invoked private concepts such as "liberty of contract," borrowed analogies from the debate over the Fourteenth Amendment, exaggerated images that drew on anticommunist and antianarchist fears, or simply ignored public criticism with an imperious, "the public be damned" attitude. But the railroads' behavior challenged deeply held notions about the priority of competition and the primacy of the logic of the market. Farmers, merchants, workers, cost-conscious entrepreneurs, and transportation competitors responded in conflicting and sometimes contradicting ways to maintain their liberty or autonomy, equality of opportunity, and just rewards as they saw them. The clash with the railroads also frequently divided communities and weakened community norms. Those who criticized the railroads invoked the older public language of the Jacksonian Era with its producerism, antimonopoly, equal rights, and democratic priorities. Some workers pursued the ritual withdrawal and renewal strategy in fraternal lodges, unions, and strikes; a few dreamed of a cooperative system or preached radical values. Those political leaders, lawyers, and self-appointed railroad experts who crafted laws to regulate rates or set standards of railroad service, who argued for the priority of the common law in court cases, and who designed and staffed the pioneering regulatory commissions followed the reform option. In so doing, a pattern for other public controversies involving businesses had been set and would be used beyond the bounds of the railroad question.

The railroads were not the only businesses that were changing the economic landscape and reshaping the legal environment, but they did provide the models and the vocabulary to defend them. The other innovators in the corporate revolution were in the manufacturing and market sectors. In describing the manufacturing sector, business historian Phillip Scranton warns against taking the models of continuous production or assembly lines as the only or even the predominant form of manufacturing in the period 1873 to 1893. In his study of the textile industry, for example, Scranton notices, on one hand, a Boston-centered system of continuous production of a standardized product utilizing semiskilled or unskilled workers and extensive mechanization. On the other hand, he points to a Philadelphia-to-Connecticut centered system of "batch" or "bulk-output" production based on constantly shifting seasonal or stylistic specialties. This system utilized skilled workers and a mixture of traditional handicraft and newer mechanized techniques. Other historians also caution against confusing the growth of technology *per se* and the expansion of industrialization. "As late as 1870," Stromquist points out, "the average American manufacturing firm employed fewer than ten workers.

Traditional skills dominated production in important industries such as iron, glass, coal mining, metal fabrication, and construction." Many factories were little more than collections of shops all brought together under one roof or in a cluster of buildings.[19]

Businesses that faced the impact of the depressions in 1873, 1884, and 1893 had a variety of options, then. The strategy called "vertical integration" appealed to those manufacturers who could standardize their products, harness the technology of mass production, utilize the techniques of temperature-controlled distribution of perishable products, or produce complex machinery with interchangeable parts. They soon found, however, that their productive capacity exceeded the ability of the current distribution system to market their goods. Gradually they expanded their operations into the distribution, advertising, sales, service, and customer financing areas. On the other hand, the strategy called "horizontal integration" brought competing productive units together either voluntarily (coordination) or by centralization (control). As Chandler has aptly summarized the differences, vertical integration "aimed at increasing profits by decreasing costs and expanding productivity through administrative coordination" within a single firm, whereas horizontal integration "aimed at maintaining the profits by controlling the price and output" of several firms. These distinctions were not so clearcut in practice at the time, however, as they later appeared to scholarly experts. They were not always understood by contemporary observers, either, and variety rather than uniformity characterized business structures and strategies in the last quarter of the nineteenth century.[20]

The event that captured the public imagination and defined the terms of the public debate over "horizontal integration," commonly called "monopoly," in this time period was, undoubtedly, the rise of the Standard Oil Company. John D. Rockefeller's Standard Oil Company had controlled the nation's largest refinery in 1872. He had concluded that pools and other voluntary agreements among competitors were unable to control price or production; therefore, Rockefeller utilized the high volume of Standard's production to demand rebates and other favorable terms from the railroads. He also exchanged stock shares with cooperating allies for better control of production, and by 1881 the Standard Oil alliance controlled almost 90 percent of the nation's refining capacity. While it set prices and production schedules, the alliance had no central administrative board and was itself threatened by new pipeline technologies and challenged by state legislatures. Accordingly, on 2 January 1882 the shareholders in the allied companies exchanged their stock for certificates in a new organization: Standard Oil Trust. A nine-member board of trustees exercised central control over the constituent companies, which were rechartered as state subsidiaries so as to minimize state taxation or regulation on "foreign" (i.e., out-of-state) corporations. Thus was created in the public mind the image of the giant, octopus-like "trust," gobbling up everything in its path and forcing competition out of the market.[21]

In the attempt to deal with this new phenomenon, lawyers, politicians, and advocates for competitive businesses turned once again to the common law for relevant concepts and legal language. In general, the common law precedents upheld "reasonable" restraints of trade by contracting parties or voluntarily cooperation, but it frowned upon any attempt to monopolize. Even if cooperative agreements temporarily raised the prices for consumers or restricted their options, such agreements were not seen as a violation of liberty under the assumption that buyers were free to go elsewhere. They could, after all, refuse to buy at the higher price. Competition in a free market would always provide an alternative or entice a competitor to enter the market at a lower price. On the other hand, attempts by contracting parties or combinations to *exclude* a third party were condemned under common law doctrine if they attempted to control prices and restrict supply. In short, some voluntary attempts to *regulate* competition among competitors were legally acceptable, but coercive attempts to *eliminate* competition or to *exclude* potential competitors were not. According to business historian Martin J. Sklar, the common law "was intended to safeguard the right of *individuals* freely to enter the market and make contracts, and to let the operations of the market determine the outcome." Thus, even for critics of the newly refashioned corporations, liberty of contract ("reasonable" restraint agreements) ranked as high as the public value of equality of competition.[22]

Having won the presidency and control of Congress by a narrow margin in the 1888 elections, Republicans in Congress wrestled with these issues in the turbulent political climate of 1889–90. Although primarily concerned with tariffs and currency issues, they also tried to fashion a viable "antitrust" act. The final product, the Sherman Antitrust Act of 1890, intrigued lawyers, baffled bureaucratic regulators, and ultimately disappointed partisans on both sides. It also set off a long-standing debate among historians and political scientists as to its meaning and intent. As Sklar has noted, the language of the act seemed straightforward: "Section 1 of the Sherman Act declared illegal 'every contract, combination in the form of trust or otherwise, or conspiracy, in restraint of trade or commerce.' . . . Section 2 declared 'Every person who shall monopolize, or attempt to monopolize, or combine or conspire with any other person or persons, to monopolize any part' of interstate or foreign trade or commerce, guilty (upon conviction) of a misdemeanor and subject to . . . punishment."[23] The phrase "every contract, combination, . . . or conspiracy, in restraint of trade" should be construed simply as the embodiment of the common law doctrine according to one of the authors of the law, Republican senator George F. Hoar of Massachusetts. The addition of the phrase "in the form of trust or otherwise" and the reiteration of the phrase "to monopolize" could be construed as a reference to recent innovations in corporate form and the fears raised by such corporate behavior. The common law language on restraint of trade was a *strategic* approach to antitrust problems, whereas the reference to trusts, combinations, and monopolies was a *structural* approach. Given these ambiguities, how the Sherman Act would be interpreted by the courts was less a question of legislative intent than it was a question of judicial inclination and priority as the courts read the statutory language.[24]

In any case, the trust *per se* as an innovation in corporate form was already obsolete. It was being replaced by the holding company, where control of subordinate companies could be achieved by purchase of their stock and by placing sympathetic representatives on their boards of directors. After 1890, the more successful mergers would be those of the horizontal integration type or where vertical integration could utilize new technologies and marketing techniques to reduce costs. In any case, by the 1890s the public mind was deeply divided and somewhat ambivalent on the subject of business organization and activities. When the giant firms emerged in the 1870s and 1880s via the routes of vertical integration (coordination and internal control) and horizontal integration (alliance, merger, trust, or holding company), the public discourse was pulled in opposite directions. To the extent that such companies lowered costs, ensured a more standard product, and provided credit, service, and product information, the American citizens as private *consumers* might believe that they had reason to be satisfied. To the extent that such companies achieved these results through internal reforms such as technological innovation, better integration of units, and efficient management of time, materials, and workers, the American citizens as public *contributors* to the dialogue on business behavior might feel that such enterprises operated within the core social values of equality of opportunity, reward proportionate to merit, or "a fair field and no favors."[25]

But the issues were not all one-sided or simple. To the extent that some companies by their innovations in organization or tactics (such as the creation of the trust or the use of secret rebates) seemed to create monopolies, to demand special privileges, and to trample upon the equal rights of other firms to compete in the marketplace, then American voters were more suspicious. They were thus willing to support the kind of legislation that created the Interstate Commerce Commission and the Sherman Act, to applaud court rulings that seemed to go against the trusts, or to vote for politicians who promised to see that economic liberty was preserved for a wider range of citizens. There was still considerable confidence in the "invisible hand" of the free marketplace, particularly among classical economists, judges, and political leaders who believed in classical economic theory. But events such as the rise of Standard Oil style trusts, holding companies, and the development of hierarchical management also raised the hope that the "visible hand" of the experts through regulatory commissions or new laws could somehow better ensure competition or protect other producers. The worker, the shipper, the community, and, ultimately, the consumer all had a stake in the outcome. But whose visible hand should it be—the business manager or the government regulators? Or did the hand that cast the ballot still hold the ultimate key?[26]

5

Civil Rights, 1883–1898:
High Hopes; Failed Promises

The modern understanding of civil rights is that they are inherent in citizenship and that citizenship defines who legally constitutes the sociological entity called the "community" and the political entity called the "nation."[1] However, the historical meaning of civil rights as a legal category was not identical in the past with these current concepts. In order to understand past presuppositions about civil rights, citizenship, and membership in the American "community" and in the United States as a "nation," this chapter will examine the situation during the period from the *Civil Rights* cases of 1883 and the end of the depression in 1897–98. The focus will be on the three groups mentioned in the debates over the Civil Rights Act of 1866: African Americans (or Freedmen), native-born Chinese residents, and some Native Americans (or Indians). The purpose of this survey of civil rights during the period 1883 to 1898 is not to imply that all white citizens enjoyed full liberty and equality in the exercise of their rights and adequate judicial protection at all levels of government while all "minorities" did not. Rather, this chapter will attempt to spell out the evolving meanings of civil rights as they emerged from the discourse between courts and contending groups and the dynamics of political debate. The story will begin with the situation of the Chinese and the Native Americans in order to compare and contrast their struggles for liberty, equality, and justice with those of the African Americans.

For over thirty years, 1853–83, the Chinese had been alternately courted by California businessmen as a source of cheap, docile labor and as merchants to form important links in the overseas trade or condemned by white California miners, underemployed workers, and politicians looking for a popular issue. The Burlingame Treaty of July 1868 between the United States and the Chinese imperial court recognized the right of immigration to the United States and provided that "Chinese subjects visiting or residing in the United States, shall enjoy the same privileges, immunities, and exemptions in respect to travel or residence, as may there be enjoyed by the citizens or subjects of the most favored nation." But, continued anti-Chinese legislation at the local and state level, the impact of the panic of 1873 on the economy, and an unsympathetic congressional investigation in 1876 had all contributed to pressure for revision of the Burlingame Treaty. The United States secured an amendment in 1880 that permitted it to limit, but not prohibit, future immigration of laborers. Then, in 1882 Congress passed the Chinese Restriction Act, which suspended for ten years such immigration (but allowed Chinese merchants and students to enter), provided for certification of resident laborers (who had entered prior to the effective date), and pledged that the United States would guarantee all the rights and immunities recognized in the Burlingame Treaty. However, it prohibited any court from admitting Chinese to naturalized citizenship. For the first time federal immigration legislation had targeted a specific ethnic group for restriction. How the courts would interpret this and subsequent legislation would be the test of the meaning of civil rights and American citizenship and of the exercise of political rights.

Chinese laborers, resident merchants, and temporary students might be excluded, restricted, regulated, and denied citizenship; but did that mean that they were also deprived of basic civil rights protection? Legal historian Charles J. McClain has pointed out that Supreme Court justice Stephen J. Field in *Ho Ah Kow v. Nunan* (1879) had "affirmed that the equal protection clause of the Fourteenth Amendment applied to all persons and not just to citizens." The lower federal courts and the western circuit courts (which included Justice Field) heard a series of habeas corpus cases that involved Chinese litigants and rendered liberal interpretations of some of the provisions of the 1882 act. West Coast congressmen, angered by these rulings, pushed through amendments in 1884 to close some of these "loopholes." In the midst of a severe economic depression, a new wave of anti-Chinese hysteria in the western states in 1885–86 led to mob action and violence against the Chinese (somewhat similar to earlier Ku Klux Klan actions in the South). Now the basis of the legal cases shifted: did the United States government under its treaty agreements with China have a responsibility to protect Chinese subjects from such actions by individual American citizens or from the failure of state and local government to protect them? Did those portions of the Civil Rights Acts of 1871 and 1875 against conspiracy to deprive others of their basic rights apply? In *Baldwin v. Franks* (1887) the Supreme Court ruled that, while Congress had the power to legislate to protect Chinese interests under treaty obligations, the Court's understanding of American federalism precluded action by the federal government. Protection of individuals from acts by other individuals rested with local and state authorities. Congress, with a presidential election in the offing in 1888, was in no mood to legislate further to protect the Chinese. Instead, in the Scott Act, it provided "that no Chinese laborer, irrespective of former residence in the United States," should be admitted.[2]

Congress had seemingly slammed the door on further Chinese immigration and litigation with the Scott Act. But historian Lucy Salyer has pointed out that a paradoxical situation soon developed. Whereas most Chinese immigrants could be denied entry by administrative fiat without any judicial appeal, those who claimed membership in the special categories established by treaty rights (merchants, students, and travelers) and those born in the United States who were returning after visits to China could claim access to judicial review. According to Salyer, "the statutes did not address explicitly the admissibility of Chinese women and children. [However,] the lower federal courts ruled in the 1880s that Chinese women and children would be allowed to enter if they were native-born American citizens." In 1888 the U.S. District Court for the Northern District of California in the case *In re Jung Ah Lung* upheld access to habeas corpus for those Chinese in the special categories. Over the next decade 80 percent of such appeals were successful, and in 1898 the Supreme Court affirmed a circuit court ruling that Chinese born in the United States were citizens and not subject to the exclusion laws. By 1901 the Supreme Court would rule that the status of wives and children would be determined by that of the husbands.[3]

How can one explain this complicated pattern between civil rights and judicial review and exclusion/inclusion in the American community? McClain has suggested that Supreme Court justices (particularly Stephen J. Field) read into the Fourteenth Amendment an essentially Jacksonian understanding of equal rights as access to economic opportunity and of federalism as state primacy. This intellectual orientation made them particularly protective of property rights; however, when the issue became one of national sovereignty and the prerogatives of Congress to override even treaty obligations, the justices deferred to Congress. In short, they saw liberty (as freedom to enact majority will) of higher value than equality (as economic opportunity) or justice (as simple procedural fairness). Salyer also found that the courts acted more out of judicial respect for orderly procedure (as opposed to arbitrary administrative fiat) and conservative respect for the sanctity of constitutional law than from any overriding belief in equality.[4]

In the contest between the Supreme Court and Congress, the legislative branch, in response to political pressure, seemed intent on *excluding* the Chinese from the American "community" and thereby *restricting* their access to legal protection of their civil rights. In the case of the Native Americans during the same time period, 1883 to 1898, Congress seemed intent on doing just the opposite; namely, it set about *including* them within the American "community" and thereby *expanding* their access to civil rights protection. But the transition of status for Native Americans was complicated by the legal understanding of the term "nation" and its meaning in the post–Civil War Era.

In legal and constitutional terms there was a distinction between, on the one hand, tribal "nations" or treaty Indians living on reservations and in the Indian Territory and, on the other hand, assimilated individuals or "civilized Indians" who paid taxes and who lived within local communities. In 1879 a federal district court had ruled in *Standing Bear v. Crook* that a peaceful ("civilized") Indian had the right to freedom of movement the same as a white person and had access to the writ of habeas corpus to uphold it. But decades of sporadic violence on the frontier between the military and treaty Indians, corruption in the administration of the reservation system, demands for change by eastern humanitarians, and political pressure by land hungry white farmers, ranchers, miners, and railroad developers had changed the mood of Congress. A consensus had emerged among white politicians and humanitarian reformers that the separate nation, treaty, and reservation system should be replaced by one that stressed individual land ownership, education for "civilization," and eventual citizenship. The Supreme Court added fuel to the fire of controversy when it ruled in 1884 in the *Elk v. Wilkins* case "that Indians were not born within the jurisdictional boundaries of the United States" in the Constitutional sense "and that Congress had never established a naturalization process for them." In short, nonassimilated Indians were not citizens. Just as the *Dred Scott* case in the 1850s had its impact on the status of the slaves and free blacks, so too the *Elk v. Wilkins* case raised a fundamental issue concerning the status of Native Americans and their civil rights.[5]

Budget cutting by Cleveland Democrats after the 1884 presidential election finally prompted Congress to act. The Dawes Act of 1887 provided for eventual elimination of much of the communal tribal land in the reservation system, the distribution of individual allotments of land, continual federal "protection" of Indians, and citizenship after a twenty-five-year trust period. When some eastern reformers and Congressmen subsequently complained that traveling "wild west" shows were recruiting

Indians contrary to the spirit of the Dawes Act, the commissioner of Indian Affairs reminded Senator Dawes that "he could not 'restrain the liberty of the law abiding person or citizen because in [his] opinion or the opinion of someone else that person or citizen [would] make an injudicious use of his liberty.'" In the end, the government officials required the wild west show promoters to post bonds for the privilege of recruiting the Indians and supervised their contracts much as the Freedman's Bureau had earlier required and supervised the labor contracts of freedmen and planters. In the Curtis Act of 1898, Congress abolished tribal government in the Indian Territory, which later became part of the state of Oklahoma, and applied the allotment principle there, too. Thus by the end of the decade, while theoretically all Indians were "legal persons" with freedom of movement and access to habeas corpus and most were assured of eventual citizenship under the Dawes Act or earlier treaties, they still remained in many respects under the "pupilage" or "wardship" of the national government. And they remained bound by the male-dominant gender assumptions that characterized the white society. While some Native American women reformers benefited from the land allotment system, more traditional women lost some of the security of the communal system.[6]

To what extent, then, did the inclusion of Native Americans within the American "community" and the extension of eventual citizenship to them reflect the core values of liberty, equality, and justice? As political theorist Alexandra Witkin has observed, "efforts to extend citizenship to Native Americans can be characterized as 'repressive emancipation.' The term describes the attempt to liberate a people from conditions they themselves do not consider oppressive." In other words, the Dawes Act and the Curtis Act reflected the assumptions of the white majority and not a negotiated consensus of both sides. While the Congressional architects of the policies were willing to grant equality to the individual Native Americans and to recognize some claims to justice (within the limits of wardship), they were not willing at this time to acknowledge unrestricted liberty. They assumed that liberty rested upon "civilization" and required assimilation into the dominant culture without worrying overly much about the psychological costs to individuals, the cultural alternatives for group relations, and the ambiguity of politically overriding one definition of "nation" by another, the encompassing nationalism of the Civil War and Reconstruction legacy.[7]

If most Chinese laborers were excluded by law and only a few categories of Chinese immigrants were granted residence rights and limited judicial protection or begrudging recognition of their citizenship based on native-born status, and if most Native Americans would eventually have citizenship but did not yet have full civil rights thrust upon them by the allotment system, what about the freedmen? What was their situation during the decade and a half after the *Civil Rights* cases of 1883? If their status as citizens was seemingly secure because of the Civil Rights Act of 1866 and the post–Civil War amendments, did this mean that their claim on civil rights was any more secure than that of the Chinese, the Native American, or even the most recent white immigrant? On 28 May 1887 the editor of the struggling black newspaper the *Freeman*, T. Thomas Fortune, brooded over the decline in African American civil rights since the end of Reconstruction. Somberly he concluded: "We think that it has been thoroughly demonstrated that the white people of this country have determined to leave the colored man alone to fight his battles; especially is this true of the treacherous, self-seeking politicians. There is no dodging the issue; we have got to take hold of this problem ourselves, and make so much noise that all the world shall know the wrongs we suffer and our determination to right these wrongs."[8] He proposed the formation of a National Afro-American League to fight for civil rights by all legal and peaceful means.

Fortune subsequently proposed a six-point program for agitation and action: (1) protection of constitutionally guaranteed voting rights, (2) action by the national and state governments against lynching of blacks by white mobs in the South, (3) equal funding for public schools, black and white, (4) abolition of the chain gang and convict lease systems in southern jails, (5) resistance to legally imposed discrimination on railroads, streetcars, and other public transportation, and (6) equal access to hotels, theaters, and other public places. The proposals found sympathy among other African American journalists (including the militant Ida B. Wells), clergy, educators, and a few political leaders. After considerable negotiation and time out for participation in the 1888 presidential campaign, Fortune and his supporters were able to convene a convention in January 1890 in Chicago to establish the National Afro-American League. One hundred and forty-one delegates from twenty-three states, North, South and West, participated in the deliberations. Conspicuous by their absence were most of the "traditional," Reconstruction Era black politicians. The constitution of the league, in fact, drew strict guidelines to keep its activities nonpartisan. The goal was "full citizenship and equality" to be achieved by educational, economic, legal, and peaceful means. The economic proposals included calls for an African American bank, an emigration bureau to facilitate black mobility, a system of farmers' cooperatives, and technical-industrial education for African American youth in the South.[9]

A host of problems confronted the National Afro-American League in 1890. Would the majority of African Americans, who lived in rural poverty in the South, listen to the leadership of the educated, urban, professionals who had created the league? Could a distinct minority within the larger American "community" afford to remain nonpartisan toward the democratic political process where they had access to it? And what did "full citizenship and equality" mean for the farmers and laborers in the South, for professionals in the North and Far West, and for women who struggled under the double burdens of racial and sexual discrimination wherever they lived?

As Fortune and his urban supporters had been laboring to put life into the proposals of the National Afro-American League, rival organizations had been spreading among white and black farmers in the South. The National Farmers Alliance and Cooperative Union had been organized in 1887 by the union of several white farmers' organizations in Texas, Louisiana, and Arkansas. The Farmers Alliance revived the equal rights rhetoric of the Jacksonian Era, the greenback proposals for monetary inflation, the producerism of the Grange and Knights of Labor and added some innovative economic and political proposals. In addition to cooperative purchase plans to reduce the farmers' costs, the Farmers Alliance called for a "sub-treasury plan" in which the government would loan money at low interest to farmers on the security of their nonperishable crops that would be stored in special government-owned warehouses. Above all, the Farmers Alliance saw itself as a vast political educational effort. As historian Theodore P. Mitchell has phrased it, they saw their effort "as the last chance for the mass of common people to gain power over the government and its laws." In the process, "for a decade, between 1888 and 1898, the Farmers Alliance challenged politics as usual in the South 'with a rapidity and clarity' that did indeed alarm the 'chronic politician.' In this challenge, the [Farmers] Alliance broadened the scope of political discourse in ways that still demand attention."[10]

The Farmers Alliance did challenge politics as usual, but it did not, at first, challenge the emerging southern system of racial separation. In 1886–87 a separate Colored Farmers Alliance had been organized in Texas and soon spread to other southern states. Initially the Colored Farmers Alliance was organized as "a secret association" with a fraternal ritual and a mutual benevolent fund for "sick or disabled members, or their distressed families." At the peak of its strength, the Colored Farmers Alliance claimed over a million members and in some areas had created cooperative stores or purchasing arrangements. Above all, it saw itself as a vast self-help effort. They intended, according to their charter, "to become better farmers and laborers, to be more obedient to the civil law, and withdraw their attention from political partisanship," and "to become better citizens, and truer husbands and wives."[11]

In their attempt to unite all producers in a common effort, the white-dominated National Farmers Alliance reached out not only to the Colored Farmers Alliance but also to the remnants of the Knights of Labor and various reform organizations. At Ocala, Florida, in December 1890, they proposed a broad platform of demands based upon the Jacksonian doctrine of "equal rights to all, and special privileges to none." Negatively, they called for the abolition of national banks, the elimination of high tariffs, the prohibition of alien landownership, the return of excess land "held by railroads and other corporations," and the outlawing of trading in agricultural futures. Positively, they called for institution of the subtreasury loan plan, an increase in the amount of currency in circulation, "the free and unlimited coinage of silver," a graduated income tax, an amendment to the Constitution for the direct election of U.S. senators, and "state and national governmental control and supervision of the means of public communication and transportation" or, if that did not remove the abuses of the current system, "government ownership of such means of communication and transportation."[12]

As the white Farmers Alliance moved inexorably toward the creation of a third party, called the Populist or People's Party, in 1891–92, they viewed the Colored Farmers Alliance increasingly as a potential source of votes. The Colored Farmers Alliance had supported the call for a strike by black cotton pickers in 1891 to protest a reduction in wages by white landowners and tenant farmers, but the effort had failed. It stirred up racist hysteria among whites, divided Alliance supporters, and was marred by some incidents of violence. The Colored Farmers Alliance leadership was, therefore, receptive to overtures from the Farmers Alliance for a political union. The People's Party would reach its peak in 1892–94 and then falter as it pursued fusion with the national Democratic Party. Eventually disillusioned with its experiments in biracial politics, the southern white Populists would join the movement to disenfranchise the remaining black voters, to further segregate the black community, and to subordinate the welfare of the poor black farmer and laborer beneath that of the poor white farmer, wealthy landowner, and merchant.[13]

The Colored Farmers Alliance was unable to protect the rights and interests of the African American farmers and laborers in the South; the

National Afro-American League didn't do much better for its more middle-class, urban and professional members. In August 1893 Fortune announced the end of the league. Numerous other claimants did try to provide leadership for African American civil rights and to keep alive their belief in equality in the 1890s. Some advocated racial pride, economic separatism ("buy black"), and cultural nationalism. A few advocated migration out of the South to the West and the North or continued to endorse the dream of colonization in Liberia. Some politically active partisans hoped for federal intervention to protect their race or to provide preferment in patronage to sustain their careers. The movements that seemed to hold the most promise for the future, however, were the self-help movement and the women's organizations.[14]

Booker T. Washington symbolized the self-help movement. The founder and principal of Tuskegee Normal and Industrial Institute in Alabama, he was anxious to provide leadership for the farmers in the "Black Belt" of the South. In January 1892 he had issued a circular for a conference to be held a month later at Tuskegee. "The aim of Principal Washington," the circular said, "is to bring together for a quiet conference, not the politicians and those usually termed the 'leading colored people,' but representatives of the masses—the bone and sinew of the race—the common, hard working farmers with a few of the best ministers and teachers." He had invited about seventy-five participants; he was overjoyed that nearly four hundred showed up. To them he was able to preach his message of self-help, hard work, and industrial education. His slogans were: pay cash, avoid debt, buy land, grow your own foodstuffs, support your own schools, encourage your best students to become teachers and ministers, and set high standards. Above all, the resolutions from the conference concluded: "we believe we can become prosperous, intelligent, and independent where we are, and we discourage any efforts at wholesale emigration and recognizing that our home is to be in the South, we urge all to strive in every way to cultivate the good feeling and friendship of those about us in all that relates to our mutual elevation."[15]

Over the next three years, Washington preached this message wherever he could, North and South, to any available audience. Finally, in September 1895, at the Cotton States and International Exposition in Atlanta, Georgia, he mounted what proved to be a national platform and delivered a short address that fixed upon him publicly the title of leader of his race. To his fellow African Americans, he stated his belief "that we shall prosper in proportion as we learn to dignify and glorify common labor and put brains and skill into the common occupations of life." To the southern whites, he seemed to say that if they would but help and encourage the former slaves, they would be promised a docile, faithful, and readily available labor force. In the most famous and frequently quoted sentence in the address, he said: "In all things that are purely social we can be as separate as the fingers, yet one as the hand in all that pertains to our mutual interests." In less frequently quoted lines he added a more somber poetic note: "There is no escape through law of man or God from the inevitable: 'The laws of changeless justice bind/oppressor with oppressed/ And close as sin [and] suffering joined/We march to fate abreast.' " To underscore this theme of justice and mutual dependence, he also included this sentence. "It is important and right that all the privileges of law be ours, but it is vastly more important that we be prepared for the exercise of these privileges."[16]

The historical evaluation of Washington's Atlanta remarks must look at both the primary text and the subtext. What the white audience heard, the primary text, seemed to confirm their current mood. Washington downplayed the political aspirations of black voters, he denied any interest in *social* equality, and he seemed to promise a docile labor force. But what the black audience heard, the subtext, was more assertive. Washington believed in the pursuit of economic power, both by individuals and by the black community as a whole. Once the white capitalists and political leaders who wanted to industrialize the "New South" became *dependent* upon such black labor, capital, property, and consumer demand, he believed that they would rationally calculate their own economic self interest and would curb the irrational, emotional excesses of racist poor whites and ambitious Populist politicians. Mutuality was a concept that implied common interest, he believed, a kind of equality between racial communities. The key to such self-advancement and economic empowerment, however modest in scale, was what Washington called industrial education. Northern white philanthropists were willing to bankroll such limited education. But the price to be paid for such largess was self-abnegation and accommodation by the black community. In May 1896 the Supreme Court dealt another blow to the civil rights of African Americans in the case of *Plessy v. Ferguson*, which upheld racial segregation in transportation on the basis of an implied "separate but equal" theory. Washington commented in June 1896 that such separation might be lawful and constitutional; however, it violated common sense. "But the colored people do not complain so much of the separation," he remarked, "as of the fact that the accommodations, with almost no exceptions, are not equal, still the same price is charged the colored passengers as is charged the white people." Such behavior was manifestly unjust.[17]

Washington's emphasis on male-dominated economic self-help, accommodation to separation, and his ostensibly evenhanded denunciation of alleged black "criminal" behavior and actual white lawlessness in lynchings did not go unnoticed or unchallenged by African American critics. Ida B. Wells, the militant journalist, had been forced to flee Memphis, Tennessee, in 1892 when she denounced the mob lynching of three black men who had achieved modest economic success. A white mob subsequently destroyed her newspaper office while she was on a business trip in the East. Befriended by Thomas Fortune, she had gathered the facts to disprove the southern white rationalization that lynchings were inevitably a retaliation for black rape of white women. Rather, she showed, lynching was a means of repression that had its roots in political and economic antagonism. In 1893 and 1894 she spoke in England and engaged in a public controversy with Frances Willard, the head of the Woman's Christian Temperance Union, who happened to be in England at the same time. Wells charged that Willard, like many white reformers, did not publicly denounce lynching and covertly acted as an apologist for southern racial attitudes. Looking back at her antilynching campaign in 1895, Wells could take some satisfaction in the fact that she had raised public awareness and political sensitivity to the issue. "This has not been because there was any latent spirit of justice voluntarily asserting itself," she observed, "especially in those who do the lynching, but because the entire American people now feel, both North and South, that they are objects in the gaze of the civilized world." Wells founded a black women's club in Chicago, edited a newspaper, married a prominent lawyer, Ferdinand Lee Barnett, and was subsequently known as Ida Wells-Barnett.[18]

Other black women, while not so outspoken or controversial as Ida Wells-Barnett, realized the need for black women to organize to promote the interests of their race. In 1895 Josephine St. Pierre Ruffin convened in Boston the First National Conference of Colored Women, which voted to form the National Federation of Afro-American Women; Margaret Murray Washington, known as the "Lady Principal" of Tuskegee Institute who had married the widowed Booker T. Washington, was deeply involved in this effort and several other "moral uplift" groups. At the same time, Mary Church Terrell, a Washington, D.C., educator, helped to form the National League of Colored Women. However, such a proliferation of organizations created confusion and competition where the deteriorating situation of African Americans called for unity, cohesion, and coordination. In 1896 the competing organizations agreed to form the National Association of Colored Women (NACW). Mary Church Terrell was the first national president, Josephine Ruffin's newspaper, the *Women's Era*, was the official organ of the organization, and Margaret Murray Washington soon wielded her influence as chair of the executive committee. While prone to acquiesce in the doctrines of separate gender spheres, the cult of true womanhood, and other Victorian stereotypes, the new organization provided a forum for protest and a means for raising hope for black women in a bleak time. While the initial strength of the NACW lay in the Northeast, it would soon expand in the South, Midwest and West. Historian Dorothy Salem has aptly summarized their situation: "As educated, elite women, they actively supported the major women's reform movements seeking moral purity, temperance, self-improvement, and suffrage."[19]

In November 1896 W. Calvin Chase, iconoclastic and vituperative editor of the *Washington Bee* newspaper, called for a resurrection of the Afro-American League under the leadership of Thomas Fortune. Fortune, pleading ill health and financial problems, begged off as would-be organizer although he endorsed the notion of a revised league. In March 1898 Bishop Alexander Walters, African Methodist Episcopal Zion Church, sent an urgent appeal to Fortune to convene a meeting to revive the Afro-American League. Still not personally convinced of the feasibility of the idea, Fortune, nevertheless, did agree to call a conference in September 1898 at Rochester, New York, ostensibly to coincide with the dedication of a monument to Frederick Douglass. At the Rochester meeting, plans were formulated to revive the Afro-American League as the National Afro-American Council by attracting existing organizations while allowing them to preserve their autonomy. Bishop Walters was elected as the new president and Ida Wells-Barnett the secretary. Shortly after the Rochester meeting, a white mob in Wilmington, North Carolina, angered by an editorial in a black newspaper about the causes of lynching and egged on by white political exploitation of the tensions, burned the offending press and shot and killed over ten blacks. As historian Emma Lou Thornbrough summarized the situation, "More prosperous blacks were given the 'opportunity' to sell out and escape the violence."[20]

Here, clearly, was a challenge to which the new organization must respond in order to be credible with the African American middle class. The National Afro-American Council called a national protest meeting to convene in Washington, D.C., in December 1898. A hostile press, both white and black, frequently attempted to portray a stark contrast between Thomas Fortune or Ida Wells-Barnett, as militant "radicals," and Booker T. Washington or Mary Church Terrell, as moderate "reformers." Fortune seemed to lend credence to this approach by an intemperate attack on President McKinley in a speech before the Racial Protective Association just prior to the meeting of the National Afro-American Council. Booker T. Washington, on the other hand, had just entertained President McKinley at Tuskegee and had made a number of conciliatory speeches. Mary Church Terrell could also sound moderate as she stressed "the elevation of black womanhood" in her activities. In reality, Fortune, Wells-Barnett, Washington, and Terrell's attitudes toward each other varied over time, but they worked together behind the scenes when possible and exploited their different public styles in the service of what they perceived to be common goals. At the meeting of the National Afro-American Council, it was Ida Wells-Barnett who publicly criticized McKinley, called for a reduction in southern representation in Congress (under the terms of the Fourteenth Amendment) because of widespread disenfranchisement of southern blacks, and expressed opposition to America's overseas expansion in the wake of the Spanish-American War. Fortune was chairman of the committee that composed the declaration of sentiments adopted by the council, signed it, but did not join the delegation that went off to present the petition to President McKinley.[21]

There was a public/private duality about the rhetoric of the leaders of this civil rights cause and their organizational pronouncements. On the one hand, they appealed to the white public on the basis of the core values that ostensibly bound blacks and whites alike in the civic and political order. Hence their essentially reformist appeal to the notions of personal liberty as *freedom from* discrimination and *freedom to* pursue individual aspiration, equal justice under law, due process, equal protection, equality of opportunity in the economic and political spheres, and the mutual reciprocity of rights and responsibilities. On the other hand, they placed before their African American audience their own middle-class notions of the private values that ought to characterize the black communities. While Mary Church Terrell's inculcation of domestic virtue or Booker T. Washington's litanies on individual effort and free labor ideology seem to modern ears to blame the oppressed rather than to condemn the oppressors, in the historical context of the 1890s such pronouncements had a different function. Such leaders as Terrell and Washington sought to create mass movements by converting individuals from the isolating perpetual *dependency* of the sharecrop and "furnishing merchant" system or the *dependency* of unskilled labor to the community enhancing *independence* of mixed self-sufficient agriculture and the *interdependence* of mutual self-help and extended family networks. Rejecting the radical alternatives of black nationalistic colonization in Africa or massive migration to the West, they proposed that the blacks stay where they were, in the rural South or urban North, and work out their destiny in fear and trembling, perhaps, but also in fervent love toward their God and one another.

There was an assumed link in such pronouncements between the private behavior of blacks and the public policy of whites. If individual blacks worked hard, lived frugally and temperately, acquired property, showed due respect and deference for southern white leadership and social customs, cultivated a Christian character and rectitude, showed fortitude under adversity, then certainly the "educated better classes" of whites would protect the black community from ignorant, "lower-class" white mob violence and political dispossession. In short, there was a vital connection between the private "is" of black achievement and the public "ought" of white acceptance of black-white equality in the economic and political realms, but not necessarily in the private social realm.

Critics, such as Thomas Fortune and Ida Wells-Barnett, were already questioning such theories on two fronts. First, just what was the factual situation? As journalists, they wanted to record the actual situation. Second, where was the evidence, they asked, that the white communities, North and South, were upholding their end of the bargain? From the president down to the local sheriff or county commissioner, where was any public respect shown for black rights except when it was politically expedient for white officials or political parties?

In summary, the evidence from 1883 to 1898 showed that the core value of liberty was not always accompanied by equality of civil rights, citizenship, and substantive justice as included in constitutional amendments and judicial interpretations. Most Chinese immigrants were excluded by law, and the few who belonged to exempted categories found their access to judicial protection gradually diminishing. Native Americans caught in the transition from communal tribalism to individual allotments found the promise of eventual citizenship and equal rights compromised by continued paternalism of federal agencies and the parochialism of white neighbors. African Americans, on the other hand, faced a more complex situation.[22]

In 1885 a federal court of appeals had attempted to define the meaning of liberty as it confronted the police power of the states to regulate the conditions of labor: "Liberty, in its broadest sense, . . . means the right not only of *freedom from* actual servitude, imprisonment or restraint, but the right of [*freedom to*] use his facilities in lawful ways, to live and work where he will, to earn his livelihood in any lawful calling, and to pursue any lawful trade or vocation. All laws therefore which impair or trammel these rights . . . or restrain his otherwise lawful movements . . . are infringements upon his fundamental rights of liberty, which are under constitutional protection."[23] Within a decade, however, the Supreme Court in *Plessy v. Ferguson* (1896) had moved away from this view of constitutional protection of rights. The state could, in effect, restrain local movements by Jim Crow laws for separate cars on transportation systems. Once again it fell to Justice John Marshall Harlan, as it had in the *Civil Rights* cases of 1883, to dissent. The Jim Crow laws should be held unconstitutional, he said, because "[in] respect of civil rights, common to all citizens, the Constitution of the United States does not . . . permit any public authority to know the race of those entitled to be protected in the enjoyment of such rights." The Reconstruction Era amendments, he believed, had "established universal civil freedom," defined citizenship, obliterated the race-line, and "placed our free institutions upon the broad and sure foundation of the equality of all men before the law." Taken historically, Harlan's dissent was an echo of Whig tradition; taken figuratively, it was a failed promise by the end of 1898 for "all men." It was even less the case for women (as shall be examined in the next chapter).[24]

6

Unity and Diversity in the Search for Women's Rights, 1888–1898

How best to bring large numbers of women, and men, into active support for women's rights? What values should guide the effort? That was the task facing a number of leaders in the period 1888 to 1898. By focusing on a few examples, the unity and the diversity among organizations can be illustrated; the continuing tensions within and between core values can be analyzed; and the relative prevalence of the roles played by reform, radical, and ritual renewal strategies can be assessed. Women confronted a host of new problems and old stereotypes as well as utopian visions, which flourished in this decade.

All women in the nineteenth century lived simultaneously in an expressive world of female support rituals and networks and a repressive world of male-superior/female-subordinate routines and institutions. As historian Carol Smith-Rosenberg has pointed out:

Uniquely female rituals drew women together during every stage of their lives, from adolescence through courtship, marriage, childbirth and child-rearing, death and mourning. Women revealed their deepest feelings to one another, helped one another with the burdens of housewifery and motherhood, nursed one another's sick, and mourned for one another's dead. It was a world in which men made only a shadowy appearance. Living in the same society, nominally part of the same culture (bourgeois, farming, or working-class), certainly members of the same family, women and men experienced their worlds in radically different ways.[1]

Women's organizations were simply an extension and institutionalization of these networks and rituals. By the 1890s two broad categories of changes were disturbing the rhythms and rituals of the polar worlds in which men and women lived. First, the expansion of educational opportunity and the increase in female employment outside the home disturbed the traditional assumption of some families that their daughters' lives would imitate those of their mothers and that the mothers' task was simply to initiate their daughters into the rituals of domestic life. Second, changed social attitudes and medical practices, particularly by the male-dominated medical and psychological professions, also challenged the patterns and routines of the female subculture of friendship, affection, and mutual support.

The largest woman's organization in 1888 was the Woman's Christian Temperance Union (WCTU); by 1892 it had 150,000 members, with another 50,000 in young women's branches. Whereas in the 1870s women's direct action crusades against excessive drinking had pushed ahead of the traditional, more cautious temperance leaders, by the late 1880s Frances Willard, the perennial WCTU president, pushed and prodded the organization into support for a wide range of tactics and issues. In doing so, she also explored the meaning of important core values. In 1887–88 Willard read Edward Bellamy's utopian novel, *Looking Backward,* and was attracted to its vision of a gender-equal, cooperative, consumer-equitable society based on technology, collective ownership, and centralized control. Like many of her middle-class coworkers, she was also intrigued with Bellamy's version of a peaceful, gradual, democratic change that incorporated the current "trusts" into one national, government-controlled trust. Willard was also attracted to his notion of cooperative solutions to the daily, practical problems of housekeeping. She supported Bellamy nationalism and urged her WCTU compatriots to study its program. According to Edith Mayo, editor of one of Willard's autobiographical works, in 1892, "shaken by the death of her mother and exhausted from years of traveling, organizing and lecturing," Willard vacationed in England at the home of Lady Henry Somerset, whom she had met through the World's WCTU. Stimulated by Lady Somerset's circle of intellectuals and activists, Willard and Lady Somerset joined the Fabian Socialists. "She declared herself a Christian Socialist and admitted that 'under the mould of conservative action I have been most radical in thought.' "[2]

A close look at Willard's 1889 autobiography, *Glimpses of Fifty Years: The Autobiography of an American Woman,* reveals a complex picture of her intellectual values. She reassured her readers that there was nothing in the book "meant to give the impression that its author undervalues the household arts or household saints." Having paid deference to the Victorian proprieties, she moved on to underscore her central point: "All that I plead for is *freedom for girls,* as well as boys, *in the exercise of their special gifts and preferences of brain and hand.* It is also my belief that the law of development will at no distant day, so largely relegate the household arts to the realm of invention and coöperation that unless *this larger liberty of woman* is fully recognized she will, during the transition period, at least, prove less useful to society than she was meant to be and must be for her own highest happiness."[3] That is, Willard defined liberty for women not simply as *freedom from* home drudgery but primarily as *freedom to* develop individually and to contribute collectively to social welfare, to expand the boundaries of the home from the private into the public realm.

On equality, Willard's thought was wide-ranging and subtle. Although women were especially interested in temperance work, she noted, they were also part of the larger movement of progress that "involves social, governmental, and ecclesiastical equality between women and men." By this she meant "such financial independence on the part of women as will enable them to hold men to the same high standards of personal [sexual] purity" as society required of women, to achieve equal political power via the suffrage, and to exercise equal roles in the church. But independence for women did not mean freedom from the interdependence of home and gender networks. Nor did it mean selfish autonomy or freedom from *mutual* dependence within marriage, what she called "equal partnership." Her conception of equality, in other words, was not so much the classic natural rights theory characteristic of the pioneers of the nineteenth century women's movement but an equality of responsibilities that rested on the Victorian symbol of the home as the primary moral institution of society. "Home protection" was more than a clever slogan for WCTU entrance into politics; it was Willard's commitment to political means to preserve a primary cultural symbol which embodied her notion of these values.[4]

On justice issues, prohibitionists did not need to read Edward Bellamy's utopian novel to become convinced that the state could be an instrument for the solution of social problems. They had come to that realization in the 1850s in the initial "Maine Law" prohibition campaign. But, whereas the traditional temperance emphasis was on the *negative* power of the state, its prohibitory "Thou shalt not" functions, Bellamy put the emphasis on the *positive* power of the state, its productive and proscriptive "Thou shall" functions. Willard misunderstood Bellamy at times; she assumed that he advocated a confederated, voluntaristic "cooperative commonwealth," modeled on persuasive moral agencies. In fact, he advocated a consolidated, centralized, elite-run, authoritarian society modeled on the military. Nevertheless, the encounter with Bellamy had expanded Willard's social vocabulary: "The cultivation of specialties [i.e. the freedom to develop one's capabilities], and the development of *esprit de corps* among women, all predict the day when, through this mighty conserving force of motherhood . . . , the common weal shall be the individual care; war shall rank among the lost arts; nationality shall mean what Edward Bellamy's wonderful book, . . . , sets before us as the fulfillment of man's highest earthly dream; and Brotherhood shall become the talismanic word and realized estate of all humanity."[5] In embracing Bellamy nationalism, Christian socialism and Fabian socialism, Willard had redefined the meaning of liberty, modified her understanding of equality, expanded her notion of justice and had, temporarily at least, taken up the radical role as a cultural critic. In doing so, she may have gotten too far ahead of the opinions of the local WCTU members.

Another organization for those women who were as concerned with respectability as they were with winning women's rights was the General Federation of Women's Clubs (GFWC). Organized in 1889–90, it claimed 20,000 members by 1892. Membership would climb to over 100,000 by 1896. Aimed at middle- and upper-class, domestically oriented women, the GFWC clubs initially stressed literary culture and self-improvement. Reflecting the social attitudes of the era, the GFWC maintained a policy of racially segregated clubs. Soon, however, the clubs were drawn into advocacy for greater educational opportunity for young women and protective legislation for working mothers and children.[6]

The values of the club women in the early 1890s can be illustrated by the activities of Berthe Honoré Palmer of Chicago. Kentucky born, Chicago raised of a wealthy mercantile family, she had married a prominent businessman, Potter Palmer. A model mother, a splendid hostess, and a beneficent patron of charitable and artistic endeavors, her views on women's rights were "advanced" but not "outrageous" by the standards of her class and conventional when it came to questions of marriage, family, and divorce. But she was especially solicitous of the needs of working women. As Mrs. Potter Palmer she accepted the private rituals of personal deference due to a woman of her status, wealth, and personal beauty but used them as means to expand her public power and influence.[7]

In preparation for a World's Columbian Exposition to be held in Chicago in 1892–93 to commemorate the four hundredth anniversary of Columbus's discovery and exploration of the New World, Congress had provided for an elaborate Board of Lady Managers to be appointed to assist the policy-making commission that was planning the event. A fascinated press and public watched as strong-minded Mrs. Palmer seized control of the Board of Lady Managers and put her personal stamp on the preparations for the fair, including plans for a Woman's Pavilion. African American women resented being shunted aside and complained about the neglect of their story, but to little avail. Mrs. Palmer used the occasion of the opening ceremonies at the Woman's Pavilion on 1 May 1893 to chide the "idealists" or "sentimentalists" who used the rituals of deference to uphold the Victorian images of women and who ignored harsh realities. The vast majority of women must work or starve, she said, and they had to work under the most degrading of conditions and for less pay than men. By means of the exhibits in the Woman's Pavilion, she hoped that the public would be enlightened as to the true potential of women. "Freedom and justice for all," she concluded, "are infinitely to be desired than pedestals for a few."[8]

Yet there was a curious ambiguity in Mrs. Palmer's rhetoric. Women's work outside the home did not constitute a rebellion against their roles as wives and mothers, she thought, but only represented a response to the desperate poverty of their families. They should be free from drudgery, unsafe working conditions, and low pay; they should be free to be better mothers and more frugal wives. However, they would remain locked in the interdependent networks of mutual obligation and duties in the home, family, and neighborhood. "We are not able to see how far-reaching may be the result of this period of change and experiment," she remarked in her closing speech at the Columbian Fair. "We feel urgently impelled to follow the highest law known to us, that of evolution and progress." But if the majority of women must work or starve, as Mrs. Palmer had said, how did a display of their "accomplishments" solve their problems? If the exhibits at the Woman's Pavilion were evidence of woman's "evolution," did they necessarily prove that all change was "progress"? It remained for fellow Chicago clubwoman Ellen Henrotin to translate such aspirations into organizational action. As historian Kathryn Kish Sklar has noted, under Henrotin's presidency of the GFWC, 1894–98, "the number of affiliated women's clubs doubled, and its 'industrial division' forged close alliances with other reform-minded women's organizations." In 1898 the GFWC resolved that every affiliated club "inquire into the labor conditions of women and children" in their area and appoint a committee "to investigate its state labor laws and those relating to sanitation and protection for women and children."[9]

Where were the working women's organizations that could have spearheaded the drive for such protective legislation? Traditional labor historians, who looked primarily at the growth of trade unions as evidence of historical trends among working women, interpreted the period 1888 to 1898 as a hiatus between the idealism of the Knights of Labor and the realism of the Women's Trade Union League of 1903, a cross-class alliance of upper-class social reformers and working-class immigrants. Historians did note that, in 1891, Samuel Gompers, the president of the American

Federation of Labor, had appointed "the daughter of Irish immigrants, Mary E. Kenney, as national women's organizer for five months" and that in 1894 Elizabeth Morgan of Chicago was nominated as vice-president of the AFL. Not until 1900, however, did the organization get around to appointing another full-time women's organizer, Eva MacDonald Valesh. A new generation of labor historians have revised this largely negative picture of the period 1888 to 1898. They point out that "ladies" federal unions were chartered by the AFL for "women's jobs," but according to James J. Kenneally, most affiliated unions "were not sympathetic to their needs. Some excluded women, others made them feel uncomfortable or negotiated inferior pay scales" for women workers. Historians of the women's movements, who have focused on cultural values and gender networks, nevertheless point to the Ladies Federal Labor Union of 1888 (chartered by the AFL) and the Illinois Woman's Alliance, 1888–94, as positive developments. They also point out that although working conditions were frequently difficult and wages notoriously low, working for wages was regarded by women as an extension of the "family economy" that characterized their working-class culture as well as an opportunity for mobility out of farms and small towns. Working outside the home also helped create informal female peer groups, women's "work space" cooperatives, and mutual support networks. The primary value of such activities was not independence but interdependence; the essential working-class demand was not individualistic equality but group justice.[10]

The tensions over women's roles outside the home were especially acute in the public debate over the so-called New Woman. Affluent, college-educated, inheritors of the previous generations' pioneering efforts in public activity, the New Woman carved out a professional career for herself and decided, largely, not to marry. Carol Smith-Rosenberg has concluded that the New Woman, by "rejecting conventional female roles and asserting their right to a career, to a public voice, to visible power, laid claim to the rights and privileges customarily accorded bourgeois men."[11]

One of the New Women who exercised a particular fascination for social commentators in the 1890s was Jane Addams. They puzzled over the route that took her from her pampered childhood in an affluent home, through the ennui and uselessness of adolescence leisure, a college education and a youthful life of genteel social graces, to the renunciation of marriage and a commitment to serving others. The key to Addams's decision was the concept of the "cultivated life." Cultivation was something more than education; it involved a training of the emotions as well as a disciplining of the intellect. A close approximation would be artistic sensitivity, a capacity to feel the hurt and pain of others and not to be

incapacitated by it; it also included an element of sympathetic understanding, empathy, or fellow feeling. In 1889 Jane Addams and her col-
league Ellen Gates Starr returned from a ritualized "grand tour" of Europe full of notions about the power of art and the grandeur of European
culture. They decided to live among the poor and to share their cultivated
life with their neighbors in Chicago. Sociologist Mary Jo Deegan has
noted that they "occupied only the second floor of the building that was
leased to them a year later," named Hull-House after the original owner.
They hung up copies of famous paintings and prepared to bring "culture"
to the working-class neighborhood. "In 1891 they built the Butler Art
Gallery on adjacent property. This two-story structure housed a branch of
the public library, had an art gallery, and space for clubs and classes." They
had thus helped to create a new social institution, the settlement house.[12]

In 1892 Addams gave a speech, "The Subjective Necessity for Social
Settlements," in which she attempted to analyze the motives of the young
men and women who were entering this new reform effort. She alluded
to the values of universal brotherhood, of democracy, of efficiency, and
spoke of the yearning for personal fulfillment. "We have in America a
fast-growing number of cultivated young people who have no recognized
outlet for their active faculties," she said. "They hear constantly of the
great social maladjustment, but no way is provided for them to change it,
and their uselessness hangs about them heavily." The settlement house,
where such young people lived in the midst of the working class and
interacted with them, provided the answer, she believed. What was the
intellectual origin of this idea? She referred to "pet phrases" of the cultivated young people: (1) the notion of common human nature, "that all
men are united by needs and sympathies far more permanent and radical
than anything that temporarily divides them and sets them in opposition
to each other"; (2) Walter Besant's notion of humanity, "not philanthropy
nor benevolence, but a thing fuller and wider than either of these"; and
(3) a renaissance of primitive Christianity. Such Christianity "has to be
revealed and embodied in the line of social progress," she said, because
"man's action is found in his social relationships in the way in which he
connects with his fellows." Social Christianity would be a way of life, not
simply a set of beliefs or rituals. "They insist," she concluded, "that it
cannot be proclaimed and instituted apart from the social life of the community and that it must seek a simple and natural expression in the social
organism itself."[13]

It was soon obvious to these pioneering social workers, however, that
the people in the neighborhood had more pressing needs than appreciation of art; they also had a culture of their own rooted in ethnic and

working-class traditions. As Jane Addams admitted in 1893 in a speech, "Domestic Service and the Family Claim," at one of the Congresses allied with the Columbian Exposition:

I have long since ceased to apologize for the views and opinions of working people. I am quite sure that, on the whole, they are just about as wise and just about as foolish as the views and opinions of other people; but that this particularly foolish opinion of young mechanics [of not wanting to marry "mere" domestic servants] is widely shared by the employing class can be demonstrated easily. It is only necessary to remind you of the number of Chicago night schools for instruction in stenography, in typewriting, telegraphy, bookkeeping, and . . . similar . . . office work, and the meager number provided for acquiring skill in household work.[14]

Her point was that young women faced a confusing set of role choices and an imperfect set of educational opportunities. For the role of "breadwinner" outside the home, whether for self-support or as a supplement to family income, there were plenty of educational programs; for the role of "bread maker" in the home, which was equally compelling in its claims on women, there were few support programs available. Over the next two years Hull-House was expanded to make room for a kindergarten, nursery, and playground along with space for a coffee shop, gymnasium, and music school. The chroniclers of Hull-House have observed that it "was in a constant state of development and remodeling; like a medieval manor house, which it vaguely resembled in appearance, the settlement added a wing here or a section there, or changed the function of a room as the need arose."[15]

The image of the medieval manor was an appropriate symbol for Ellen Gates Starr and Jane Addams's philosophy and roles in the women's rights movement. In her autobiography, *Twenty Years at Hull-House*, Addams noted that in college "a curious course of reading I had marked out for myself in medieval history seems to have left me fascinated by an ideal of mingled learning, piety, and physical labor." Ellen Gates Starr, influenced by an artistic aunt who had converted to Roman Catholicism, was attracted to the aesthetic aspects of religious rituals and gradually moved from her austere Unitarian background into the "Anglican Catholic" movement. There was a widespread fascination with medievalism and Roman Catholic liturgical practices among such middle- and upperclass American Protestants of the late nineteenth century. These Protestants found in medieval Catholic piety a childlike intensity of belief, spontaneous innocence, and communal cohesion that was so lacking in their own overly rational religion and routine lives. To many of the residents and sympathetic supporters, Hull-House resembled a medieval monastery combined with a college dormitory. How else could contemporaries describe the communal arrangement of a community of largely unmarried women, and a few men, that mingled learning, in a broad sense, with practical piety in acts of love for others, and physical labor, in spite of "weak" backs and "feminine" frailty than to call it a medieval cloister?[16]

Widespread women's networks and separate cultural institutions such as Hull-House reinforced the role of ritual withdrawal and renewal among such New Women advocates and activists. Jane Addams was adamant when it came to assertions of women's independence; she was politically active when it came to legislation for protection of women workers; and she was personally involved in agitation for temperance and antiprostitution "social purity" legislation. But, periodically, she would withdraw from the daily routine of administration and public controversy into the rituals of renewal—Chautauqua lectures, lively Hull-House debates around the dinner table, attendance at ethnic festivals in the neighborhood, or a social tea with wealthy clubwomen. While her cultural ideas stressed women's "maternal instincts" and the positive contributions of women to social evolution, they were distinct from the older doctrine of separate spheres. Nevertheless, there was enough overlap between her ideas and conventional notions that she could participate in these supportive rituals and return to her institutional roles feeling refreshed rather than isolated or ignored as was the fate of some of her more militant contemporaries.[17]

Jane Addams, and the thousands of women who joined settlements, had an institutional base of operation. In 1891 there were only six settlements in the United States; by 1900 there were over one hundred. Whether young women stayed a few months, a summer, or a lifetime, the settlement house provided them with a support network, rituals of withdrawal and renewal, and female, separate "space" in which to work for a particular cause. These advantages can be seen by comparing the relative stability of the settlement movement with the chronic insecurity of the suffragist cause in the 1890s.[18]

Competing for membership and influence with the WCTU, the General Federation of Women's Clubs, trade unions, and the settlement movement was the divided woman suffrage movement. Disappointed by progress and prompted by younger members, Elizabeth Cady Stanton and Susan B. Anthony's National Woman Suffrage Association and Lucy Stone and Julia Ward Howe's American Woman Suffrage Association united in 1890 to form the National American Woman Suffrage Association (NAWSA), which officially listed 13,000 dues-paying members in 1893. In a moment of candor, Anthony told an audience in 1893, "I will tell you frankly and honestly that all we number is seven thousand." Why were the suffragists so few? "I would philosophize," she said, "it is because women have been taught always to work for something else than their own personal freedom; and the hardest thing in the world is to organize women for the one purpose of securing their political liberty and political equality." It was easy to mobilize women in the cause of temperance, or education, or amelioration of the needs of the poor she observed, "but it is a very difficult thing to make the masses of women, any more than the masses of men, congregate in great numbers to study the cause of all the ills of which they complain; to organize for the removal of that cause; [and] to organize for the establishment of great principles that will be sure to bring about the results which they so much desire." Anthony spoke from experience, but not all the younger suffragists agreed with her analysis.[19]

The merger of the two suffrage organizations in 1890 did not bring a flood of new members as had been anticipated. A convergence of factors, however, seemed to promise an opportunity. The largest untapped pool of potential converts to the suffrage cause were the white women of the South. After the Civil War, they had been confined to the pedestal of Victorian gender stereotypes and lived in a rigid version of the separate spheres doctrine from which they had only gradually extracted themselves through charitable, WCTU, and religious activities. A few elite white women who were suffragists thought they could use the elite white male voters' fears of populism and black voting to their advantage. By enfranchising women, or at least property-owning, tax-paying, or educated ones, the white supremacists of the dominant Democratic Party could counterbalance black voting in ways that would avoid Congressional intervention to uphold black male voting under the Fifteenth Amendment (as had been threatened in 1890 by the Lodge election bill). These elite white women suffragists persuaded the leadership of the NAWSA to pursue a southern strategy, but the price was to tacitly acquiesce in southern segregation laws and racist rhetoric. Even Susan B. Anthony was enticed to support the strategy.[20]

As Adele Logan Alexander, an expert on black women suffrage, has noted, when the NAWSA held its national convention in Atlanta, Georgia, in 1894, Anthony personally asked the aging black abolitionist and women's rights advocate Frederick Douglass not to attend "as a matter of expediency" in order not to acerbate white fears of social equality. " 'Not only that,' " Alexander observes, Anthony admitted to Ida B. Wells-

Barnett, " 'but when a group of colored women asked that I come to them and aid them in forming a branch of the suffrage association among the colored women, I declined to do so on the grounds of the same expediency.' " But expediency was not a word that impressed Ida B. Wells-Barnett as a militant spokesperson for black rights. She had protested the neglect of African American situations and achievements at the time of the Columbian Exposition, the subservience of women's clubs and WCTU leaders to southern racial prejudices, and the failure of the federal government to act against lynching. Whether supporting woman suffrage or civil rights, Wells-Barnett was uncompromising. Little came of NAWSA's expedient strategy, however. The white supremacists preferred to disenfranchise black men by legal subterfuges than to enfranchise any white women.[21]

Black club woman Margaret Murray Washington complained in 1896 about the growing tension between black and white women's organizations. White southern women's organizations would not join the National Council of Women if "colored" organizations were represented. Furthermore, the National Council of Women leadership was slow to protest against the injustice of Jim Crow travel. "I have no cencure [sic] for the northern white women," Washington wrote, "but the great organizations such as the W.C.T.U.[,] the national Council, the Federation [GFWC] &c managed by northern white women if they were inclined, could do more in the direction of correcting evils or indignities against the colored women than they" did. Anthony eventually regretted the expediency policy that had prompted her role in the NAWSA convention and welcomed black suffragists. She attended Thomas Fortune's meeting in Rochester, New York, in 1898 that resulted in the creation of the National Afro-American Council. Anthony also encouraged the National Association of Colored Women to maintain its membership in the National Council of Women. But the damage had been done. At the NAWSA annual convention in 1899 a black delegate moved a resolution condemning segregation in transportation. The motion was tabled following vigorous protests by southern white delegates. The 50,000 black women who joined the National Association of Colored Women over the next decade were, thus, largely alienated from the white-dominated suffrage associations. Furthermore, such white suffrage associations rarely condemned the disenfranchisement of black men or the rising tide of violence against them. The old alliance of abolitionists and woman suffrage advocates, broken in 1867–70, was still not healed, to the detriment of both causes.[22]

Elizabeth Cady Stanton also antagonized many of the more cautious suffragists, both North and South, by her reversal of orthodox attitudes toward women's roles and her attacks on authoritarian religion. In 1892 in a speech, "The Solitude of the Self," she argued that woman's highest natural goal was selfhood or autonomy, not dependence, and that "it is only the *incidental relations of life,* such as mother, wife, sister, daughter, which may involve some special duties and training." When she published *The Woman's Bible* in 1895, a critical evaluation of Judeo-Christian scriptures in terms of their attitudes toward women, the national convention of the NAWSA passed a resolution to distance the organization from it. "They meant to dissociate their middle-class propriety from anything controversial," according to historian Kathleen Barry. But, "without universal principles of justice and equality, the demand for suffrage was merely an appeal to self-interest. And now these reform-minded women seemed to be chiefly concerned with not alienating religious authorities and Christian women." Was woman suffrage a symbol of her goal of selfhood and autonomy, or was it simply a means to protect her social roles and self-interests? Leaders and followers seemed to be divided on this crucial issue.[23]

The tensions between roles and values, between suffrage as a symbol and as a means, was also seen in the career of Charlotte Perkins. Born in 1860 and raised on the fringes of the New England based, reform-minded Beecher clan, she was intellectual, artistic, athletic, and "neurasthenic" (subject to nervous prostration). She experienced a "broken" home when her father separated from her mother. Thereafter her mother led a precarious, nomadic existence among sympathetic relatives. Perkins also experienced economic dependence before her marriage to artist Walter Stetson in 1884. But neither motherhood nor trial separation could save the marriage, and they were divorced. This was followed by her "abandonment" of their child, whom she entrusted to the care of her former husband and his new wife. Both friends and critics were outraged. Thus she knew both public adulation and condemnation all before she was thirty-five. Like Frances Willard, she was influenced by Bellamy nationalism and Christian socialism but added to them a stronger commitment to feminism. Whereas Willard harnessed the expanded meanings of liberty, equality, and justice found in such intellectual developments to the traditional images of the Victorian home, Perkins took some of the same new meanings and began to transform the concept of the home. If women could not achieve autonomy while tied to individualistic household drudgery, she said, then abolish the individual home by collective, cooperative, or socialized housekeeping.[24]

In 1898 Perkins published her masterpiece of feminist scholarship, *Women and Economics.* In it she observed:

Economic independence is a relative condition at best. In the broadest sense, all living things are economically dependent upon others,—the animals upon the vegetables, and man upon both. In a narrower sense, all social life is economically interdependent, man producing collectively what he could by no possibility produce separately. But, in the closest interpretation, individual economic independence among human beings means that the individual pays for what he gets, works for what he gets, gives to the other an equivalent for what the other gives him. . . . As long as what I get is obtained by what I give, I am economically independent.[25]

Where could women radicals such as Charlotte Perkins find an organizational "home" in 1898? The German-immigrant-dominated Socialist Labor Party, which had "courted" native-born women sympathizers in the late 1880s and early 1890s, retreated into ideological dogmatism during the depression, 1893–97, and denounced middle-class women activists as agents of capitalism. Populism, Bellamy nationalism, and Christian socialism, while still providing inspirations for women activists, could not provide institutional continuity as the movements faded after the elections in 1896–98. Philosophical anarchism, which had a long tradition among native-born intellectuals, could have served as an alternative base for women radicals because it combined individual liberty, mutual cooperation, and hostility to coercive authority. However, a few acts of violence by immigrant anarchists against symbols of the economic order had created a confused image in the public mind of anarchists as terrorists and had led to official persecution and public repudiation. So Charlotte Perkins remained what one of her biographers has called "a free lance radical." By 1900 she had remarried and was known thereafter by friends and foes alike as Charlotte Perkins Gilman.[26]

In summary, if the varied activities of women's organizations and leaders of the 1890s indicated one point, it was the enormous *potential* of women. Against the dramatic background of widespread suffering due to economic depression, rapid industrialization, endemic labor violence, racial strife, and unprecedented power lodged in new and unfamiliar institutional forms, women had expanded their networks, created new organizations, and pioneered in new life patterns. The old concept of the separate spheres was being transformed almost beyond recognition as clubwomen, settlement house residents, and a new generation of cautious but active suffragists all claimed wider public roles precisely because they cherished their private virtues, maternal instincts, or homes. In settlement houses, college sororities, and women's club meetings, they created female "space" for their rituals of withdrawal and renewal. But other events of the 1890s—the ambiguity of the meaning of the women's exhibits at the Columbian exposition, the segregation of black women into separate organizations, the acquiescence in Jim Crow discrimination by northern white suffragists in order to attract southern white women, the repudiation of radical attitudes by cautious reformers, the diffusion of WCTU strength, the gap between the values of older leaders and younger followers in numerous organizations, and the isolation of socialist and anarchist women—all these indicated that the dream of *all* women being united on the basis of common gender experiences was a myth, an illusion. Class, generation, race, religion, ethnicity, ideology, and personality divided women as it did men.

Common core values had different meanings for those leaders who played divergent roles in women's organizations. Liberty meant independence as *freedom from* the dependence of marriage to the New Woman such as Jane Addams or to the radical feminist such as Charlotte Perkins Gilman. Liberty meant primarily *freedom to* develop one's talents and to be a better mother to Frances Willard of the WCTU or to achieve autonomous selfhood to Elizabeth Cady Stanton of the NAWSA. Liberty might mean *freedom from* the drudgery of housework to be achieved by Willard's dream of Christian socialism and Bellamy nationalism or by Gilman's blueprint for cooperative, communal housing with the cooking, cleaning, and child care being provided by experts. It meant *freedom from* low pay, unsanitary work conditions, and job discrimination to women's club leader Mrs. Potter Palmer or to women trade unionists.

Equality also had varied meanings. It meant partnership in marriage to Willard, the right to vote to Susan B. Anthony, and equal pay for equal work to trade unionists. Justice meant achieving protective labor legislation to GFWC president Ellen Henrotin, to AFL organizer Mary E. Kenney, and to Hull-House activist Ellen Gates Starr. Justice meant ending Jim Crow segregation in transportation to Margaret Murray Washington of the National Association of Colored Women, but according to many white women in the GFWC or the WCTU, justice meant maintaining social separation. As Ida B. Wells-Barnett noted bitterly: "When the negro has appealed to the Christian and moral forces of the country—asking them to create a sentiment against [lynching,] this lawlessness and unspeakable barbarism; demanding justice and the protection of the law for every human being regardless of color—that demand has been met with general indifference or entirely ignored."[27] But intertwined with all these variations on the theme of independence and dependence as goals, of suffrage as symbol and as means, of duties and desires, of justice and equality, was the overriding fact of interdependence. Whether in the home, the extended family, the kin network, the ethnic community, or in various organizations, women's lives were characterized by interdependent rituals of consolation and routines of mutual support.

While women debated the meaning of these core values and built new institutions, the disruptive forces of urbanization, industrialization, technological innovation, and specialization in the workplace were transforming the context of their lives. These developments affected women's hopes, dreams, and ambitions as drastically as they did men's. And the primary agent of such changes in the social and economic context was seen increasingly to be the business corporation. The struggle to reconcile core values with new realities was sharply evident in the 1890s in the attempts to regulate and to restructure this behemoth, the corporation.

7

Business and Labor in the 1890s: Regulation, Resistance, and Reorganization

In the 1890s people over the age of thirty could remember the events in their lifetime that accompanied the emergence of the modern business corporation and the early attempts to regulate them. The multiple facets of the corporate growth meant, in turn, that there were many different voices in the debates over the proper public policies and the most effective private strategies with which to respond to the revolutionary disruptions of traditional assumptions caused by corporate behavior. These debates touched on one of the deepest polarities in American thought: competition and cooperation. Both competition and cooperation had deep roots in American social, religious, economic, and political life. But, in terms of institutionalized core values, of operative rhetoric, of legal pronouncements and legislative enactments, the balance in the late nineteenth century had tipped decisively toward competition. The antimonopoly rhetoric of the Jacksonian Era had presupposed that the public good of free competition (equal rights) ranked higher than the private benefits to be derived from cooperation within the state-chartered limited-liability corporate form (special privilege). Carried into the post–Civil War Era and transformed into antitrust rhetoric and protest language, the same ranking of values persisted. The enactment of the Granger laws in the 1870s, their partial judicial endorsement in the *Granger* cases, the establishment of the Interstate Commerce Commission in 1887, and the passage of the Sherman Antitrust Act in 1890 all represented attempts to more firmly embed the primacy of competition into the legal and institutional framework of the country. The public good of free competition between businesses was of greater social worth than the private good of some forms of corporate cooperation, now prohibited in the Sherman Act as "every contract, combination . . . or conspiracy, in restraint of trade."

Intertwined with this belief in the primacy of competition was the notion of individualism. It was a question of where lay the ultimate responsibility for the daily welfare of the person—whether they would eat or not, have suitable clothing to wear or not, and shelter over their head or not. Individualism rested that responsibility squarely on the sovereign self. Only if some *personal* tragedy befell—insanity, crippling handicap, or destitution due to sudden widowhood or death of one's parents—would *public* assistance be offered by appropriate legal institutions or *private* support be given as an act of charity. Individualism was reconciled with the need for social order in the late-nineteenth-century community in the legal doctrine of "liberty of contract." Persons voluntarily agreed to conform to certain conditions or to perform certain acts for one another in light of their mutual calculations of self-interest. Such voluntary cooperation undergirded community cohesion but did not imperil the reign of competition. The operant meaning of the common law and antitrust language was that private individuals could not by agreement or covert cooperation do something "unreasonable" in restraint of trade that was contrary to the greater public good of the competitive system. Even religious communitarians who held property in common as liminal utopian groups had to resort to the "liberty of contract" doctrine as a legal basis for their existence or to protect their collective property from suits and claims by dissident former members.[1]

This chapter will examine two developments in the 1890s that had the potential to challenge the primacy of competition over cooperation in the ranking of core values: (1) the regulation of the corporation by government agencies and courts, and (2) the emergence of socialism and other forms of worker solidarity in response to the hardening of class lines during the depression of 1893–97. Why these challenges to the corporate forms of cooperation failed in the 1890s will also be examined, and the consequences of corporate behavior in the merger movement will be briefly indicated.

First, attempts at regulation of corporations must be seen in the context of the various strategies adopted by businesses. Some corporations followed the logic of the system by vertical integration with centralization of planning and decision making or by horizontal integration through the creation of trusts and holding companies. Both strategies could have been seen by public officials as attempts to elevate corporate cooperation above the logic of the market or competition in the ranking of core values. But this reality was masked, in part, by the attitudes and actions of the regulatory agencies themselves. Understaffed, underfunded, and unwilling to risk their careers or reputations on legal cases that seemed doomed to failure, the regulators did little to clarify the law. The regulatory agencies placed a premium on stability in the industries to be regulated and adopted quasi-judicial, case-by-case responses to specific complaints rather than quasi-legislative, industry-wide rule making or preemptory procedures. They thereby performed largely symbolic or ritualistic functions with inadequate technical information and gradually subordinated the legislative preference for competition to the presumed needs for consolidation, coordination, and control within the industry.

When the federal courts took up the first cases under the Sherman Antitrust Act in 1890–95, they turned for guidance to familiar common law doctrines. Common law doctrines rested on such distinctions as the *intent* to monopolize rather than the intensity of monopoly conditions that existed, the *effects* of the alleged business behavior on community welfare, and whether the temporary monopoly was maintained by "reasonable" means (voluntary agreement) or "unreasonable" means (intimidation or violence). Many judges also believed that all attempts at monopoly would be temporary because their very profitability would tempt other competitors to enter the field against them. The cure for monopolies, in other words, was in such judges' opinion simply more competition. Also, some judges developed the line put forth originally by Justice Stephen Field in his dissenting opinion in *Munn v. Illinois* (1877) that business rights were matters of private property and due process and, as such, were subject to judicial, not legislative, supervision. The corporation—a collective, cooperative social institution—was metaphorically subsumed as a private "person" into the familiar language of individualism, liberty of contract, competition, cooperation, and the community as a collection of sovereign, self-interested individuals.[2]

Middle-class moralists, academic economists, small entrepreneurs, farmers, politicians, labor leaders, engineers, and would-be "scientific" managers all vied for public attention or private power in the debate over the corporation and its relation to core values. For Henry Demarest Lloyd, a middle-class investigative journalist, the causes of the rise of the corporation were neither impersonal technological factors nor rational management choices but rather *personal* greed and lack of compassion for others. In 1881 in the *Atlantic Monthly,* Lloyd published an exposé article on Standard Oil called "The Story of a Great Monopoly." Because Standard Oil regarded its business activities as private matters and released little public information, Lloyd was not always accurately or completely informed, but he kept plugging away on the topic for over a decade. He finally published his book in 1894 under the title *Wealth against Commonwealth.* Lloyd's story was essentially a morality tale or melodrama complete with a cast of stereotypical characters. For Lloyd, and others who shared his viewpoint, the problem was one of enforcing personal morality. If "the people" knew the facts, they would rise up in righteous indignation and demand regulation of such unethical business behavior and restore the moral purity of an earlier America. If denominational religion could no longer curb the individual businessman and the corporate appetite for money and power, then a secular equivalent had to be found. A mass conversion was necessary that would put the good of the many (commonwealth) above the greed of the few (wealth).[3]

If Lloyd and those who shared his essentially ethical condemnation of the corporation were primarily concerned with the *burdens* it placed upon others—competitors, workers, investors, public officials—and regarded corporate behavior as a deviation from acceptable standards, other social critics were concerned with the potential *benefits* that could flow from the corporate form. Using the scientific language of evolution, they regarded the emergence of the giant corporation as inevitable, the working out of the natural laws of competition in a changed economic environment. The question was not how to prohibit the formation of trusts, but how to better distribute the resulting products. As has been noted in chapter 6, Edward Bellamy in his novel *Looking Backward* (1888) regarded excessive competition as wasteful and disorderly. Evolution would produce one giant corporation with hierarchical authority, a military-like industrial army, and technological efficiency that promised a peaceful, orderly, and prosperous utopia. "The people" at some vague moment in the future simply would take over the huge corporation and run it not for the conspicuous consumption of the elite but for the comfort and convenience of all. A new breed of evolutionary socialists, such as Lawrence Gronlund, also saw the trend toward trusts as inevitable as was the democratization of administration. Rather than seize power by revolution and class solidarity as the old Marxian socialists had envisioned, the new advocates of the cooperative commonwealth believed that they could achieve their goals by evolution and democratic politics.[4]

Another social critic of the evolving industrial order was Henry George, a California journalist. Like Henry Demarest Lloyd and Edward Bellamy, he was a moralist and a visionary. But George assumed the persona of a hard-hitting, logical economist. Using the traditional languages of eighteenth-century classical economics, Jeffersonian agrarianism, and Jacksonian democratic rhetoric, he expressed the experience of his generation in a book, *Progress and Poverty*, which he completed in 1879. A central image summed up his idea. As settlers moved into unoccupied land and plotted farms and cities, as railroads connected them with distant markets, and as factories were built and products exchanged, "civilization" expanded and "progress" was achieved. The social product of these combined efforts was to be divided between landowners in the form of rent, workers in the form of wages, and businessmen in the form of interest on their investments. But landowners who monopolized the land demanded a disproportionate share in the form of higher rents. Workers and businessmen, who should cooperate in mutual harmony, fell to squabbling over the remainder of the social product. Thus progress was accompanied by poverty. George had a simple solution to the problem. Rather than have the state seize the land and divide it equally, let the "community" expropriate the "unearned increment" on land values by collecting a single tax on it. Thus, landowners would still have private ownership of their property, workers could avoid the loss of individual liberty that characterized socialist systems, and businessmen could maximize their capital because they no longer had to pay onerous taxes to support large government bureaucracies. All sectors of the economy could work in harmony and receive their proportionate share of prosperity. It was a compelling vision that attracted workers, middle-class moralists, and some urban businessmen.[5]

Eugene Debs, a railroad union leader who had started his career in the 1870s, shared the prevailing views of harmony of interest between workers and owners/managers, of the possibility of individual social mobility, and of the need for unions to be limited to skilled craftsmen. His experience in the 1880s had broadened his views somewhat as he saw the impersonal management of distant owners replacing the man-to-man, mutual respect of the small-scale, locally owned enterprise. He also saw workers undercutting each other by taking vacant jobs during strikes and by unions refusing to support each other's strikes. As his biographer Nick Salvatore has pointed out, while Debs was "deeply affected by the writings of Henry George, Lawrence Gronlund, and [Edward] Bellamy," up to the 1890s he was still primarily concerned with the possibility of individual social mobility. He retained the old image of the worker who eventually became the owner of his own shop. As Salvatore has concluded, "Debs remained at this point less concerned with class formation than with the fulfillment of America's promise."[6]

Samuel Gompers, president of the American Federation of Labor (AFL), had been exposed to Marxian socialism in the 1870s and 1880s in the cigarmakers union and the internecine warfare of New York City's labor and socialist parties. He retained a deep commitment to economic organization and self-protection for all kinds of workers via trade unions, labor councils, and federations but developed a growing wariness of political coalitions with farmers, middle-class reformers, or independent socialist-labor parties. In an 1893 pamphlet, *What Does Labor Want?*, Gompers could still use traditional Marxist terminology to explain the "separation between the capitalistic class and the laboring mass" in terms of the capitalist class being "in possession of all the tools and means of labor" and the working class "begging for the opportunity to labor."[7]

The events that transformed the lives and ultimately the opinions of Henry Demarest Lloyd, Eugene Debs, Samuel Gompers, and others were wrapped up in the impact of the depression that gripped the nation from 1893 to 1897. As a reformer, in the 1880s Lloyd had shared many of the prevalent assumptions of his day about individualism, liberty of contrast, and the basis of community. In the 1890s he came increasingly to advocate a different version of cooperation, a variety of Christian socialism as a solution to the ills of a business-dominated society. He took up the role of the radical. It was not simply that he sought to use cooperation as a means or to restore an earlier balance between cooperation and competition; rather, in making cooperation the goal or end of his social vision, he challenged the current basis of community. In its starkest form, it was the question of the ultimate unit of the community. Was it the individual or the group? There was no denying the fact that Lloyd was a wealthy suburban land investor and something of a dilettante who was more at home with intellectuals from Hull-House than with the workers and trade unionists at a neighborhood saloon. As historian Peter J. Frederick has expressed it, "his socialism was grounded not on dialectical materialism and the conflict of classes but on Christian principles of moral concern for the welfare of others." That is, Lloyd's sense of what "ought to be" did not so much grow out of an analysis of the fats (the "is") of the working-class situation as his proposals represented an attempt to impose his own definitions of meaning and moral order upon the data of the workers' daily lives. In a similar fashion, Lloyd misread the agrarian Populist movement. In 1894 he tried unsuccessfully to fashion an alliance between the minuscule, rural People's Party of Illinois and the workers of the urban industrial areas. By 1896 he had abandoned the Populists and had converted to the gradualist, elite version of radicalism, or Fabian socialism.[8]

Eugene Debs also crossed the line from reformer to radical during the period 1894–97. In an ironic sense, Debs's efforts to build a more effective union of railroad workers mimicked the efforts of the corporations to curb competition by pools, trade agreements, and trusts. Debs's newly formed American Railway Union (ARU) tried to bring skilled and unskilled workers into one system-wide union; it represented "vertical integration" applied to worker competition. For one brief moment in 1894 Debs confronted James J. Hill of the Great Northern Railroad and forced him into binding arbitration because the workers stood united and the business leaders in the railroad towns were divided. But when the ARU decided in 1894 to boycott Pullman railway cars in support of a strike by Pullman manufacturing workers, the confrontation proved to be disastrous for the union. This time the railroad managers were well organized, determined to break the power of the unions, supported by federal troops, and armed with antistrike injunctions based on the Sherman Act and issued by sympathetic judges. Debs and his national union officers were convicted of contempt of court in November 1894 for violating an antistrike injunction. Although conspiracy charges were heard in a separate trial, that trial adjourned on a technicality. Debs served a six-month sentence in Woodstock jail on the contempt charge.[9]

Debs talked vaguely about supporting something like Gronlund's notion of the cooperative commonwealth, but he refused to be publicly identified with any of the current socialist organizations. Upon release from jail, 22 November 1895, he rededicated himself to the American tradition of individual liberty and collective redemption through the use of the ballot. In the 1896 election he supported the People's Party for its democratic promise, but, like Lloyd, soon moved beyond it. If neither trade unions, nor strikes, nor third parties could curb the corporation, what then? On 1 January 1897 Debs announced his decision: "The issue is Socialism versus Capitalism. I am for Socialism because I am for humanity." For the next year he talked vaguely about a cooperative colony somewhere in the West to provide a temporary haven for blacklisted Pullman strikers and about a "grand co-operative scheme." When forced to make a choice in June 1898, however, he abandoned the economic colonization idea for more orthodox socialism and a political commitment to the new Social Democratic Party. Debs crossed the line between reformer and radical when he ceased being simply the labor organizer and advocate of political action to preserve citizen's rights. He became a radical when he sought to be the architect of the cooperative commonwealth and the apostle of socialist solidarity. What was at issue was not the means he was willing to use to combat the intrusions of the corporation upon traditional working-class communities, but the goals that he now envisioned. Cooperation was not simply a means to an end, cooperation was now an end in itself and the hallmark of a new kind of community. Debs talked about humanity rather than class, but he, too, raised the fundamental issue: what was the basis of community in America—individual competition or class cooperation?[10]

While Lloyd and Debs moved from the role of reformers to that of radicals in the 1890s, Samuel Gompers moved in the opposite direction.

Gompers maintained in the late 1880s that he was a radical in terms of goals, that trade unionism as a means to achieve these goals was sanctioned by Marxist philosophy, and that solid economic organization by workers must precede political action according to a Marxian understanding of labor history. But events of the 1890s wrought a subtle shift in his position. At the 1890 convention of the AFL, Gompers argued forcefully and successfully against allowing the Socialist Labor Party to become a member of the AFL. "Unions, pure and simple," he said in a famous phrase, "are the natural organization of wage workers to secure their present material and practical improvement and to achieve their final emancipation." In 1893 midwestern socialist trade unionists moved a series of resolutions at the AFL convention, including Plank 10 that called for "the collective ownership by the people of all means of production and distribution." They secured the referral of these resolutions to the membership on a close vote. Gompers opposed Plank 10. At the 1894 convention Plank 10 was defeated on a parliamentary maneuver, but Gompers was ousted as president. A year later Gompers was reelected president, set his face resolutely against the hard-line Marxist socialists, and continued to ignore those members of the AFL who wanted cooperation with the Populists. Gompers could be ideological about the class basis of government and the need for workers to rely on their own voluntary organizations (i.e., trade unions), and he could be liberal as he publicly opposed racially exclusive union charters; but, above all, he was pragmatic. Gompers supported some protective legislation for children and women, acquiesced in racially discriminatory practices in some local unions when necessary, and tolerated local labor politics.[11]

By the end of the 1890s it was clear to all but the most diehard ideologues that no grand antimonopoly movement had emerged to stem the process by the corporations in reshaping American life. Regulation via independent agencies, legislative enactment, or judicial interpretation had proven to be ineffective. Resistance in the form of farmer-labor alliances, working-class community solidarity, strikes, unions, third parties, and consciousness-raising by middle-class moralists and idealists had been shown to be inconclusive. The evidence from the voting patterns of the decade was that although third parties such as the People's Party could draw unprecedented numbers and historically high percentages in some areas, they could not shake the loyalty of most farmers, workers, small-town merchants, or newly enfranchised immigrants to the two major parties. The specter of armies of workers voting for Republican presidential candidate William McKinley, the high tariff, and the gold standard in 1896 while fusionist Populist farmers went down to defeat behind Democratic contender William Jennings Bryan would remain fixed in the popular imagination for decades.[12]

If the attempts of those who were *external* to the life of the giant corporations to either reform them or to provide radical alternatives failed, those who were *internal* to the life of the corporations and who wished to restructure them also experienced frustration and a sense of futility as the decade of the 1890s ground through the cycle of depression and recovery.

The problem, according to Frederick W. Taylor, a mechanical engineer and pioneer of scientific managements, was that the modern corporation was *not* efficient. Their factories were little more than conglomerations of old-fashioned shops; their so-called managers were "rule of thumb" amateurs who knew little about the capabilities of the machinery. Stockjobbing financiers only wanted quick profits on their investments rather than long term economic stability and highly productive systems. Workers were more concerned with controlling the pace of production by their craft prerogatives than they were in working to their maximum capacity. What was needed was a reorganization of the corporation. A scientifically trained engineer, Taylor believed, could determine the optimum mixture of machine, labor, guidance, record keeping, and coordinated control. Because he believed that workers would respond more readily to monetary rewards or penalties, Taylor advocated a differential piece-rate system of payments to replace the standard hourly or day wage system, crew-based subcontracting, and ad hoc discipline by untrained foremen.[13]

The context for Taylor's heightened concern was a new wave of corporate mergers between 1895 and 1904. Unlike earlier attempts to achieve vertical integration or coordinated control *within* a firm, this new wave of consolidations was predominately an attempt to achieve horizontal integration and coordinated control *between* competitive firms. In addition, the pace and scale of consolidation seemed unprecedented. As economic historian Naomi Lamoreaux has noted: "In 1895, four consolidations were organized; in 1897 there were six. Then, in 1898, the number of new combines suddenly rose to sixteen, and, in 1899, to a high of sixty-three. By the next year the movement began to taper off. Twenty-one consolidations were formed in 1901, seventeen in 1902, and a scant three in 1904. . . . All told, more than 1,800 firms disappeared into consolidations, many of which acquired substantial shares of the markets in which they operated."[14] What caused the great merger movement? Two factors stand out in recent historical analysis of the merger movement: (1) the economic environment, and (2) the legal climate.

Lamoreaux in her study of the merger movement found that, contrary to the myth of the heroic empire-building entrepreneur, most mergers occurred in particular kinds of industries. These industries were: (1) capital-intensive, (2) engaged in mass production of standardized products across a wide range of markets, (3) characterized by numerous firms closely matched in size or competitiveness, (4) had recently completed periods of rapid expansion, and (5) were subject to price fluctuations. Caught at the beginning of the depression in 1893 with high fixed costs for maintaining their productive facilities, these firms adopted the strategy of "running full" to drive down per-unit costs. They also engaged in price-cutting in order to dump their inventories on the declining market. That is, those firms that could afford to play the game at all during the depression had enough financial resources to maintain production even at low prices and to absorb losses in the short run. However, the firms that were "running full" could not afford to continue such a strategy indefinitely. Merger promised a solution that would coordinate production and raise prices to profitable levels.[15]

Contrary to public opinion then and popular imagery later, not all mergers were equally successful. Running productive facilities at full capacity during the depression years meant that the machinery wore out faster. Or the machinery might become technologically obsolete as more specialized firms sought efficiency in newer techniques. Emerging companies, therefore, were faced with heavy capital needs to replace worn-out or outmoded equipment. To save capital, they frequently closed older facilities outright or consolidated activities into a few plants in order to minimize costs. Two patterns of postmerger behavior soon emerged. If the merged firm could operate at lower prices and maintain its market position, it could undercut its rivals. If, on the other hand, the merged firm did not achieve sufficient efficiencies, it could lose its market position and be undercut by lower-priced rivals. And, as Philip Scranton has reminded historians, batch and specialty manufacturers had economic survival strategies not found in the bulk production industries that favored mergers. Thus, while the merger movement was disturbing to contemporaries and had a significant input on competition, not all mergers were as successful in the long run as their initiators had hoped.[16]

The legal climate was important in stimulating much of the merger movement. It was created by the federal courts and the Supreme Court in a series of cases, 1895–98. Preoccupied with the priority of competition *between* firms and the technical question of whether the business behavior in the case at hand fell under the commerce clause of the Constitution that governed *interstate* commerce, the judges were less concerned with the consequences of cooperation *within* a single firm, whether it resulted from a merger or by contract. As William Letwin has explained, in *United States v. E. C. Knight Company* (1895), Chief Justice Melville W. Fuller focused on two questions: "first, whether the Sherman Act could destroy a monopoly of manufacture, and, second, whether [the] attempt to dissolve the contracts involved" was the appropriate remedy. Although the E. C. Knight Company did control over 90 percent of sugar-refining production, Justice Fuller held that this fact only "incidentally and indirectly" affected *interstate* commerce because the manufacturing took place within states rather than between them. On the second point, Fuller, on a strict reading of the facts in the case, ruled that the company did not unduly diminish competition. The case established a precedent and an anomaly: a single coordinated firm could do something that a combination of separate firms could not do, namely, control production and prices. This provided an incentive to mergers. Soon, however, the courts modified this position. In the *Trans-Missouri Freight Association* case (1898), the *Joint Traffic Eastern Trunk Line Association* case (1898), and *Addyston Pipe and Steel* case (1899), the courts ruled that combinations that attempted to fix prices or divide markets violated the Sherman Antitrust Act if they did so in "unreasonable" ways.[17]

An opportunity for innovations in corporate structure and management philosophy, therefore, existed during the period 1895 to 1900. But the merger mania was sometimes conducted in a manner that frustrated these internal efforts at reform or doomed them to failure. A case study can illustrate these conditions and contradictions between corporate mergers and business innovation. For example, Arthur J. Moxham, inventor of a steel-rolling technique, began to manufacture light weight rails for electric street railway systems. Moxham formed a company with Tom L. Johnson, who owned or controlled a number of street railways. The Johnson Company, as it was called, established its headquarters in Johnstown, Pennsylvania. Moxham concluded in 1893 that building a technologically advanced steel mill at Lorain, Ohio, west of Cleveland, would benefit the firm by reducing costs and freeing it from dependence on its steel suppliers. Moxham wanted to achieve vertical integration through technological efficiency and coordinated management.[18]

Moxham's strategy ran counter, however, to the interests of the established steel rail manufacturers and their voluntary trade organization, the Rail Association. In 1895 the Rail Association, which controlled prices and production, made a deal with the Johnson Company. The Johnson Company promised not to produce heavy rails for steam railways; in exchange, the Rail Association allocated one-half of the production quota for lighter-weight rails for electric street railways to the Johnson Company. During the building of the new facility at Lorain, the Johnson Company had moved its subsidiary electric motor operations to its plant in Johnstown, Pennsylvania. In 1896 Moxham hired Frederick W. Taylor, the pioneering management expert, to make the Johnstown plant more efficient. Taylor thus found himself introducing in the context of a continuing depression and a capital strapped company the innovations in management that he had developed earlier in more prosperous times and with more tolerant company attitudes. Taylor replaced the older subcontractor system with salaried foremen, brought in lower wage women workers for some jobs, and imposed differential piece-rate pay systems. By early 1897 Taylor had turned the Johnstown plant into a profitable operation. But neither Taylor's innovations, financial contributions by Pierre DuPont, nor Moxham's deal with the Rail Association could save the Johnson Company. In 1899, Johnson, Moxham and the DuPonts sold their interests in the Johnson Company to the newly created Federal Steel Company, which itself would soon be swept up in another merger among steel producers.[19]

In summary, the merger movement among the large-scale, administratively coordinated corporations in the last decade of the nineteenth century had raised a number of troubling questions. To middle-class moralists, such as Henry Demarest Lloyd, the question had been how to restrain the individual greed responsible for corporate misdeeds and to reassert traditional communal norms. To utopian dreamers, such as Edward Bellamy and Henry George, or socialist theoreticians, such as Lawrence Gronlund, the question had been how to retain the benefits of this product of social evolution. How could they peacefully tax the benefits of social evolution or transfer the ownership of the giant "trust" to the state or to the "working people"? To politicians, whether in the Republican, Democratic, or Populist Party, the question had been how best to regulate the public economic behavior of the corporations. How could they either preserve the widest margin of private "liberty of contract," protect the equality of opportunity of smaller-scale entrepreneurs, farmers, and skilled workers, or promote the public interests of all "producers"? To mechanical engineers, and pioneering scientific managers, such as Frederick W. Taylor, the question had been how to restructure the corporation and the workplace so as to achieve not only maximum productivity and profitability but also the most efficient combination of human and technological resources. By the end of the decade of the 1890s the corporation, particularly in its consolidated or horizontal merger form, seemed to be triumphant. External reformers had been rebuffed, radicals isolated, and those within the corporation who advocated scientific management had been put on the defensive and temporarily forestalled.

The rise of the corporation and the merger movement threatened to erode core values rather than simply to reverse the priorities among them. Few could deny that there were fewer *independent* firms and that equality of competition *between* firms had been replaced by oligopolistic competition in which a few firms dominated their industries. And who could deny that "smaller" firms, such as the Johnson Company, were *dependent* upon the forbearance of their larger competitors and their trade associations for price stability or market shares? In other words, by the end of the 1890s there was less overall competition and less equality among competing firms. The same process seemed to be at work among the workers. The skilled craftsman who enjoyed the "liberty of the trade," who moved from city to city on the upward journey from apprentice to master craftsman, who controlled the pace of work in the shops, who set traditional communal standards by social rituals, and who bargained equally for wages—such a heroic figure, as Debs, Gompers, and ordinary workers knew, was an "endangered species." Dependence, not independence, was the growing lot of all workers, skilled and unskilled.

By the time the corporate lawyers and federal judges had elevated "liberty of contract" into a legal defense of corporate rights and a barrier to local and state regulation, the basic premise on which such freedom rested was already a myth. The *equality* of the worker and the employer to enter into a mutually satisfactory arrangement no longer existed on a personal, one-to-one basis. It was not, then, that the corporation claimed the core value of liberty for themselves while denying the core value of equality with others but that the impact of the corporation seemed to diminish *both* liberty and equality, *both* competition and cooperation, and *both* individualism and community. The struggle *among* corporations for dominance in the market, the struggle *between* corporate employers and workers for control in the labor market, the struggle in the press, the political platform, the legislative chambers, and the courtroom *between* reformers, radicals, and corporate spokesmen for cultural legitimization, the struggle *within* the corporation for authority, expenditures, and priorities between managers and financiers—these were all struggles for power.

Power in modern society includes not only control over the *means* of production and exchange relationships but also the power to define *meaning*. That is, what was at stake in the conflicts of the 1890s was the ability to determine whose semantic categories would shape social perceptions, define legal and linguistic conceptions, and establish the parameters of permissible behavior. The struggle for power also involved the question of how to, and who would, deal with the unintended consequences of social actions. The corporations in the 1890s had won the political skirmishes, and they had dumped the undesirable consequences of consolidation upon workers, competitors, and communities. But in spite of self-serving rhetoric, they had not quite convinced important sectors of the public. The persistence of moralistic critiques, of populistic appeals to equality and democracy, of trade union consciousness, of socialist alternatives and utopian visions, of mercantile appeals to regional equity or fairness in trade, and the invocation of common law restraints all showed that the corporation might be a dominant cultural institution, but it was not fully hegemonic in the culture. The lingering doubts among clubwomen, settlement house workers, and popular writers about "mere money-making" and the appeal for humanitarian protection for women, children, and immigrant workers also called attention to other cultural traditions. If any group was to win this tug and pull of cultural constructions, then an intellectual revolution as vast and as far-reaching as the economic transformation of the past thirty years and the institutional revolution of the merger movement would have to take place. And, perhaps, it would take just as long. The corporations might have won the institutional struggle in the 1890s, but they had not won the intellectual one.[20]

PART II

New Languages and Old Realities

To the participants who lived through the period from the 1890s to the 1920s, there was an indefinable quality of excitement, tension, and high drama in the private achievements, public politics, and cultural conflicts of the period. Their languages and memories were charged with certain characteristic words and images: "insurgent," "movement," "muckraker," "trust buster," "crusade," "rebellion," and "crossroads." Above all, there were endless variations on the words "progress," "progressive," and, after 1912, "progressivism." Historians subsequently coined the phrases "the Progressive Era" or "the Progressive Movement" in an attempt to encompass the entire episode. However, the notion of progressivism as a single mass movement or a coherent set of ideas cannot accommodate the diversity and complexity of the historical data.

Historian Daniel T. Rodgers, in a review of this problem, has suggested that the focus should be on the social languages and rhetorical strategies used by different groups and individuals. He has isolated three such overlapping social languages in the early twentieth century. First, the language of antimonopoly drew on notions of equality of opportunity in the economic realm, belief in equity or economic fair play within the boundaries of the common law, and reassertion of community norms. Second, the language of social cohesion emphasized "social bonds and the social nature of human beings." While couched in the neutral terms of social science, the language of social cohesion reflected the religious values and emotional memories of a generation that had moved from farms and small towns to the growing urban areas. Third, the language of efficiency, initially the province of highly trained professionals such as scientists, engineers, architects, and accountants, focused on the rational relationship of effort to outcome in social affairs. It was based on experiences of professionals in the growing hierarchies of corporations, educational systems, and regulatory agencies of government. Social languages, in short, provided the vocabulary for talking about core values in rapidly changing situations; rhetorical strategies, on the other hand, provided the ways to reach the potential audience.[1]

The study of *who* used the vocabulary of various social languages, *when*, and *how* they used them rhetorically shows more about the nature of the Progressive Era than attempts to fit the multitudinous activities of the era into a single abstract model. Because social languages were *means* to achieve social change, they could be harnessed to a variety of ends or goals: reformists, radical, or ritualistic renewal. Linking social languages and rhetorical strategies to organizations, interest groups, and political coalitions illuminates the historical *context* of progressive social movements; linking language and rhetoric to core values, especially liberty, equality, and justice, will also clarify the *content* of ideas and their *meaning* for American history.[2]

This flexibility in the use of language raised a perplexing question, however, about the relationship of language to values during the period 1898 to 1932. If values were abstract and absolute and language merely descriptive, then the function of words was simply to convey and confirm the meaning of values apart from the ebb and flow of transient experience. Philosopher John Dewey thought otherwise. "There is, in truth," he wrote, "a certain real fact—an existent reality—behind both the word and the meaning it stands for. This reality is social usage." Because social usage, or custom, changed over time, language, particularly a new social language, was both a means to clarify values and a way to change social reality so as to achieve these values.[3]

Those caught up most intimately in attempts to change social reality had to struggle, therefore, with this tension between the old abstract values and new ways of talking about them in social languages. Woodrow Wilson, for example, in a speech before the Democratic Club of Philadelphia on 21 February 1911 said:

> It is very interesting to see how an audience like this responds and thrills at those old words, consecrated throughout many generations, . . . , those old formulas of liberty that have rung in this country from generation to generation on the lips of public orators. I believe, and hope, that my own pulse leaps to respond to them as yours does, but what I am interested in is the translation of liberty into experience, and my blood would leap much more quickly to the details by which we were to get it, than to the general statement of what it is we want to get. . . . It is all very well to say what we want. We want liberty. Of course, we want liberty, but what is liberty?[4]

Wilson was part of that generation of progressives who, from the 1890s to the 1930s, attempted to redefine the meaning of liberty, equality, and justice. In confronting anew the issues of civil rights, women's rights, and the regulation of business, they also encountered certain old realities of human prejudice, institutional inertia, and cultural conservativism. These stubborn forces frequently thwarted their attempts to translate the new social languages and their versions of values into institutions and individual inspirations.

8

Women's Rights, Feminism, and the Social Gospel, 1898–1912

The diversity of situations among men and women during the period 1898 to 1912 presented a problem for those who worked for social reforms, including women's rights. Increased access to education, including higher education, had opened up new lines of employment and possible professional careers for women. Technological innovations in office equipment and communications had shifted clerical work from male clerks who copied documents by hand to female "typewriters" who prepared them on machines and from male telegraph operators to female switchboard operators. Mass production and distribution of consumer items, including commercially prepared food and bakery items, freed middle-class women from the kitchen and laundry so that they could participate in women's clubs or reform organizations. The application of machine production to consumer items brought women into factories and realigned some jobs along gender lines. Immigrant women supported their families' incomes by working in small tenement "sweatshops," on "piecework," or by peddling goods in street markets. African American women experienced urbanization and industrialism as well but found their options limited by racism and gender stereotypes. The net result of this variety among women's situations was the need for new leadership and a diversity of organizations. This chapter will explore the new patterns of leadership, the social language and ideology used to communicate their understanding of core values, the organizations that were created, and the tension these developments created among men and women, particularly in the social gospel movement. Above all, it will explore the question of whether in this plethora of competing interests and organizations, of conflicting priorities of men and women, and of contested religious roles and social sanctions there was sufficient unity to constitute an effective women's rights movement and to create coalitions for change.[1]

By the end of the 1890s some familiar leaders of the women's rights organizations were passing from the scene. Frances Willard died in 1898, and the Woman's Christian Temperance Union (WCTU), which had followed her "do everything" philosophy for so long, backed away from her commitment to woman suffrage. They focused more strictly on the prohibition issue because they were being elbowed aside on that issue by the aggressive, male-dominated Anti-Saloon League. On the woman suffrage scene the pioneers were dying off: Lucy Stone in 1893, Elizabeth Cady Stanton in 1902, and Susan B. Anthony in 1906. The one organization that claimed to speak for women's rights since the reunion of the divided woman suffrage movement in 1890, the National American Woman Suffrage Association, seemed to be in the doldrums. The presidents of the NAWSA, Carrie Chapman Catt and Anna Howard Shaw, were not able to maintain the momentum of the organization. Catt had decided to resign in 1904 to care for her seriously ill husband and to concentrate on international women's issues; Shaw was an eloquent speaker but an indifferent administrator, and NAWSA suffered accordingly. The General Federation of Women's Clubs, which under president Ellen Henrotin, 1894–98, had focused on investigating the conditions of working women and children, soon drifted into internal squabbles and seemed to be emphasizing once again literary self-culture more than social reform until the election of Sarah Platt Decker, a western suffragist, in 1904. Mary Church Terrell, president of the National Association of Colored Women, 1896–1901, stepped aside in conformity with the organization's constitution (which limited the president to two *consecutive* terms). When she ran for president again in 1906, she was rebuffed by delegates who resented her elite status and social abilities. Thereafter she put her energies into the issue of interracial understanding. Thus the organizations that had represented large groups of women in the 1890s, that had pioneered in municipal housekeeping and protective programs for working women and children, and that had spoken in the old languages of the nineteenth century seemed stymied for the moment in the face of the diversity among women's life situations.[2]

Leadership, particularly the roles of articulating ideas, planning strategies of action, and creating organizations, passed to a new generation of women. One of the new style leaders was Harriet Stanton Blatch, the daughter of Elizabeth Cady Stanton. With her experience in England in a variety of women's causes and her contacts with working women in the United States, she helped to redefine the scope of the woman suffrage movement and to relate it to a larger audience of women. In New York she urged the existing middle-class suffrage organizations to realize the potential of working women and their need for the vote. When the traditional organizations were too slow to take up the idea, she formed a new suffrage organization in 1907: the Equality League of Self-Supporting Women. The advantage of the phrase "self-supporting" was that it could encompass both working-class, wage-earning women and middle-class, salaried or fee-earning professional women. The Equality League, and another new organization, the American Suffragettes, also pioneered in the use of militant tactics to promote the suffrage cause: parades, outdoor rallies, newspaper publicity, trolley car campaigns, and support of striking workers. Such tactics also helped to bring some upper-class, reform-oriented women into the suffrage cause. Thus the breach that had opened in the late 1860s and 1870s between middle- and upper-class women suffragists and working-class trade unionists began to close. But the efforts of the suffragists also provoked the upper-class men and women who opposed woman suffrage to pull together their local efforts in 1910 and form the National Anti Suffrage Association.[3]

Another example of a leader who rose to prominence during 1898 to 1912 was Florence Kelley. Born in Philadelphia in 1859, the daughter of a prominent entrepreneur and politician, William D. (Pig-Iron) Kelley, she had studied at Cornell University and at the University of Zurich. There she embraced socialism, translated Friedrich Engels' *The Condition of the Working Class in England in 1844*, and in 1884 married a Russian socialist. But the marriage failed. In 1891 she found a refuge with Jane Addams at Hull-House. In 1893 she was appointed "factory inspector" for the State of Illinois to enforce antisweatshop legislation for women and children. But opposition to her efforts and a political change after the 1896 elections soon ended her brief career as a public official. Eventually she moved to New York City, where she had found an alternate role as executive secretary of the newly organized National Consumers' League (NCL). The league was a cross-class effort that brought the consumer purchasing power and social consciousness of middle- and upper-class club women to bear in support of working-class women in garment manufacturing and retail sales. "Under her politically principled and technically expert leadership," sociologist Theda Skocpol has concluded, "the National [Consumers'] League became a persistent and remarkably effective advocate of child labor legislation as well as protectionist legislation for women wage-workers." By 1905 the NCL could claim sixty-four local leagues but no more than a few thousand members. What they lacked in numbers the NCL made up in the political influence of its elite members and the tenacity of Kelley's executive skills.[4]

Along with the emergence of new leadership and the creation of new organizations or revitalization of old ones was a change in thought and language symbolized by the new term "feminism." Historian Nancy Cott has pointed out that "people in the nineteenth century did not say *feminism*. . . . Most inclusively they spoke of the woman movement, to denote the many ways women moved out of their homes to initiate measures of charitable benevolence, temperance, and social welfare and to instigate struggles for civil rights, social freedoms, higher education, remunerative occupations, and the ballot." Whereas the nineteenth-century advocates used the singular term "woman" to symbolize the identity and unity of the female gender in a single, all encompassing social movement, the early twentieth-century activists increasingly used the plural term "women" to symbolize the diversity of interests among members of the female gender. In articulating feminism, for example, Blatch shifted the basis of unity among women from the home and their family duties to the workplace and their numerous roles in it. Kelley shifted consumerism from a passive role to a positive one for both club women and workers. Such shifts threatened, however, to explode the notion of a single woman movement into a host of competing causes and organizations.[5]

Feminism was primarily a set of ideologically defined *goals*. Feminists talked about the goal of *independence* as indicative of economic self-support, about conscious choice between marriage and career, about self-expression in the arts, and about the frank acknowledgement of women's sexual natures and needs. In so doing, these thinkers were redefining the cultural concept of liberty as it applied to women. Women's *freedom from* traditional restraints, particularly in life-choice expectations, sexual behavior, and economic opportunity, was intimately linked with their *freedom to* explore the new opportunities of an expanding consumer-oriented economy. For example, Charlotte Perkins Gilman, the radical feminist thinker and writer, argued that women would never be free to enjoy equality of opportunity as long as they bore the double burden of home and child care *and* a career. Only some form of cooperative sharing of household "chores," professional child care, restructuring of domestic relations, and new architectural arrangements could achieve such "domestic liberty." Emma Goldman, the anarchist theoretician, argued that women would never be free from the "tyranny of biological destiny" and free to explore their sexual natures until they had access to birth control information and devices. Mary White Ovington argued that women would never enjoy the freedom to use equal political power wisely until they enjoyed freedom from unequal economic power; she thus linked feminism and socialism. Louise Bryant argued that women would never be free to be radicals until they were free from conventional notions of marriage.[6]

If feminism as an ideology defined one end of a spectrum on the issues of marriage, home, work, education, and sexuality during the period 1898 to 1912, maternalist views defined the other end. By "maternalist" historians and legal scholars such as Seth Koven and Sonya Michel refer to "ideologies and discourses that exalted women's capacity to mother and applied to society as a whole the values they attached to that role: care, nurturance, and morality." Thus, maternalist rhetoric sounded similar to traditional concepts such as separate spheres for the genders and the special roles of women in reference to children. For example, the National Congress of Mothers, organized by socially prominent, white women in 1897 disavowed any intention to further women's rights or to be a "sex movement," but it was willing to work for child labor laws. Maternalist rhetoric, on the other hand, could be used to support protective legislation for women. It was so used by local coalitions of women's groups and consumer organizations, by African American churches and benevolence organizations, by the National Consumers' League and the General Federation of Women's Clubs, and by settlement house workers, both white and black. Even though many settlement house social workers were single women, they regarded themselves as symbolic mother figures or held that all women embodied maternal instincts and values whether they had children or not. Women who shared this maternalist perspective, according to Koven and Michel, "transformed motherhood from women's primary *private* responsibility into *public* policy."[7]

Whether women's leaders aligned themselves with the feminist ideology or with maternalist rhetoric, they all shared a sense of urgency over the issue of protecting working women and children. This sense of urgency facilitated the creation of coalitions of organizations that worked together on the issue. While the needs of self-supporting professional women were complex and ambiguous, working-class women's demands were more direct and explicit: income stability and employment security, public recognition and legitimacy for unions, legal intervention by government to protect women from exploitation and hazardous working conditions, and some reversal of negative stereotypes in the media and in public rhetoric about the morality of working women. Some women workers were involved in large-scale industry and, hence, subject to the more impersonal corporate discipline, others were involved in small-scale production in "sweatshops," piece-rate home labor, retail shops, or domestic service. They were subject to the frequently humiliating conditions of personal supervision and sexual harassment. To deal with these problems, middle- and upper-class women's rights advocates joined with women workers in 1903 to establish the Women's Trade Union League. The WTUL focused on the need for laws to limit the number of hours that women could work, to raise their minimum wages, and to protect their health. Settlement house workers provided support and encouragement, women's club matrons provided money, and working-class young women provided the pickets for strikes. But even such cross-class efforts to achieve common goals could not mask other tensions and continuing conflicts: (1) between male-dominated trade unions and female workers, (2) between the income needs of immigrant families and the middle-class preconceptions about the nature of childhood and the priority of preparatory education, (3) between black aspirations and white ethnic loyalties, (4) and between consumer protection proposals and the precarious market positions of small-scale ethnic entrepreneurs.[8]

These tensions between the needs of women workers and the ambiguities of progressive rhetoric can be illustrated by the famous case of *Muller v. Oregon* (1908). The prevailing legal doctrine held that under liberty of contract employers and employees could agree on mutually satisfactory terms without interference by the state. The Supreme Court affirmed this view in *Lochner v. New York* (1905), which overturned a New York law limiting male bakers to ten hours a day. When it came to the issue of protective legislation for women and children, state laws limiting the hours of work for women had been passed or improvements in existing laws had been made by ten states before the Supreme Court agreed to hear an appeal on an Oregon law. The burden of defending the Oregon law fell to Florence Kelley and the NCL staff. In November 1907 Josephine Goldmark, an associate of Kelley, asked her brother-in-law Louis Brandeis, the famous "people's lawyer," to join the case. While most legal commentators on *Lochner v. New York* believed that it presented an absolute barrier to protective legislation for women, Brandeis realized that the Supreme Court had allowed for the police power of a state to be invoked in such cases if "reasonable" circumstances required it. Brandeis used Goldmark and Kelley's data on the impact of long hours of work on women's health and "women's biological vulnerabilities" (i.e., their childbearing physiology). Brandeis's brief argued that the state had a reasonable basis for the regulation because, in fact, prolonged hours of work were detrimental to women's maternal roles and responsibilities. The Supreme Court agreed. Thus, a progressive concession had been won from a conservative court by appeals to maternalist rhetoric that was compatible with traditional stereotypes of female "weakness," their special maternal and nurturing roles, and the need for (masculine) public protection. The brief had argued, in effect, that the public's interest in having healthy mothers outweighed the private rights of employers and employees to engage in liberty of contract, in which the contract assumed an equality of status between the consenting parties. Thus, a conservative court could invoke the core value of justice to counterbalance liberty and equality.[9]

Simultaneously with these changes among women, there were widespread anxieties among urban, middle-class white men. Old familiar landmarks were disappearing. A man could no longer assume that he would pass on to his sons his knowledge of nature, his artisanal skills, or his business enterprise in the tradition of the proprietary mode. The merger movement among corporations and the growth of mercantile chain stores restricted his options. The rituals that marked the transition from boyhood to manhood—the hunting trip, first long trousers, graduation from high school, apprenticeship, the male bonding of the militia, fire company, or fraternal lodge meeting—all seemed threatened. Fraternal orders lamented the waning of the golden age of widespread membership. They worried about the seeming reluctance of younger men to join the lodge, or, if they did, to devote much time to its elaborate rituals. Public figures such as Theodore Roosevelt bemoaned the passing of the frontier and the loss of the martial spirit. They sought in the violence of collegiate sports an antidote for the ennui and "effeminacy" of urban life. Suburban lifestyles, in which the father was absent during the workday while the children were required by mandatory attendance laws to spend more and more time in school among women teachers, undercut paternal authority. Anxiety over the "temptations" of the city, the "effeminate" influences of popular culture, and the "delinquent" behavior of urban boys found expression in the boys club movement. This concern for "character building" was symbolized by the founding in 1910 of the Boy Scouts of America and by the professionalization of boys work in the Young Men's Christian Association and similar organizations.[10]

These tensions between men and women put additional stress on one of the foundations of social reform during the late 1890s and early 1900s— religion. As historian Robert M. Crunden has put it: "Americans remained dominated by patterns of religious thought. Some were explicit, giving rise to what became the social gospel movement. Most were implicit, shaping ideas that seemed to be about secular matters." The term "social gospel" had been first used in 1886 by a preacher to describe Henry George's *Progress and Poverty*, and gradually the term took on wider meanings. The notion of redeeming society, of creating the heavenly kingdom on earth, or, at least, of rescuing working men, women, and children from the hells of urban life and industrialism had motivated a whole generation of liberal theologians and activist believers. Some Protestants saw the social gospel as simply a variation of Christian socialism, a way to realize the cooperative commonwealth or to counter the excessive materialism and greed of corporate capitalism. An African American trend emphasized racial justice as well as social reform. A Roman Catholic version of the social gospel stressed the need for "piety, religion, education, and charity" among recent immigrants. Some ecclesiastical authorities saw the need for social justice efforts among working men to woo them away from socialism. Both religious tendencies took organizational form in the first decade of the twentieth century. An interchurch conference in 1905 laid the groundwork for the inauguration of the Federal Council of Churches among thirty Protestant groups in 1908. By 1912, the Federal Council had adopted a lengthy Social Creed, which included protective laws for working women, abolition of child labor, and wide ranging welfare proposals. Similar Catholic conferences in 1899–1900 had led to the creation of the American Federation of Catholic Societies in 1901 and eventually to the creation of the National Conference of Catholic Charities. Building on recent papal encyclicals, the Catholic version of the social gospel also endorsed a wide variety of welfare ideas.[11]

Both men and women had been involved in the social gospel since the late 1880s, but by the end of the 1890s a new assertiveness among men about their role in religion became evident. Books appeared in profusion with such titles as *The Manliness of Christ* (1900), *The Manly Christ, a New View* (1904), *The Masculine in Religion* (1906), *The Manhood of the Master* (1911), and *The Masculine Power of Christ* (1912). The sincere social gospel minister was, then, caught in a conflicting situation. On the one hand, he felt pulled to support women in their efforts to bring in the kingdom by welfare activities and protective legislation; on the other hand, he felt tugged by masculine solidarity to support institutional expressions of social Christianity. For example, one of the preeminent social gospel theologians, Walter Rauschenbusch, published *Christianity and Social Crisis* in 1907. The book was a compendium of progressive proposals and an articulate exposition of liberal theology. When it came to the relations between men and women in the early church in Corinth, he cautiously echoed St. Paul:

[Paul's] prophetic strains asserted that in Christ all the old distinctions of race and social standing would disappear, including the difference between man and woman. The spirit of Christianity has accomplished that result in the slow progress of centuries, *and our women are now free and our equals. If these Corinthian women tried to take at once that heritage of liberty which was to be theirs eventually, we cannot help sympathizing with them.* But we can also understand the unusual vexation and distress in Paul's mind when he heard of this disorder, and agree with his prudence in biding them keep within the bounds of customary modesty and restraint.[12]

In his sequel, *Christianizing the Social Order,* published in 1913, Rausch-enbusch also endorsed woman suffrage, but when it came to women working outside the home and the need for protective labor legislation, in both books he echoed maternalist sentiments and "the priority of the home and maternal roles and values."[13]

Other social gospel advocates also supported a masculinist response to the perceived "crisis of feminization" of mainline Protestantism. They called for imitation of business structures and techniques in the churches in the Men and Religion Forward Movement of 1911. As historian Gail Bederman has noted, "the Men and Religion Forward Movement itself should be seen as merely one manifestation of a much broader cultural trend. When the consolidation of a consumer-oriented, corporate capitalism made Protestant men feel that their identity as men was uncertain and their religion was effeminate, many middle-class men moved to re-codify religion as especially manly."[14] This highly publicized, centrally directed crusade for manly religion failed in its overly ambitious goal of bringing three million "missing men" back into the Protestant churches; in fact, according to Bederman, "in 1912, 15,000 *fewer* people had joined the church than had joined in 1911." Nevertheless, behind the Men and Religion Forward Movement and the increasingly ritualized woodcraft/ Indian lore activities and regimented "character building" activities of the boy scouts, YMCAS, and boys clubs lay a hunger for "old-time" values and secure gender identities. If the new social language of masculine bonds and assertiveness as used by social gospel advocates could not heal all the anxieties of men in the face of radical feminist ideology and maternalist rhetoric of reform-minded women, then perhaps organizations could provide the opportunity for ritual withdrawal and renewal. Those who served as scout leaders, YMCA boys' work executives, or publicists in the Men and Religion Forward Movement could preserve older values, re-store their sense of worth, or reinvigorate their dedication to core values. Even some of the traditional fraternal orders began to heed the call to simplify their time-consuming rituals, to diversify their gender specific activities, and to become more public spirited.[15]

In summary, in the first decade or so of the twentieth century a grad-ual socioeconomic reorientation touched all areas of women's life experiences. Women's rights advocates in the period 1898–1912, therefore, had to face the fact of diversity. Divided by class, generational, racial, economic, educational, and even tactical considerations within the suffrage campaign, the older rhetorical fiction of a single, comprehensive woman movement gave way before two new developments. First, there was a new self-assertiveness of self-supporting women at all levels of society (from retail clerks, factory workers, and clerical workers to educated professionals). This assertiveness found expression in the Women's Trade Union League, the Equality League of Self-Supporting Women, the ranks of settlement house workers, and in the public image of the New Woman. Second, a distinctive ideology, feminism, was being articulated, which redefined the relationships between women and society. The new feminists broadened the cultural concept of liberty to encompass *independence* as economic self-support, artistic self-expression, freer sexual development, and conscious choice between career or marriage. But the feminists, as cultural radicals, were a distinct minority.

Maternalist rhetoric used maternal images of women's special nature and nurturing roles even as they stressed the mutual support of women's *interdependence* in the family and neighborhood. Such reformers used the social language of social bonds and human nature to reach out to all uncommitted men and women. Equality for women meant primarily equal rights—to education, employment, and equal pay for equal work. But, increasingly social claims were raised in terms of justice—for protection in the workplace, for the right to vote, for equitable promotion and professional advancement, and for the right to form unions and strike, if necessary, for better working conditions. The time for periodic ritual withdrawal into separate spheres and women's clubs activities devoted to high culture, polite conversations, and genteel fund raising was passing; the time for united action in a self-conscious women's movement was at hand. The revival of the woman suffrage movement under new leadership, and the shift in maternalist rhetoric from merely justifying women's *private* roles to legitimizing their *public* policy proposals, upset the hitherto sacrosanct masculine public sphere of politics. Calls for "municipal housekeeping" by women's clubs and settlement house social workers challenged long-held masculine self-concepts about their governing roles.

Many middle-class urban men watched these developments and were beset by a number of anxieties. A host of boys clubs, boys' work departments in social agencies, and scouting organizations emerged to build "character" in boys. Conservation and hiking clubs, social gospel activities, and renewal interest in "manly" religion challenged young men to get involved. Popular entertainments and professional sports created new forms of fellowship and fraternity. Liberty, for such men, might mean nostalgia for the youthful *freedom from* adult responsibilities and *freedom to* exploit the resources of nature for self-development. Equality might mean the fraternal companionship, brotherhood, and camaraderie of the team, the hunting trip, or the street-corner "gang." Justice might mean primarily obedience to law, respect for the rules of the game, and keeping one's word and pledge. The values were admirable but somewhat archaic in the highly competitive, workaday world of corporations and civic causes that was clashing all around them. If periodic withdrawal and renewal in liminal group or liminoid cultural activities were not enough, if men could not escape from the corporate world, could they fashion new meanings of liberty, equality, and justice in pursuing reform or radical alternatives within that world?

9

Regulation of Business: Progressivism, Socialism, and the Gospel of Efficiency, 1898–1912

Why did several varieties of progressivism emerge in the late 1890s primarily in the rapidly growing urban areas? These cities were experiencing the double impact of industrialization and population growth related to immigration from abroad and migration from the rural areas. Among the middle-class professionals, small-scale entrepreneurs, and white-collar clerical and supervisory ranks there was a growing sense of frustration, fear, and irritation at their perceived loss of independence. Living in the new suburbs or in residential neighborhoods distant from the centers of work and commerce, they were *dependent* as commuters on streetcars, trollies, or commuter trains owned by franchised monopolies or by financial speculators. These middle-class citizens also demanded better public services, such as clean water, sanitary sewers, police and fire protection, garbage removal, up-to-date education for their children, parks and recreational space, museums, and cultural events. They were *dependent,* however, upon antiquated municipal departments run on the patronage systems by political bosses, who exchanged jobs and services for votes by immigrants and poor workers. The city councils listened more to the corporate interests or speculators who could pay bribes or "boodle" than they did to suburban commuters or residential customers. The city relied upon an arbitrary tax system that extracted more in property taxes from home owners than it returned in public services. At the same time, the city gave preferential treatment on tax assessment to corporations and utilities.

After the economic recovery in 1897 as prices began to rise, such middle-class citizens began to experience the impact of inflation, which eroded the value of their savings, life insurance, or bank accounts. Inflation raised their cost of living while their salaries remained relatively fixed or increased only incrementally through occasional promotions.

This made them *dependent* as consumers on the pricing policies of distant corporations, "trusts," or "monopolies" rather than on competition in local markets. In their own eyes, the urban middle-class families were caught between domineering businesses above them who were in alliance with corrupt political bosses and their political machines and militant workers and immigrants below them who espoused unionism and socialism. This chapter will focus, therefore, on middle-class progressivism and working-class socialism to test these perceptions against certain realities. It will also examine a variation of the social languages that emerged from the interaction of these two developments—the "gospel of efficiency."[1]

This pervasive feeling of dependence occasioned by the predominant role of corporations put the issue of regulation of business at the forefront of public concerns during the period 1898 to 1912. And the railroads were at the center of many of these concerns because they made shippers, consumers, passengers, and communities *all* feel dependent. The question in the Progressive Era, therefore, was not *whether* the government should regulate the railroads, but *who* and *how*. Roughly speaking, there were three options: (1) the legislature by law, (2) the judiciary by legal doctrines, or (3) the executive branch by bureaucratic judgment in independent commissions. From the point of view of later events, the legislative solution has appeared to be more "democratic" as it could accommodate the concerns of a multitude of private economic interests. Legislation could also enact prohibitions against specific business practices. The judicial solution, on the other hand, appeared to be more "conservative" in that it respected private property rights, liberty of contract, and market mechanisms. The executive solution, above all, appeared to be more "progressive" or liberal because it invoked rational expertise, greater public accountability, and disinterested, elite control. But legislation, litigation, and bureaucratic legerdemain are all means, not ends in themselves. They must be evaluated historically in relation to values, and contingencies, in order to draw a fair judgment on their meaning in this period of our history.

What was at stake in the question of business relationships with the economic and political process, in the eyes of the middle-class progressives, was the viability of the notion of liberty as inherited from the nineteenth century. The gap between official rhetoric and current realities seemed overwhelming. It was not that government interfered with business; it was that business interfered with, i.e., "corrupted," government. It was not that one business used unfair competitive tactics against another; it was that giant mergers seem to have *eliminated* competition altogether. It was not that "confiscatory taxation" by the many based on their democratic political power denied proportionality of economic rewards to the few; rather, it was that disproportionality of economic power by the few in the form of bribes, "boodle," or graft denied the equality of political power of the many, that is, it was "undemocratic." It was not that legal grants of privilege by charters of incorporation to investors denied equal entry into a field of economic endeavor for others; it was, rather, that the economic privileges of the giant corporations in the form of rebates, discounts, patent monopolies, and economies of scale precluded entry into new areas by smaller firms. Popular confusion on these issues was evident in current discourse and terminology: (1) the word "trust" was used as a synonym for monopoly; (2) "monopoly" (or dominance by *one* firm) was used as an inaccurate description for oligopoly (or dominance of a *few* firms); (3) "Big Business" was a term used for all corporate activity; and (4) "Wall Street" was a shorthand symbol for financial capitalism. Even humor reflected these confusions. "A trust is a body of men who don't trust anybody so they get a whole lot of people to trust them [with their money]," quipped vaudeville comedians Joe Weber and Lou Fields. Behind these confusions of language usage, however, there lurked a significant intellectual shift of attitudes and a desperate search for political remedies. If those citizens called progressives supplemented their rhetorical emphasis on liberty as a core value with additional appeals to equality or justice, it was not because of any great depth of commitment to these two social values (as shall be shown in the next chapter) but rather because of a pervasive feeling of discontent with the current status of liberty.[2]

However much these predominantly middle-class citizens might talk about restoring government to "the people," putting power in the hands of "good citizens," or in restructuring local government to achieve the moral good of the "community," they were, in fact, but one more competing interest group among many in the complex urban environment. They picked up the language of antimonopoly formerly directed against the railroads by disgruntled farmers and crossroads merchants or against Standard Oil by pioneering muckraking journalists and pipeline shippers, in part, because they were experiencing similar disadvantages on a miniature scale from trolley lines, commuter trains, and public utilities. Also, in the aftermath of the great merger movement in business from 1895 to 1904, they discovered that business could manipulate local power centers, thus challenging their sense of community and democracy. What bothered the nascent progressives was the realization that the corruption could not be explained away simply as the singular "sin" of an errant individual who violated community norms; rather, it was *systematic*, the product of seemingly impersonal economic forces and political realities, and it seemed to be so widespread.[3]

In opting for more democratic innovations in government and increased reliance on governmental regulation by commission, progressives of 1898–1912 stretched the language of antimonopoly to its logical limits. Instinctively, they also incorporated elements of the language of social bonding and human nature into their rhetorical strategies and political coalition building. For example, Robert M. La Follette, a Republican congressman from Wisconsin, had cast about in 1897 for a way to revive his lagging political career. He had picked up some of the rhetoric that had been developing among individualistic businessmen, community-oriented religious evangelicals, safety-conscious workers, and tradition-oriented ethnic farmers. Historian David P. Thelen has noted that "in the desperate economic depression of 1893–1897, these groups [had] found a common voice . . . , which incorporated their hatred of combinations, hostility toward materialism, and longing for a united community into a new tone of resentment toward large-scale industrialism." La Follette championed some of their causes (direct primaries, equitable taxation, and restriction of free railroad passes), waited when the machine-dominated Republican Party ignored him, and, behind the scenes, assured wealthy railroad leaders that he was not as dangerous as he sounded on the platform. Finally the party nominated him for governor. He was elected in 1900. He had used the social languages of antimonopoly and social cohesion to gather together a diverse group of political supporters, and he wove their concerns into a viable political platform.[4]

Another political leader who combined the languages of antimonopoly, social bonding, and efficiency was Theodore Roosevelt. The popular Spanish-American war hero was elected governor of New York in 1898. To the issues of business regulation and protection of workers, Roosevelt added a passionate commitment to the environment. He saw in the middle-class anxiety about conservation of the land both a symbol of past moral values and a concern about future economic opportunities. As governor, Roosevelt supported civil service reform, a franchise tax on corporations, minor concessions for workingmen's welfare, tenement "sweatshop" restrictions, and conservationist "game law" amendments. Elected Republican vice president in 1900, he assumed the presidency following the assassination of President William McKinley. As president, Roosevelt moved cautiously but symbolically to revive the Sherman Antitrust Act by having the Justice Department file suit to dissolve the Northern Securities Company, a railroad holding company, in 1902. If "producers," that is, small-scale entrepreneurs and farmers, cheered these moves, "consumers," that is, middle-class urban families, were heartened by his threatened federal intervention in an anthracite coal strike in the winter of 1902–3. Conservationists were also pleased with his support of western irrigation projects.[5]

Elected to the presidency in his own right in 1904 over a hapless Democratic opponent, Roosevelt urged more progressive regulation of business. In a January 1905 speech before the Union League Club in Philadelphia, he sounded the appropriate note: "[T]he great development of industrialism means that there must be an increase in the supervision exercised by the Government over business-enterprise. . . . Neither this people nor any other free people will permanently tolerate the use of the vast power conferred by vast wealth without lodging somewhere in the Government the still higher power of seeing that this power is used for and not against the interests of the people as a whole."[6] In spite of the vague terminology, the notions of social bonds and human nature (community as "this people" and "the people as a whole") and of antimonopoly ("supervision exercised by the Government over business-enterprise") were blended together. (The limits of Roosevelt's conception of the nature of community, social bonds, and human nature will be dealt with in chapter 10.)

There were tensions *between* the social languages of antimonopoly and social bonds and human nature that complicated the process of political coalition building to deal with the issue of business regulation. When La Follette was elected to the United States Senate in 1906, he hoped to duplicate on the national scene his exploitation of the antimonopolistic belief in free competition. In brief, La Follette, who favored the democratic legislative option for business regulation, genuinely believed that it was possible and desirable to "bust up" the trusts. He wanted to restore a semblance of equal competition by vigorous governmental intervention. On the other hand, Roosevelt, who favored the executive administrative option for business regulation, was increasingly listening to the advice of a group of academic specialists, financial experts, and administrative veterans. They believed that market regulation by large corporations was inevitable. They supported proposals that would sanction some corporate restrictions on competition, provided they were supervised by sympathetic government agencies or, at least, by the federal judiciary. The final result of the sparring over these differing viewpoints between members of Congress, the White House, and the federal bureaucracy was the Hepburn Act of 1906, which strengthened the Interstate Commerce Commission's rate-making powers. La Follette also wanted the ICC to evaluate railroad property values as a necessary step toward the determination of fair rates; Roosevelt, however, tended to favor the approach of the Bureau of Corporations. The Bureau advocated a cautious policy of publicity about corporate activities, federal licensing of interstate corporations, and public-private cooperation to police markets in the interests of justice and community service. The difference between La Follette's structural approach to antimonopoly and Roosevelt's procedural approach seemed to be simply this: did "trust busting" mean *restoration* of competition or *recognition* of corporate self-regulation under government *regulatory* supervision? Which meaning would best restore liberty or ensure equality and justice?[7]

The issue was not quite so simple or two valued, however. The complexity of the issue was evident in 1907–8 when the National Civic Federation, a progressive business, labor, and public interest coalition, tried to steer through Congress a series of amendments to the Sherman Antitrust Act. Behind these proposed amendments stood a widespread consensus that had emerged among some business leaders, farm organizations, labor unions, and administrative bureaucrats. Congressional leaders were sympathetic to public complaints and seemed willing to act. According to historian Martin J. Sklar, "the common outlook favored (1) the legalization of reasonable restraints of trade; (2) effective federal regulation of interstate commerce to prevent unreasonable restraints and unfair methods of competition; and (3) the establishment of some federal administrative agency clothed with authority to carry out such regulation." In spite of the consensus, the effort failed. The National Association of Manufacturers, representing the interests of small-scale manufacturers, wanted to invoke the Sherman Act against strikes and boycotts by labor unions. Samuel Gompers of the American Federation of Labor, at the same time, wanted exemption from judicial interpretations that applied Sherman Act provisions to labor union activities. Some business leaders, unnerved by a bank panic in 1907 and uneasy about the upcoming elections in 1908, had second thoughts about strengthening the role of the president in economic matters. Congressmen, caught in the crossfire of conflicting opinions, decided to let the issue die. Meanwhile, Roosevelt decided not to seek another term and left the unresolved issues to his handpicked successor, William Howard Taft. In short, the social language of antimonopoly, even interpreted narrowly as governmental restraint on unreasonable corporate behavior rather than broadly as restoration of competition, was not sufficiently flexible to encompass all the relevant and conflicting economic interests and, at the same time, satisfy the social language of common bonds by a single legislative consensus.[8]

By 1908, then, the electorate seemed poised at a strategic moment on the issue of regulation of business. Republican William Howard Taft defeated his Democratic challenger, William Jennings Bryan, and assumed the mantle of presidential leadership. Whereas Roosevelt had been willing to confront congressional conservatives in order to achieve limited progressive gains, Taft believed that he had to work with the Republican congressional leadership in order to achieve further reform. On the issue of railroad regulation, proposals endorsed by conservative leaders and by Taft were amended by insurgent Republicans. The resulting compromise, the Mann-Elkins Act of 1910, was passed with bipartisan support but plenty of bruised political egos as well. The act empowered the Interstate Commerce Commission to suspend "unreasonable" railroad rates, to prohibit pooling, and to strengthen the limits on short-haul/long-haul rate discrimination. But there was another option between legislative prohibitions and empowered regulatory commissions. That third option was judicial interpretation. In 1911 the Supreme Court in the *Standard Oil* case and the *American Tobacco* case enunciated its "rule of reason" in which it returned to the common law standards of liberty of contract, right of competition, and protection of private property rights. The Sherman Act, the basic antitrust law, the Court said, prohibited only "unreasonable" agreements in restraint of trade. By implication, some agreements in restraint of trade were acceptable if they met the "rule of reason." The courts, not the elected legislators or the appointed regulators, would ultimately decide the difference.[9]

If the progressive reformers had difficulty in using the social languages of antimonopoly and social bonds to further their interests in the regulation of business, in the face of congressional compromises and judicial "rule of reason" standards, so too did the socialist radicals when they confronted the issue. In the decade from 1898 to 1908 Eugene Debs struggled to find a suitable social language to supplement his socialist ideology and to convince fellow Americans that his dream of socialism was feasible. The inherited European Marxist vocabulary of class warfare, social revolution, capitalist exploitation, proletarian solidarity, and working-class internationalism grated on the sensitivities of Americans nurtured on the rhetoric of individualism, social mobility, harmony of interests, and equal political rights. Debs rejected the language of antimonopoly as a petit bourgeois complaint by crossroads merchants and small-scale manufacturers against corporate capitalism. He believed that the trusts were an inevitable stage in the evolution of capitalism; trusts paved the way for the eventual socialist appropriation of the means of production, distribution, and exchange. Nor was it simply a matter of socialists rejecting capitalistic competition and embracing communal cooperation. The trusts, he believed, marked the point at which even the capitalists had abandoned classical laissez-faire competition in favor of economic cooperation. The question was not how to "reform" the system in order to achieve capitalist defined values; rather, it was a question of "revolution," of replacing the system with a new one. It also involved a radical transformation in the meaning of values. Equality would no longer be confined to the legal and political realm nor would it be defined simply as the opportunity to enter business (a "fair chance") or the right to compete with other entrepreneurs (a "fair field"). Economic equality under socialism would mean equal ownership in the means of production, equality of obligation to labor, and an equitable share in the social product of industry ("full value of labor").[10]

Although Debs condemned the current system for its inherent waste and maldistribution of wealth, his primary concern was not making the current system work better; rather, it was to achieve social unity. Liberty was an empty promise when the goal of personal independence was contradicted by the reality of workers' dependence. Instead of proclaiming such illusory "independence," Debs preached social *interdependence.* His most eloquent and emotional passages spoke of the social bonds that united "wealth and want," "millionaires and mendicants," "masters and slaves." Debs could be quite sentimental and conventional at times about motherhood, womanly virtues, and social equality, but the revival of socialism under his rhetoric provided a rallying point for a variety of women radicals in independent groups, party auxiliaries, and the activities of the Woman's National Committee of the Socialist Party of America. Debs refused to draw the colorline against black workers and advocated equality for women. He welcomed both the newly arrived immigrants and the native-born workers and farmers into the working class. "By the working class," he said, "I mean all useful workers, all who by the labor of their hands or the effort of their brains, or both in alliance, as they ought universally to be, increase the knowledge and add to the wealth of society." Beyond the trade union, beyond the Socialist Party, beyond the working class, Debs believed that the socialist *movement* represented the last best hope for a more humane social order. The problem was how to get the political power to achieve this social order.[11]

The role and limits of social language in the building of a political coalition and in the creating of such a socialist movement was evident in Debs's political campaigns. He ran for president in 1900 on the Social Democratic Party ticket and in 1904 on that of the newly unified Socialist Party of America. In 1900 Debs had drawn fewer than 100,000 votes, in 1904 just over 400,000 votes, and in 1908 he drew 420,000 votes. Remembering that women could join the Socialist Party of America but could not vote for the most part in the larger society, a ratio of 1:10 can be calculated between the number of dues-paying, card-carrying, Socialist Party members and the number of sympathizers of the socialist movement, who cast their votes for Debs. Thus the 41,000 Socialist Party members in 1908 represented a core of the 420,000 socialist voters who cast their ballots for Debs, whether out of commitment to his beliefs or out of disgust with the traditional parties is not clear from the historical records. What held together the men and women, the middle-class intellectuals, the working-class trade unionists, the former Populist farmers, the radical immigrants, the idealistic college-educated professionals, and the muckraking journalists who comprised the socialist movement? Certainly it was not the frequently cantankerous, feuding, and parochial internal politics of the Socialist Party of America. Nor was it the running rhetorical battle between the Socialist Party of America and its rivals such as the hard-line Marxist Socialist Labor Party and the syndicoanarchist, rowdy-romantic Industrial Workers of the World (IWW, "the Wobblies"). Most observers then, and historians now, agree that the socialists were bound together largely by the symbolic figure of Eugene Debs. The impact of the corporation on the economic, political, cultural, and social life of the country may have created the potential audience, but it was Debs's rhetoric that molded them into a social movement.[12]

In this confusing political environment, some progressives looked for additional intellectual resources to bolster their favorite cause. One was Louis Brandeis, the "people's" lawyer, who in 1910 was involved in a number of highly publicized, public-issue law cases involving federal regulation of the railroads. In a case before the Interstate Commerce Commission, railroad corporations had petitioned for an across-the-board freight rate increase to raise needed capital. Brandeis, who believed in competition more than cooperation among corporations, looked for a way to counter the railroads' arguments. He thought that he had found it in the scientific management theories of Frederick W. Taylor. Yes, Brandeis conceded, the railroads did need more capital, but they didn't need to raise their rates to generate it! The railroads were too inefficient; by adopting Taylor's techniques of scientific management, they could lower their costs and realize the needed capital through such savings. The ICC agreed with his argument. By adopting this "if you can't raise the bridge, lower the river" strategy, Brandeis had not only stymied the railroads, he had also stimulated public interest in what could be called the "gospel of efficiency."[13]

Frederick W. Taylor, the pioneer of scientific management, had spent the first decade of the twentieth century struggling to overcome labor union hostility toward his innovations, political distortions of his ideas, public misunderstandings, and even professional jealousy. But Taylor, too, had his blind spots. His real love was mechanical efficiency, how to run the machines in the shop under optimum conditions. His views on what were later called personnel management were rudimentary and amounted to little more than a cash reward and punishment system. He was more interested in machines than in workingmen and saw women workers essentially as cheap labor. And, as historian Samuel Haber has noted, the word efficiency was inherently vague. It could refer to a personal attribute (productive use of time), to a mechanical measure (energy input-output ratio), to an economic criteria (profitability ratios for investments of capital), or to a preference for social harmony and leadership by the "competent" elite over social conflict and leadership by "incompetent" politicians. Where Taylor and Brandeis might use the term efficiency in its primarily engineering or economic senses, the progressive audiences might understand it primarily in its social sense. A society guided by scientific experts on regulatory commissions could promise more social services at less public cost. Productivity could replace the old-fashioned tariff as the politicoeconomic symbol of the new harmony of interests that would bind employers and employees together in a mutually beneficial relationship. President Taft's political bungling on the tariff reform issue in the unprecedentedly high Payne-Aldrich Tariff of 1909 and his subsequent defense of it only underscored this point for many progressives.[14]

In spite of, or perhaps because of, such ambiguities in the meaning of the key concept of efficiency, organizations dedicated to scientific management proliferated: the Society to Promote the Science of Management (known after 1915 as the Taylor Society), the Efficiency Society, portions of the American Society of Mechanical Engineers, the Harvard Graduate School of Business Administration, and the Frederick W. Taylor Cooperators. And the concept of efficiency could be applied to a number of progressive issues. Taylor's *The Principle of Scientific Management* (1911) carried an introduction that linked the idea of scientific management to Theodore Roosevelt's call for conservation of natural resources: "We can see our forests vanishing, our water-powers going to waste, our soil being carried by floods into the sea; and the end of our coal and our iron is in sight. But our largest wastes of human effort, which go on every day through such of our acts as are blundering, ill-directed, or inefficient, and which Mr. Roosevelt refers to as a lack of 'national efficiency,' are less visible, less tangible, and are but vaguely appreciated."[15] Taylor lamented the lack of a social movement dedicated to "greater national efficiency." There were some conservation organizations, and a shadowy penumbra of believers existed, but as yet, no charismatic leader had emerged to focus this diffuse discontent.

Taylor's linking of the conservation issue with the hunger for rational order and efficiency was farsighted. The Ballinger-Pinchot controversy of 1909–10 had pitted Chief Forester Gifford Pinchot, a Roosevelt protégé, against Secretary of the Interior Richard Ballinger, a Taft appointee. Progressives accused Ballinger of being subservient to corporate interests in the matter of coal leases on government land in Alaska. The politics of the issue, and President Taft's narrowly procedural bureaucratic backing of Ballinger, had made the conservation fight a symbol for progressive anxieties. Mixed in the conservation issues was an inherent tension between eastern, elite views of scientific management of natural resources, midwestern middle-class nostalgia for nature as a source of values, beauty, and inspiration and western interest in exploitation of resources or, at least, control of land policy. The word "conserve" could mean to preserve *for* future use (by private corporations or by public agencies), to preserve *from* future use (by prohibitions on private actions or by protection of public lands), or to promote efficient use so as to minimize waste of current resources. Who should conserve what for whom, and why, remained unresolved issues.[16]

The anxiety over the conservation issue, the vague hunger for "greater national efficiency," and the emotions aroused by the seemingly rapacious appetite of the giant corporations for natural resources were all indicative of a crisis of confidence, particularly among the urban middle class. Corporate business impacted on the daily lives of such men and women. They felt the psychological discomfort of the corporate redefinition of selfhood and success. The older definitions of liberty as *independence* had praised the individual entrepreneur or professional. To own one's own business, to move up from the ranks of master craftsmen, to open one's own retail shop, to hang out one's sign or "shingle" as a lawyer, doctor, or engineer, to own one's own farmland, to become a teacher— these had been the traditional goals for middle-class citizens in the last quarter of the nineteenth century. But the growth of the corporations made working for someone else, the fact of *dependence*, a common and expanding experience. It took time for men and women to adjust their psychological reactions and career expectations. At best the corporate structure could become the new arena of self-advancement. As some of the disciples of Taylor's scientific management realized, the social language of efficiency was capable of defining a new criteria for such success. Productivity—whether measured by input-output ratios, profitability, or simply the reduction of social chaos—became their master metaphor for social order. If the factory-as-a-system was like a well-calibrated machine, then society-as-a-whole could be run on similar lines by engineer-experts. Social harmony, conservation of natural and human resources, reduction of waste and fraud, consumer abundance, and increased wages and salaries, all would flow from the reform of business from within. At its best, then, the revitalized corporate structure could serve as a model for other institutions in society.[17]

In the conservation cause and in the mystique of scientific management, some middle-class men and women extended the social language of efficiency beyond the narrow boundaries of their professional specialties and turned it into a series of metaphors for the need for social order, rational decision making, and elite/expert guidance in this chaotic period of change. Liberty as *freedom to* exploit natural resources might have to be curtailed in the interest of the *equal rights* of other citizens to enjoy the renewing beauty and solitude of the wilderness or to claim a share of the common resources. Liberty as *freedom from* unreasonable restraint of trade seemed to be losing out in the chaos of competing options or ways of dealing with the problem. Equality of opportunity required some form of government action to ensure justice, but which form was most efficient? A few radical cultural critics raised the specter of a utopian, *interdependent*, self-actualizing, natural, artistic, and democratic urban society. They wanted to ensure by the use of the concept of productivity that social rewards would be proportional to talent, skill, or socially useful work. Thus, some who believed in the "gospel of efficiency" dreamed of conservation as a way that would either lead back to the promised land of renewed opportunity or on to a new Edenic garden city.[18]

Whereas efficiency had long been a *criteria* for social decisions for progressives, the "gospel of efficiency" turned it into a *cause*, an overarching vision of social and political renewal. But if there was a "gospel" that promised salvation, who was the "messiah"? And who were the "chosen people"? Did the progressives' middle-class perceptions of core values encompass all Americans or only some? And how far would the demand for justice reach?

10

Civil Liberty and Civil Rights, 1898–1912

Today writers speak of "civil liberties" as "those freedoms or liberties found in the first ten amendments of the Constitution (Bill of Rights)" and "civil rights" as referring to any law or regulation "that expressly forbids discrimination on the basis of race, color, religion, national origin and, in employment, sex."[1] But a hundred years ago political theorists, popular essayists, reformers, lawyers, and librarians used the terms "civil liberty" (or simply liberty) and "civil rights" (or citizenship) somewhat differently. The term "civil liberty" referred to a *status,* a condition of freedom characteristic of participation in "civilization," citizenship in the Republic, or membership in a "modern" society (as opposed to the un-freedom of feudalism, tribal society, or "primitive" conditions). According to a prevalent political science theory in the 1890s, the state was the creator and guarantor of this status of freedom through the rule of law. Subordinate rights such as liberty of conscience, freedom of speech, and liberty of the press were also protected by the state but were not un-limited in their scope. This chapter will explore the question of whether the experience of some of the groups studied so far—African Americans, Asian immigrants, Native Americans, and southern and eastern Euro-pean immigrants—coincided with this conception of liberty during the period 1898 to 1912. In particular, it will trace the effective meaning of the term "civil liberty" in legal discourse and the role played by social lan-guage in defining civil rights.[2]

If civil liberty was a secure status to be protected by the rule of law, there were still those who needed to know how to determine the meaning of the law. Oliver Wendell Holmes Jr., a legal scholar, remarked in an 1899 essay that "it is not true that in [legal] practice . . . a given word or even a given collocation of words has one meaning and no other. A word gener-ally has several meanings, even in the dictionary." The good lawyer as researcher had to understand the history of legal concepts and the logic that bound various decisions together, but above all, the lawyer as practitioner had to attend to the experience of the community. The law was not an abstract expression of sovereign will; it was a prediction of what the courts would do in certain circumstances and what penalties it would impose for particular forms of behavior. Holmes was one of the pioneers working out the new language of legal realism that would characterize the early twentieth century. Judges did not simply discover the law or the content of rights, he argued, they helped to shape the meaning of the law as practice. Therefore, the law could be adapted to the changing needs of the community as it evolved.[3]

There were also thinkers and activists who were concerned with the changing nature of the community and its relationship with the state (or government). The true basis of rights, they believed, was in the community; government only intervened to protect these rights. The crucial link between the community and the government was the concept of citizenship. The good citizen was as concerned with responsibilities as with rights. These responsibilities included being informed about public issues, joining voluntary associations or civic leagues, signing initiative petitions, voting for candidates in primaries, for referendum or for recall petitions, and, above all, subordinating self-interest to the common good. But such a definition of the good citizen implied that there were those who did not measure up to the mark and could be restricted or limited in their participation in the government. Social Darwinism, racism, and pseudoscientific eugenics arguments could be used to disenfranchise, to exclude, and to limit some groups. Even as progressive and as typically "middle class" a thinker as President Theodore Roosevelt was not immune to some of these tendencies.[4]

This, then, was the context in which African Americans, recent Asian immigrants, Native Americans, and "new" immigrants from southern and eastern Europe confronted the question of the status of civil liberty and the meaning of civil rights at the turn of the century. The combination of political theory, evolutionary assumptions, and legal language that they confronted was a curious mixture of positive and negative inferences, a self-consistent system that served best the interests of those who articulated it, the white middle class. Dr. W. E. B. Du Bois, an African American scholar trained in history and sociology at Harvard and the University of Berlin, was as skeptical of claims that civil liberty was a secure status for all as he was of Booker T. Washington's homilies to the black community about racial progress and pious hopes that someday civil rights for all would be respected by the white community. Du Bois had taken a teaching position at Atlanta University in 1897. He had experienced the psychological shock of learning that a poor African American farmer named Sam Hose had been lynched and grisly evidence of his death displayed in a shop window. In September 1899 Du Bois reported in the *Independent* magazine on the conventions of the National Association of Colored Women and the National Afro-American Council: "There can be no doubt as to the wave of intense feeling which has recently stirred American Negroes. Events of grave significance to them have followed fast and faster in the last ten years; the Wilmington riot, the murder of Postmaster Baker, the crucifixion of Hose, continued lynchings and disturbances, progressive disfranchisement, the treatment of Negro soldiers, and the hostile attitude of trades-unions—all these things have profoundly moved these people, and to the student of race problems their action under such conditions is of great interest."[5] While Du Bois acknowledged the "evident intelligence and air of good-breeding" among the women delegates and called them "the aristocracy among the Negroes," he found the "candid earnestness and faithful striving" of the mostly male delegates to the National Afro-American Council conference "a far more reliable reflex of the mental attitude of the millions it represented." Heatedly debated resolutions called upon Congress to pass antilynching legislation, condemned rape by either black or white offenders, urged blacks to become skilled artisans and businessmen, called upon President McKinley to denounce mob violence, accepted suffrage restriction based upon "intelligence and property" but denounced disenfranchisement based on race alone, and laid claim to all "the rights and . . . duties of American citizenship."[6]

Du Bois's male bias notwithstanding, the convention of the National Association of Colored Women also addressed the meaning of recent events for black women. In her presidential address, Mary Church Terrell pointed to some of their accomplishments and looked to the future. "In short, what our hands have found to do," she concluded, "that we have cheerfully done." She urged the delegates to stress their "duty to the children" through kindergartens, day nurseries, and children's clubs. She also urged them to organize reform efforts, study the labor situation, particularly that of single women who supported families, and train young women for domestic service. "To stem this tide of popular disfavor against us," she proposed mutual self-help, high moral standards, and "purification of the home." But she was not willing to rest content with these self-reformative and ameliorative projects. "Against lynching, the convict lease system, the Jim Crow car laws, and all other barbarities and abuses which degrade and dishearten us," she concluded, "we must agitate with such force of logic and intensity of soul that the oppressor will either be converted to principles of justice or be ashamed to openly violate them."[7]

To what extent the National Association of Colored Women and the National Afro-American Council reflected the attitudes of the African Americans in the rural South remains unclear; however, after a decade of earnest efforts and repeated failures, the urban, professional, educated elite had created viable institutional and organizational structures and the collective means to express their considered opinions. If the middle-class professionals did not always appreciate or understand the modest achievements of the poor in just surviving economically and psychologically in an atmosphere of repression, if the secularized elite underestimated the role of the churches, and if the club women remained locked in Victorian gender stereotypes, nevertheless, their organizations were a means of creating a cohesive black community in order to protest their treatment by the larger white community.[8]

As a sociologist, Du Bois realized the limits of social languages in holding together communities—both white and black—and the impact of certain events. For example, he believed that the Spanish-American War had had a devastating influence on attitudes. "There has come a significant change in public opinion," he wrote in May 1900, "a growing indifference to human suffering, a practical surrender of the doctrine of equality, of citizenship, and a new impetus to the cold commercial aspects of racial intercourse."[9] And the problem was not confined to the United States. Worldwide imperialism also cast its shadow on the future. In a speech given in London in July 1900 at a Pan African Congress, he said: "The problem of the twentieth century is the problem of the colour line, the question as to how far differences of race . . . are going to be made, hereafter, the basis of denying to over half the world the right of sharing to their utmost ability the opportunities and privileges of modern civilization. . . . If, by reason of carelessness, prejudice, greed and injustice, the black world is to be exploited and ravished and degraded, the results must be deplorable, if not fatal, not simply to them, but to the high ideals of justice, freedom, and culture which a thousand years of Christian civilization have held before Europe."[10] In his classic work, *The Souls of Black Folk* (1903), Du Bois also spoke of another dividing line, the double consciousness that divided the African American self into two spheres: an African heritage and an American promise.[11]

In *The Souls of Black Folk*, Du Bois included "two chapters [that] studied the struggles of the massed millions of the black peasantry," as he called them. But neither the poetic interludes, the chapter heads of music from the black spirituals, nor the chapter on the "sorrow songs," could hide the fact that the book was primarily an attack on Booker T. Washington's philosophy and on his influence. Du Bois made an impassioned plea for a broader, more comprehensive higher education for the elite of the African American population who would provide the leadership for the future. "The foundations of knowledge in this race, as in others," he argued, "must be sunk deep in the college and university if we would build a solid, permanent structure. . . . Is there not, with such a group and in such a crisis, infinitely more danger to be apprehended from half-trained minds and shallow thinking than from over-education and over-refinement?" And Du Bois was not alone in his criticism of Washington's educational philosophy. "Does this mean that the Negro objects to industrial educa-tion?" Ida Wells-Barnett asked rhetorically in her critique of Booker T. Washington. "By no means," she replied. "It simply means that [the Negro] knows by sad experience that industrial education will not stand him in place of political, civil and intellectual liberty, and he objects to being deprived of fundamental rights of American citizenship to the end that one school for industrial training shall flourish."[12]

The time to act had come. In paragraph seven of "Credo," published in October 1904, Du Bois summed up his synthesis of conflicting claims: "I believe in Liberty for all men; the space to stretch their arms and souls; the right to breathe and the right to vote, the freedom to choose their friends, enjoy the sunshine and ride on the railroads, uncursed by color; thinking, dreaming, working as they will in a kingdom of God and love."[13] In 1905 a group of African American journalists, educators, religious leaders, and professionals rallied to Du Bois's call. They, too, were dis-satisfied with Booker T. Washington's accommodationist public rhetoric and behind-the-scenes private power brokering. Washington's so-called Tuskegee Machine was favored by influential white politicians, including President Roosevelt, and by northern white philanthropists. Neverthe-less, a group of twenty-nine "anti-Bookerites," gathered in July 1905 on the Canadian side of Niagara Falls. Hoping to revive the full civil rights claims of the Reconstruction Era and to overcome the self-imposed lim-itations on their status of Washington's approach, they called themselves the Niagara Movement. The objects of the movement, as set forth in its Constitution, were:

(a) Freedom of speech and criticism.
(b) An unfettered and unsubsidized press.
(c) Manhood suffrage.
(d) The abolition of all caste distinctions based simply on race and color.

(e)   The recognition of the principles of human brotherhood as a practical present creed.

(f)   The recognition of the highest and best human training as the monopoly of no class or race.

(g)   A belief in the dignity of labor.

(h)   United effort to realize the ideals under wise and courageous leadership.[14]

In August 1905 Du Bois, as one of the initiators of the new organization, wrote candidly: "Today we have a growing enthusiastic organization of nearly 75 members, educated, determined [and] unpurchasable men." Du Bois's rhetoric was excessively masculine in explaining the Niagara goals, but he appealed especially to "the young men and women" of the nation. Membership in the Niagara Movement would remain small in number, and controversial, but in the mind of Du Bois the Niagara Movement spoke to and for the nine to ten million African Americans who could not or who dared not speak in public for themselves.[15]

In spite of Du Bois's claims, the Niagara Movement was but one of several civil rights and humanitarian organizations, black and white, progressive and socialist, male dominated or female initiated, that were working to attack discrimination, school segregation, Jim Crow transportation, exploitation of black workers, and the scourge of debt peonage in the South. In May and June 1909 a National Negro Conference was held, and from this conference came a temporary Committee of Forty to plan for the future. Diverse spokespersons were drawn into the effort: black activists such as Du Bois and Ida Wells-Barnett, black religious leaders such as Bishop Alexander Walters and Rev. William Henry Brooks, white inheritors of the abolitionist tradition such as Oswald Garrison Villard and Moorfield Storey, white socialists such as Mary White Ovington, Charles Edward Russell, and William English Walling, and white social workers and intellectuals such as Jane Addams, Arthur Spingarn, Joel Spingarn, Rabbi Stephen S. Wise, and Henry Moskowitz. At the second conference in 1910 a permanent organization was created and the name changed to the National Association for the Advancement of Colored People. The founding members represented an elite and were initially drawn mainly from the North. Local membership in the NAACP seldom enlisted much more than 2 percent of the national African American population. Nevertheless, over the years the NAACP increasingly acted as the symbolic focal point of the more widespread, loosely coordinated, and frequently divided, civil rights movement.[16]

What did the NAACP stand for in its early years? Through its first president, Moorfield Storey, the tradition of Charles Sumner and the

Reconstruction Era Civil Rights Act of 1866 lived on in the new organization. (In 1867–69 Storey had served as Sumner's personal secretary.) Equality before the law, equal access to public accommodations and transportation, equal suffrage (at least for males), equal education, antidiscrimination—such was the legacy of Charles Sumner and the Reconstruction Era. According to legal historian William B. Hixon Jr., Storey's role was limited, but vital: "Unlike W. E. B. Du Bois, Villard, Ovington, and Joe and Arthur Spingarn, Storey had little to do with the day-to-day problems of the NAACP. Any organization devoted to securing complete equality before the law, however, would be largely dependent upon litigation for the realization of its goals, and here someone with Storey's legal skill and professional prestige was invaluable." While relying on careful research and preliminary legal work by others, Storey, like Holmes's model lawyer, was able to frame the legal language that would begin to counter the judicial limits of the Supreme Court's narrow interpretation of the Fourteenth Amendment. And the Supreme Court was beginning to rethink some of its positions. Between 1910 and 1912 it overturned a southern peonage law, a "grandfather clause" voter discrimination law, and a residential segregation ordinance (which discriminated against *white* owners' "due process of law" for their property rights).[17]

Not everyone in the organization agreed with Storey's cautious goal of securing equality before the law by means of patient litigation. Du Bois, editor of the NAACP journal, the *Crisis,* and director of research, was sensitive to slights and patronizing attitudes by whites such as Villard. Du Bois was frequently at odds with other NAACP executives as well. Above all, he wanted the NAACP to embody within itself equality *and* justice. Without strict justice there could be no liberty, no *freedom from* lynch law and "judicial murder." Without strict justice there could be no equality between the races. Without equality for *all* groups—an end to the inequality of caste, color, gender discrimination—there could be no liberty as *freedom to* develop one's talents. Without the freedom to make mistakes and to take responsibility for them and to be judged by the same criteria as one's coworkers there would be no liberty *within* organizations and no movement toward any of these goals within society as a whole. There were, of course, other groups who also had claims on the notion of liberty, justice, and equality: Asian immigrants, Native Americans, and recent southern and eastern European immigrants. They, too, had pressing needs for their civil rights to be protected or for their status under civil liberty to be secured.[18]

Du Bois's observation in 1900 that the Spanish-American War had had a negative influence on American public opinion was particularly pertinent for Asians. The annexation of Hawaii, Puerto Rico, and the Philippines meant that large numbers of Asians and other indigenous peoples were now under American control. Did they automatically fall within the political theory of the secure status of civil liberty? Were their civil rights to be protected by the constitution and judicial process? Japanese laborers, who had been recruited as contract laborers in Hawaii since 1868 and who in some cases had replaced the excluded Chinese laborers in the United States, presented a case in point. In April and May 1900 anti-Japanese protest meetings were held in Seattle and San Francisco, organized by leaders associated with the American Federation of Labor. James D. Phelan, a progressive Democrat, was blunt and outspoken. "Chinese and Japanese," he said, "are not the stuff of which American citizens can be made." All three political parties in 1900—Republican, Democrat, and Populist—supported at least Chinese labor exclusion and, in some instances, the exclusion of all Asians as well. In 1901 the Supreme Court in the *Insular* cases ruled that the new possessions such as Puerto Rico were not territorial acquisitions in the model of earlier continental acquisitions and, therefore, their inhabitants did not automatically possess the constitutional rights of citizenship. This confirmation of the colonial status of Puerto Rico had important implications for Hawaii and the Philippines, and for Japanese immigrants in the United States.[19]

Two factors differentiated the treatment of Japanese in the United States from the earlier treatment of Chinese workers and residents. First, Japan, as a rapidly modernizing and industrializing nation with a major military victory to its credit in the Russo-Japanese War of 1904–5, was viewed with cautious respect by Western nations. President Theodore Roosevelt, who had brokered the Treaty of Portsmouth (1905) that ended the Russo-Japanese War, was not anxious to antagonize Japan. Second, economic issues in the United States and regional political tensions accompanying the rise of progressivism complicated the issue of Japanese status. Like the Chinese immigrants before them, Japanese immigrants, particularly laborers in California, encountered hostility from labor groups and politicians. A 1906 school segregation order in San Francisco aimed at Japanese students prompted President Roosevelt to point out that it violated an 1894 treaty. He negotiated a Gentlemen's Agreement with Japan to restrict immigration of Japanese laborers and, in an executive order, prohibited Japanese immigrants from entering the United States via Hawaii, Canada, and Mexico, although parents, wives, and children of resident Japanese would be eligible for passports to the United States. Roosevelt also secured concessions from California officials. However, anti-Japanese riots in San Francisco in June 1907 undercut the compromise between state and federal officials. In the Gentlemen's Agreement, the Japanese government had a responsibility for verifying the socioeconomic status of Japanese immigrants and issuing the relevant documents; in response, the Japanese diplomatic representatives in the United States created the Japanese Association of America in 1909. Ostensibly a self-supporting organization, the JAA was, in fact, a semiofficial agency of the Japanese government. It was, therefore, a further cause of misunderstanding about the status of Japanese immigrants and residents between progressive politicians and the Japanese community. Finally, in 1911, the Bureau of Immigration and Naturalization in response to political pressure issued a directive declaring most Asian immigrants to be "aliens ineligible for citizenship."[20]

If the question of civil liberty as a secure status had been answered largely in the negative for African Americans and Asian immigrants between 1898 and 1912, the status of the Native Americans was equally complicated. As Alexandra Witkin has pointed out: "Critical to American political discussions about extending citizenship to Native individuals or nations has been the question of 'civilization.' United States citizenship meant membership in a 'civilized' community characterized by productive, profitable, monogamous, family units, in contrast to communal, 'tribal' societies."[21] This had been the rationale for the Dawes Act of 1887 and the attendant assimilationist education programs. By the end of the 1890s the self-appointed humanitarian guardians of Native American civil liberty and civil rights, those who had been largely responsible for the Dawes Act, lost influence in Congress. More efficiency-minded, pragmatic bureaucrats took charge of Indian affairs. Congress in the Curtis Act of 1901 granted citizenship to members of the Five Civilized Nations in the Indian Territory, which subsequently became incorporated in the state of Oklahoma. The Supreme Court in *The Matter of Heff* (1905) held that Native individuals became citizens when they received their allotment. Thus, by 1906 there were 166,000 Native Americans who had become citizens either by the Dawes Act allotment process, by separate treaty with their "nation," or by the grant to the Five Civilized Nations. However, Congress, in order to ensure continued federal "protection," passed the Burke Act of 1906. As Francis Paul Prucha has pointed out, the Burke Act "amended the Dawes Act by making discretionary the period in which the allotted lands were held in trust for the [Native Americans] and providing for the granting of United States citizenship *at the end* of the trust period instead of at the beginning." Furthermore, the Lacey Act of 1907 "required [a Native American] to apply for his [pro rata] allotment before any action could be taken." Thus, while the attributes of "civilization" brought the Native American within the status of civil liberty, the process of acquiring citizenship was extended and was not seen by the courts as being incompatible with federal "protection" or wardship.[22]

By the end of the first decade of the twentieth century, then, comparisons could be drawn as to the status of the three groups studied so far. African Americans were citizens by birth and within the status of civil liberty by constitutional amendments but did not enjoy their full civil rights. They had formed numerous organizations to protest the situation and propose remedies. Most Asian laborers were barred either by the Chinese Exclusion Acts, by the Gentlemen's Agreement, or by various executive orders and were outside the status of civil liberty. Those born in the United States, members of the various exempt categories, or wives, children, or parents of these categories could claim some civil rights, but the rest were "aliens ineligible for citizenship." Native Americans had been promised citizenship and the status of civil liberty by the allotment process or by specific treaty provisions (at the price of minimizing their tribal culture or communal autonomy); their civil rights were limited, however, by the judicial doctrine of wardship or government protection. How does one account for this pattern of variation in the status of civil liberty? Certainly racial prejudice played a major role in the story but was not the only factor. Economic competition, particularly by labor unions, and media stereotypes, particularly when combined with political opportunism, added complexity to the pattern. Cultural differences acted as countervailing pressures, especially for middle-class white citizens who had different attitudes toward different racial and ethnic groups.

This can be seen by looking briefly at the status of southern and eastern European immigrants. In the confused terminology of the time, ethnic groups were frequently called "races" and ranked hierarchically in the Darwinian fashion; in the economic situation of the day immigrants were "cheap labor"; and in the political arena, they were prime candidates for machine politics of the urban area. But the cultural standards (life style, religion, and behavior) of the "new" immigrants differed from those of the "old" immigrants and "native-born" citizens many of whom voted Progressive. Many "old line" citizens had, in fact, joined restrictionist leagues. In 1906 Congress, responding to pressure from restrictionists and from the White House, created the Dillingham Commission to study the immigration "problem." After three years and forty-two volumes of reports, the Dillingham Commission endorsed most of the stereotypes of the day. It concluded that the "new" immigrants were not as desirable as the "old" immigrants and that such immigration ought to be restricted. The trade unions of the AFL were increasingly hostile to the largely unskilled and semiskilled, young, male workers who made up a large percentage of the new immigrants between 1900 and 1910. Trade union membership criteria, high union initiation fees, and skill or competency tests, like the literacy tests proposed periodically by immigration restrictionists, served to discriminate against the new immigrants in the labor market.[23]

Given their common problems, why did not African Americans, Asian Americans, Native Americans, and new immigrants band together to protect their rights? Perhaps no single organization could have encompassed such a diversity of situations. However much the NAACP might claim that its principles were universal, its focus was, as its activities suggested, the advancement of the cause of a particular race. The socialists might proclaim the universality of the working-class and welcome black workers, women, and recent immigrant groups with radical traditions into their camp, but in socialist parlance "red" meant socialist, not Native American, and "black" sometimes meant anarchist, not African American. In 1907 the Socialist Party national executive committee went on record as opposing all Asian immigration. African American editorials condemned on principle the exclusion of any group on racial grounds, but on pragmatic grounds they could also hope that anti-Asian policies might create economic opportunity for black workers in the West. Korean workers were recruited for Hawaiian sugar plantations when Japanese workers proved too assertive of their rights. In sum, before these diverse groups could join together to protect their civil rights, they needed to discover their own identities, build their own organizations and find a common language of protest.[24]

When middle-class, white, Protestant progressives talked about restoring government to "the People," they meant to people essentially like themselves. Their desire for administrative efficiency sometimes overrode predilections for "equal justice under law" or "due process of law." The "privileges or immunities" of state citizenship varied widely from region to region under the federal courts' interpretations of the Fourteenth Amendment. And some progressive social scientists and pragmatic thinkers were busy redefining the concept of liberty. They put the emphasis on the *freedom to* achieve one's capabilities rather than on *freedom from* social or government restraint. Ironically, they thereby assumed that the children of immigrants, Native Americans, Asian Americans, African Americans, and even some native-born, working-class whites needed a period of tutelage under professionally trained social workers and teachers to become "Americanized" by the public school system and the neighborhood settlement house. The bonds of social cohesion were essentially to be defined initially by the established, white middle class, not by a consensus of all the groups involved. Liberty for many middle-class progressives, in other words, did not necessarily mean security of civil liberty for all groups, equality of civil rights, even within the working class, or justice for all minorities. But there were other voices and other values that insisted on being heard or considered in the ongoing public discourse occasioned by the events of 1912 to 1916 and the impact of World War I.[25]

11

Progressivism and Power: Lobbying and Institutional Change, 1912–1916

According to a standard textbook analysis, the presidential election of 1912 provided the electorate with unique, clear-cut ideological choices. On the pressing economic issues of the day—how to deal with trusts, labor unions, monetary policy, tariffs, conservation of natural resources—the positions were neatly packaged, labeled, and prophetic of later controversies in the twentieth century. Republican William Howard Taft, seemingly lethargic and an inept follower of Roosevelt's early policies, ostensibly supported a high tariff, exploitation of natural resources by big business, and judicial interpretation of antitrust laws. Theodore Roosevelt, an energetic and dynamic advocate of government action on the Progressive Party ticket, advocated the New Nationalism: "regulation of corporations, physical evaluation of railroads, a graduated income tax, a refurbished banking system, labor legislation, the direct primary, and a corrupt practices act." Woodrow Wilson, scholarly but eloquent, disciplined and inspirational candidate for the Democratic Party, was influenced by Louis Brandeis's version of the New Freedom: "a dismantling operation that would ensure the survival of regulated business competition by shoring up the small business, breaking up the new conglomerates, returning the market to free enterprise, dispersing wealth more widely, and reaching out a helping hand to the workingman." Eugene Debs, charismatic champion of the Socialist Party condemned the excesses of capitalism, proclaimed the coming millennium under socialism, and advocated a host of pragmatic, piecemeal proposals to help the workers. The electoral results were dramatic but unusual: Taft had 3.5 million votes (and 8 electoral votes), Roosevelt had 4 million votes (and 88 electoral votes), Wilson had 6 million (and 435 electoral votes), and Debs had close to 1 million votes (and no electoral votes). Wilson, with only 42 percent of the popular votes, was a "minority" president but an impressive one.[1]

This chapter will show that the realities behind some of the major achievements of the Wilson administration, 1912–16, were more complex than such an analysis of political ideologies would indicate. The issues of regulation of business, trade union rights, woman suffrage, and civil rights involved not only conflicting values but also fortuitous events and clashing personalities and institutional interests. The limits of social languages to create and sustain political coalitions were also evident. But in the end, there were significant institutional changes in American life, some of which have persisted up to the present. There was also a price to pay, so to speak. The meanings of core values—liberty, equality, and justice—were narrowed from the more wide-ranging debates of the previous decade and, in the case of civil rights, there was considerable erosion from the precarious status under previous Republican administrations.

To understand these developments, the political and institutional *context* of the times must be examined. First, the electorate was changing as black males were being disenfranchised in the South and some women were being enfranchised at the local, state, and even the presidential primary level in a few states, primarily in the West and Midwest. Second, nonpartisan, progressive changes in voting registration procedures, primary elections, and long ballot formats were reducing the previously high ratios of voting based on strict party loyalty. In the North, voter turnout declined from 65 percent in the 1904–8 presidential elections to 59 percent in 1912. In the South, the average voting rate for the period 1900–1916 was only 32 percent of the electorate. Between 1912 and 1916 over half of the states adopted the presidential primary system; yet, the voter turnout in 1916 increased only slightly to 62 percent and declined in the 1920 presidential election to 49 percent.[2] Third, a case study of electoral behavior in New Jersey, 1880–1920, has shown that the progressive reforms also recast the nature of the political parties. They changed from being informal, loose coalitions of local interests into centralized, hierarchical organizations that cut the candidates loose from older forms of party discipline. Fourth, the reforms tended to disenfranchise the poor and recent immigrants.[3]

Accompanying the decline of old-fashioned partisanship was the rise of special interest groups. Thousands of trade associations organized by businessmen, hundreds of trade unions allied largely with the American Federation of Labor, the Women's Trade Union League, and the railroad brotherhoods, a growing number of organizations of white-collar professionals, numerous women's groups (GFWC, NAWSA, National Consumers'

League, WCTU, settlement houses, and the NACW), and a scattering of ethnic and religious fraternal orders had all learned the same lesson by the early twentieth century. They could bypass the political party, lobby elected officials directly, draft legislation, propose referenda, and conduct publicity campaigns with a tolerable return of achievement for the time and money invested. Technological changes in local transportation and in public media, such as photogravure "Sunday Supplement" sections in newspapers, silent films, newsreels, and the popular phonograph records created new ways for special interest advocates to reach potential supporters. Much of the old-time fervor, excitement, public pageantry, and emotional tension of the partisan campaign now flowed into the efforts of these special interest groups, particularly those for women suffrage, prohibition, and civil rights. For example, in March 1913 a woman suffrage parade in Washington, D.C., was attacked by hecklers and reaped a bonanza of publicity. The male-dominated Anti-Saloon League used a "Grand Remonstrance" parade on 10 December 1913 to present a petition for national prohibition to Congress. The National Association for the Advancement of Colored People (NAACP) in 1915 protested against the racist and negative portrayal of Reconstruction Era blacks in the silent film *Birth of a Nation* and tried unsuccessfully to raise funds for a counter film, *Lincoln's Dream*.[4]

The people who benefited the most from these changes in the electoral system were the experts, the lobbyists, and the spokespersons for social movements. Through their advice, help in drafting legislation, and ability to generate publicity, they helped to shape the legislative, institutional, and cultural changes of the period. Their influence ran far beyond the numbers of their supporters or their roles in organizations. The legitimization of their power was seen in their access to public officials or their appointment to bureaucratic positions. This process of interaction between lobbyists and political leaders was vividly illustrated by institutional change in the Wilson administration, 1912–16.

Woodrow Wilson was an astute student of the theory of congressional government but was sympathetic to the progressive emphasis on executive leadership, administrative prerogative, and symbolic public action. In 1913 he startled traditionalists by calling Congress into a special session, addressing it personally on the need for tariff reform, and guiding the revised tariff through the thicket of protectionists by judicious use of patronage, party discipline, and publicity. The resulting Underwood Tariff lowered duties by an average of 10 percent, added an income tax to make up for lost governmental revenue, and put manufactured items produced by "trusts" on the free list where they would have to compete with foreign competition. The Underwood Tariff would be rendered largely symbolic by the outbreak of war in Europe in August 1914 and later by America's wartime revenue needs. In 1913, however, it stood as a symbolic act marking the end of a fifty year period of partisan wrangling and highly charged public debate over high protectionist trade barriers.

If on the tariff issues Wilson had largely kept his own counsel, on the issue of banking and currency reform he was more willing to listen to others. Lobbyists for the banks supported the Glass-Willis Plan which called for a decentralized banking reserve system, privately controlled by the banks themselves and empowered to issue paper currency. Wilson insisted on the addition of a federal reserve board in Washington to supervise the system. In May 1913 he submitted the plan to scrutiny by his advisors. William Jennings Bryan, titular leader of the agrarian wing of the Democratic Party, and secretary of state in the Wilson cabinet, objected to two provisions. Bryan wanted a government-controlled board with the sole power to issue paper currency. In a quandary, Wilson called on Louis Brandeis whose antimonopoly views had helped to shape the rhetoric of Wilson's New Freedom campaign.[5]

The issue, as Brandeis saw it, was one of concentration of power. The banking system was like a vast pyramid. Local banks deposited their reserve funds in larger urban banks. These banks then deposited their reserves in a few regional metropolitan banks in Boston, Chicago, and New York City. These few kingpins at the top then used "other people's money" to dominate the economic system. Given his predilection for democratic control of power, Brandeis (inaccurately) saw the major banks as a "trust," who used their power to benefit a few large industries. He called for public control of this private power. Furthermore, the power to issue paper currency, he believed, should remain a function of the central government regardless of whether the currency was backed by private commercial paper or traditional gold or silver deposits. Wilson was convinced. On 23 June 1913 he sent the revised bill to Congress, helped steer it through Congress, and signed it into law before the end of the year.[6]

The Federal Reserve Act, with its careful balance of private ownership and public control, its decentralized operation via regional banks and centralized policy-making located in the Federal Reserve Board, its carefully crafted institutional independence, its flexibility in meeting various credit needs and countercyclical role in economic growth and stability, has long been regarded by historians as a monument to the Wilson-Brandeis version of progressive reform. Recently, however, some commentators have questioned this view. Thomas K. McCraw has analyzed Brandeis's regulatory philosophy. Brandeis's antipathy to bigness, his nostalgic preference for small-scale enterprise, and his lawyer's love of adversarial confrontation made his economic analysis inconsistent and his policy advice rhetorically excessive.[7] Furthermore, as Martin J. Sklar has pointed out, Wilson's *economic* analysis was different on key points from Brandeis's analysis.[8] In the Federal Reserve controversy, Brandeis's role seems to have been to convince Wilson on primarily *political* grounds of the need to accept Bryan's suggestions.[9]

If Brandeis's role in the Federal Reserve Act had been that of a political advisor, he played less of a role in the next set of business issues and ultimately abdicated his advisorial role in favor of an outside lobbyist. By January 1914 Wilson, having expended some of his political capital with Congress in the tariff and banking fights, was anxious about the prospect of Democratic Party losses in the upcoming congressional elections in the midst of an economic downturn. He decided to offer the olive branch to business. In a conciliatory speech, he called on government and business "to meet each other halfway in a common effort to square business methods with both public opinion and the law." The Wilson administration accordingly endorsed the Clayton Antitrust Bill, which provided for criminal sanctions against a long list of prohibited business practices, and the Covington Trade Commission Bill, which proposed to expand the Roosevelt Era Bureau of Corporations as an information gathering, public publicity or "sunshine" agency. Both bills passed the House of Representatives in early June 1914. The Chamber of Commerce surveyed business opinion and found substantial support for a federal trade commission but hostility to some of the prohibitions in the Clayton Bill.[10]

Brandeis, preoccupied with a railroad rate case before the Interstate Commerce Commission, asked his old friend George Rublee, a dilettante Wall Street lawyer, to help. As historian Thomas K. McCraw has noted: "Rublee subscribed to [Theodore Roosevelt's] Progressive Party plank that called for a very strong interstate trade commission, quite unlike the sunshine agency favored by Wilson and Brandeis and contemplated by the provisions of the Covington bill." Rublee sensed an opportunity to craft a bill more in keeping with his own views. Accordingly, he collaborated with another Brandeis supporter, Representative Ray Stevens of New Hampshire. The Rublee-Stevens draft was turned down by a Democratically controlled House committee and found no support among Wilson's cabinet members. But Brandeis endorsed the idea at a crucial meeting between Wilson, Rublee, and Stevens. Wilson then asked the House committee to substitute the Rublee-Stevens version for the re-

cently passed Covington Bill. After heated debate, and personal intervention by Wilson, both the House and Senate agreed to adopt the Rublee-
Stevens version.[11]

Once again, political considerations had overridden economic analysis.
Antimonopoly social language proved too imprecise to limit legislative
behavior. Businessmen had gotten what they wanted: a strong trade commission to reduce some of the uncertainty stemming from the 1911 Supreme Court "rule of reason" cases and a weaker Clayton Act. The Wilson
administration had apparently gotten what it wanted: proof for the electorate that it could regulate business behavior. The heart of the Federal
Trade Commission's (FTC's) authority, inserted by George Rublee, was the
power to determine and declare "unfair methods of competition" to be
unlawful and to issue "cease and desist" orders. Unfortunately for Rublee,
and for future commissioners, the phrase "unfair methods of competition" did not have the specificity and clarity he naively assumed that it
did. In the long run, then, the Federal Trade Commission Act would prove
to be a flawed experiment in Progressive Era politics and ambiguous social
languages.[12]

The Clayton Act revealed another aspect of the role of special interest
groups in the legislative process and the limits placed upon them by
political considerations. The trade unions associated with the American
Federation of Labor and the railway brotherhoods wanted a specific exemption from the antitrust laws because of recent adverse court decisions.
Having supported the Democratic candidate Wilson in 1912, they now
expected support regardless of tension within the party. The provisions
included in the final version of the Clayton Act because of trade union
lobbying were either traditional, largely symbolic, or ultimately ineffec-
tual. Historian Martin J. Sklar has noted that "Labor received, in the
Clayton Act, an unactionable declaration, rooted in the socialist and populist traditions, that 'the labor of a human being is not a commodity or
article of commerce,' and it received a restatement of the existing law that
trade unions and farm organizations were not, per se, illegal or in violation of the antitrust laws." The provision limiting court injunctions
against strikes looked back to the Pullman strike of the 1890s, but Gompers hailed the Clayton Act as labor's "Magna Carta" and looked forward
with hope.[13]

African American leaders, on the other hand, could look neither backward with self-congratulations nor forward with much confidence in
1912. Neither Taft's strategy of supporting "lily white" southern Republicans in 1912, nor Roosevelt's Progressive Party renunciation of federal intervention in race relations in the same election in a bid for south-

ern support had promised much for civil rights. A few northern black leaders, led by Bishop Alexander Walter of the African Methodist Episcopal Zion Church and W. E. B. Du Bois of the NAACP, had supported Wilson's 1912 Democratic Party candidacy. According to John Milton Cooper Jr., in his study of Wilson, "for a white man born and raised in the nineteenth-century south, Wilson held surprisingly mild racial views. . . . Although he had rarely written or talked much about racial matters, Wilson believed that blacks were not innately inferior to whites and would eventually, probably in two or three centuries, achieve a measure of economic and political, if not social, equality in America." And, with support in the 1912 campaign from some civil rights leaders, Wilson had earned the largest number of African American votes for a Democratic Party candidate up to that time.[14]

However, civil rights lobbyists were soon disappointed. Oswald Garrison Villard of the NAACP thought that he had convinced Wilson to support the idea of a privately financed public inquiry into race relations by a National Race Commission; however, Wilson backed down out of deference to southern Democratic senators whose support Wilson needed for his legislative program. The president also allowed Postmaster General Albert S. Burleson and Secretary of the Treasury Willard G. McAdoo to institute racial segregation among government employees in their departments and to eliminate or reduce in rank those African Americans who had previously worked for the government. Protests in the press and by prominent social workers, church leaders, and civil rights advocates checked, in part, the spread of such official segregation in other governmental agencies and partly reversed it in the Treasury Department, but relations between Wilson and civil rights groups deteriorated rapidly thereafter.[15]

Particularly revealing was the so-called Trotter affair. On 12 November 1914 William Monroe Trotter, Boston-based, militant African American leader of the National Independent Political League, had led a delegation to meet with Wilson at the White House in order to protest segregation in Washington. Both Trotter and Wilson lost their tempers; Wilson excused the segregation in government agencies and summarily ordered Trotter out of his office. While more moderate African American leaders had tried to repair the damage or had used the incident to denounce Trotter and ingratiate themselves with the Wilson administration, the damage was irreparable. Part of the problem was the differing views of core values held by such organizations as the NAACP and by Wilson. While the NAACP meant by equality the promotion of opportunity for a disadvantaged *group* and protection against *group-oriented* discrimination, Wilson meant something closer to traditional nineteenth-century liberalism: equal opportunity for the *individual* with reward proportionate to talent or merit. While justice in the immediate context of the times meant to the NAACP protection of the laws and recognition of citizenship rights, Wilson had a more paternalistic view. He would "do the right thing," as circumstances warranted, grant some favors out of charity or goodness, resist crudely racist legislation, or extend judicial clemency in individual cases. Basically, he favored separate, parallel development of the races. The progressive language of social bonds and human nature had its limits when it came to the issue of civil rights in the face of such fundamental disagreements.[16]

What was the meaning of equal rights for women in the midst of these events in the Wilson administration? Many women had responded in the 1900s to the rhetoric of self-appointed spokespersons who had articulated their grievances, primarily for equality and justice in terms of the social languages of social bonds and human nature and of efficiency. In social movements the leaders tried to advance their causes in the centers of power. The Progressive Party of Theodore Roosevelt had endorsed woman suffrage and supported it halfheartedly. As a result of the 1914 midterm congressional elections, in which the Democrats suffered numerous defeats and the Progressive Party began to falter, the Wilson administration became peculiarly sensitive to pressure as the 1916 presidential election loomed over the horizon. In the case of the woman suffrage movement, however, relations with the Wilson administration were complicated in 1914–15 by the creation of the Congressional Union (CU), a semi-independent offshoot of the National American Women Suffrage Association (NAWSA). The CU used militant tactics that its leaders, Alice Paul and Lucy Burns, had learned initially in England and had used against the Democrats in the 1914 elections. With the outbreak of war in Europe in August 1914 some woman suffrage supporters had shifted their activities to peace concerns. President Wilson had indicated to suffragist delegations in the past that, while he might *personally* be sympathetic toward woman suffrage, until his *party* made a commitment, he was not at liberty to recommend any action. In October 1915 Wilson finally endorsed a New Jersey woman suffrage amendment but only as a private citizen. Carrie Chapman Catt, reelected president of the NAWSA in December 1915, moved quickly in 1916 to separate her more moderate organization from the CU militants and to downplay her own involvement in the international women's peace movement.[17]

Catt called an emergency convention of the NAWSA in September 1916 to revitalize the suffrage forces, to capitalize on the (admittedly weak) endorsement of woman suffrage by the reunited Republican Party and the state-by-state approach to enfranchisement endorsed by the Democratic Party in deference to its southern wing. President Wilson addressed the last night of the NAWSA emergency convention. He was courteous, complimentary, and cautious, but he did give the woman suffrage movement some political advice:

[W]e rejoice in the strength of it, and we shall not quarrel in the long run as to the method of it. Because, when you are working with masses of men and organized bodies of opinion, you have got to carry the organized body along. The whole art and practice of government consists not in moving individuals, but in moving masses. . . .

I have not come to ask you to be patient, because you have been, but I have come to congratulate you that there was a force behind you that will, beyond any peradventure, be triumphant and for which you can afford a little while to wait.[18]

The CU leaders were not prepared to wait, however. They organized a Woman's Party that ran against Wilson in the 1916 presidential election. Wilson campaigned on a platform of peace, preparedness, and moderate progressivism. Democrats in Congress helped Wilson by passing a spate of legislation aimed at special interest groups: farm credits, eight-hour workday for federal workers, and an antichild labor bill. When the returns were counted, Wilson had won reelection over his Republican challenger, Charles Evans Hughes, 9 million popular votes to 8.5 million popular votes (277 electoral votes to 254 electoral votes). The Socialist Party had been badly divided by the European war and nationalistic divisions. Debs, too sick and tired to run again in 1916, watched as the socialist vote declined to 585,000 for candidate A. L. Benson. Woman suffrage leaders such as Catt could assume that some progress had been made during Wilson's first term (1912–16) and that his victory rested, in part, on women voters in the West. They could also look forward to ready access to the White House, and, perhaps, to more public endorsements of woman suffrage during his second term to counter the growing organization of antisuffrage forces.[19]

By the end of 1916 the question of the operative meaning of liberty was clearer than it had been in the 1912 presidential campaign. Institutional changes had narrowed or delimited the terms of public discourse. Wilson in his 1912 campaign rhetoric had still carried some of the intellectual baggage of classical liberalism that defined liberty as *freedom from* external restraint, although it was corporate rather than governmental restraint he complained about. He had, at the same time, used some of Brandeis's antimonopoly language to express his desire for a New Freedom. The Underwood Tariff probably came as close to embodying this notion of liberty as *freedom from* dependence on "trusts" for consumers as did any of the subsequent congressional actions. The Federal Reserve Act, the creation of the Federal Trade Commission, and the passage of the much-amended Clayton Act, were closer to the spirit of Theodore Roosevelt's New Nationalism than to Wilson's initial political predilections. Liberty as the *freedom to* have access to credit on equitable terms, to reduce the legal uncertainties surrounding certain forms of competition or business activity, to bargain for better wages and working conditions through trade unions on equal terms with employers seemed to be protected by governmental structures or specific legal prohibitions. A measure of private self-regulation by member banks, by competing firms, and by trade unions seemed compatible in this synthesis with the "public interest," provided it was supervised by governmental agencies or the courts. Even critical social theorists such as the philosopher John Dewey and the political pundit Walter Lippmann warmed up to President Wilson once they saw the apparent "mastery" of his administration over the previous "drift" of the country and of Wilson's own earlier rhetoric. Dewey's notion of effective freedom, the freedom of an agent armed with the instrumental means to achieve socially beneficial goals, seemed to be satisfied by reforms in the Wilson administration. The old empty notion of the formal freedom of an agent simply set free from restraint seemed to have been overcome by this more activist approach.[20]

The situation confronting the NAACP and other civil rights organizations during the Wilson administration had raised anew the question of the meaning of equality. The assumption that equality was guaranteed by the link between citizenship and due process of law under the Fourteenth Amendment and the right to vote under the Fifteenth Amendment (for men) had been weakened even before Wilson took office. But the strength of the southern wing in the Democratic Party and in Congressional leadership, Wilson's acquiescence in segregation in federal employment, and the pervasive racism among progressive voters had narrowed the bounds of public discourse. W. E. B. Du Bois tried to rally African Americans with an editorial in the *Crisis,* the NAACP journal, in April 1915:

The American Negro demands equality—political equality, industrial equality and social equality; and he is never going to rest satisfied with anything less. He demands this in no spirit of braggadocio and with no obsequious envy of others, but as an absolute measure of self-defense and the only one that will assure to the darker races their ultimate survival on earth.

These involve both negative and positive sides. They call for freedom on the one hand and power on the other.[21]

In defense of political rights, the Supreme Court in 1915 did overturn an Oklahoma constitutional requirement of a literacy test for voters that exempted the descendants of those who had voted in 1866 (popularly known as a "grandfather clause"). The defense of industrial equality involved the supporters of African American education in a struggle with Congress for equitable funding for land-grant colleges and agricultural extension work. In defense of social equality, historian Rayford W. Logan has pointed to negative victories: the defeat of numerous anti-intermarriage laws during the period 1912 to 1916. Thus, by the end of the first Wilson administration, the African American community was still separate and barely equal.[22]

Ironic as it might seem to later generations, the issues of women's rights, particularly woman suffrage, was debated more in terms of justice and expediency in the early twentieth century than in terms of equality. Maternalist claims for protective legislation for women workers were justified less in terms of equality of individual economic opportunity than they were in terms of the social needs of the community and the injustices of the current treatment of women. Suffragists marched in parades for the right to vote under banners that proclaimed, "we demand justice." Given the racism of the era, the demand for the vote for women was frequently justified as strengthening the white community, particularly in the South, or of correcting the "injustice" of denying the vote to educated, middle-class professional women while granting it to illiterate, working-class immigrant men. Working-class trade union women might raise the cry of "equal pay for equal work," but, at the same time, they supported militant strikes, demanded welfare legislation, and worked for the right to vote on social justice grounds.[23]

The meaning of justice was also narrowed in the debates over institutional innovations. The radical socialists had raised the issue of "substantive" or class-based justice and the inherent "unfairness" of the entire capitalist system. The progressive reformers' actions in the Federal Trade Commission Bill, however, with its "cease and desist" orders and quasi-judicial procedures made the workings of the corporate-dominated, consumer-oriented economy more a matter of "procedural" justice and "fair competition" than of "substantive" justice. Businessmen, who hoped to avoid the uncertainties of court-based, "rule of reason" antitrust decisions, still had to contend with judicial review, but they found that FTC administrative "justice" was more expeditious than the courts. The trade union leaders who had hoped that the Clayton Act's pro-labor provisions would afford them a measure of "justice" could point to the implied exemption for unions from antitrust provisions and the more explicit prohibitions on the use of antistrike injunctions by the courts. But in the context of the times, trade union leadership's lobbying efforts on the Clayton Act represented more a ritual withdrawal and renewal to reinforce old values than a reform-minded strategy to deal with current realities. Although management reformers used the social language of efficiency and radical socialist leaders used the language of social bonds and human nature, the trade union leaders persisted in using ritualistic antimonopoly social language and the rhetoric of "liberty of contract." Wilson's reelection in 1916 still left him a "minority" president in the sense that he received less than 50 percent of the popular vote (49 percent for Wilson, 46 percent for Hughes). Whether he would be able to uphold the current meanings of liberty, equality, and justice as expressed in the social languages of efficiency, social cohesion, and antimonopoly in the debates over business regulation, civil rights, and women's rights, depended, in large part, on America's involvement in the European war and Wilson's ability to handle its impact on American society and economy.[24]

12

Progressivism and Power: The Impact of Wartime Mobilization and the Gospel of Efficiency, 1916–1920

By the end of 1916 it was clear that American involvement in the European war was only a matter of time and the accidents of wartime strategy by the belligerents, particularly after Germany resumed unrestricted submarine warfare in February 1917. By April 1917 Wilson would call upon Congress for a declaration of war, and Congress would vote for the declaration (82 to 6 in the Senate and 373 to 50 in the House of Representatives). This chapter explores the impact of wartime mobilization as it became the context in which progressivism was tested anew, and in which public values, progressive social languages, and the private agendas of special-interest groups clashed. It was also the context in which women's rights and civil rights organizations maneuvered for postwar advantages or reeled under repeated blows of adversity. In the process of wartime mobilization some newly created institutions were battered and buffeted, but they survived. New issues were added to the political and cultural agenda, and the meanings of core values were further defined and narrowed.

The first impact of the European war on progressivism was on the antimonopoly movement and its rhetorical strategy. The Federal Reserve Board, for example, was authorized to provide a "flexible currency" based upon gold and silver currency, acceptable commercial paper, government bonds, bank notes, drafts, and bills of exchange. It was also required to facilitate the credit needs of regional banks and to supervise the banking system so that the highly criticized "monopoly" of a few central banks didn't dominate the economy. But both business and government needed large amounts of capital quickly and in concentrated form. The net effect of wartime conditions was to vastly increase the money supply as gold flowed into the United States from Allied purchases and as government securities flooded the banking system. This contributed to successive rounds of inflation that increased both workers' wages and consumers'

prices. It also subtly transformed the Federal Reserve banking requirements and, hence, its regulatory ability. Meanwhile, antimonopoly politicians, including Senator Robert M. La Follette, turned their attention to
other issues such as wartime profits by corporations, skyrocketing taxes,
the military draft, and the erosion of personal freedom. Left to its own
devices, the Federal Reserve Board acted mainly to shore up the Treasury
Department's vast borrowing through the sale of Liberty bonds and did
not attempt to restrain the banking "monopoly."[1]

The Federal Trade Commission, recently created to monitor unfair
competition and to police business behavior, was battered by the wartime
mobilization, too. Even before the United States entered the war, Congress had created a loosely structured Council of National Defense, composed of cabinet officers, businessmen, and spokesmen of organized labor.
The CND soon spawned a host of new agencies. The War Industries Board
was ostensibly empowered to control production, allocate resources to
priority industries, standardize government contracts, and regulate labor
conditions and relations. A Food Administration, a Fuel Administration, a
War Trade Board, a United States Shipping Board, and a Railroad War
Board soon crowded onto the scene, jostled each other in bureaucratic
infighting, and pushed the FTC aside.

By November 1917 the National Industrial Conference Board, a business organization representing 50,000 manufacturers, recommended
"that a commission be appointed, with equal representation by the Government, the employee and the employer, . . . to settle all questions
arising" from the war effort and that strikes and lockouts be declared
illegal during wartime. The Board of Directors of the Chamber of Commerce was even more direct. It called for the creation of a "Department of
Munitions or War Supplies, War Supply Board, or similar agency of
whatever name, able to bring about centralized control or cooperation
between the various government activities engaged in procuring war materials and supplies." Furthermore, the chamber said, "the Government
should have the power during the period of War to control prices and
distribution of production for public and private needs to whatever extent
may be necessary for our national purpose." They even granted that this
new department, or super agency, should have exclusive right to "com-
mandeer plants, material, equipment [and] supplies" and have "final
authority regarding all priority matters both as to production and distribution." Cabinet members bluntly warned Wilson that it might be
necessary for the government "to take over [the chaotic] railroads."
Within a year, the president and Congress moved along these lines: a

stronger War Industries Board, government operation of the railroads, and curtailment of the power of the FTC.[2]

Centralization, coordination, combination, price-fixing, rate setting, profit margin regulation—all the old antimonopoly bugaboos were back but in a new guise. Such government-sanctioned activities, businessmen now argued, would promote national efficiency. Some businessmen and a few progressive publicists found in wartime conditions new rhetorical justification for old realities in business behavior. Of course, there had to be some coercion during the wartime mobilization, they argued. But it should be directed more toward consumers, farmers, coal miners, reluctant Liberty bond buyers, striking workers and draft-avoiding "slackers" than toward patriotic and profit-making businessmen. Other businessmen, progressive politicians, and some public officials who served in the new government agencies saw in the wartime effort a momentary realization of the dreams of the "gospel of efficiency." They urged businesses to standardize the products of industry, to eliminate "waste" and duplication, to conserve fuel and energy by a daylight saving time system, and to "rationalize" the movement of war supplies by a government-coordinated transportation system. The war ended too soon for many of these efforts to be fully implemented, but the image remained of a brief millennium of efficiency. In addition to the appeal for efficiency, the language of social bonds and human nature, in the form of the rhetoric of patriotism, could be put to wartime purposes. The activities of the agencies of conformity, such as the vigilante-style, self-constituted American Defense Society, the National Security League, or the Commission of Public Safety, and the policies of some official public agencies, such as the Committee on Public Information, all used the social language of social bonds to reinforce the old social structure.[3]

Labor leaders also learned how to use the wartime mobilization to further their interests under the rubrics of efficiency and social cohesion. Samuel Gompers, president of the American Federation of Labor (AFL), who had lobbied for trade union exemption from antitrust laws in the Clayton Act, now worked just as hard for trade union inclusion on wartime agencies. He even supported government mediation of strikes. In July 1917 Gompers helped to set up the American Alliance for Labor and Democracy (secretly funded by the Wilson administration through the Committee on Public Information), which included trade unionists and a number of prowar socialists. And Gompers carefully distanced the AFL from the call by Russian socialists in October 1917 for an international conference of workers and socialists.[4]

Gompers' triumph in such lobbying efforts seemed to come in November 1917 when President Wilson agreed to address the AFL convention. Wilson was perfectly blunt with the audience of trade unionists:

If we are true friends of freedom, our own or anybody else's, we will see that the power of this country and the productivity of this country is raised to its absolute maximum, and that absolutely nobody is allowed to stand in the way of it. . . .

It means, not only . . . that the conditions of labor are not rendered more onerous by the war—but also that we shall see to it that the instrumentalities by which the conditions of labor are improved are not blocked or checked. . . .

To put it concretely, that means this: nobody has a right to stop the process of labor until all the methods of conciliation and settlement have been exhausted.[5]

But Wilson and Gompers were like two cooks in a kitchen trying to hold down the lids on too many boiling kettles. Inflation, syndicalist or worker control sentiment, spontaneous local labor grievances, official and quasi-official oppression of dissent—all these developments contributed to wartime strikes in spite of Gompers's "no strike" pledge. Finally, in April 1918 Wilson established the National War Labor Board, under former president William Howard Taft and progressive labor lawyer Frank P. Walsh, to hear grievance cases. Eventually, a War Labor Policies Board, under Felix Frankfurter, was also established to set wartime labor standards.[6]

In short, many of the prewar progressives who had wanted to reform business from *outside* the corporation through antitrust legislation and government regulation had fallen by the wayside in the wartime mobilization or had shifted their efforts elsewhere. They now stressed such issues as (1) taxing wartime "excess profits," (2) advocating government operation of munitions factories, shipping lines, and railroads, and (3) exercising control of public opinion by government-sponsored publicity, propaganda, and patriotism. Those businessmen and progressive professionals who had wanted to reform business from *inside* the corporation by the implementation of scientific management, by standardization of products and rationalization of procedures, and by combination, coordination, and interfirm cooperation were riding the crest of the wave of wartime mobilization. They extended the language of the "gospel of efficiency" to legitimatize their efforts. Other businessmen, who wanted neither to be regulated nor to restructure the way they conducted their affairs, were willing during the wartime emergency to countenance some centralized government direction. They supported such government regulation on the condition that they had a strong representation in it, that labor unions were bound by it, and that the antimonopoly publicity of the prewar era be replaced by fulsome praise and public recognition for their patriotic efforts. Trade union leaders, and some farm organization lobbyists, supported whatever government proposals suited their economic interests, tried to preserve or extended their protective legislation, and lobbied for guaranteed access to credits. They, too, basked in the light of the public approval by government officials. They relished their access to the top levels of the Wilson administration and tried to distance themselves from any taint of earlier populism or socialism.[7]

While business, labor, and agricultural lobbyists invoked the rhetoric of patriotism or the "gospel of efficiency," the majority of semiskilled or unskilled workers, family farmers, tenant farmers or sharecroppers, and urban consumers on relatively fixed incomes bore the brunt of warfare inflation, military conscription, rationing, taxation, and the public pressure to purchase Liberty bonds. They did so with a curious mixture of patience, resignation, occasional rebellion, and skeptical humor that defied easy categorization. As shall be shown in later chapters, the weight of repression, both official and quasi-official, fell heaviest on certain groups: (1) immigrants, particularly German Americans; (2) radicals, particularly the Industrial Workers of the World, syndicalists, a few militant unions, various anarchist groups, and antiwar socialists; (3) civil libertarians, pacifists, and religious "conscientious objectors"; and (4) any outspoken critics of the war effort who happened to run afoul of the vague perimeters of the Espionage Act of 1917 and the Sedition Act of 1918.[8]

If the antimonopoly movement was the first progressive cause to feel the pressure of the wartime mobilization, then the women's rights movement and the quest for black civil rights soon followed. The results for women's rights, including woman suffrage, were largely positive and dramatic; the impact on African American civil rights were more negative but equally dramatic. For women the wartime mobilization was both an opportunity and an additional burden. Because women were divided along the lines of work—whether they worked primarily in their own home, outside their home or in someone else's home—their responses followed the same lines. Women who already worked outside the home, whether as unskilled or semiskilled industrial employees, retail clerks, or as skilled handicraft workers, and women who worked in other people's homes as cooks, maids, and domestic servants, found the range of wartime opportunities expanding. Industries scrambled to replace male workers drafted into the military, and governmental agencies looked for clerical workers as they expanded. Although the total number of women employed in such occupations did not increase dramatically during the war effort, the locus of their efforts shifted. As J. Stanley Lemons has summarized the situation: "Surveys showed that women came from other industries into the war industries, not from the ranks of the unemployed. One study found that 65 percent had come from other factories, 25 percent from domestic service and restaurant work, and 5 percent from laundries; only 5 percent had never worked before." As white women shifted from domestic service or low-paying industrial jobs, opportunities expanded for black women to take their places. The minuscule National Women's Trade Union League, headed by social worker Margaret Dreier Robins, used the leverage of the situation to counteract some of the discriminatory practices of male-dominated trade unions. The NWTUL lobbied vigorously to secure or maintain protective labor regulations for women workers against business pressure to reduce them in the name of national efficiency. Congress established a Woman in Industry Service as part of the Department of Labor, but it had to rely on the National War Labor Board for power to protect women workers.[9]

Middle-class and upper-class women, who did not work outside their homes for wages or salaries, and some business and professional women, who did work outside the home for salaries or fees, responded to the wartime effort through a bewildering variety of voluntary organizations: the American Red Cross, the YWCA, the General Federation of Women's Clubs, the National Consumers' League, the National Federation of Business and Professional Women's Clubs, local Councils of National Defense, Women's Liberty Loan Committees, the Medical Women's National Association, and the National Association of Colored Women. Those women who had previously put their efforts into preventing war and forestalling American involvement in the European war now shifted their focus to providing a mechanism to prevent *future* wars or of ending the current war by negotiations as soon as possible. The net result of the efforts of such women's organizations was a tremendous amount of volunteer activity: knitting, bandage rolling, food conservation, fund-raising, Liberty bond sales, volunteer nursing, doughnut and coffee dispensing to soldiers, and aid and comfort given to widows, families of servicemen, and victims of the war abroad. They could rightly claim that they had contributed to the efficiency of the war effort.[10] Along with these positive contributions there were some negative aspects: bombastic patriotic propaganda, some not-so-subtle pressure for "100 percent Americanism" directed toward immigrants, and a few sensationalistic "social purity" episodes. Antiprostitution campaigns, antivenereal disease publicity, and some pressure for racist restrictions around military camps, embarkation posts, and training facilities characterized these negative efforts.[11]

Since woman suffrage had been the one overarching cause that had attempted to unite prewar women's groups, it was not surprising that it continued to be a primary factor in women's activities during the wartime mobilization as well. The National American Woman Suffrage Association (NAWSA), headed by Carrie Chapman Catt, pursued a dual policy of vigorous support of the war effort and persistent, quiet, moderate lobbying for state suffrage victories and passage of the federal suffrage amendment. By 1916 Catt had also come to the conclusion that the suffrage drive would have to accommodate itself to white southern sensitivities about states' rights and race relations in spite of the fact that twenty African American woman suffrage organizations enthusiastically supported the cause and the NAACP had officially endorsed woman suffrage. The militant Congressional Union and its successor, the National Woman's Party (NWP), headed by Alice Paul, concentrated single-mindedly on pushing for suffrage by picketing the White House. The women pickets were arrested, jailed under abysmal conditions, and brutally force-fed when they went on hunger strikes. By 1919 the National Woman's Party was also turning a cold shoulder to African American concerns about the vote for women and racial equality. In spite of these tensions among the suffragists, a combination of factors worked to push woman suffrage: (1) NAWSA behind the scenes lobbying, (2) the example of women's sacrificial service in the war effort, (3) the NWP's exploitation of the jailing of the pickets and the attendant publicity, (4) Wilson's "arm twisting" of recalcitrant Democrats, and (5) the threats of future political retribution against reluctant politicians, particularly by potential women voters. The stubborn antisuffrage forces in the Senate finally gave way. On 4 June 1919 the Senate approved the Susan B. Anthony woman suffrage amendment. After some dramatic cliff-hanger votes in state legislatures and unsuccessful court challenges by die-hard "antis," women would be granted the right to vote—just in time for the 1920 presidential election.[12]

But what would women do with the ballot? What did women want? How would women as full citizens armed with the vote relate to each other? At the height of the suffrage campaign, NAWSA claimed to represent over two million members. At the 1917 NAWSA convention, Catt had referred to the need for a postsuffrage victory organization to maintain women's unity as a force for further progress. After the distractions of the final war efforts, the NAWSA convention in March 1919 voted to launch an auxiliary organization, in enfranchised states only, that Catt proposed be called the League of Women Voters. Opposition to the proposal came largely from women allied with the major political parties, particularly Ruth Hanna McCormick of Illinois, leader of the Women's Division of the Republican Party. If women had fought so long to be integrated into the political process, she asked, why maintain a separate organization? In typical progressive fashion, Catt had opted for a nonpartisan, educational and lobbying format for the proposed organization. Newly enfranchised women voters needed to be educated, Catt maintained: first, in the sheer mechanics of registering, voting, and guarding against vote fraud, and, second, in the complicated issues facing the postwar reconstruction of American society. At its 1920 convention, the NAWSA formally agreed to reconstitute itself as the National League of Women Voters.[13]

The leaders of the National Women's Party wrestled with a similar question: "What—if *anything*—next?" At its peak in 1919 NWP probably had fifty thousand adherents. As historian Christine A. Lunardini has pointed out, the leaders of the NWP were dedicated to the goal of equality for women: "The immediate goal would be the 'removal of the legal disabilities of women.' The organization, the planners determined, would 'continue to work for that object until it is accomplished.' " Thus, just as during the height of the suffrage campaign, there were several rival organizations dedicated to securing equal political and legal rights for women. Together they could claim to represent two and one-half million out of the twenty-seven million women who became eligible in 1920 to vote.[14]

Women experienced a wide range of new opportunities in the wartime labor force (however briefly the situation lasted). Women's rights had been protected by government agencies such as the National War Labor Board or had been promoted by Council of National Defense (CND) women's committees and by the Woman in Industry Service. Above all, the war had been the context for the final achievement of the long-sought goal of the right to vote. Much still remained to be done, and the divisions among organizations dedicated to achieving women's rights persisted, but at least they could point to the fruits of their labors. For the African American quest for civil rights, however, the story was more complex and less positive. As with women, the context was the impact of the wartime economy and military mobilization on the African American communities. For several decades, black workers had been moving from the South to the North and the West in search of economic opportunity and to escape Jim Crow segregation and lynching. American involvement in the war simply accelerated this "Great Migration"; from 1916 to 1918 approximately a half million African Americans followed the new "underground railroad" to the northern and western cities. Subject to military conscription, 342,277 African Americans served in the military. They were limited to segregated units in the army, restricted to working in food service in the navy, and excluded completely from the marine corps. Nevertheless, approximately 200,000 served overseas, with almost 30,000 in the combat areas. Thus, war created a dynamic that both mobilized the black communities and frustrated them.[15]

Two cities in particular seemed to symbolize this dynamic: Harlem and Chicago. If Harlem symbolized intellectual and cultural ferment, a wideranging debate on ideas, and competition among individuals for leadership, Chicago symbolized institutional conflict and interracial tension. Harlem was known as the "cultural capital of black America." It was a heady mixture: (1) Caribbean refugees fleeing European and American imperialism, (2) New Negro artists and intellectuals who exemplified Du Bois's "talented tenth," (3) established African American businessmen and businesswomen, real estate developers, aspiring politicians, and charismatic clergy, and (4) bewildered rural migrants from the South trying desperately to adjust to a volatile urban setting. Wandering down Lenox Avenue, a newcomer to Harlem might stop at a newsstand and pick up a copy of the *Crisis*, the magazine of the NAACP. In the July 1918 issue he or she might read the editorial by W. E. B. Du Bois entitled, "Close Ranks." Du Bois urged African Americans to support the war effort: "Let us, while this war lasts, forget our special grievances and close our ranks shoulder to shoulder with our white fellow citizens and the allied nations that are fighting for democracy." Du Bois's editorial reflected the strategy of a white NAACP officer, Joel E. Spingarn, who hoped to convince the Military Intelligence Bureau of NAACP loyalty. He wanted to use that loyalty and support of the war effort by blacks to combat racial discrimination in the military, to expand economic opportunities for blacks, and to strengthen their claim for full citizenship. Membership in the NAACP rose by the end of 1918 from 9,869 to 43,994. However, Du Bois's prowar editorial proved controversial among some of his colleagues and failed to convince the government's "antiradical" watchdogs in the Military Intelligence Bureau.[16]

Continuing to look through the newsstand offerings, the newcomer on Lenox Avenue in 1918 might pick up a copy of the newly established newspaper *Negro World*. Selling at five cents a copy, boasting of a circulation of 50,000, the newspaper carried lengthy editorials by Marcus Garvey addressed to "Fellow men of the Negro Race" and a column "Our Women and What They Think" by Amy Jacques Garvey, Marcus Garvey's wife. Garvey, a charismatic Jamaican immigrant, had founded a Harlem-based branch of his Universal Negro Improvement Association (UNIA) in 1916. He advocated a complex mixture of black nationalism, racial pride and self-help, anticolonialism, and black capitalism. He espoused plans for a black-owned steamship line to facilitate a return-to-Africa movement and created a mass following by the use of colorful parades, rituals, regalia, and the paraphernalia of a fraternal order. Garvey would claim over two million followers by the middle of 1919, but his critics were dubious of the claim. (Recent scholars put the figure at one million.) No one could deny, however, that large numbers of African Americans and recent Caribbean immigrants from all classes were listening to Garvey's message.[17]

If the newcomer to Harlem stopped at the corner of Lenox Avenue and 135th Street, he or she might listen to the soapbox oratory of A. Philip Randolph, Chandler Owen, and Hubert Harrison. They preached socialism and working-class solidarity. The black citizens' problems were primarily class based, they argued, and only socialism could save them. Racial discrimination was just a means used by the owning class to divide the working class. When the United States entered World War I, Randolph and Owen, through their journal, the *Messenger*, urged African Americans not to support the war effort. Patriotism, according to the *Messenger's* editorial line, was just another tool of the capitalists to manipulate the emotions of the masses and to exploit them for profit. Hubert Harrison, through his magazine, the *Voice*, attacked Du Bois's "Close Ranks" editorial, particularly his admonition to forget "special grievances." Harrison countered by pointing out that these grievances included "lynching, segregation, and disfranchisement" and that African Americans could not "preserve either their lives, their manhood or their vote . . . with these things in existence." The government took a dim view of such "subversive" activities, suppressed editions of socialist journals, and arrested outspoken socialist leaders.[18]

Du Bois puzzled over these competing calls for black self-separatism ("purity") and for cooperation with the white-dominated society and government ("compromise"). He defended the NAACP policies and his own role in them: "Unless we had fought segregation with determination, our whole race would have been pushed into an ill-lighted, unpaved, unsewered ghetto. . . . Unless we had welcomed the segregation of Fort Des Moines [for training of black officers], we would have had no officers in the National Army. Unless we had beaten open the door of northern universities, we would have had no men fit to be officers."[19] Traveling to Paris as a journalist to cover the peace conference and to participate in a Pan African Congress, Du Bois investigated on his own the treatment of the African American soldiers by the military. In a May 1919 editorial in the *Crisis*, Du Bois sounded a militant note:

[W]e are cowards and jackasses if now that the war is over, we do not marshal every ounce of our brain and brawn to fight a sterner, longer, more unbending battle against the forces of hell in our land.

We return.

We return from fighting.

We return fighting.[20]

As far as Du Bois and numerous Harlem leaders were concerned, the place to make the "world safe for democracy" was at home.

Chicago was a symbol of the tensions confronting African American society. (Let it also stand as a symbol for Springfield, East St. Louis, Washington, D.C., Knoxville, Omaha, Pittsburgh, and numerous other towns that experienced racial tension.) From 1910 to 1920 Chicago's black population increased from 44,103 to 109,594, at a time when its white population increased more slowly and foreign immigration diminished. Competition for housing, jobs, social services, political patronage, and recreational space divided the city into warring neighbors along informal, psychologically defined lines. In the African American newspaper *Chicago Defender* recent migrants from the South found articulation for their grievances, and the circulation grew from 50,000 to 125,000. Then, on 27 July 1919 a black youth swam across one of the informal boundaries on a Lake Michigan beach that separated "white" and "colored" recreational sections. The target of rocks thrown by angry whites, he let go of the railroad tie he was using as a float and drowned. Rumors spread quickly, violence flared, and Chicago was plunged into thirteen days of racial lawlessness, in spite of the efforts of the hastily called state militia to restore order. As historian E. David Cronon has summarized the situation: "At the end of the reign of terror at least thirty-eight persons were dead and hundreds more injured. More than a thousand families, mainly Negroes, were homeless as the result of the worst outbreak of racial strife in the nation's history." Two years earlier, in 1917, the East St. Louis, Illinois, riot had left a similar number dead and $400,000 in property destroyed. Du Bois had investigated that incident and had denounced it in his editorials in the *Crisis*. The NAACP had organized a silent protest march to muffled drums by eight to ten thousand African Americans down Fifth Avenue in New York City to bring pressure on the Wilson administration. Now the Chicago riot in 1919 indicated that the NAACP's work was not over; it had just begun—again.[21]

In summary, what was the meaning of the wartime experiments in government regulation, the protection of women's rights, the achievement of woman suffrage, the participation of African Americans in the war mobilization, and the assaults on their civil rights in the period 1916 to 1920? Much has been made by historians of the wartime slogan: "To make the world safe for democracy." But there was another theme that was embodied in the name "Liberty bonds." Liberty had been the primary core value of the prewar progressives. Whether understood primarily as *freedom from* corporate competition via "trust busting" or from excessive competition via government-sanctioned corporate coordination, as *freedom to* secure equitable credit or to bargain collectively through trade unions, or (in Dewey's instrumental "effective freedom") as the *freedom of* an agent armed with the appropriate social resources to achieve self-development, liberty had been the touchstone of Roosevelt's New Nationalism, Taft's faltering efforts, and Wilson's New Freedom program. True, there were those, particularly among the conservatives and the Supreme Court, who saw "liberty of contract," the legal fiction derived from the Fourteenth Amendment, as the summum bonum. Even Gompers of the AFL and other traditional trade unionists, in their ritual withdrawal and renewal phase in the face of rapidly changing economic realities, invoked their own version of "liberty of contract" and claimed *freedom from* antitrust strictures on restraint of trade. Progressive reformers, conservatives, and trade unionists all believed that liberty was the ultimate goal and the primary good (even as they disagreed as to its meaning). Woman suffragists had marched to victory under the banner of liberty but raised the issues of equality and justice as well, particularly for working women. Civil rights advocates had benefited from the equality of opportunity created by war mobilization, had willingly endorsed the equal burdens of citizenship, and had reminded the government of their right to justice as well.

There were those, such as the radical socialists, syndicalists, and anarchists, who pointed out that such "liberty," equality, and justice, however defined, were illusionary for the mass of workers, farm tenants or sharecroppers, recent immigrants, and disenfranchised blacks. They offered alternate definitions of liberty as *freedom from* capitalism or from the state and *freedom to* share equitably in the ownership of the means of production, distribution, and exchange, to enjoy secure employment and the social benefits of technology, and to join the ranks of a self-governing, socially recognized, all-encompassing working class. They redefined equality as something beyond mere individualistic equality of opportunity and advocated a communal-based equality. They also defined justice as something more than obedience to correct judicial procedures or reliance on the courts to interpret the substance of the current law. Above all, they wanted justice to be emblematic of class-based obligations to work for the benefit of all as embodied in a socialist system.

The wartime public discourse on the meaning of core values of liberty, equality, and justice resulted in a narrowing of these terms as they became embodied in institutions, in the political distribution of power, and in individual and group consciousness. These meanings had been particularly evident in the attempts to regulate and restructure business in the name of efficiency, to expand the rights of women in the name of social bonds, and to claim civil rights in the language of equality. This fact will become clearer when compared with the fate of the core value of justice in the simultaneous debates over another development: the shift from civil liberty to civil liberties.

13

From Civil Liberty to Civil Liberties, 1914–1928

If students had been sent to the library in 1914 or 1915 to do research for a paper on the defense of the rights found in the Bill of Rights, they would have encountered an anomalous situation. The new reference tool, the *Readers Guide to Periodical Literature*, did not have a category "civil liberties." Under the heading "Civil Liberty" the reader was directed to see the category "Liberty," with subcategories "Liberty of Conscience," "Liberty of Speech," and "Liberty of the Press." If, about ten years later, students on a similar assignment looked in the *Readers Guide*, they would still find the category "Civil Liberty" with the notation to see "Liberty." But something subtle had begun to happen in the *content* of the articles listed. For example, an article by Upton Sinclair, the former muckraker, published in the *Nation*, 4 July 1923, was entitled "Protecting Our *Liberties*." In 1925 Oswald Garrison Villard, grandson of the abolitionist William Lloyd Garrison and an officer in the National Association for the Advancement of Colored People (NAACP), published an article in *Harper's* magazine entitled "New Fight for Old *Liberties*." What had transpired in the ten years or so was the beginning of an intellectual clarification and reconceptualization of what civil liberty meant in the modern world. Confusions of terminology, persistence of old categories and habits of thought, the introduction of new terms, subtle shifts in semantic meanings, the emergence of new organizations, the narrowing of legal implications—all these developments were indicative of a gradual shift in thought and contributed to the emerging definition of civil liberties. This chapter will focus on the introduction of the term "civil liberties," the experiences during World War I and immediately after it that shaped the meaning of the term, and the institutions that emerged, 1914–28, to implement the new meanings.[1]

The precipitating event in the transformation of the meaning of the concept "civil liberty" was undoubtedly the outbreak of war in Europe in 1914. The war was a challenge to all the easy assumptions of progressivism. Even before American entry into the war, popular writer Raymond B. Fosdick had argued that the problem with most Americans and their reluctance to support a military buildup, or "preparedness," lay in their "conception of liberty" [compared to the efficiency of the "Prussian ideal"]. By liberty he meant excessive individualism, belief in equality, resistance to restraint on personal freedom, and a sense of self-centered independence. Preparedness, on the other hand, he said, required "disciplined co-ordination," elevation of the needs of the state, and subordination of individual interest to the general interest. "[If] liberty and discipline [i.e., individualism and hierarchy] are incompatible," he wrote, "if democracy cannot conceive of the subordination of individual interests, then freedom needs refining." American participation in the war and its wartime mobilization did just that. Suddenly, the freedoms that had been taken for granted were challenged by governmental action and by public opinion. Conscription challenged liberty of conscience for pacifists, censorship curtailed freedom of the press, and the Espionage Act (1917) and Sedition Act (1918) "conscripted" free speech and personal liberty for the war effort.[2]

An American Union Against Militarism had been organized in 1914 by a loose coalition of pacifists, social workers, feminists, social gospel advocates, and conservative lawyers who were worried about the implications of the preparedness debate on the prospects for peace. The AUAM had formed a subordinate "Civil Liberties Bureau" based on the model of British pacifists and anticonscription groups. When in April 1917 Congress voted to enter the war and President Wilson argued that, once "the people" had spoken through their elected representatives, there was no room for dissent, the AUAM leadership divided. One group rallied to create a National Civil Liberties Bureau in October 1917. Crystal Eastman, feminist and socialist, who had helped organize the AUAM's original Civil Liberties Bureau, Roger Baldwin, a socially elite, progressive social worker who had served as secretary of the Liberty Defense Union, Harry Weinberger, a lawyer who represented the Legal Defense League, and social gospel ministers Norman Thomas, John Haynes Holmes, and Harry F. Ward all united around the National Civil Liberties Bureau. Roger Baldwin later recalled that the organization of the Civil Liberties Bureau in 1917 was "the first time the phrase 'civil liberties' had been so used in the United States" and that they had borrowed it "from a British war-time Council for Civil Liberties, whose leaders we knew." But what did this phrase mean in the immediate context of wartime America? A writer for the *Dial* warned in October, 1917 that "freedom of action, of speech, even of conscience, all are subjected to violent shifts by military undertaking and its régime."[3]

Wartime tensions provided the *context* for restrictions on personal freedom, but the *content* of the debate reflected prewar controversies. For example, the Anti-Saloon League in the 1900s had "found a way of uniting the moral effort of the evangelical Protestant churches with the political power of the overrepresented rural areas [particularly in the South] by stressing the classic mixture of nonpartisanship, singleness of purpose, and centralization of authority." Sensing an opportunity to exploit anti-immigrant nationalism, middle-class desire for social control of minorities, and social gospel humanitarianism, the ASL put pressure on Congress to do something about wartime alcohol consumption. In 1917 Congress "passed the Lever Food and Fuel Control Act (forbidding the use of foodstuffs for distillation and regulating beer and wine production); the Eighteenth Amendment for national prohibition; and, in 1918, the War Production Act, outlawing the manufacture and sale of beer and wine." By January 1919 the necessary two-thirds of the states had ratified the Eighteenth Amendment. In spite of widespread voter support, the issues raised were serious enough for former president William Howard Taft to publish a popular article entitled, "Is Prohibition a Blow at Personal Liberty?" His answer was no: "Reasonable restraint of personal liberty of action for the common welfare" was justified. Anti-immigration groups also provided an example of prewar continuity. In 1913 Congress had been pressured to pass a literacy test for immigrants only to encounter a veto by President Wilson. In 1917, responding to wartime tensions, Congress passed an omnibus immigration restriction act, which included a literacy test, only to encounter another veto by President Wilson. This time they were able to override the veto. However, the law did not specify literacy in English so it was not as much of a barrier to immigration as some restrictionists had hoped. These attacks on personal freedom were a sign of the times and a foretaste of further restrictions.[4]

The groups that bore the brunt of wartime restrictions were the socialists and anticonscriptionists. The Socialist Party had split into prowar and antiwar factions. Many of the prowar socialists were native-born or of "old" immigrant background. As they left the Socialist Party, the balance of power in the party tended to shift toward more radical "new" immigrants, particularly in the foreign language federations with European orientations. The shifting character of the Socialist Party membership was accompanied by a radicalization of viewpoint in response to repression at home and revolutionary events abroad. As Nick Salvatore has noted in his biography of Eugene Debs: "The Bolshevik Revolution in November 1917 convinced many on the left that all that stood between them and the establishment of American soviets was a purge of conservative leaders and the restructuring of the party on proper revolutionary principles along the Russian model." Debs, shaken by the arrest of many of his comrades, seized upon the Russian revolution as a ray of hope. In an antiwar speech in Canton, Ohio, in June 1918, Debs shouted: "Our hearts are with the Bolsheviki of Russia [who] by their incomparable valor and sacrifice added fresh lustre to the fame of the international movement." Nevertheless, Debs concluded his speech by identifying his opposition to the war with the American tradition of dissent: Thomas Paine, Thomas Jefferson, John Adams, William Lloyd Garrison, and Abraham Lincoln. A zealous U.S. attorney sent a stenographic copy of the speech to the Department of Justice in Washington. In spite of a cautious appraisal of the speech by department officials, the attorney decided to seek a federal grand jury indictment and charged Debs with violating the wartime Espionage Act. In a trial in September 1918, Debs was found guilty and sentenced to ten years in the federal penitentiary. Also sentenced to ten year in prison for antiwar activity was socialist Rose Pastor Stokes.[5]

In September 1918, the same month as the Debs trial, the liberal journal the *Nation* published an article entitled, "Civil Liberty Dead." The article referred to a recent "round up" of 75,000 young men in New York and New Jersey by troops, Justice Department agents, and quasi-official patriotic organizations. The ostensible purpose was to locate "slackers," young men who had not registered for the draft or who were not carrying their conscription classification cards. Only 3 percent were ultimately found to fit this category, but the trampling on the rights of all of these citizens prompted an outcry even from some conservative senators. President Wilson promised an official inquiry. "But, after all," the *Nation* article observed, "the worst feature of the affair is not the official anarchy. It is the fact that personal liberty and freedom have disappeared in America, and that the bulk of our vocal patriots thoughtlessly approve of it in the earnestness of their desire to win the war." An editorial in the *Independent*, also in September 1918, was somewhat less sanguine about the opinion that the war had "Prussianized" American institutions. Once the war was over, the editorial asserted, the "common sense" of the American people would return. Besides, the writer said, "normal curtailments of individual liberty—normal because incidental to social evolution, to civilization itself—were well begun in America before we entered the war, and they will continue after we return to the habits of peace." The war ended with an armistice in November 1918. But events in 1919 showed that the status of civil liberty was as precarious after the war as it had been during the war.[6]

On 10 March 1919 the United States Supreme Court unanimously upheld Debs's conviction and sentence, as it had upheld a week earlier the conviction of Charles T. Schenck, general secretary of the Socialist Party, for mailing antiwar and antidraft leaflets. The *Debs* and *Schenck* cases were expressions of the political-legal theory that civil liberty, as the secure status of freedom based upon collective membership in a civilized society, was *primary* and that individual liberty—of speech, press, or religion—was *secondary* to the common good. Justice Oliver Wendell Holmes Jr. laid down the classic exposition in *Schenck v. U.S.* (1919):

[T]he character of every act depends upon the circumstances in which it is done.... The most stringent protection of free speech would not protect a man in falsely shouting fire in a theater and causing a panic.... The question in every case is whether the words used are used in such circumstances and are of such a nature as to create a clear and present danger that they will bring about the substantive evils that Congress has a right to prevent.... *When a nation is at war many things that might be said in time of peace are such a hindrance to its effort that their utterance will not be endured so long as men fight and that no court could regard them as protected by any constitutional right.*[7]

In *Debs v. U.S.* (1919) Holmes likewise declined to uphold a defense based on freedom of speech (First Amendment). Holmes referred to the Anti-War Proclamation and Program adopted by the Socialist Party in April 1917. "Evidence that the defendant [Debs] accepted this view and this declaration of his duties at the time that he made his speech," Holmes said, "is evidence that if in that speech he used words tending to obstruct the recruiting service he meant that they should have that effect." To the "clear and present" *danger* criteria, in other words, Holmes had here added a "clear and present" *intent* doctrine to protect government needs from proscribed individual deeds.[8]

The fateful year 1919 also found the trade union movement in disarray. With a postwar recession, renewed inflation, rising unemployment, public apprehension over labor unrest, and the Wilson administration virtually leaderless on domestic issues, an ambivalent situation developed. Labor leaders such as Samuel Gompers of the American Federation of Labor (AFL) tried to repudiate the radicals in their own ranks and to reassure the anxious public of their patriotic devotion to American values. At the same time, Gompers upheld the right of workers to strike for better wages, shorter hours, and collective bargaining rights. But such strikes only fed popular fears and created opportunities for radicals to exploit the turmoil for their own purposes. Left-wing radicals, wanting to magnify the image of their support among workers, injected revolutionary rhetoric into the volatile strike situations. A simultaneous series of unexplained bomb attacks, general strikes, and riots only fanned the flames of public suspicion and resentment.[9]

A number of business associations and right-wing "law and order" groups seized the opportunity to wage a campaign for the "open shop" to undermine the trade unions (who favored the "closed shop") and used the strikes to pin the red tag of "bolshevism" (or communism) on *all* labor unions. Newspapers circulated wild rumors, created nonexistent conspiracies, and oversimplified complex issues by hurling the word "bolshevism" about. As Robert K. Murray noted in his classic work, *Red Scare: A Study of National Hysteria, 1919–1920,* "There was no attempt at any time to understand what the word 'bolshevism' actually meant or what its relationship was to other isms such as socialism or anarchism. Instead, all such isms were lumped together as being the same. . . . It was automatically assumed that anyone who was not a 'conservative' was a 'radical,' and hence even those who advocated the mildest reforms were dumped into the 'Red' classification."[10] Thus, by the middle of 1919 Gompers and other trade union leaders were like persons trying to outrun their own shadows: the harder they tried, the more the shadow of "bolshevism" stuck to them.

Meanwhile, those socialists who thought of themselves as the true Bolsheviks, the inheritors of the Russian revolutionary tradition, were further isolated from the mass of American workmen and women. On 13 April 1919, the day that Eugene Debs arrived at a federal prison, the right-wing leaders in the New York Socialist Party voted to oust the left-wing revolutionary socialists. In May the national executive committee of the Socialist Party likewise expelled the left-wing, foreign-language federations and the "revisionist" Michigan state organization. Those 26,000 members expelled promptly split among themselves over the best course of action to follow throughout the summer of 1919. The ousted left-wing leaders formed two rival Communist parties. John Reed, Benjamin Gitlow, William B. Lloyd (son of Henry D. Lloyd, the antimonopoly muckraker of the 1890s) and other native-born radicals formed the Communist Labor Party (CLP). The Communist Labor Party's manifesto called for "the organization of the workers as a class, the overthrow of capitalist rule and the conquest of political power by the workers." By the end of 1919 the CLP claimed 10,000 members. Meanwhile Louis Fraina, Nicholas Hourwich, and Charles Ruthenberg, representing the left-wing, foreign-language federations, formed the American Communist Party.

The ACP took a hard-line position in its manifesto and called for "proletarian revolution, the overthrow of capitalism and the establishment of the dictatorship of the proletariat." By the end of 1919 the ACP claimed 60,000 members. The Socialist Party, now under the domination of its right-wing and moderate leaders, such as Victor Berger and Morris Hillquit, dropped to 30,000 members.[11]

Thus, a year after the *Nation* and the *Independent* had worried editorially about the state of civil liberty in America, the situation had changed dramatically. In Paris in March 1919 a caucus of American military officers and enlisted men had determined to form a new veterans organization, to be called the American Legion. The draft of the preamble of the proposed constitution stated their purpose: "We, the members of the Military and Naval Services of the United States of America in the Great War, desiring to perpetuate the principles of Justice, Freedom, and Democracy for which we have fought, *to inculcate the duty and obligation of the citizen to the State;* to preserve the history and incidents of our participation in the war; and to cement the ties of comradeship formed in service, do propose to found and establish an Association for the furtherance of the foregoing purposes."[12] Alice Edgerton, writing in the *Nation* in October 1919, raised a troubling question about such pressures for conformity in the postwar situation: "But are we indeed normally free? Is not the easy loss of freedom in time of stress a measure of the thinness of our 'freedom'?" The scope of her concern was wider than wartime conscription, free speech, or censorship of the press. She noted a number of other problem areas: rigid sexual norms and conformity, the educational system and its "Americanization" programs, the press's support of the status quo out of timidity or economic dependence, the state's use of its "police power" to intrude into a variety of private matters under the guise of protective legislation, and the power of business to dominate society. To blame the war was inadequate, she concluded. The issue of free speech had predated the war (she cited the 1912 free speech cases from the troubled labor history of San Diego, California). "In other words," she concluded, "a great mass of the American people, possibly the majority, are spiritual autocrats. We do not want individual liberty for the dissenters; to that extent we do not want democracy."[13]

Walter Lippmann, a former socialist and wartime advisor to Wilson's foreign policy staff, agreed. "From our recent experience," he noted in November 1919, "it is clear that the traditional liberties of speech and opinion rest on no solid foundation." Indeed, the traditional Anglo-American liberal theory of civil liberty, going back to John Milton and John Stuart Mill and recently represented by the English philosopher

Bertrand Russell, was inadequate. Civil liberty, according to Lippmann, was not an abstract ideal, a fixed status, or an absolute value. Rather, "a useful definition of [civil] liberty is obtainable only by seeking the principle of liberty in the main business of human life, . . . *in the process* by which men educate their response and learn to control their environment." Instead of being a formal concept or an attribute of civilization, he noted, "liberty is a condition under which activity takes place, and men's interests attach themselves primarily to their activities and what is necessary to fulfil them." Freedom, in other words, was not a comfortable unitary status but a constant *struggle* to protect certain specific rights or *liberties.* The modern concept of "civil liberties" meant that individual rights were *primary* and the collective rights of society and the prerogatives of the states were *secondary.*[14]

But how could the process of protecting civil liberties be implemented? Richara Roberts, writing in the social work journal *Survey* for 15 November 1919, observed that "during the war, in Great Britain and America, small companies of people banded themselves together to do what they could to help save the traditional liberties of the English-speaking people from being altogether lost" in the wartime mobilization, but, she noted ruefully, most of these advocates were "heretics respecting the war," that is, they were pacifists. Now that the war was over, and the pacifist issue had faded somewhat, she continued, "there is a very real tendency to stretch-out the war-time restrictions to cover other heresies that appear to be more immediately dangerous," especially economic dissent. She had little to offer by way of a solution to the problem but a mea culpa for her generation and a cautious note that "those of us who are neither reactionaries nor revolutionaries must cry loud and long, and affirm our liberty resolutely by using it."[15]

The year 1920 started with well-coordinated state and federal raids, supervised by Attorney General A. Mitchell Palmer's Justice Department, which arrested 4,000 suspected radicals. If the more moderate Socialist Party members thought that they were immune to governmental actions, they were mistaken. Victor Berger, a Socialist Party member and duly elected congressman from Wisconsin, was expelled from the United States House of Representatives. Five Socialist Party members of the New York State legislature were similarly disbarred and expelled. According to historian Robert K. Murray, under state antisocialist, sedition, criminal sydicalist, and "red flag" legislation, "no fewer than 1400 persons, both citizens and aliens, were arrested under this state legislation and of this number about 300 were ultimately convicted and sent to prison," many of whom were simply socialists, not communists. And the government lumped together bolshevism, anarchism, and immigrant radicalism indiscriminately and deported 249 alien radicals on the aging ship *Buford* in December 1920, including the anarchist orator, antiwar activist, and birth control advocate Emma Goldman. Thus the "Palmer raids," imprisonment or isolation of socialist leaders, and the deportation of immigrant radicals narrowed the meaning of core values such as liberty, equality, and justice. Those who had alternate definitions, rankings, or understanding of such terms were shunted aside from the postwar public discourse.[16]

Roger Baldwin, a member of the wartime National Civil Liberties Bureau (NCLB), had been radicalized by his wartime experiences and by the postwar repression. He had been jailed for resisting conscription on grounds of "individual freedom, democratic liberty and Christian teaching." He planned to join a radical worker's organization while in jail. Upon his release from jail, Baldwin and other civil liberties advocates decided the time had come to reorganize the wartime NCLB into a permanent organization. On 19 January 1920, just after the Palmer raids, the American Civil Liberties Union was formed. By the end of the year the ACLU would claim 1,000 "correspondents" and 800 cooperating attorneys, figures which Samuel Walker, an historian of the ACLU, concedes "were probably exaggerated." In fact, the degree of support for the ACLU position among lawyers was hardly encouraging. The *Nation* magazine had sent an urgent letter to New York lawyers about recent events and asked if it wasn't time for the bar "to speak out against the denial of the Constitutional rights of free speech and public assembly in this country." The results—in those instances where lawyers would even allow their answers to be printed—were published in April 1920 under the title "Are American Liberties Worth Saving?" Attorney Paul D. Cravath said bluntly, "[that] citizen anarchists should be punished and [that] alien anarchists should be deported." George W. Wickersham, who had served as attorney general under President Taft, was equally forthright: "There is no absolute right of free speech, despite the language of the First Amendment of the Constitution." He cited Justice Holmes's "clear and present danger" criteria from the *Schenck* case. Several other lawyers waffled on the issue. Only Harlan F. Stone, dean of the School of Law at Columbia University, took a strong stand in favor of a watchdog role for the bar. He predicted, "[W]e shall soon witness a reaction in public sentiment in favor of adequate protection of the rights of minorities and of insuring to individuals, even though they be foreigners, justice according to law administered by the courts."[17]

Harlan Stone's prediction came true sooner than he might have expected. The very excesses of government repression, newspaper hysteria, and vigilante-induced conformity raised serious questions about the meaning of justice, the basis of representative democracy, and the protection of individual rights. In May 1920 the National Popular Government League issued a report, written by twelve prominent lawyers, which was entitled *Report upon the Illegal Practices of the United States Department of Justice*. The spectacle of former Republican presidential candidate Charles Evans Hughes, representing the New York Bar Association, denouncing the disbarment of duly elected Socialist Party members from the New York State Assembly because it was a danger to representative government caused many newspaper editorial writers to reconsider their reflexive antiradicalism. Senator Warren G. Harding, the Republican presidential candidate, feared the erosion of American core values by government power more than any threat to those values posed by radical organizations or rhetoric. But if lawyers were divided among themselves about the best way to protect specific liberties, the ACLU was similarly divided. On the one hand, lawyers and constitutional experts such as Walter Nelles, Walter Pollack, and Felix Frankfurter (an independent advisor) believed in the legal process of slow, patient pursuit of strategic cases and the building up of legal precedents. On the other hand, activists such as Roger Baldwin, Normal Thomas, and Scott Nearing argued for direct action to support harassed labor and radical movements. Events would soon push the ACLU in a definite direction.[18]

Not everyone agreed with the National Popular Government League or with the ACLU and their concern for equal rights and protection of individual liberties. John Corbin, an immigration restriction advocate, candidly wrote in December 1920, that "above equality is liberty, and liberty rests upon the superiority of the citizen." By this he meant the superiority of the Anglo-Saxon, middle-class, "old stock" citizen. In 1921 Congress, responding to such nativist, antiracial, and racial fears, set annual quotas on immigration by nationality: only 3 percent of the foreign-born from any European country listed in the 1910 census would be admitted as an annual quota. Asians in the excluded zone were already barred from entry, but some belonged to exempt categories. In the case *Ng Fung Ho v. White* (1922), Justice Brandeis reversed an administrative deportation order so that a judicial review of a claim to citizenship could be made. "To deport one who so claims to be a citizen," he wrote, "obviously deprives him of liberty" in the constitutional meaning of the term. The Supreme Court would hold in 1923, however, that restrictions on alien landownership did not violate the Fourteenth Amendment's equal protection clause because it affected all persons placed in a category for a "reasonable purpose" in the same way. In 1924 Congress adopted an even more comprehensive and restrictive immigration quota law. Total immigration per year was limited to 150,000, with the quota for each European country based on 2 percent from that country listed in the 1890 census. Also in 1924 Congress, which in 1919 had granted immediate citizenship to Native Americans who had served in the military in the war, now recognized that citizenship of all Native Americans born in the United States did not infringe on their property rights under tribal control. Thus, by 1924 the concept of civil liberty as a secure status was a patchwork of categories, exemptions, exclusions, and contested claims that could enhance or undercut claims to individual liberties.[19]

Supporters of the ACLU and other writers in the early 1920s appealed to the "average American citizen" to realize what was happening to their rights, to join in the effort to protect the Constitution's guarantees of their civil liberties, and to understand the key terms in the public discourse in the same way that the ACLU did. Walter Lippmann, in *Public Opinion*, published in 1922, pointed out that the progressives had hypostatized the "public" and "public opinion" in their own middle-class images. But the wartime propaganda and the postwar red scare showed that the public was not a collection of well-informed citizens who decided rationally what to do on the basis of the common good. "The people" were dependent on the information they received from the newspapers and not simply on their own experience. Furthermore, the information that they received was always partial, partisan, and stereotypical. If American democracy rested on the foundation of an enlightened public and the public was not, in fact, enlightened, then the protection of rights and civil liberties rested on shifting sand. And it did no good to appeal to the constitution as an expression of popular sovereignty because the same criticism would apply. "The democratic fallacy," Lippmann concluded, "has been its preoccupation with the origin of government [in the popular will] rather than *with the process* and results." A similar article in the *Nation* in 1923 held that, above all, liberty included "the liberty to know, to utter, and to argue, and to argue freely according to conscience"; it required toleration and mutual respect for the rights of others. But if neither public discourse nor case-by-case litigation could uphold individual liberties, what then?[20]

The ACLU emerged in the 1920s as the primary organization dedicated to raising questions about civil liberties, providing some tentative support for victims of excessive use of power, and monitoring governmental procedures. It was an organization without a viable constituency, however. The groups that the ACLU defended did not, or would not, support it. The ACLU was thus caught in the awkward position, for example, of defending freedom of speech for the Communists in the case of Benjamin Gitlow, a founder of the Communist Labor Party, while recognizing that the Communists didn't believe in free speech for those who they called "reactionaries." The ACLU repudiated the Communists' tactics of secrecy, their refusal to tell the truth under oath, and the way they manipulated defendants in legal cases for propaganda purposes; however, the public didn't necessarily notice the ACLU's criticisms in its defense of Gitlow's freedom of speech. Nevertheless, the ACLU achieved a symbolic victory in *Gitlow v. New York* (1925). Supreme Court Justice Edward T. Sanford, a conservative, acknowledged that "for the present purposes we may and do assume that freedom of speech and of the press—which are protected by the First Amendment from abridgement by Congress—are among the fundamental personal rights and 'liberties' protected by the due process clause of the Fourteenth Amendment from impairment by the states." Thus, the Supreme Court, speaking through Justice Sanford, seemed to agree in part with the ACLU brief on this point. Although Gitlow's conviction was upheld, this dictum had important implications for the future.[21]

How then to protect civil liberties if the ordinary process of government should not do so? Walter Lippmann's prescription in his 1927 book, *The Phantom Public,* sounded like a description of the work of the ACLU: "[T]he public interest in a problem is limited to this: that there shall be rules, which means that the rules which prevail shall be enforced, and that the unenforceable rules shall be changed according to a settled rule. . . . The interest of the public is not in the rules and contracts and customs themselves but in the maintenance of a régime of rule, contract and custom."[22] That the public interest was equivalent to the rule of law and that the protection of rights and civil liberties was equal to the proper processes put the ACLU in a strategic role. The ACLU, conscientious lawyers, prosecutors, judges, and organizations concerned with proper legal procedures, were the "phantom public." They acted as surrogates for the old progressive notion of the good citizen. Whereas the progressives had put their trust in either the democratic legislature or the efficient executive branch, the emerging civil liberties "lobby" put its faith in an enlightened judiciary.

The process of the shift in emphasis from "civil liberty" as a status to "civil liberties" as a process was not completed by the end of the 1920s. But the meaning of the key terms had been clarified. Civil liberty as a status meant that freedom, as embodied in the collective entities known as the society and the state (or government) and in the rule of law, was primary and the exercise of specific individual rights was secondary. Civil liberties, on the other hand, meant that freedom was a process of constant vigilance and effort in which individual liberties were primary and the prejudices and prerogatives of both society and the state were secondary. The institutional actors involved in the process were the law schools, the private organizations such as the ACLU, the judiciary, and the journalists. Like the developments of the Gilded Age, the developments of the Roaring Twenties were always multifaceted, mainly misleading in their popular images, and frequently tragic as new social languages clashed with stubborn old realities.

14

Limits to Change in the New Era, 1920–1924

With the end of the war in November 1918 and the "red scare" of 1919, two of the key issues of progressivism were put into sharper contrast—the regulation and restructuring of business and the rights of women in light of their changing roles in society. The popular images of the Roaring Twenties, which highlight the unprecedented prosperity, the adulation of the business leaders, the consumerism, and the changed lifestyles of middle-class, young, college educated women, all have an element of truth to them, but they also obscure some equally important developments. There were numerous "bumps" on the road to modern society, particularly as they relate to the political process. Some of these need to be examined in detail. This chapter will explore, first, the fate of various attempts to restructure and regulate business and, second, the divisions among women's rights advocates over the meaning of equality and the proper role of protective legislation for women workers. It will follow the railroad reorganization or Plumb Plan, Herbert Hoover's attempt to restructure business-government relationships, the Sheppard-Towner Maternity and Infant Protection Act, and the equal rights amendment through the crucial period of 1919 to 1924. In the process, the progressive social languages of antimonopoly, efficiency, and social cohesion will be shown to be in conflict with the rhetoric of antiradicalism, the realities of the self-interest of business organizations, and the divisions among women.

A good example of the dilemma of the times can be found in the efforts of trade unions and railroad brotherhoods to propose a restructuring of the railroad industry. The wartime discussion of government operation of the railroads within the Wilson administration had turned on the question of efficiency. The overriding concerns of Wilson's advisors were the effect of government operations on investor confidence, the role of railroad securities in the banking system, and the need to compensate owners for repairs to the roads and their equipment. Wilson's declaration of government operation was based on narrow legal grounds (he cited a 1916 military appropriations act amendment as authorization) and justified it as a wartime necessity. He was congratulated by numerous railroad executives for his prompt action. The only doubts among Wilson's closest advisors concerned the ability of Secretary of the Treasury Willard G. McAdoo to handle the assignment efficiently. Nevertheless, Wilson was careful to keep the public focus on government *operation* of the railroads and to avoid any prolonged discussion of government *ownership*.[1]

At the American Federation of Labor (AFL) convention in June 1919, Samuel Gompers worked hard to disassociate the trade union movement from radicalism in general and "bolshevism" in particular. Yet all his effort could not stop the delegates from endorsing the Plumb Plan, which had been devised earlier by the railroad brotherhoods. The Plumb Plan, drafted by Glenn R. Plumb, a legal counsel for the brotherhoods, called for the purchase of the railroads by the federal government and the establishment of a fifteen-member operating authority. This authority would have five representatives each from management, labor unions, and "the public." Profits would be divided similarly between management, workers, and the federal government. Backed by the AFL and the railroad brotherhoods, the Plumb Plan was introduced in Congress in August 1919. Government *operation* of the railroads in wartime had been discussed dispassionately within the Wilson administration in the language of efficiency, financial guarantees, and investor confidence. Government *ownership* of the railroads had been debated for over thirty years from a variety of political and philosophical positions. The Plumb Plan, however, was dismissed by angry Congressmen and conservatives in the emotional language of antiradicalism and charges of bolshevism. A real "bolshevik" of 1919–20 would have talked about seizure or expropriation of private property rather than its purchase by the government. A real "bolshevik" would have advocated operation "by the workers" rather than shared responsibility with management. Such subtleties, however, were beyond the vociferous critics of the Plumb Plan. As historian Robert K. Murray has summed up the situation: "Employer and business magazines urged the nation to resist firmly such a 'revolutionary proposal.' Editorials appearing in the public press echoed these assertions and further suggested that the principle [of government ownership and operation] might next be applied to banks, natural resources, and public utilities."[2]

Such criticism shocked the trade union and railroad brotherhood leaders out of some of the previously narrow and nostalgic preoccupation with the autonomy of the skilled craftsman and his control of the shop floor or the prerogatives of their railroad brotherhoods. In upholding the right of workers to strike for better wages, hours, and collective bargaining, in repudiating radical goals, and in endorsing the Plumb Plan, such trade union leaders as Gompers and railroad brotherhood advisors such as Plumb assumed the role of reformers. In the process, the goal of independence, the autonomy of the worker, was recast from individual to group terms as the drive by business associations for the "open shop" destroyed or reduced the older techniques of worker control. Scientific management techniques and assembly line production methods reduced even skilled craftsmen to a lower status. Independence meant increasingly the autonomy of the union, workers' right to self-government within the union, and the right to try to persuade others to join the union. Unions would lose a number of spectacular strikes in 1919, and a series of court decisions would subsequently undercut the supposed safeguards of the Clayton Act. The courts, for example, would uphold the "yellow dog" contract in which a worker agreed *not* to join a union as a condition of employment. In two years the unions would lose more than a million members. The Transportation Act of 1920 returned the railroads to private control with a provision for employee representation plans, which quickly turned into "company unions." The very fact that trade unions of the AFL and the railroad brotherhoods survived at all and continued to champion the economic rights of workers, their claims to equal dignity, and their role in control of the *pace* of work made them a foundation for the future. Nevertheless, part of the tragedy of the Plumb Plan proposal, 1919–20, was its inability to explain its concerns for liberty and justice for workers in a social language that would replace the shopworn antimonopoly rhetoric, fend off the charges of bolshevism of its critics, and undercut the primacy of business's narrowly focused definitions of efficiency (as maximum productivity or profitability).[3]

How fared the genuine radicals? What role could they play in the immediate postwar debates about restructuring business? Moderate Socialist Party leaders such as Morris Hillquit struggled with the relationship of socialism to the American economy and business in 1920. The Socialist Party nominated Eugene Debs as its standard bearer for the 1920 presidential election and sent a formal committee to the Atlanta federal prison to notify him of the honor. Historian Nick Salvatore has noted that Hillquist sent Debs a letter outlining the party's new platform and "defended its 'systematic omission of our favorite Marxian terminology' on the grounds that such language remained incomprehensible to most Americans: 'I am now more convinced than ever that in order to get our message across we must divorce ourselves from the worship of phrases, and talk the plainest possible English.' " Debs, in the isolation of his prison cell and in deepening depression over the failure of American workers to act like a class-conscious proletariat, gradually lost his infatuation with the Bolshevik Revolution. He repudiated their call for armed insurrection and reaffirmed his lifelong belief in democratic means, even as he conceded that "the people" wanted too little out of life and voted accordingly. Although Debs's vote total in the 1920 presidential election, 920,000, exceeded his 1912 effort, there was little evidence that newly enfranchised women had flocked to the cause in appreciation of the role played by numerous women in the socialist movement. In spite of the election of numerous Socialist Party members to local office and the continued circulation of socialist newspapers, there was little evidence that the electorate was interested in socialist ideas for business and labor. The language of social cohesion, of brotherhood, and of working-class solidarity might encourage faithful party members but it did little to achieve the power they needed to change the economic system.[4]

To judge, then, from the results of the November 1920 presidential election, the vast majority of voters (men and women) apparently wanted neither reform proposals such as the Plumb Plan nor radical alternatives such as those espoused by the Socialists. Rather, over 60 percent voted for Republican Warren G. Harding, an unprecedented victory over the Democratic candidate James Cox of Ohio. What did the voters want? The restoration of past values and priorities, repudiation of Wilsonian progressivism, ritual withdrawal and renewal, and reaction against any new proposals seemed to be their priorities. Historians have increasingly come to the realization, however, that while President Harding and many of his cabinet officers represented a return to pre–Progressive Era values and attitudes in their public actions, others, including Secretary of Commerce Herbert Hoover and his loyal band of supporters, represented continuity with progressive values and attitudes in the early 1920s. Hoover's supporters, for example, spoke of a "new era" of economic and political possibilities. Crucial for this group of government officials, academic economists, and private businessmen was the wartime experience of mobilization and regulation of the American economy. It was not that Hoover and his associates wanted to revive the coercive power of government to command the economy that they had experienced in wartime; rather, they wanted to adapt the lessons learned in the wartime mobilization to a new, more democratic system based on voluntary cooperation by private businesses and unobtrusive coordination by government experts and regulatory agencies.[5]

During his first year as secretary of commerce, 1921–22, Hoover moved energetically to implement a revised version of the wartime program to deal with the problems of postwar recession and reconstruction. He ran into resistance from some members of the Harding cabinet and conservatives in Congress who relied primarily upon the rhetoric of anti-radicalism, the political tradition of states' rights, and a belief in economic "natural laws." For Hoover, the advantage of the progressive social language of efficiency in such a situation was its capacity for expansion. As an engineer, he was quite familiar with the technical definitions of efficiency as energy input/output ratios and, as a wartime administer, he had proven to be adept at administrative efficiency in terms of the delegation of authority, clarification of objectives, and coordination of effort by centralized command and decentralized operations. In 1920, as head of the Federated American Engineering Societies, he had commissioned an investigation into "waste" in American industry. He authored the introduction to the report published in 1921. American industry *as a system* was not producing at its potential, he noted. "In part the results were attributable[,]" according to historian William J. Barber, "to the unsatisfactory functioning of the microeconomic system (in deficiencies in managerial skills and practices, in labor-management frictions); in part they were traceable to macroeconomic phenomena ('the wastes of unemployment during depressions; from speculation and over-production in boom'). The task of the future was 'to do a better job of it.' Inefficiency, whether writ large or writ small, was the enemy." Efficiency, therefore, became the master metaphor for a new era of social harmony and expanding productivity under government-business cooperation and expert coordination.[6]

If Hoover's vision of the new era was to be realized, however, certain changes were necessary in the attitudes and practices of government regulatory agencies. First, the Department of Justice would have to revise its antitrust limitations on trade associations, particularly on the sharing of production and pricing information among association members. Hoover "recognized that there was a latent danger in trade associations if members abused the information at their disposal to engage in price-fixing conspiracies, but he regarded this risk to be minor. . . ." To those who argued that deemphasizing antitrust legislation gave bigger firms an advantage, Hoover countered by arguing that data gathering and publication gave smaller firms a better chance to compete. Efficiency, in the long run, had to be won in fair competition, not by collusion. The Supreme Court decided in December 1921, however, that the statistical activities of an industry trade association amounted to a conspiracy to fix prices. This decision was implicitly a challenge to Hoover's encouragement of government-private cooperation via trade associations. He tried to get Attorney General Daugherty to agree to certain clarifications about *government*-sponsored statistical collection and publication as opposed to *private*-sponsored efforts, but the Justice Department insisted on using the criteria of economic intent and effect to determine antitrust issues. Senator Walter Edge sponsored legislation favorable to Hoover's views, but "opposition from antitrusters, dissident businessmen, and conservatives fearful of opening the path to new governmental controls" defeated all attempts to pass such legislation.[7]

Second, if efficiency was to become a byword of business, then Hoover believed that the Federal Trade Commission (FTC) would have to change its procedures. Instead of the Brandeis-style preference for adversarial, "after-the-fact" findings by regulators, Hoover favored advisory, "before-the-fact" guidelines set by administrators. Support for such an advisory role for the FTC went back to 1911, in the wake of the Supreme Court's *Standard Oil* and *American Tobacco* "rule of reason" decisions. As has been shown earlier in this book, the legislation creating the FTC in 1914 (by substituting the Rublee/Stevens version for the original Covington Bill) had empowered the agency to determine "unfair methods of competition" and to issue "cease and desist" orders. By 1920, however, the Supreme Court had held that the statutory language was too vague and that the federal courts would ultimately determine what the phrase "unfair methods of competition" meant. Barber has noted that W. E. Lamb, solicitor of the Department of Commerce, recommended to Hoover in August 1921 that "there should be some governmental agency to which the commercial interests of the country could go for the determination of the legality of proposed plans of consolidation and cooperation." He doubted, however, that the FTC was the appropriate agency.[8]

Hoover tried in the 1920s to make the Department of Commerce itself into an efficient substitute for the FTC. In effect, he told businessmen not so much what they *could* do as what they *should* do in his opinion to rationalize their industries and make them more efficient. He pinned his hopes on the trade associations and did all he could to help them. Finally, in 1925 the Supreme Court would agree with some of his ideas in the *Maple Flooring Manufacturer's Association* case. The majority opinion, written by Justice Harlan F. Stone, held "that the public interest is served by the gathering and dissemination, in the widest possible manner, of information with respect to the production and distribution, costs and prices in actual sales, of market commodities, because the making available of such information tends to stabilize trade and industry, to produce fairer price levels and to avoid waste which inevitably attends the unintelligent conduct of economic enterprises."[9]

If the Federal Trade Commission failed to live up to Hoover's expectations, and the Supreme Court gave only grudging support for trade association activities, the Federal Reserve banking system also disappointed Hoover and his supporters in the early 1920s. The Federal Reserve system had its own internal problems and didn't welcome outside advice. From mid-1920 to mid-1921 the economic system experienced a sharp decline. The Federal Reserve Board was criticized for having acted "too late and too much" in raising the rediscount rate (the rate at which member banks could borrow from the reserve banks). As prices fell dramatically, the Federal Reserve Board was blamed for its deflationary policies. In a 1921 White House Conference on Unemployment report, Hoover advocated countercyclical spending for public construction during such downward swings of the business cycle, and, bypassing the Federal Reserve Board, he encouraged commercial banks during upward swings of the economy to dampen inflationary pressures by restricting loans. At the same time, Hoover worried about international trade. He asked Benjamin Strong, governor of the Federal Reserve Bank of New York, to take steps to stabilize European currencies. In Hoover's view, such a move would bypass political complications, restore the gold standard as the means for international trade, and help American trade. But Strong, locked in his own power struggle with members of the Federal Reserve Board, had other considerations on his mind. Not until 1925 would the Federal Reserve Bank of New York take action along the lines that Hoover had recommended.[10]

Hoover's desire to encourage others to follow his advice took the form in 1922 of a short book called *American Individualism*. Rather than attempt to use forthrightly the progressive social languages and their vocabularies, he borrowed some of the current rhetoric of the Harding administration's conservatism and insinuated into it his own values of mutual cooperation, public service, and efficiency. "We have grown to understand," he wrote, "that all we can hope to assure to the individual through government is liberty, justice, intellectual welfare, equality of opportunity, and stimulation of service." But to use the language of laissez-faire conservatism to attack the consequences of "the great wastes of overreckless competition in production and distribution" and to warn against "the forces in business which would destroy equality of opportunity" was to invite misunderstanding. Hoover's justification of individualism was cast in terms of *private persons* and their needs, but his rationalization for his policies was cast in terms of *public institutions* such as "the chambers of commerce, trade associations, labor unions, bankers, farmers, propaganda associations, and what not." No wonder Hoover's biographer, Joan Hoff Wilson, has concluded that *American Individualism* "left his contemporaries confused and uncertain; the term had long been familiar in another context. In fact, Hoover meant to describe Americans and their institutions as they ought to be, not as they actually were."[11]

If Hoover had difficulty using the metaphor of efficiency for his purposes when he tried to smuggle it into conservative rhetoric, so too the social language of social bonds and human nature proved to be unsuitable when progressives tried to use it for their purposes in the early 1920s. The prewar urban progressives had tried to counteract the isolating individualism of the urban environment by a nostalgia for the rural, small town, neighborly, participatory democracy and its politics of deference that they remembered. They had also insisted that standards of personal morality be carried into public affairs. Progressive educators had focused on the plasticity of social nurture rather than the supposed rigidity of biological nature. They looked upon the school as a means to forge new social bonds to hold society together. Political theorists had tried to devise ways to articulate the common welfare that would overcome the alleged divisiveness of partisan politics, ethnocultural loyalties, and economic class. A new generation of political realists, however, were tempered by the failures of prewar urban progressivism, the excesses of wartime propaganda, and the postwar repression of dissent. Such theorists were coming to some sobering, tentative conclusions. Irrationality, emotion, and misinformation ruled the day according to this interpretation. As Robert Westbrook has observed: "[T]hey argued that it was best to strictly limit government by the people and to redefine democracy as, by and large, government for the people by enlightened and responsible elites." Hoover's notion of functional groups—workers, farmers, businessmen, government experts—held together by voluntary cooperation and submitting to government coordination for the sake of greater productivity and social harmony was a mixture of progressive nostalgia and technocratic, elite innovation that he used to confront a divided society.[12]

If Hoover used the progressive social language of efficiency and the conservative rhetoric of individualism in his attempt to restructure business-government relations in the interest of refurbishing liberty, there was a simultaneous debate going on among women activists about the meaning of equality. The issues touched on the question of restructuring business but in a tangential way. The primary question was whether equality meant that women and men were *equal and identical* and, therefore, ought to be treated the same or did it mean that they were *equal but different* and, thus, ought to be accorded separate treatment or protection in those areas where the differences were relevant to public purposes? Academic orthodoxy at the turn of the century had held that differences between the sexes were biological in origin, and, therefore, both inevitable and unchangeable or capable only of slow, evolutionary change. However, pioneering research by women in anthropology, sociology, psychology, and ethnology in the first two decades of the century argued that differences were more social or cultural in origin and, therefore, neither inevitable nor immutable. The implications for the new feminism of the women associated with the National Woman's Party (NWP) was that, potentially at least, men and women were *equal and identical* in essential characteristics. Laws were, thus, *not* primarily instrumental *means* to overcome disabilities; rather, they were formal acknowledgements or symbols of such equal status. Hence the emphasis was on *removing* certain barriers to equality in the law according to Alice Paul of the NWP. She also admitted the thrust of Crystal Eastman's and Charlotte Perkins Gilman's radical analysis that, unless undergirded by economic and social *independence*, mere legal equality would be inadequate. On the other hand, Florence Kelley, of the National Consumers' League, stressed the *differences* in the factual situations of men and women; therefore, working women, particularly mothers or mothers-to-be, needed "special protection." For those who shared this view of men and women as equal but different, the law was instrumental, a means of achieving equitable treatment. The necessity to work outside the home, moreover, did not free women from the bonds of familiar *interdependence*. The line between these intellectual positions did not initially run between organizations but rather within each, and the conflict could rage even within a single individual.[13]

The issues that clarified the debate and drew the intellectual lines closer to organizational boundaries were the Sheppard-Towner Bill and the proposed equal rights amendment. In 1920 the newly organized National League of Women Voters drew up its agenda for action:

1. Sheppard-Towner (Maternity and Infancy Protection) [Bill].
2. Constitutional amendment to abolish child labor.
3. Adequate funding for the Children's Bureau.
4. A federal Department of Education.
5. Federal aid to combat illiteracy and to raise basic teachers' salaries.
6. Compulsory civic education in the schools.
7. Federal regulation of food marketing and distribution.
8. Federal aid for home economics training.

9.   Women representatives on all federal commissions.

10.   A federal-state employment service with a women's department (headed by a woman).

11.   An end to discrimination against women in the Civil Service.

12.   Public funding for sex hygiene education.

13.   American citizenship for American-born women who married alien men and identical naturalization procedures for men and women.[14]

Many of the issues had long histories of agitation and support by women's organizations behind them.

The Children's Bureau, for example, had been recommended in 1903 by social settlement workers and finally established in 1912, with Julia Lathrop as its head. The Children's Bureau had immediately launched investigations into the causes of maternal and infant mortality. It found that 80 percent of expectant mothers received no trained care or expert advice. Julia Lathrop drafted a bill to provide for federal aid for maternal and infant health training. She toured the states that had woman suffrage in 1917 to generate support for it. The bill, modeled on the Smith-Lever Agricultural Extension Act, would have provided federal money to the states to conduct the maternal and infant care. Congresswoman Jeannette Rankin introduced the bill in July 1918, but it languished with little support from the Wilson administration and expired at the end of the Congressional session.[15]

The enfranchisement of women by the Nineteenth Amendment and the political uncertainties that this introduced into the 1920 presidential and congressional elections breathed new life into the effort. Senator Morris Sheppard (Democrat of Texas) and Congressman Horace Towner (Republican of Iowa) reintroduced the bill in the Sixty-sixth Congress. They proposed an initial appropriation of $4 million with $10,000 to each state to help start the program. Nevertheless, the bill remained locked in committee from May to December 1920, in spite of endorsement by the Democratic, Socialist, Prohibitionist, and Farmer-Labor Parties. It also had the strong personal endorsement of the Republican presidential candidate, Senator Warren G. Harding of Ohio. The Senate committee finally passed the bill on 18 December 1920, and the House committee cut the appropriation to $1 million but did send the measure on to the Rules Committee, where it promptly died. President-elect Harding promised women's groups that he would bring the measure up in a special session along with pressing tariff and budget matters as the economy stumbled through the severe postwar depression.[16]

The Sheppard-Towner Bill, and the whole complex of issues concerning infant mortality, child labor, maternity health care, and protective labor legislation for women and children encompassed a wide variety of beliefs about women and equality. A conservative, or cultural traditionalist, who might not believe in the equality of men and women, could, nevertheless, vote for such a bill out of a paternalistic sense of the need to protect "helpless" children and "delicate" mothers. A women's rights advocate, who played a reform role and who believed that men and women were equal but different, could support the bill because of crucial gender role differences. Thus, maternalist rhetoric could enhance the images of women's child-bearing capacity, child-nurturing role, and special moral sensitivity. A feminist, who played a radical role and who believed that men and women were equal and identical, would have a harder time supporting these bills. She could make an exception regarding the proposal as a temporary measure until women achieved greater legal equality and economic independence, or she could choose to remain silent on the issue.[17]

The hearings on the resubmitted Sheppard-Towner Bill in July 1921 did not examine such questions in depth, however. The Senate passed the bill by a vote of 63 to 7 and sent it to the House. The chairman of the House Committee on Interstate Commerce and Foreign Commerce, Samuel Winslow, a die-hard antisuffragist, allowed a continual parade of hostile witnesses—antisuffragists, states' rights advocates, medical lobbyists, and extreme conservatives—to prolong the proceedings. The Women's Joint Congressional Committee, a lobbying effort that represented ten women's organizations who claimed over ten million members, put pressure on reluctant congressmen. No one knew whether newly enfranchised women voters would vote as a bloc or not. Nervous Republicans looked to President Harding for guidance. Supposedly the women's vote had been one of the factors in his lopsided victory. Harding continued to support the Sheppard-Towner Bill, and it passed the House by a vote of 279–39. The final version was weaker than the earlier Rankin proposal, but at least it had passed.[18]

The rationale for such protective legislation as the Sheppard-Towner Act, maximum hours for working women, minimum wage laws, and prohibitions on child labor had been developed over the years by people such as Florence Kelley, Louis Brandeis, Julia Lathrop, and Felix Frankfurter to circumvent the Supreme Court's limited liberty of contract doctrine and to exploit the court's exception based on the police power of the state as developed in *Muller v. Oregon* (1908). Such "sociological" or instrumental jurisprudence took into account the consequences of the law as well as the logic of such constitutional guarantees as due process and privileges or immunities. Sometimes advocates of protective legislation used maternalist images and rhetoric; sometimes they used the language of equal rights. That is, equality arguments said that women as citizens should have the *same rights* as men to vote, own property, enter into contracts, sue and be sued, or serve on juries. Such rights should be granted *regardless* of their gender. Technically speaking, on the other hand, some advocates used equity arguments. Equity notions said that, because men and women were different in important biological, social, or cultural factors, the law could treat women *as a group* "unequally" or equitably *according* to their gender because of the greater good for society that would result. A mixture of "equality" and "equity" (or "justice") arguments might be logically inconsistent, but it had been effective in the final stages of the suffrage campaign. Such arguments had helped to bring a diverse spectrum of women into support of the vote.[19]

But the suffrage campaign was over. Alice Paul, head of the National Woman's Party, was initially concerned with *eliminating* those common law restrictions that treated women *differently* than men in order to establish their legal identity. From November 1920 to May 1921 she had solicited advice from her contacts. She had been persuaded of the need to draft a constitutional amendment to secure the goal of equality before the law. The language of the various drafts of the proposed equal rights amendment set off a prolonged and bitter feud between "protectionists" and "formalists" that threatened the unity of the women's rights movement. By November 1922 the die was cast. The United States Court of Appeals struck down a minimum wage law for women. Paul, and National Woman's Party members, believed that an equal rights amendment and liberty of contract doctrines would adequately protect women's *freedom to* pursue their own interest. Florence Kelley, and members of such organizations as the National League of Women Voters, feared such doctrines. They believed that an equal rights amendment would not provide women with meaningful liberty as *freedom from* exploitation. The Supreme Court majority, in *Adkins v. Children's Hospital* (1923), affirmed the Court of Appeals' ruling: a minimum wage law for women violated liberty of contract.[20]

In summary, between 1917 and 1920 many women had united behind the goal of enfranchisement even though they disagreed, sometimes vehemently, on the means to achieve it. Between 1920 and 1922 women activists divided not only on questions of means—whether to work in partisan or nonpartisan fashion, whether to seek integration into male-dominated political institutions or separation in their own single-sex organizations—but also on the goals of feminism and maternalism, the meaning of equality, the requirements of justice for women, and whether liberty rested on similarities or differences between men and women. To the extent that the National League of Women Voters and allied women's organizations that supported protective legislation argued from the position that men and women were equal but different, they fulfilled the role of reformers. They accepted the current meanings of core values and measured recent events against them. (Some were even operating from a modified Victorian "separate spheres" philosophy.) The separation between the gender spheres was not simply private versus public as it had been in the Victorian Era but also public-as-protective versus private-as-exploitive in the 1920s. Ironically, those who fulfilled the radical role of proposing new values or meanings for current ones seemed to be moving beyond the group-conscious feminism of the prewar period and toward a redefined individualism. In the dialogue between dependence, independence, and interdependence, Alice Paul and her NWP colleagues rejected the first option vehemently, embraced the second firmly, and increasingly ignored the third. Furthermore, as Rosalyn Terborg-Penn has noted, "the [National Woman's Party] felt no obligation to defend the rights of black women." Interdependence was a race issue in their view and not necessarily a gender issue. The progressive languages of social bonds and human nature had been stretched to their limits. In the process, a dynamic of legal controversy had been unleashed that would challenge the meaning of equality for the next decade.[21]

The institutions and inspirations of progressivism lived on in the early 1920s in such development as the Plumb Plan, Hoover's attempts to restructure business along the lines of voluntary cooperation and government coordination (but not control), in the Sheppard-Towner Act, and in the debate over the proposed equal rights amendment. All this happened in spite of the reputation of the Harding administration for its emphasis on laissez-faire economics, political conservatism, immigration restriction, and instances of constitutionalized inequality. There were obvious setbacks for the advocates of women's rights and the regulation of business in the period 1900 to 1924; some the most significant setbacks came from court rulings. Supreme Court decisions such as the restrictions on trade associations and labor unions and the overturning of minimum wage laws for women in *Adkins v. Children's Hospital* indicated that the formalist view of liberty of contract was stronger than it had been a decade before. Whether the heritage of progressivism among men and women in confronting claims to equality and justice in civil rights would suffer similar institutional and legal restrictions in the 1920s is the next topic for investigation.

15

Which Way for Civil Rights? Separation and Cooperation in the Jazz Age, 1920–1928

The year 1920 was a somber one for people of good will—black and white, men and women, North and South—who reviewed recent events. The signs of the time were ominous. The Ku Klux Klan had been reestablished in 1915 by William J. Simmons, a former minister, promoter of fraternal orders, and a businessman. The order grew modestly until two public relations experts, Edward Young Clarke and Elizabeth Tyler, applied the recruiting techniques they had learned promoting the Anti-Saloon League and the Red Cross. From 5,000 members in 1920, the organization would claim 5 million members by 1925. To the traditional theme of white supremacy, the Klan added hypernationalism, anticorruption, and hostility to Catholics, Jews, and recent immigrants. Another sign of the times was the prevalence of lynching of blacks. In 1916, four whites were lynched while fifty blacks were so murdered; the numbers dipped in 1917, but in 1918, four whites and sixty blacks were lynched. Mob violence against African Americans was frequently urban in location, but in rural Arkansas in late 1919 blacks had organized to secure higher prices for cotton grown by tenant farmers and higher wages for cotton pickers. White landowners clashed with the blacks; five whites and approximately two hundred blacks were killed. Federal troops had to intervene. Seventy-three African Americans were subsequently indicted for murder; sixty-seven received jail terms and twelve received death sentences. No whites were indicted.[1] This chapter will examine separation and cooperation as strategies to deal with the strained relations between the races, and to protect the civil rights of African Americans, during the period 1920 to 1928.

Where in the plethora of organizations, competing ideologies, and cultural conflict in the 1920s was there a secure basis for civil rights? Was it the group or the individual? Race or class? What was the best means to protect civil rights in an era of governmental repression and political conservatism? One option was racial self-separation, which was advocated by Marcus Garvey and his Universal Negro Improvement Association (UNIA). Many professionals, recent southern migrants, and Caribbean immigrants followed Garvey. They all had one thing in common: a culturally radical rejection of the psychological sense of racial inferiority stamped upon their psyches by the predominately white culture. They resonated to Garvey's clarion call for black pride: "Up, You Mighty Race!" He taught a generation to think of themselves not as members of a despised minority within the United States or colonial empires but as members of a dynamic race equal to other races on the world scene. Garvey even dreamed of a black-owned steamship line to facilitate an eventual back-to-Africa movement.

Not all African Americans agreed with Garvey. In September 1919 Garvey announced that his proposed Black Star Line was about to purchase its first vessel and encouraged all his supporters to buy stock in the venture. The *Chicago Defender* newspaper, edited by Robert S. Abbott, attacked Garvey and sniped that he was not even an American citizen. "His organization [UNIA], too, is composed mainly of foreigners," the editorial continued, "and certainly does not represent one iota of the American Race man[.]" When Garvey attempted to speak in Chicago in September 1919, a detective promptly arrested him on a warrant charging him with selling stocks without a proper license under a recently passed law. Freed on $1,000 bond, Garvey was subsequently brought to trial. Federal agents, who had been following Garvey's activities for some time, noted in their report the conflict between Garvey and the *Chicago Defender*. At the trial, Garvey's lawyer entered a guilty plea; Garvey was fined $100 plus court costs.[2]

In August 1920 Garvey's UNIA held a convention that adopted a Declaration of Rights of the Negro Peoples of the World. Some of the numbered points in the Declaration of Rights provided a glimpse into the meaning of key values for the Garvey movement:

1. Be it known to all men that whereas all men are created equal and entitled to the rights of life, liberty and the pursuit of happiness, and because of this we . . . , do declare all men, women and children of our blood throughout the world free denizens, and do claim them as free citizens of Africa, the Motherland of all Negroes.

5. We assert that the Negro is entitled to even-handed justice before all courts of law and equity in whatever country he may be found, and when this is denied him on account of his race or color such denial is an insult to the race as a whole and should be resented by the entire body of Negroes.

16. We believe all men should live in peace one with the other, but when races and nations provoke the ire of other races and nations by attempting to infringe upon their rights[,] war becomes inevitable, and the attempt in any way to free one's self or protect one's rights or heritage becomes justifiable.

41. We believe that any limited liberty which deprives one of the complete rights and prerogatives of full citizenship is but a modified form of slavery.

46. We demand of all men to do unto us as we would do unto them, in the name of justice; and we cheerfully accord to all men all the rights we claim herein for ourselves.

54. We want all men to know that we shall maintain and contend for the freedom and equality of every man, woman and child of our race, with our lives, our fortunes and our sacred honor.[3]

Liberty, equality and justice were invoked as values, but given radically different meanings than current American understandings of these core values. They were cast in terms of extranational racial citizenship, black nationalism, and group-based claims. Given the contemporary treatment of African Americans in the United States, the document also sounded a warning note to American society.

Attention must be turned to the context of the times and the divisions *within* the black communities in order to understand the Garvey movement. The period of rapid growth of UNIA, 1919–20, coincided with the onslaught of a postwar depression, the wave of lynching, mob violence, and official harassment directed against blacks, "reds," and recent immigrants, and the growth of the Ku Klux Klan. Garvey had to fight a two-front war against white officials, on the one hand, who suspected his movement of planning violence and organizing paramilitary defense forces, and black critics, on the other hand, particularly in the *Chicago Defender* and the NAACP. They disagreed with Garvey's separatist nationalism, back-to-Africa dreams, narrow version of black capitalism, and the steamship scheme. Garvey could also be his own worst enemy at times. His rhetoric could be excessively macho (but feminists such as Ida Wells-Barnett supported UNIA). Dictatorial, sensitive to criticism from within UNIA, seemingly incompetent in financial and business matters, attuned more to the colonial situations in the Caribbean, Central America, and Africa than to the constitutional realities of the American scene, Garvey squandered massive amounts of goodwill and capital in support of the Black Star shipping line. In February 1922 Garvey and three of his Black Star officials were indicted on twelve charges of fraudulent use of the mails in the sale of stocks. When Garvey entered into negotiations with the leaders of the Ku Klux Klan on the basis of parallel ideologies of separation of the races, and when a number of Garvey critics were either threatened or intimidated, a group of prominent black leaders arose against him. This group included Robert S. Abbott of the *Chicago Defender*, William Pickens of the NAACP, and Chandler Owen, the socialist. They sent a letter in January 1923 to the United States attorney general urging that he disband UNIA and vigorously prosecute the mail fraud case. In May 1923 Garvey was brought to trial, found guilty on shaky evidence, fined $1,000 and sentenced to five years in a federal prison.[4]

Self-separation as a political, economic, and cultural strategy during a period of rapid change was not confined to the black communities that rallied to Garvey and the UNIA. In a parallel fashion, the revival of the Ku Klux Klan exemplified similar tendencies among some white communities. In the 1920s contemporary liberal writers and civil liberties advocates dismissed the Klan as just another aberration of the Roaring Twenties, a reaction against modern life by isolated, ill-educated, and insecure rural folk and small-town bigots. Later generations of political scientists, sociologists, and historians portrayed it as "a complex of political, social, and moral attitudes [that] established itself, compounded of nativism, fundamentalism, prohibitionism, and a conviction that the American character resided in the farm and hinterland town." Strongest in the South, Midwest, and Northwest, the Klan found supporters in urban areas as well as rural but seemed to self-destruct after 1924 by internal bickering, corruption, and partial success of its political agenda.[5]

Recent social history studies of the Klan in the 1920s have revised some of these older historical interpretations. As historian Michael Kasin has noted: "The principal argument of this [revised interpretation] is a straightforward one: the KKK of the 1920s was not the bastion of displaced, provincial failures portrayed by most observers and scholars since H. L. Mencken. It appealed to the normative beliefs of ordinary, native-born white Protestants and primarily sought to exert those beliefs within its own ethno-religious community. The Klan's racist, nativist, and often violent rhetoric was a poor guide to its behavior."[6] Kazin also pointed to studies of women in the Klan (WKKK), which had chapters in two-thirds of the states. They show that the WKKK "encompassed thousands of women who viewed the organization as furthering the same reforms—Prohibition, woman suffrage, and a moral housecleaning of public life—that most self-described 'progressives' had favored before World War I." Klan women also supported consumer boycotts of Catholic- and Jewish-owned businesses and kept alive antiprostitution drives. It was precisely this harking back to prewar conditions and invocation of older understandings of values that marked the Klan as a ritual withdrawal and renewal mechanism in the face of new postwar realities.[7]

On what basis have historians concluded that Marcus Garvey's appeals to black racial pride, separatism, and self-development projects in the Universal Negro Improvement Association were culturally radical but overall a positive development? On what basis have they concluded that William Simmons's, Edward Young Clarke's, or Elizabeth Tyler's appeals during the same time period to racial pride, white supremacy, and community control in the Ku Klux Klan were a ritual withdrawal and renewal option but a negative development overall? Both organizations used similar techniques (or *means*) to promote their causes: parades in uniform and regalia, newspapers, fraternal insurance programs, special music and ritual, and political pressure. While some Klans engaged in, or condoned, violence outside the law, UNIA members also advocated forceful self-defense and remained conspicuously quiet about violence directed against their critics within the black community. If historical attention is shifted from the *means* to an examination of the *goals* and their relationship to institutional core *values*, then the basis of the historians' judgments becomes clearer. If the litmus test of the meaning of core values—liberty, equality, and justice—is applied to the case, some significant differences emerge. Garvey argued that if *both* races were to *equally* enjoy full liberty, then they must ultimately separate. The Garvey movement's values as spelled out in the Declaration of Rights of the Negro Peoples of the World were similar to the core values of American society but shifted their basis from the individual to the group: race, racial community, or "nation." It also played a positive role in rejecting the white cultural premise of racial inequality of minorities that had hampered black consciousness since the failure of Reconstruction.[8]

The Ku Klux Klan, on the other hand, proclaimed its adherence to America's core values—liberty, equality, justice—but narrowed their focus to their own group. Liberty for whom? The Klan rhetoric excluded Catholics, Jews, and certain immigrant groups as well as blacks. Equality for whom? The Klan engaged in economic boycotts and "unfair competition" with local white insurance salesmen through fraternal insurance as part of Klan membership. They put pressure on school systems to fire "undesirable" educators. They divided local communities into "superior" (white, Protestant, "dry") and "inferior" (black, immigrant, Catholic or Jewish, "wet") groups. The Klan also insisted on elaborate public displays of the American flag and enforced public respect for it, but did they practice "liberty and justice *for all*"? The resort to whipping, tar-and-feather tactics, threats and violence, political control of local police, and intimidation of juries and courts undermined the standards of justice. Through ritual evocation of a rural, small town, commercial, frugal, temperate, homogeneous Protestant past (that had, in fact, never existed in such pristine purity), they sought to hold on to the past. Such activities did not *narrow* the gap between America's core values and current realities; rather they *widened* the gap and tended to denigrate the very values, and flag, they invoked.

If UNIA defined the radical response of some African Americans to their situation in the early 1920s, and the KKK represented the ritual withdrawal and renewal option on the part of many whites, the NAACP and other interracial groups represented the reform response for those whites and blacks who supported some version of equal civil rights. Their conceptions of what constituted civil rights were shaped largely by events. For example, in 1918 the problems of black migration from the South to the North, the racial tensions that resulted, and the revival of the Ku Klux Klan had shocked a number of white moderates and African American religious and educational leaders. In December 1918 a group of moderate southern white men, with the support of some northern white philanthropic foundations, created the Commission on Interracial Cooperation. Paternalistic, ameliorative, and cautious, the CIC challenged neither segregation nor the prevalent white fear of social equality. Nevertheless, as historian Jacquelyn Dowd Hall has pointed out, the CIC was concerned "that white violence could have extremely disruptive social consequences [for the South] if blacks fought back, turned to the federal government for protection, or chose migration as an alternative to victimization." The South as a region could lose not only its cheap labor supply but its political autonomy as well if the federal government intervened.[9]

Concern among white church women also prompted efforts to deal with the strained relations between the races. In 1919 ten prominent African American women associated with "colored women's clubs," YWCA, and educational institutions addressed a statement to the Women's Missionary Council of the American Missionary Association: "First of all, we wish to express our sincere gratification in the fact that race relations in the South have advanced to the place where the white women of the South are conscious of the part which colored women must play in any successful effort to adjust the unhappy conditions which have distressed the hearts of all lovers of right and justice, and dangerously threaten the common welfare and the safety of the Nation."[10] The statement included detailed practical suggestions for mutual reform efforts in the areas of domestic service, child welfare, Jim Crow travel, education, woman suffrage, antilynching, and press coverage of racial matters.[11]

The NAACP, meanwhile, was pursuing its own strategy to combat lynching and mob violence. First, it had launched a sustained lobbying effort in support of the Dyer Bill, a proposed federal antilynching law. Second, NAACP officials joined the efforts of two Arkansas lawyers, one white and one black, to secure justice for those convicted in the Arkansas riot cases. The hope of the NAACP leadership was that its dual efforts would mobilize support among African Americans. They were somewhat cautious, therefore, in responding to the invitation of the Commission on Interracial Cooperation. Some women activists had also been cool to the CIC because it did not recognize their efforts or role in interracial dialogue. In February 1920 prominent African American leaders, including Robert R. Moton of Tuskegee Institute, John Hope of Morehouse College, and Bishop R. E. Jones of New Orleans, were added to the CIC. This eased some suspicions among African American activists and earned the endorsement of the CIC by W. E. B. Du Bois and the NAACP. The creation of a Women's Committee by the CIC also eased tension. The Women's Committee tapped the wellsprings of the Protestant social gospel (particularly in the Methodist Episcopal Church, South), the activism of the YWCA, and the leadership of the National Association of Colored Women (NACW).[12]

The CIC Women's Committee sponsored a conference for southern women at Memphis, Tennessee, in October 1920. Four southern African American women—Margaret Murray Washington, Charlotte Hawkins Brown, Elizabeth Ross Haynes, and Jennie Dee Moton—addressed the ninety-some southern white women and reiterated their concerns, which were similar to the 1919 statement to the Women's Missionary Council. Charlotte Hawkins Brown of North Carolina electrified the audience with a frank recital of the humiliation she had suffered at the hands of a Jim Crow mob on her way to Memphis. "Will you just put yourself in my place," she pleaded. "Just be colored for a few moments, and see yourself sitting down in a seat, helpless, with twelve young white men sitting around."[13] The result was a "breakthrough" experience. Historian Jacquelyn Dowd Hall has captured the significance and meaning of the event: "Confronted by proud and articulate black women, exhorted passionately, yet in acceptable generalities and in the language of a shared religious tradition, to accept responsibility for the plight of women whose aspirations were so much like their own, the white women present responded with an outpouring of emotion that would become the paradigm for—and often the only accomplishment of—interracial meetings for a decade [1920–30]."[14] But emotional repentance could also revivify language and enhance communication. Whereas the prewar white progressive social workers, social scientists, and educators had used the seemingly neutral, objective, and scientific social language of human nature and social bonds to shape the conduct and culture of immigrants and "minorities" in their own middle-class image, the postwar women of the CIC, YWCA, and NACW found in the empathetic, emotional, and religious language of their southern communal traditions a new basis for interracial cooperation and tentative tolerance amidst the ritualistic aspects of their efforts.[15]

Added to this religious language of social cohesion was the cooperation and ritualized interactions of the women activists who ran the League of Women Voters' citizenship education programs, who lobbied for child welfare and labor protection legislation, and who worked within the CIC, YWCA, and religious institutions for genuine autonomy and equality for African American women. In 1922 African American women formed a Committee of Anti-Lynching Crusaders to support the NAACP's campaign. However, while the Dyer Bill was before the House of Representatives in 1922 and passed in 1923 (231 to 119), it died in the Senate. Admittedly lukewarm Republican support faded after the fall elections and southern Democrats threatened to filibuster. All was not lost, however. The Supreme Court in the Arkansas riot case, *Moore v. Dempsey* (1923), held that the "mob-dominated trial" had violated the due process clause of the Fourteenth Amendment. Justice Oliver Wendell Holmes Jr., delivered the opinion of the Supreme Court: "[I]f the case is that the whole proceeding is a mask—that counsel, jury and judge were swept to the fatal end by an irresistible wave of public passion, and that the State Courts failed to correct the wrong, [then no argument of necessity or minor correction] can prevent this Court from securing to the petitioners their constitutional rights." *Moore v. Dempsey* marked a crucial point in the gradual movement of the Supreme Court toward a stricter use of the Fourteenth Amendment to protect the rights of citizens from state or local actions or from failure to act to protect their rights.[16]

Even though Marcus Garvey's movement declined following his imprisonment and the number of lynchings also declined in the late 1920s in spite of the defeat of the Dyer Bill, the issues of racial separation and interracial cooperation remained alive. This can be seen in two incidents in 1927–28: A. Philip Randolph's efforts to organize an all-black trade union and Herbert Hoover's involvement with Mississippi River flood victims in the South. The situation of African American workers in the 1920s was symbolized by the plight of the railroad sleeping car porters. The Pullman Company had set up an employee representation plan under the Transportation Act of 1920. Given the confusion in labor union circles following the failure of the Plumb Plan for government ownership and cooperative operations of the railroads, many of the sleeping car porters had agreed to accept the Pullman Company plan. But the Pullman Plan made no provision for genuine collective bargaining. After pro forma discussions, the company would present a "take it or leave it" wage offer. In 1924 an attempt to organize a bona fide labor union failed. Disgusted with the Pullman wage offer for 1925, one of the elected representatives under the Pullman employee representation plan, Ashley L. Totten, approached the only man in Harlem he believed could help the porters break out of the deadlock—A. Philip Randolph.[17]

Randolph was one of the several prewar socialists who had drifted away from socialist radicalism during the 1920s, cooperated briefly with Marcus Garvey's Universal Negro Improvement Association, and then became a critic of Garvey's movement. With Randolph's radical dreams smashed, his career as a journalist in the doldrums, his belief in Garveyism over, he was receptive to Totten's suggestion that he organize an independent union of sleeping car porters. The passage by Congress of the Railway Labor Act in 1926 seemed to create a favorable opportunity. The legislation provided for joint conferences between employers and employees' representatives, for elections without "interference, influence, or coercion," and for negotiations on such matters as pay rates, work rules, and working conditions. The law also provided for a Board of Mediation to settle any unresolved disputes.[18]

Building up a base of membership proved to be the more feasible part of Randolph's task; keeping it together as a union—the Brotherhood of Sleeping Car Porters—turned out to be more difficult. In December 1926 the Brotherhood claimed approximately 5,000 members out of the estimated 11,000 porters who worked the Pullman cars on the nation's trains. The membership rose to over 6,000 in May 1928, when Randolph threatened a strike against the recalcitrant company. The Pullman Company, which claimed all along that it had an employee representative plan already and that the Brotherhood did not represent the majority of its porters, refused to arbitrate and doubted that the Brotherhood could disrupt its service. The Board of Mediation agreed with the company and declined to intervene or to invoke provisions of the Railway Labor Act for a presidential emergency board. William Green, president of the American Federation of Labor (successor to Samuel Gompers), was sympathetic to the porters' cause, but urged Randolph to call off the strike. The Brotherhood was not strong enough to win, he said. Randolph reluctantly agreed.[19]

The whole incident clarified for Randolph a number of points. In July 1928 the Catholic Industrial Conference of Cincinnati invited him to speak but withdrew the invitation when it learned of his radical past. In a letter to the Brotherhood member who would substitute for him on this occasion, Randolph wrote: "One thing I would stress very fundamentally . . . and that is never again will Negroes permit white people to select their leaders for them. I would make it very emphatic that upon that principle we shall not compromise, not only with respect to the Pullman porters but with any Negro movement. . . . Of course, we want the support of everybody we can get, but not at the price of surrendering principles that are vital to our existence."[20] These were also the principles upon which William Green convinced the AFL to allow the Brotherhood to affiliate with the AFL as an independent union in 1928, thus bypassing the jurisdictional claims of the segregated Hotel and Restaurant Employees' Alliance, a rival union.[21]

Beset on the right by the Pullman Company, which fired, suspended or demoted many of the union members and local leaders, the Brotherhood was also attacked from the left by some of Randolph's old radical compatriots who were now allied with the communist-front American Negro Labor Congress. However, like Susan B. Anthony and Elizabeth Cady Stanton in 1869 when they created a woman-directed, separatist suffrage organization, Randolph had learned some bitter lessons: black workers would have to go it alone to form their own unions, elect their own representatives, pay their own bills (not depend on white foundations for grants or on white unions for loans), repudiate the efforts of radical communists to infiltrate their organizations or create rival ones, and insist on equality within the predominantly white trade union movement. All of the passion of his radical days of the prewar era, all the pride of black separatism and cultural awareness of his Marcus Garvey phase, all his renewed respect for the role of the churches and religious language in the black community, and all the practical experience of his union organizing, strike leadership, and anticommunist activities would come together in his subsequent prose, oratory, and role as a civil rights leader. While justice might be denied at the moment, independence could be earned daily by individual self-sacrifice. Equality could be demanded and defended by group effort within the framework of the institutions of American society.[22]

These changes among civil rights advocates would ultimately touch Herbert Hoover and involve him in their fate. This development began in the spring of 1927 when a devastating flood swept the entire Mississippi River basin. Over one and a half million people were displaced. With his reputation as a humanitarian in World War I and in the Soviet Union in the early 1920s, Herbert Hoover was called upon to organize and coordinate a massive public-private relief effort. Soon disturbing reports began to surface in the African American press, particularly the *Chicago De-*

fender, and in reports to Hoover by black Republican leaders in the South. In some areas, local Red Cross supplies were given to white landowners who used them to hold their sharecroppers in virtual peonage. African American tenant farmers were held in some relief camps under armed guard to prevent their leaving the South. The NAACP dispatched investigators to confirm the reports and filed a protest with Senator Arthur Capper of Kansas, a Hoover supporter.[23]

At first Hoover tended to dismiss the reports, to defend the Red Cross, and to issue general instructions to correct any abuses. Persistent pressure from African American leaders, however, caused him to appoint an all-black investigating commission. As head of the team, Hoover selected Robert R. Moton, the principal of Tuskegee Institute and symbolic inheritor of Booker T. Washington's mantle of leadership (at least in the eyes of northern philanthropists and Republican politicians). Because NAACP representatives were not included on the investigating team, Moton was mistrusted by the NAACP leadership, by Monroe Trotter of the militant National Equal Rights League, and by the *Chicago Defender*. Nevertheless, the Moton Commission's report was critical of abuses found in the relief camps, particularly the role of white national guard troops, and recommended a number of changes that Hoover immediately adopted. Historian Donald J. Lisio has summarized the meaning of this experience for Hoover: "Having worked closely with black leaders for the first time, Hoover had come to believe that 'full interracial cooperation' was both desirable and necessary for future programs. He looked to the prestigious voluntary organization, the Commission on Interracial Cooperation [CIC], to achieve significant future progress."[24]

The Mississippi Valley flood and the Moton Commission report expanded Hoover's range of experience and touched his sympathies, but it did not alter his values or change his favorite progressive means to achieve them. Economic independence via black ownership of land became Hoover's primary goal; practical education on the Tuskegee model, private philanthropy, and political development of a two-party system in the South were the means by which he hoped to achieve it. In effect, Hoover had privately adopted the model advocated by the Freedman's Bureau in the Reconstruction Era and harnessed it to Progressive Era values. Justice and efficiency were the primary values, but he made little mention of equality. Therein lay the problem with Hoover's overall approach to civil rights. The unspoken assumption was that liberty was the great desideratum, but liberty meant initially *freedom from* "undue" government (public) interference and, therefore, a primary reliance on private effort supplemented by philanthropic aid. Liberty also meant *freedom to* pursue one's own self-interest in voluntary cooperation with others. Whether dedication to these values could frame workable solutions—for southern black sharecroppers, for northern white businessmen, for unemployed men and women of both races, for militant veterans, for women and children in need, for every sector of American society—would soon be tested in the fire of the Great Depression.[25]

In summary, the strained relations between the races in the period 1920 to 1928 evoked a debate among those concerned with the civil rights of African Americans. Should they recognize that racial interests were so disparate that only self-separation could ensure dignity and advancement—either permanently as in Garveyism or temporarily and strategically as in Randolph's black trade unionism? Or did the precariousness of the situation require that interracial cooperation or, at least, mutual communication was necessary to protect the self-interest of both races—either institutionally as in the CIC Women's Committee conferences for southern women or governmentally as in Hoover's efforts to work with the Moton Commission? The UNIA and KKK had frequently invoked similar core values but meant totally different things by them as their different roles—radical and ritual withdrawal and renewal—would indicate. Randolph's Brotherhood of Sleeping Car Porters adopted a reform stance but had to confront the radical option of the communist-backed American Negro Labor Congress. There were, thus, tensions among black leaders as well as tensions between whites and blacks.

African American leaders also probed issues deeper than simply the best *means* to achieve change. They also explored current values. As W. E. B. Du Bois perceived, a reform stance must appeal beyond equality of opportunity to a demand for justice. And justice had to be understood not simply as favors granted by paternalistic or patronizing power out of a sense of charity or duty. Rather, justice must be seen as a matter of rational rights recognized by law and undergirded by equal participation in the political process. In appealing to the heritage of equal protection of the law in the Fourteenth Amendment in the Dyer Bill and in petitioning for due process of justice for the Arkansas riot prisoners, the NAACP had touched on another pertinent fact. None of the social languages of the Progressive Era were particularly sympathetic to the plight of the black community in the 1920s. Senator Robert La Follette, the advocate of antimonopoly, was personally supportive of civil rights, but other whites who espoused the same rhetoric were not. The prewar language of inclusive social bonds and human nature had been twisted and narrowed by wartime superpatriotism and the postwar red scare. It was further distorted by the Ku Klux Klan and immigrant restriction legislation into an exclusionist rhetoric of ritual retreat in defense of a conservative power structure and a prewar pietistic moral code. The language of social efficiency, fortified by the supposedly scientific data of wartime intelligence testing on army recruits, simply reinforced racist assumptions hidden in the eugenics movement and immigration restrictions.[26]

The NAACP, the CIC Women's Committee, and the antilynch crusaders, 1920–28, needed to articulate social languages that would inspire supporters and guide actions, that would provide positive black identities and appeal to white consciences, and that would act as a lever for lobbying efforts and judicial encounters with entrenched doctrines. Here, perhaps, was the most difficult task of the intellectuals, artists, and writers of the famous Harlem Renaissance of the 1920s. "The task of Negro intellectuals, as they had addressed themselves to the issue of race in American life," historian Nathan I. Huggins pointed out, "has been to delineate Negro character and personality in the American context. . . . The problem was to define the Negro as a part of the American future; few were willing to touch the American past." Huggins highlighted the dilemma: If the black intellectual concluded that there was no place for him in the American Dream (or future), then the intellectuals were irrelevant to the needs of the black "masses." For the "masses" had no practical escape from American society, no expatriate flight to France in the 1920s, no elite, artistic withdrawal into the liminoid space of the cabarets, night clubs, and dance halls and their artificial black-white communitas. If, on the other hand, the black intellectuals concluded that there was a place for blacks in the American Dream (or future), because they were similar to or identical in nature with their white neighbors, then what happened to their claims of difference, their African identity, black "soul," and distinctive culture?[27]

Furthermore, in order to demonstrate *individual* achievement, as the American Dream required, African American intellectuals had to appeal to *group* consciousness and a hypersensitivity to *collective* behavior. If every individual achievement was to be touted as an example of racial merit, "a credit to the race," then did not every individual failure indicate a group failure as well? Du Bois's divided soul notion had come back to draw the color line in their consciousness. In order to be treated on the basis of personal merit, in other words, the black artists and intellectuals had to work for equality of opportunity and justice for the racial group, because it was membership in that group that was the basis of the denial of their individual talent or merit by the white society. How then to link liberty, equality, and justice to civil rights in social languages that would communicate positively with whites of goodwill and create interracial coalitions? That was the challenge facing black intellectuals, artists, writers, and civil rights leaders. Psychologically, they could offer a definition of liberty as *freedom from* mutual fear, prejudice, and self-limiting stereotypes. Economically, they could expound liberty as *freedom to* develop one's talents in ways that would stimulate growth for all in the industrial society. Politically, they could hold up an image of equality to enhance community by fostering civil participation and the common good. Ethically, they could offer a definition of justice as "fair play" and the strengthening of protection for *all* citizens. In short, they could appeal to the core values of liberty, equality, and justice; but would white Americans listen to African American meanings of these values amidst the hustle and bustle of the emerging consumer society or the clamor and confusion of antiradicalism, nativism, and racism of the Roaring Twenties?

16

Progressivism in Transition and on Trial, 1924–1932

American society in the early 1920s was, as has been shown in the preceding chapters, a divided society. The ideological conservatism and "100 percent Americanism" of the day saw only "aliens" and "Americans" or "classes" and "consumers." Classes in this context meant not only the sociological phenomena but also any organized interest group: the "Farm Bloc," "trade unions," and "manufacturers." Consumers meant not only families but also any purchaser of materials. For example, President Harding's attorney general, Harry M. Daugherty, was hostile to Secretary of Commerce Herbert Hoover's trade association voluntarism as being unfair to "consumers" (i.e., corporations that purchased raw materials or component parts). The expansion of "consumers" to include corporations and purchasers of finished products was ironically akin to the earlier socialist expansion of the category of "working class" to include some white-collar employees ("brain" workers as distinct from "hand" workers) and some farmers (tenants, day laborers, sharecroppers).

But a social language can "break down" when stretched too far in the attempt to create a political coalition or social movement. The language of social bonds and human nature, for example, with its implicit promise of pluralism, broke down in the immigration restriction debate, the prohibition experiment, and the civil liberties cases of the 1920s. The mutual goodwill and tolerance that the prewar progressives had assumed would characterize the democratic community, particularly in the thought of someone like Jane Addams or John Dewey, broke down in the wartime experience. It was replaced by the mutual suspicion, intolerance, and repression of the Ku Klux Klan, the American Legion, the Anti-Saloon League, and anti-immigrant groups who set so much of the public tone in the 1920s. This chapter will explore some of the social, economic, and cultural realities of American life and the limits of political language in the period 1924 to 1932. It will focus on the third-party presidential campaign of Senator Robert La Follette in 1924, the Hoover and Alfred Smith presidential campaign of 1928, and Hoover's response to the Great Depression, 1929–32. In the process, some attention will be paid to the language of liberty, the fate of women's rights and civil rights, and the limits of government in these trying times.

The recession of 1921–22, falling farm prices, the "open shop" campaign by manufacturers, the failure of the Plumb Plan for the railroads, the use of court-ordered injunctions in major strikes, and the splintering of the Socialist Party were all factors in the disillusionment of many voters with the Democratic and Republican parties. The result was the creation of a Conference for Progressive Political Action during the 1922 congressional elections. Senator Robert M. La Follette emerged as the leading spokesman for the CPPA. The death of President Harding on 2 August 1923 brought the conservative Vice President Calvin Coolidge into the White House amid growing evidence of corruption in the Harding administration. The Democratic Party split between its rural and urban wings in the 1924 convention and nominated a weak compromise presidential candidate, John W. Davis, a Wall Street lawyer. These developments all combined to encourage the CPPA supporters. La Follette welcomed representatives of a wide range of dissenting organizations: farm, labor, socialist, civil rights, civil liberties, women's rights, and social gospel. The only group he specifically excluded were the communists. La Follette had visited the Soviet Union in 1923 and was appalled by the suppression of civil liberties, the dictatorial decision making, and the capacity of the militant communists to subvert organizations from within. He wanted to have nothing to do with them, and the CPPA organizers agreed.[1]

As if by some providential "hidden hand," the CPPA convention in Cleveland on 4 July 1924 assembled in one place many of the persons discussed in this book or who were linked to social movements analyzed earlier: Morris Hillquit for the Socialist Party, Harriet Stanton Blatch for women voters, self-supporting women, and trade unionists, Senator Lynn Frazier for populist-oriented midwestern farmers, Peter Witt for middle-class urban progressives in the tradition of Cleveland's Tom Johnson, George Lefkowitz for the Farmer-Labor Party, William Pickens of the National Association for the Advancement of Colored People (NAACP), and Fiorello La Guardia, a New York urban progressive. La Follette had wanted Louis Brandeis as his vice presidential running mate, but Brandeis refused to leave his position on the Supreme Court. Therefore La Follette selected Senator Burton K. Wheeler of Montana, congressional investigator of corruption in the Harding administration and a renegade Democrat. Resurrecting the name Progressive Party, La Follette launched a vigorous but underfunded and poorly organized campaign. With Eugene Debs's concurrence, the Socialist Party endorsed La Follette. Samuel Gompers's American Federation of Labor (AFL) and the railroad brotherhoods gave sporadic support. Some civil rights, civil liberties, feminists, and 1912-style progressives rallied to the cause as well: W. E. B. Du Bois, James Weldon Johnson, Margaret Sanger (birth control advocate), Jane Addams, Amos Pinchot (conservationist), and Louis F. Post (assistant secretary of labor under Wilson who had resisted "red scare" attacks on civil liberties).[2]

The platform of the Progressive Party of 1924 did not represent any ideological realignment. Rather, it attempted to unite the antimonopoly rhetoric of the past with the consumerism and special interest politics of the early 1920s. The day before the convention La Follette announced that the purpose of his campaign would be "to break the combined power of the private monopoly system over the political and economic life of the American people." The preamble to the Progressive Party platform echoed this sentiment. The platform called for government ownership and operation of water power and the railroads, and it recognized the right of farmers and workers "to organize and bargain collectively through representatives of their own choosing for the maintenance or improvement of their standards of life." La Follette in public letters condemned the Ku Klux Klan and "any discrimination between races, classes and creeds." These courageous statements won the support of the NAACP but alienated prohibitionists. La Follette's attacks on the Supreme Court, designed to appeal to labor groups, only alienated religious groups with court-protected parochial schools who feared Klan-dominated, state legislatures. Workers and farmers were *both* members of a class, defined economically, *and* members of various racial, creedal, and ethnic configurations, defined culturally. Workers and farmers were *both* producers *and* consumers.[3]

The rhetoric of antimonopoly could not encompass the contradictions of La Follette's coalition. There were, in fact, two kinds of antimonopoly in the 1920s. First, there was the strategic antitrust policy invoked by the Department of Justice against peripheral, horizontal combinations and trade associations. These were the kinds of antitrust cases that government attorneys thought they could win, and the kind that Herbert Hoover saw as a threat to his plans for coordination of the economy. Second, there was structural antimonopoly policy directed against central, vertically integrated oligopolies that dominated their markets. This policy sought to restore competition by returning to comparably sized units. It was this kind of structural antimonopoly advocated by La Follette and, on occasions, by Justice Brandeis. But the integrated corporate form of business organization was so completely woven into the fabric of American life by the mid-1920s that the prospect of "breaking up the monopolies" created anxiety among clerical, supervisory, distributive, and retail workers who depended upon them for job security and income stability. They looked to "welfare capitalism," or company unions, not to independent trade unions and antimonopoly to protect their rights.[4]

La Follette's campaign speeches were packed with specific proposals for the repeal of current legislation that worked against the interests of farmers, laborers, and independent businessmen. He also attacked the conduct of American foreign policy, particularly Wilson's involvement in World War I: "The great war which began ten years ago is now generally admitted to have been an imperialistic war, born of the greed of financiers, exploiters of foreign lands, imperialists who conquered defenseless peoples in order to protect their numerous loans and destructive concessions. They made war on foreign peoples as they profiteered and made *war on liberties of the people at home*."[5] Whether dealing with domestic policy or foreign policy, several themes were evident: (1) equality, whether between citizens of the nation or between nations, (2) equity among economic groups, (3) justice by adherence to law, whether nationally or internationally, and (4) liberty, as protection of constitutional rights and the priority of human rights over property rights.[6]

The Republican-dominated press charged that La Follette's "radicalism" would endanger the prosperity currently being enjoyed by the country or would bring about a financial and industrial panic. The results of the election seemed to reflect these fears. La Follette received 16.6 percent of the popular vote (and 13 electoral votes), John W. Davis, the Democratic candidate, carried 28.8 percent of the popular vote (and 136 electoral votes), and Calvin Coolidge earned 54 percent of the popular vote (and 382 electoral votes). La Follette had won most of the old Socialist voters, fewer farm votes than anticipated (some farm prices had risen just before the election), and many urban, immigrant workers who had voted Republican or Socialist in 1920 and now protested against Wilsonian Democracy. According to historian David P. Thelen, "clearly [La Follette] did not win the support of a majority of the nation's workers, perhaps because they feared that they would lose their jobs, perhaps because ethnic commitments led them elsewhere." Wherein lay the power of Calvin Coolidge's appeal to the American electorate? Political analysts, then and now, have stressed the divisions within the Democratic Party, the handicaps of its lackluster candidate, and the relative strength of the Republican Party's appeal for peace, prosperity, and minimal government. Others have called attention to the influences of cultural issues, such as the enforcement of national prohibition and immigration restriction, that pulled workers one way according to their ethnic and religious identifications and economic issues that pulled them another way according to their skill levels, trade union membership, or dreams of individual mobility and success.[7]

Historians of the women's movement have also called attention to divisions among women as voters. The National League of Women Voters (NLWV) had by 1924 reduced its initial thirteen-point program to four basic areas: (1) training for citizenship, (2) protective legislation, (3) efficiency in government, and (4) international cooperation. It could congratulate itself on some successful lobbying efforts: the Sheppard-Towner Act, the Cable Act granting a woman citizenship independent of her marital status and the nationality of her husband, and the establishment of the Women's Bureau and the Bureau of Home Economics. But, for two years, 1922–24, the NLWV had been battered from the right by antiradical "red tagging" rhetoric of former antisuffragists (now turned superpatriots) who accused them of being bolsheviks and by military preparedness advocates and War Department personnel who feared women's peace and international cooperation efforts. At the same time, the NLWV was attacked from the left by the increasingly militant advocacy of the equal rights amendment by members of the National Woman's Party. The new women voters, it seems, were as divided as the rest of the electorate.[8]

To understand the situation, the relative roles played by various groups in the 1924 election and their various interests need to be examined in some detail. The demise of the Socialist Party as a viable political alternative, the "underground" political status of the Communist Party, the strength of patriotic organizations, and the effectiveness of antibolshevik rhetoric removed the radical option from public discourse for most people. La Follette, a reformer at heart, accepted the support of the moderate socialists and AFL trade unionists, rejected the communists, proposed structural antimonopoly, supported a variation of the Plumb Plan, and advocated congressional restraints on the federal courts in labor law cases. Nevertheless, the Republicans raised the hue and cry of radicalism against him. Historian Donald R. McCoy has emphasized that "repeatedly the Republican vice presidential nominee [Charles Dawes] would demand of his audiences: 'Where do you stand? With President Coolidge on the Constitution with the flag, or on the sinking sands of Socialism?'" Having pinned the label of "radical" on La Follette and dismissed the Democrat's platform suggestions for reform, Coolidge could unite the routine acceptance of the economic status quo of many contented consumers with cultural reassurance by invoking old values to deal with current issues for anxious voters.[9]

The tactics and rhetoric of the Coolidge campaign had about them a quality of ritual and symbolism. The linking of Coolidge with the flag in the Dawes quote was more than a tried and true political gimmick. The American Legion had sponsored a national flag conference in 1923–24 as part of its 100 percent Americanism campaign. The conference changed the wording of the original 1892 pledge from "I pledge allegiance to *my* flag" to "I pledge allegiance to *the* flag of the United States of America." Fraternal orders with their elaborate private rituals were declining in numbers or were being challenged by more purely social organizations, country clubs, and patriotic lodges. Some fraternal orders occasionally entered public controversies, such as the Masonic orders who supported the proposal for a federal Department of Education in the 1920s. The fraternal orders also joined the growing number of patriotic organizations in their public rituals of civic conformity. Thus, the Republicans, in identifying their candidate with the ritual celebration of the Constitution and the flag, tapped into the current forces of ritualism and cultural uniformity.[10]

These political rituals and pageants yield insights into the values and priorities of the 1920s as much as books, speeches, and editorials. There was something comforting for many Americans when they saw photographs of Henry Ford, Thomas A. Edison, and Harvey Firestone, "the aging symbols of the technological miracles of modern times," as they sat on the White House veranda with President Coolidge "discussing great affairs" during the 1924 election campaign. Even trade unionists in the 1920s adapted their traditional Labor Day parades and rituals to the mood of the public audiences and adjusted their publicity to the nationalizing tendencies of a new media—the radio. The National League of Women Voters under its president Belle Sherwin, a former National Consumers' League advocate and suffragist, settled into a nonpartisan, public education approach to current issues. The National Woman's Party, isolated from the moderate women's groups, periodically indulged in the rituals of defending its "no-special treatment" equal rights amendment and of opposing protective legislation for women.[11]

The rhetoric of the 1924 presidential campaign revealed the range of meanings associated with key terms. Trade unionists championed the need for justice, understood as the right to bargain collectively through unions of the workers' own choice. Some women workers also believed in the need for a decent income, or "family wage," sufficient to participate in the consumer society. Women's rights advocates demanded equality but based it upon different visions: (1) the equal-but-different strategy of protective legislation, (2) the equal-and-identical strategy of the equal rights amendment, and (3) the equality of opportunity needs of educated professional women and skilled clerical workers. La Follette revived briefly the old progressive antitrust rhetoric based on equal competition and the socialist emphasis on public ownership and operation of transportation and utilities. The NAACP continued to call for equality of rights and government protection of justice in spite of the failure of the Dyer Bill.[12]

Some cultural critics also tried to stretch the meaning of the term liberty beyond its current economic and political connotations. Nebraska novelist Willa Cather lamented the passing of immigrant culture under the pressure of Americanization and the consumerism of the young. "Too much prosperity, too many moving-picture shows, too much gaudy fiction," she complained, "have colored the taste and manners of so many of these Nebraskans of the future." If Cather decried the current ways in which the young used their liberty, their *freedom to* conform to a consumer society, H. L. Mencken, the acerbic critic, took a different tack: "I am against forbidding anyone to do anything, or say anything, or think anything so long as it is possible to imagine a habitable world in which he would be free to do, say, or think it." Such liberty as *freedom from* prohibition, social restrictions, or middle-class mores was especially attractive to some of the young people that Cather criticized.[13]

The Coolidge campaign showed the Republican hierarchy of core values and the range of meanings among them. The Republican campaign stood for *freedom from* "excessive" income taxes, government regulation, and "unnecessary" expenditures, particularly in the minds of Secretary of the Treasury Andrew Mellon and President Coolidge. The Republicans also advocated *freedom from* international "entanglements" in the continuing refusal to join the League of Nations. In the mind of Herbert Hoover, on the other hand, Republicans also stood for *freedom to* regulate production, allocate markets, and achieve greater efficiency via voluntary cooperation under government auspices. The electorate made its priorities obvious in 1924: liberty ranked higher than equality or justice. Conservatism and ritualism ("100 percent Americanism"), both as *descriptive* categories for current realities and as *prescriptive* norms for acceptable public behavior and private priorities, proved to be stronger than the inherited social languages of progressivism in their antimonopoly, social bonds and human nature, and social efficiency versions in the first half of the 1920s.

If there was to be any change in priorities or implementation of new social policies, it would not be under the Coolidge administration. The years from 1924 to 1928 were largely a repeat of the Harding years: (1) prosperity for the upper class and portions of the middle class (augmented by consumer credit), (2) an influx of capital from abroad and tax cuts for business in 1927 fueling stock market speculation, and (3) new forms of consumerism and popular culture masking serious structural inequities in the economy. President Coolidge vetoed farm relief (McNary-Haugen Plan) in 1927 and 1928 as "class legislation." Civil liberties advocates denounced the execution of two Italian-born anarchists, Nicola Sacco and Bartolomeo Vanzetti, in 1927 on what the experts regarded as inadequate evidence, improper judicial procedures, or simply antiradical and class bias. Civil rights advocates continued to push the antilynching Dyer Bill, but to no avail. Women's rights advocates were concerned about preserving protective legislation such as the Sheppard-Towner Act (undercut by conservatives in Congress in a funding bill) and differed among themselves over the proposed equal rights amendment. Social gospel activities in Protestant churches were in decline. When Coolidge announced that he would not be a candidate for another term in the 1928 presidential election, the possibility of change seemed to improve. But, that would depend on who would be the candidates.[14]

For the moment in 1928 the prospects seemed brightest for Herbert Hoover. The presidential election of 1928 pitted the phlegmatic Hoover as Republican presidential candidate against the flamboyant Alfred E. Smith for the Democrats. With the death of Robert La Follette in June 1925, the remaining supporters of the Progressive Party of 1924 drifted into the two main political parties or supported Norman Thomas in a new Socialist Party. Jane Addams supported Hoover because she didn't like Smith's antiprohibition stance. Some farm leaders, dissatisfied with Coolidge's veto of farm relief legislation, turned to the Democrats (only to be disappointed by the unsympathetic attitude they perceived in Smith's consumer-oriented, domestic policy advisor, Belle Moskowitz). John Dewey, although he favored Norman Thomas's ideas, supported Smith. Felix Frankfurter (an ally of Louis Brandeis) also abandoned Hoover. However, such disaffections among progressives didn't influence the conduct or the outcome of the election. As historian Joan Hoff Wilson has remarked: "The 1928 presidential campaign between Al Smith and Herbert Hoover brought out the intellectual best in the two men and the worst in their supporters." Fear, suspicion, rumor, racial innuendo, and anti-Catholic bigotry, big budget negative advertising, and general prosperity definitely influenced the final outcome: Hoover received 21 million popular votes (and 444 electoral votes) and Smith received 15 million popular votes (and 87 electoral votes).[15]

The personal attacks in the campaign on Smith and Hoover obscured the similarities between the two candidates and the common background of their closest advisors. Both were self-made men who had embraced the progressive goals of the prewar and postwar period, but they differed as to the best means to achieve those goals in the late 1920s. Furthermore, Hoover used the 1928 campaign to reiterate the themes of his 1922 book, *American Individualism*, now buttressed by examples or statistics from his career as secretary of commerce. Still using the borrowed language of excessive individualism to mask his dedication to voluntary cooperation by special interest groups and the government's role in regulatory agencies, Hoover put additional emphasis on his conception of liberty. He equated his view of liberty with what he called true liberalism, "a force proceeding from the deep realization that economic freedom cannot be sacrificed if political freedom is to be preserved." False liberalism, he implied, was synonymous with rule by bureaucracy "that interprets itself into government operation of commercial business." Smith, on the other hand, had been influenced by social workers and public policy advisors, such as Belle Moskowitz, Eleanor Roosevelt, and Frances Perkins, who encouraged him to embrace the emerging civic liberalism of the late twenties. It combined maternalist social welfare programs, governmental efficiency and restructuring, reaffirmation of civil liberties and civil rights, and a preference for planning and publicity by experts. This liberalism tended to confine democratic participation by citizens in decision making to periodic elections or referenda. Smith also stressed *personal* liberty as *freedom from* restive laws such as prohibition and *freedom to* practice one's religion unhindered by majority pressure for conformity.[16]

Hoover had little opportunity after his inauguration in March 1929 to realize his ambitions for social harmony and economic growth. A stock market crash in October 1929 sent the economy tumbling. To meet the crisis of the depression, Hoover moved in 1929–30 to implement the economic plans that he had formulated in 1919–21 to deal with the post-war recession. His recovery program rested on three principles: (1) increased construction by public agencies (local, state, and national governments), (2) lower interest rates by banks to stimulate capital spending by businesses and to stimulate residential builders and buyers, and (3) voluntary maintenance of wages and prices by business to indirectly stimulate consumer demand. But Hoover had to confront the economic legacies of the 1920s and the weakness of some of the institutions of the Progressive Era. Mergers among corporations had continued throughout the 1920s; indeed, Willard Thorp of the National Bureau of Economic Research charged that the Sherman Antitrust Act and the Clayton Act, as interpreted by the Supreme Court, had encouraged such combinations because *interfirm* cooperation was legal whereas *intrafirm* cooperation was not. The Federal Reserve Board had pursued low-interest policies during the prosperity of 1927–28 but had switched to a high-interest policy to protect the gold reserve following the stock market crash. As local, state, and national tax revenues declined, so did the willingness of public agencies to commit themselves to long-term construction projects or borrowing for such proposals. Businesses that had voluntarily maintained wage rates and prices for half a year, in response to Hoover's appeal at a White House conference, now slashed them as unsold goods piled up in the warehouses. Thus, Hoover's attempts to reconstruct business from *within* by encouraging corporate voluntary cooperation and to rescue it from *without* by encouraging low interest rates to stimulate construction had both failed.[17]

In the areas of women's rights and civil rights, too, Hoover's well-meaning gestures and overtures faltered before the harsh realities of the depression. As historian J. Stanley Lemons has pointed out: "[T]he advent of the Great Depression intensified prejudice against working women, especially married women. While the attack was centered on married women, there was always the lurking presumption that every woman worked for 'pin money' and kept a family man out of a job." With the failure of his initial recovery program by 1931, Hoover advocated higher taxes and reduced government spending to hold down Treasury borrowing. When Congress passed the Economy Act of 1932, a section "required personnel reductions to be made at the expense of persons [i.e., married women] whose spouses were employed by the government." Hoover protested but signed the bill anyway. Women were forced out of government employment and into competition for lower-paying jobs.[18]

The pressure against working women in government employment highlighted the division among women's rights groups over the issue of protective legislation versus equal rights. Business and professional women's organizations, disappointed by their progress during the 1920s and under pressure from militants of the National Woman's Party in their ranks, turned increasingly against protective legislation and in favor of the equal rights amendment. In spite of the NWP's endorsement of Hoover in the 1928 presidential election, they had little to show for their support except some changes in the Cable Act concerning the determination of a married woman's citizenship. Supporters of protective legislation were also disappointed with Hoover's perfunctory but futile pronouncements in favor of renewing the Sheppard-Towner Act after its funding ended in June 1929. Hoover did raise appropriations for the Women's

Bureau and the Children's Bureau, but it was a case of too little, too late. The National League of Women Voters in 1928 had supported the development of inexpensive public electric power in the Norris Plan for the Tennessee Valley area only to see it vetoed by Coolidge in 1928. Hoover vetoed the same plan in 1931. Thus, on the eve of the 1932 presidential elections, Hoover, in spite of goodwill and progressive sentiments, had alienated both wings of the women's movement and many nonpolitical working women.[19]

In the area of civil rights, Hoover pursued a paradoxical strategy in 1928. He favored southern "lily white" progressive, reform-oriented elites, in order to "revolutionize" the Republican Party in the South. He opposed the traditional "black and tan," patronage-oriented Republican politicians in the South, while ignoring powerful African American leaders in the North. The strategy backfired. In spite of private assurances by Hoover, neither northern blacks nor southern whites fully trusted him. According to historian Donald J. Lisio, "in August 1930, Hoover had condemned lynching as 'undermining the very essence of justice and democracy'; although his statement had been reported in the press, it had gone almost unnoticed." In October 1930 Walter White of the NAACP pointed out to the president that lynching was once again on the rise and urged that he call a conference of southern governors. Hoover, who mistrusted the NAACP leaders, did not act. He did meet, however, in November 1930 with Monroe Trotter of the National Equal Rights League and a delegation from an antilynching congress. Unlike Trotter's famous confrontation with Woodrow Wilson, the meeting was amicable, but again, Hoover did not act.[20]

While these events were taking place, the NAACP's efforts to pass the Dyer Bill and to correct specific injustices by pursuing selective court cases seemed equally frustrating. The antilynching issue continued to serve as a reminder for all African Americans in the South of their precarious position. It also rendered the NAACP's slow-paced efforts vulnerable to criticism. As historian Jacquelyn Dowd Hall has observed, when racial violence flared in 1930, it was Jessie Daniel Ames, director of women's work for the Commission on Interracial Cooperation, who "seized the opportunity to launch a women's campaign against lynching: single-issue in focus, elaborately organized, [it was] part of a larger movement" for change in the South. It was called Southern Women for the Prevention of Lynching (SWPL) and worked alongside efforts by African American women. Whereas the male-dominated NAACP program increasingly stressed black *independence* and racial cooperation, the southern white women of the SWPL and black women's groups stressed racial *interdependence* and attacked cultural stereotypes, which were regarded as derogatory to both races. Thus, by the end of the 1920s the heritage of women's political campaigns, feminism, and social gospel activism came together to supplement and stimulate the NAACP campaign against lynching. The civil rights movement was refurbished in the process, and the social language of social bonds and human nature was somewhat rejuvenated.[21]

In 1931, shocked by a report on lynching and prodded by a second meeting with Monroe Trotter's delegation, Hoover drafted an ambitious plan to use military units to curb lynch mobs where state and local police failed to act. In effect, Hoover advocated an updated version of the Reconstruction Era "force bills," which had divided the Republican Party in the distant past. When his political and legal advisors cautioned Hoover not to adopt the policy, he quietly dropped it. In 1932 the Republican Party would also drop from its platform its promise to work toward elimination of lynching. Such inactivity and public silence, in spite of good private contacts with African American leaders such as Robert Moton, made a mockery of Hoover's promise in October 1932 "that the Republican party would 'not abandon or depart from its traditional duty toward the American Negro' and [his reassurance to African Americans] that the 'right of liberty, justice, and equal opportunity is yours.' "[22]

Hoover's ranking of values in the October 1932 statement to black Republicans was instructive: liberty, justice, and equal opportunity—in that order. As the depression deepened, as the macroeconomic recovery plan (based on experiences in 1919–21) failed, as the goodwill and confidence in his leadership vanished among women's rights advocates and civil rights leaders, Hoover's thinking was increasingly dominated by budget cuts and tax increases. He showed great creativity in designing new institutional *means,* but he stayed with the goals and values that had long guided him. Hoover accentuated the concept of liberty in his rhetoric and used it increasingly as a rationale for actions *not* taken. But it was a pinched and peculiarly narrow conception of liberty that was increasingly at odds with current realities. Hoover believed that unemployed and destitute *individuals* should not be aided *directly* by the federal government lest such aid diminish their independence; but *institutions* (such as banks, railroads, insurance companies, savings and loan associations, and farm marketing cooperations) could be aided *indirectly* by grants of credit, government contracts, or changes in the banking system's acceptability of commercial paper. Justice, particularly economic justice, would be achieved by maintaining the gold standard, stabilizing world trade relations, foregoing international debt payments temporarily, and keeping the federal budget in balance. Recovery would not be served by granting bonus payments to war veterans, nor by strikes for union recognition, nor by "raids" on the Treasury by selfish interest groups. Racial justice would have to wait until the depression was conquered. Equal opportunity was the hallmark of Hoover's conception of liberty, but married women would have to give up their government jobs. African Americans would have to work out their own destiny through practical education and self-help. Unemployed men and women at the bottom of the economic ladder would have to be patient until the benefits of recovery programs "trickled down" to them.[23]

The fault was not so much in Hoover's *personal* commitments or his *private* background; indeed, those who knew him best and most intimately stood in awe of his grasp of American values and the complexities of economic problems. For all of his difficulties with public communication, the peculiarities of his terminology, and his use of private meanings for public terms such as American individualism, Hoover was not so different from many of his contemporaries. As Joan Hoff Wilson, Ellis Hawley, Donald J. Lisio, and other interpreters of Hoover have pointed out, he was essentially a progressive in his values and attitudes. If he used the social language of antimonopoly less than Robert La Follette, if he adapted the language of social bonds and human nature to include his notions of voluntary business-government coordination and cooperation, if he expanded the language of efficiency beyond the limits of the Taylorites or of Louis Brandeis, Hoover was simply doing more than some other progressives of his generation were doing. President-elect Franklin Delano Roosevelt, former Democratic presidential aspirant Alfred E. Smith, the social welfare advocate Belle Moskowitz, president Belle Sherwin of the NLWV, A. Philip Randolph of the Sleeping-Car Porters' Union and others were also trying to apply the social languages of progressivism to the problems of the period 1924–32. But the legacy of progressivism was being tried in the ordeal of the depression and ultimately would be found wanting. In the process, the basis of a new liberalism would be articulated and would become institutionalized in the next decade, but the old progressive coalitions would be shattered in the process.

Afterword

"In particular, this book will argue that, during the period 1865 to 1932, the history of the attempt to achieve civil rights, women's rights, and the regulation of business was, for the most part, a story of failure. Yes, there were victories and some notable achievements by the heroic pioneers of these three social movements. . . . The thesis of this book, however, is that the failures and disappointments of these three social movements stemmed primarily from the fact that so many Americans ranked liberty (for themselves) higher than equality (with others) and justice (for all)."
—Introduction

Having looked at the evidence in support of this main argument, some final reflections are in order. These comments will be on the interaction between the attempts to secure civil rights, to extend women's rights, and to regulate business and the core values of liberty, equality, and justice during the period 1865 to 1932. They will be neither a comprehensive summary nor a confirmation of a tentative hypothesis; rather, they will be a brief resume of themes, observations, and questions raised in the inquiry.

Part 1. Old Languages and New Realities, 1865–1898: A Reprise

Liberty and Civil Rights
In the aftermath of the Civil War, the task of defining the legal, constitutional, and political meaning of liberty for the former slaves and former Confederates fell to the Republican Party leadership and their Union supporters, both North and South. Drawing on the old languages of biblical-evangelical abolitionism, the natural rights republicanism of the Revolutionary Era, the prewar "free labor" ideology, and the Whig

tradition of positive state action, they created a compelling synthesis to confront the new realities unleashed by the war and by industrial-technological growth. The institutional embodiment of their understanding of core values was found in the Thirteenth, Fourteenth, and Fifteenth Amendments and in the Civil Rights Act of 1866 and subsequent acts up to 1875. The Republican actions extended these concepts of citizenship and civil rights not only to former slaves but also to "assimilated" Indians and to resident Chinese in certain categories and to their native-born children. Legal scholars and historians of Reconstruction regard these achievements as a "constitutional revolution" (albeit an incomplete one) because these institutional changes extended the protection of the national government over civil rights when the states failed to uphold them.

Yet within twenty-five years, from the *Slaughter House* cases (1873) to the end of the depression in 1897–98, the "constitutional revolution" was turned back by judicial interpretation and political pressure. The Reconstruction experiment in biracial democracy in the South was overturned by violence, economic coercion, and political divisions that were symbolized by the Compromise of 1877. The abandonment of African Americans by northern Republicans, the exclusion of Chinese workers largely because of pressure from western Democrats, and the forced assimilation of Native Americans and the reduction of the reservation system by a bipartisan coalition of eastern humanitarians and western land interests in the Dawes Severalty Act of 1887 reduced the impact of the constitutional amendments and civil rights acts. Too many white Americans saw these groups as impediments to reconciliation between the regions, as potential competitors for economic opportunity, or as defeated foes to be remade in their own cultural and economic images.

What were the options that faced those groups that were being discriminated against? African Americans in the South faced three options: (1) migration or "exodus" to the North or West (or, perhaps, to Liberia in Africa), (2) accommodation to second-class citizenship in order to concentrate on individual economic self-advancement and cooperative group help through churches and schools (the philosophy of Booker T. Washington and women's clubs), and (3) militant protest, creation of civil rights organizations, and continued use of political rights where possible (the philosophy of Ida Wells-Barnett and Thomas Fortune). Chinese residents turned to whatever protection the courts would grant and the support of their own extended families and clan organizations. Some Native Americans farmed their allotment of land, attended the special schools, and learned the new ways of life; others clung desperately to traditional cultures or drifted back to the reservations after selling or losing their allotment. In the eyes of most white Americans, all citizens enjoyed the formal status of civil liberty (that is, they were free) and equal justice under law, but civil rights varied according to class, ethnicity, and gender.

Equality and Women's Rights

Women had the same formal status of civil liberty as men, that is, of citizenship and membership in the nation, but they did not have equality of rights. This was particularly galling to Susan B. Anthony and Elizabeth Cady Stanton, pioneer suffragists, who pointed out that the Fourteenth and Fifteenth Amendments, by making the term voter synonymous with male citizen, denied to women the possibility of the right to vote without further amending the Constitution. Some suffragists tried the tactic of claiming that the right to vote was inherent in citizenship (or civil liberty) and suing to gain recognition of it or acting as if they already had the right to vote. But the courts ultimately rejected their argument. Others tried to change state laws to protect married women's property rights or to protect their wages from improvident husbands. They made some progress on these issues in the period 1865 to 1898 but did so by appealing to cultural stereotypes that stressed women's inequality, dependence on men, or special maternal roles.

Whoever wanted to challenge the limits that American society placed on women had to find a social language that would communicate with a potentially large but increasingly diverse audience. Suffragists drew on the language of Revolutionary Era natural rights. For them suffrage became both a symbol of their quest for independence and a means to correct current legal disabilities. While they agreed on goals, the suffragists split in 1869 into two organizations over the question of tactics: (1) the American Woman Suffrage Association, which stressed state level enfranchisement and sharing leadership with men, and (2) the National Woman Suffrage Association, which advocated a national constitutional amendment and leadership directed by women. An attempt to form an alliance between middle-class suffragists and working women failed, too. Working women confronted the new realities of industrialism and had immediate and pressing economic needs. Their working-class culture stressed interdependence in support of their families and communities more than the individual independence advocated by middle-class suffragists.

Other middle-class women confronted the new realities of urban growth or changing agricultural communities but remained dependent upon the older languages of separate spheres, the cult of domesticity, and the Victorian sexual and ethical ethos. They saw service to others as a liberation from selfish desires or priorities and dedicated themselves to doing their maternal duty to others as a way of redeeming their changing communities. Under the leadership of Frances Willard of the Woman's Christian Temperance Union, they pushed the strategy of a separate female *public* sphere into new areas and stretched the language of maternal duty to its logical limits. African American women of the middle class, caught between the strictures of racial segregation and the inherent limits of Victorian respectability, found ways to serve their communities by church work, educational endeavors, and quiet moral example. The one event which symbolized, both positively and negatively, the diversity among women in this period was the creation of a Woman's Pavilion for the Columbian Exposition in 1892–93 under the leadership of socially elite women such as Berthe Honoré Palmer. At the same time, many women sought periodic withdrawal from a rapidly changing world and thereby found renewal through study clubs, women's clubs, professional sororities, fraternal lodge "auxiliaries," and the private rituals of mutual support.

Out of these various tensions and activities, women advocates who wanted equal rights found that they could best communicate with others by broadening the concept of liberty. It could mean *freedom from* the dependence of having to choose marriage and *freedom to* pursue a profession or a career of service to others (the "New Woman" such as Jane Addams); it could mean *freedom to* develop one's talents in the woman's club movement. Liberty could also mean the right to extend one's maternal duties into the public sphere (Frances Willard), or to achieve autonomous selfhood (Elizabeth Cady Stanton). Liberty to some meant *freedom from* the drudgery of housework by cooperative endeavors (Charlotte Perkins Gilman), *freedom from* the degradation of Jim Crow transportation (National Association of Colored Women), and *freedom from* the exploitation of low paying, "sweatshop" labor (women's trade unions). Intertwined with all these variations on the old language of liberty as *freedom from* dependence and *freedom to* seek independence and the yearning for equality of rights, there was the persistent reality of women's interdependence in their families, neighborhoods, and communities.

Justice and the Regulation of Business
The emergence of the modern limited-liability, stock-issuing corporation during the 1850s to the 1890s was not determined by the natural forces of technological imperatives; it was, rather, the product of trial and error decisions, adaptations of existing legal codes, and rigorous application of hierarchical models borrowed from the military and the railroads. And

such new corporate forms coexisted with, and intermingled in, family control of firms, traditional methods of shop production (with variable batch systems, as well as assembly line techniques), and various forms of worker's control. The corporate organizers, managers, legal experts, and investment advisers responded positively to what they saw as the logic of the system (the economics of "running full" to drive down unit costs); they also experimented with vertical integration, horizontal coordination, or mixed modes. As managers, they tried to fend off predatory investors and to subordinate tradition-oriented unions. When all else failed, they evoked the language of private property rights and liberty of contract to cover their situation or they invoked the emotional images and fears generated by the bloody Paris Commune of 1871, the Great Railroad strike of 1877, and subsequent strikes and violence in the 1870s–90s.

But the growth of the business corporations violated traditional norms of community control of economic life, created new forms of competition, and challenged deeply ingrained images of independence held by skilled craftsmen, family-owned businesses, and partnerships. The advocates of business regulation, therefore, drew on the common law notions of the logic of the market (the economics of equal and fair competition) and the acceptability of "reasonable" restraint of trade based upon voluntary cooperation by competitors. The priority of communal norms would be maintained, they believed, by the natural workings of the unfettered market and the occasional necessity of lawsuits to determine the amount of punitive damages. In order to reach the political audience of citizens and voters, advocates of regulation drew on the antimonopoly rhetoric of Jacksonian democracy ("equal rights for all, special privileges for none") and the producer psychology of agrarian and artisanal communities.

In the end, the public mind was deeply divided by the clash between the old languages of regulation and common law notions of competition and the new realities of corporate growth, consolidation, and attempted cooperative control of markets. Did the corporate behavior warrant retribution by the application of common law restraints, restructuring by antimonopoly statutes, or sympathetic regulation by knowledgeable experts? The state of the public discourse was evident in the confusions of terminology, the ambiguity of legislative enactments, and the tentativeness of administrative and judicial rulings. The Granger laws of the 1870s were upheld by the court in *Munn v. Illinois* (1877), but were subsequently limited to *intrastate* commerce because only the national government could regulate *interstate* commerce. Congress was reluctant to act until political exigencies prompted the creation of the Interstate Commerce Commission in 1887. Business experiments with new forms of organization ("trusts," holding companies, vertical and horizontal mergers) once again prompted Congress to act in the Sherman Antitrust Act of 1890. But no grand coalition of anticorporate forces emerged. Neither strikes by labor unions, complaints by communities, lawsuits by injured competitors, radical rhetoric by socialists, nor reform proposals by Populists could curb the corporations as a wave of mergers accompanied the depression of 1893–97 and swept on into the new century.

The corporations and the merger movement threatened to erode traditional core values. It was not simply that corporations claimed liberty of contract for themselves while denying equality of competition to other forms of business. It was not simply that business jeopardized justice for workers, their unions, and the communities that depended upon them by their alliance with government and their dependence on antistrike injunctions issued by sympathetic judges. Rather, the impact of the corporate economy seemed to diminish the reality of both liberty and equality, both competition and cooperation, both individual mobility and community autonomy, both the "privileges or immunities" of ordinary citizens and the "equal protection of the law" for all. The corporation might be regarded as a legal "person" in the eyes of the courts but not as a "citizen" in the laws of some states; it might be regarded as an independent legal person with the right to life (in perpetuity), liberty (of contract), and protection of private property (by the courts and the militia) and still not exhibit the interdependence that was believed to be essential to maintaining a democratic community. This to the critics of the corporations was the greatest injustice of all.

Part 2. New Languages and Old Realities, 1898–1932: A Rescript

The Languages of Antimonopoly and Efficiency and the Regulation of Business
Progressivism emerged in the late 1890s and early 1900s among middle-class consumers and commuters in rapidly growing urban areas, among skilled craftsmen and artisan workers in trade unions and self-managed shops, among professionals in the scientific and engineering societies, among independent businessmen and small entrepreneurs who wanted to counter the corporations' growing power, and among members of women's clubs, consumer leagues, and settlement house activists who were concerned with working conditions of women, children, and recent immigrants. In various ways they adapted the social languages of antimonopoly and efficiency that had been used earlier by producer-oriented farmers, merchants, and moralists, putting these languages on a new

basis. The new languages reflected a consumer-oriented psychology, a preference for interfirm competition (as opposed to intrafirm coordination and cooperation), and a belief in the power and beneficence of experts and well-informed citizens. These consumers-citizens-competitors complained that the newly merged corporations, "monopolies," or "trusts" and their corrupt alliance with the "boss system" in politics (that exploited immigrants and unskilled workers) made the upper working-class and middle-class voters feel dependent upon distant, impersonal, and hierarchical institutions rather than independent in their own right and interdependent with their community norms.

But how to restore such independence and interdependence? How to regulate the power of business without jeopardizing its benefits for the consumer? The social languages of antimonopoly and efficiency were sufficiently elastic to encompass three possibilities: (1) restoration of competition by "breaking up the trusts" into smaller competitive units by democratic, legislative action; (2) regulation of corporate behavior under executive branch supervision by elite-staffed commissions, bureaus, and agencies; and (3) restraint of business behavior by judicial determination and application of "rules of reason" on a case-by-case basis. In the end, political influences, personal factors, and lobbying by self-interested groups created a constantly shifting pattern of attempts to use all three options. Their incremental achievements included some largely symbolic but still significant antitrust lawsuits, passage of consumer protection legislation, pioneering conservation measures, limited railroad regulation, and some measures to protect working men, women, and children. The institutional additions to these progressive reforms included the reduction of the tariff (until wartime needs intervened), the creation of the Federal Reserve banking system, the establishment of the Federal Trade Commission, and the passage of the Clayton Antitrust Act.

Wartime mobilization of the economy also provided an opportunity for those advocates of the "gospel of efficiency" to standardize aspects of industry, coordinate production, reorganize the transportation system, and eliminate some "waste" in industry, government, and society. Participation in the war effort did not last long enough to give these ideas a fair test; however, they did provide a model for some aspects of postwar reconstruction and later attempts to deal with the great depression during 1929–32. But the resurgence of laissez-faire conservatism and the growth of a consumer society in the 1920s indicated the continuing strength of some old political and economic realities. The railroad system was returned to private control and ownership (despite the proposed Plumb Plan backed by labor unions) and struggled on with technological competition, labor representation experiments, and inconsistent regulation. The Federal Reserve system had its own priorities in the early 1920s and ignored Secretary of Commerce Herbert Hoover and his ideas. The Treasury Department favored high tariffs and low taxes; the Federal Reserve banks allowed capital to flow into stock market speculation. The Federal Trade Commission was quiescent in the 1920s, and the Supreme Court limited trade association activities and hindered Hoover's plans for business-government cooperation.

In 1924 Robert La Follette attempted to unite progressives who believed in women's rights, civil rights, democratic socialism, and governmental farm-labor support under the banner of antimonopoly. His third-party effort failed before Coolidge's appeals to self-interested liberty and antiradicalism. In 1928 Hoover was more successful in his presidential bid by blending the "gospel of efficiency" with his own redefinition of individualism. He soon stumbled, however, on his self-imposed limits in dealing with the depression after 1929. Hoover's ideas of business-government voluntary cooperation, "trickle-down" support of financial and business institutions, countercyclical public construction, and loan-based relief programs all faltered against the old realities of budget cuts, tariff increases, and Hoover's inability to communicate his ideas and priorities clearly. On the eve of the 1932 elections, neither antimonopoly rhetoric nor plans for business-government efficiency swayed the voters who had more pressing personal, community, and human needs on their minds.

Women's Rights and the Language of Social Bonds and Human Nature
Progressivism as a historical term for the renewal of American society and values during the period 1898 to 1932 encompassed a wide range of intellectual trends relating to women. Feminism, a new set of goals that emerged during the 1910s, stressed independence in the choice between marriage or career, economic self-support, artistic self-expression, and recognition of women's sexual nature and needs. Maternalism, an older set of goals, stressed women's maternal roles and nature, care for others, and didactic functions. Maternalism transformed the dependence of private familial roles into a vision of interdependent public responsibilities. Suffragism, too, was transformed in the Progressive Era as a new generation of leaders responded to the diversity of women's economic life situations. The combination of middle-class activists (National American Women Suffrage Association), working-class trade unionists (National Women's Trade Union League), African American women's club leaders and educators (National Association of Colored Women and National

Association for the Advancement of Colored People), upper-class ideologues and militant suffragist tacticians (Congressional Union and National Woman's Party) pushed the suffrage campaign forward by a variety of means. Women's participation in support of wartime mobilization also put the suffrage campaign in a more favorable political context. The Nineteenth Amendment was finally passed in June 1919 and ratified by the necessary number of states in 1920. Women also secured some protective legislation during the Progressive Era; wartime mobilization also expanded their range of economic opportunities.

In all of these developments women were aided by the social language of social bonds and human nature. This new language reflected the social gospel theology, the belief in the plasticity of the changing nature of social reality, the cultural shaping of personality, and the malleability of social roles. Such views facilitated the building of political coalitions to secure protective legislation for women workers and children, consumer laws, and the right to vote. But not everyone agreed with these frequently amorphous and constantly changing descriptions of reality. Antisuffragists believed in fixed gender boundaries and the futility of trying to change roles that they believed were set by nature. Some men were uneasy with the predominance of women in the Protestant churches and in the social gospel. Such men attempted to reassert masculine roles and "character building" models for boys and young men in ritual activities, fraternal lodges, and service-oriented organizations. Wartime patriotism, antiradical sentiment, and immigration restriction sentiment also challenged feminism and any links among women's rights advocates and socialism and pacifism.

What did equality mean, then, for women once they had secured the vote in 1920? They divided on the goals to be achieved next. And their tactics or means depended on their basic orientations toward men and women. For the National League of Women Voters and allied organizations, men and women were equal but different in nature; therefore, society was justified in passing protective legislation such as the Sheppard-Towner Act (infant and maternity care). For the National Woman's Party, men and women were equal and identical in civil status; therefore, the political system should pass an equal rights amendment in order to remove all legal barriers between them. The generation of the "New Woman" of the 1890s and the feminists of the 1910s were being surpassed in the 1920s by a new generation of middle-class consumers, by youthful "flappers," and by aspiring professionals—who forgot about the struggles of the past. But old realities intruded themselves into the political process as the courts invalidated some protective legislation with liberty of contract arguments. Antisuffragists (converted into superpatriots by the postwar "red scare"), laissez-faire conservatives, and medical associations undercut the Sheppard-Towner Act by negative publicity, budget cuts, and bureaucratic infighting. The onslaught of the depression in 1929–32 further undercut women's economic opportunities. Both legislation and bureaucratic rules meant that some women could not hold a government job (if their husbands did), that many women must take lower pay, or that priorities in relief employment would go to men with families. The social bonds that the progressives had assumed would work best in a democracy to unite a community and ensure its welfare unraveled in the late 1920s and early 1930s as traditional views of rigid, gender bound human nature reasserted themselves.

Civil Liberty, Civil Rights, and Civil Liberties

In 1898 a prevalent understanding of the term "civil liberty" was that it meant a fixed status, a condition of freedom linked to "civilization" in the cultural sense and "citizenship" in the political sense. The state was the creator and the guarantor of civil liberty through the rule of law. Some progressive social thinkers believed, on the other hand, that the true basis of rights was in the community, an evolving, adapting entity. The link between the community (sociological concept) and the state or government (political-legal concept) was the notion of citizenship. The good citizen enjoyed civil rights (which were protected by the state) but exercised civil responsibility as well. How well did these theories accord with the facts?

By the year 1912 the prevalent political theory was that African Americans were citizens by birth and, therefore, enjoyed the status of civil liberty; but, in fact, they did not enjoy full civil rights. Therefore, African Americans and their supporters formed numerous organizations, such as the Niagara Movement (1905), the National Association for the Advancement of Colored People (1910), and federations of women's clubs and religious-based social welfare programs. Most Asian laborers were barred by the Chinese Exclusion Acts or by the Gentlemen's Agreement with Japan. They were regarded as being outside the status of civil liberty; however, those Asians born in the United States, in exempt categories, or who were family members of people in these categories had some judicial access to civil rights protection. The rest were regarded by administrative edict as "aliens ineligible for citizenship." Native Americans had been brought into the status of civil liberty by inclusion within the notion of "civilization" through the reduction of the reservation system, assimilationist education, and allotment of land under the Dawes Act and similar laws. Citizenship depended upon receiving one's allotment of land; however, civil rights could still be limited by the legal "wardship" exercised by the government. Thus, whereas the African Americans were "separate, but equal" in the eyes of the courts, the Native Americans were "integrated, but not yet equal," so to speak. Asians were either excluded by law or executive agreement or "separated, but occasionally equal" if they belonged to the appropriate exempt category or were citizens by birth.

Events during World War I and the early 1920s helped to create an intellectual division between the older concept of civil liberty and the newer concept of civil liberties. The prewar concept of civil liberty had held that the needs and prerogatives of society and the state were primary and the rights of individuals were secondary, even those included in the Bill of Rights. Once the U.S. Congress declared war, instituted a conscription system, and passed the Espionage Act (1917), and the Sedition Act (1918), the prevalent assumption was that debate, dissent, and personal desires were all subordinate to the common will. The Supreme Court affirmed this view in such cases as *Schenck v. U.S.* (1919) and *Debs v. U.S.* (1919). A coalition of pacifists, social workers, social gospel advocates, some feminists, and conservative lawyers who worried about constitutional guarantees of rights banded together in various temporary organizations during 1914–17. They borrowed the phrase "civil liberties" from English anticonscription and pacifist groups to describe their attempts to defend individual rights on constitutional grounds. The suppression of antiwar socialist newspapers, the jailing of Eugene Debs and other socialist orators, and the excesses of the postwar "red scare" prompted second thoughts among many political and legal leaders. A permanent organization was formed in 1920, the American Civil Liberties Union. By the mid-1920s supporters of their efforts had begun to articulate the language to describe the core concept of "civil liberties": the constitutional rights of individuals are primary and the needs of society and the state are secondary. The Supreme Court gave gradual and limited acceptance to these views in such cases as *Moore v. Dempsey* (1923) and *Gitlow v. New York* (1925). The notion of a static, secure civil status (civil liberty) was being challenged by the notion of a constantly shifting process of protecting individual rights (civil liberties). There were also a few radicals who responded to the language of bolshevism (or communism) and dreamed of placing the American socialist movement on a new revolutionary basis or of influencing the labor movement from within.

But war and the postwar "red scare" prompted a resurgence of some old realities or enabled lobbyists to exploit the drive for social control to their advantage. The Anti-Saloon League helped to secure passage of the Eighteenth Amendment for national prohibition. Immigration restrictionists overrode President Wilson's veto to secure a literacy test for immigrants and the passage of immigration restriction legislation in 1920 and 1924. Even "right-wing" socialists and moderate trade unionists of the American Federation of Labor used the turmoil of the postwar recession to oust the "left-wing" radicals in the Socialist Party or to separate themselves from militants in the labor movement. The American Legion, created in 1919, used nationalism, patriotism, and antiradicalism to inculcate duty and loyalty to the state. The Ku Klux Klan grew rapidly in the postwar era in the South, Middle West, and Northwest. It tried to reinforce the values of white, Protestant, rural and urban citizens by relegating African Americans, Catholics, Jews, and recent immigrants to second-class citizenship. Conservative views of limited government, antiradicalism (in the convenient political label of anti-"bolshevism") and Klan-influenced conformity contributed to divisions in the Democratic Party in 1924. Coolidge was able to defeat the revived progressivism of Robert La Follette in 1924 by denouncing it as radicalism and declaring his own stand to be for liberty.

While the concept of civil liberties was being articulated in the 1920s, the question of how to achieve civil rights for African Americans was also undergoing significant change. There were two prominent options: (1) racial self-separation, and (2) interracial cooperation. The first option was evident in Marcus Garvey and the Universal Negro Improvement Association (UNIA). Garvey invoked the core values of liberty, equality, and justice but gave them radically new meanings in terms of extranational racial citizenship, black nationalism, racial pride, and group-based self-help projects. Whereas a radical such as Garvey stressed strict racial separation, a reformer such as A. Philip Randolph attempted to form a black trade union (Brotherhood of Sleeping Car Porters) that stressed racial separation but also advocated cooperation with the white-dominated American Federation of Labor. The second option, interracial cooperation, was also pursued by the moderate Commission on Interracial Cooperation, its women's committee, the YWCA, "colored women's clubs," and the NAACP. The focus of their efforts was antilynching legislation and improved interracial communication. Interracial cooperation was also evident in Herbert Hoover's humanitarian relief efforts during the 1927 Mississippi River flood in his appointment of the Moton Commission to investigate complaints of violations of African Americans' civil rights by local relief agencies and state governments. Hoover's values of justice and efficiency guided his efforts in support of black landownership (similar to the Freedmen's Bureau of Reconstruction) and in proposals for federal civil rights enforcement. But as W. E. B. Du Bois had pointed out earlier, without equality, all such attempts at justice ended up in paternalism and dependence. As the 1920s ended in depression, the dilemma of the African American intellectuals and civil rights leaders was simply this: none of the progressive social languages met their needs; none of Hoover's relief priorities strengthened their claims on equal civil rights. To seize their share of the American Dream as individuals, African Americans had to stress their group-based accomplishments and needs. But such group-based claims clashed with the "individualism" of whites who seemed increasingly reluctant to engage in interracial cooperation as the depression deepened.

Final Perspective

How to account for the pattern of achievements and failures indicated in the brief summaries of Parts 1 and 2 of this book? Who was responsible for the repeated patterns of failure? Those who resisted all specific proposals for change, who reacted out of racist perspectives and negative cultural and gender stereotypes, who routinely allowed inordinate self-interest to cloud their perception of the common good, who thwarted the implementation of protective laws and constitutional rights, and who violated common decencies and fair play in lynchings, race riots, and "red scare" hysteria must bear a major share of responsibility for these historical failures. But the past covered in this book was not a simple story of "good" victims and "bad" predators. The period 1865 to 1932 was one characterized by numerous contested social constructs, clashing priorities, changing meanings of key terms, and shifting institutional dynamics. The past was a complex tragedy in which all the actors "sinned" to some degree and fell short of the demands of democratic mutuality.

Core values, as contested social constructs, were at the center of these three-way struggles for power, for meaning, and for protection from unanticipated consequences. Controversies that involved core values were part of the transition from a producer-oriented society with a relatively homogeneous (but restricted) political order in 1865–98 to a consumer-oriented society with an increasingly heterogeneous polity in a culturally complex society in 1898–1932. There was a mixture of "good" and "evil" on all sides of these historical controversies; there was disappointment inherent in the very process of conflict and consensus. Liberty, equality, and justice were not just slogans or shibboleths that can be ignored by students of history in favor exclusively of the "hard data" of social science; rather, these core values were the very substance of the intellectual and cultural conflicts that were played out within the "souls" of the participants and the "bodies" of their institutions.

Traditional notions of liberty, equality, and justice were based primarily on notions of individualism in the period of the 1860s to the 1890s. These ideas became distorted when the contending parties became organizations, corporations, trade associations, unions, civil rights and civil liberties organizations, ethnic or religious groups, or government regulatory agencies. The gradual shift in emphasis from "procedural" definitions of justice to judicial determinations of "substantive justice," "reasonableness," or "fairness"; toward the priority of individual civil liberties; toward group-based civil rights; toward protective legislation for women and children; toward the demands for equal constitutional rights; and toward liberty as effective freedom to realize one's potential—all these demands created a cacophony of conflicting claims. The cry for equality and justice from minorities, women, small entrepreneurs, consumers, and endangered communities too often could not be heard above the clash of corporate and group-based conflicts. Most Americans between 1898 and 1932 had not yet learned that, however admirable and desirable might be the goal of liberty for themselves, equality denied and justice deferred for others in the long run undercut the very basis of ordered liberty—the democratic community.

The problem lay not simply in the *meaning* of the core values, but in the persistent *ranking* of them as well. As the end of the drama that had begun in 1865 appeared in 1932, the situation seemed all too familiar. With a minuscule radical option, with ritual withdrawal and renewal tendencies so prevalent, with limited reform options and organizations, and with a fearful majority clinging to familiar routines of the fading "consumer paradise," Americans wrestled anew with the conflict between the priorities of liberty and equality and the practical meaning of justice. Only gradually would some begin to understand the point made by the old socialists, the interracial commissions, the struggling working-class families, and the women's rights and justice advocates, that in liberty *interdependence* was more important than individual *independence* in maintaining cultural traditions and social institutions. Only painfully would a few people face the issue that liberty as a social goal was something more than *freedom from* external governmental restraint. It could also include freedom from segregation, discriminatory employment, or negative stereotypes as well. Liberty also meant the *freedom to* develop one's potential or talent. Such freedom entailed equality as guaranteed *access* to the means (education, credit, the ballot) necessary to achieve one's potential. Only haltingly, case by case, precedent by precedent, controversy by controversy, did the American political system and culture begin to recognize that justice was not simply adherence to a set of procedures (due process) or a tenuous equity (reward proportionate to effort or "fairness"). Justice was also a matter of the standards, of the expectations applied to all levels, of constitutional phrases turned into daily practices, protected by courts and undergirded by a sense of community. Liberty, equality, justice—the core values still stood. Whether these values could guide the nation as the trauma of the Great Depression deepened depended not only on their meaning in public discourse but, above all, on the priorities that Americans would assign to them.

Notes

Introduction

1   The Bradley Commission on History in Schools, *Building a History Curriculum: Guidelines for Teaching History in Schools* (Washington, D.C.: Educational Excellence Network, 1988), 1–2 (quotation); Lloyd Kramer, Donald Reid, and William L. Barney, eds., *Learning History in America: Schools, Cultures, and Politics* (Minneapolis: University of Minnesota Press, 1994), 1–24.

2   For the debate during the New Deal era on the concept of liberty, see Merrill D. Peterson, *The Jefferson Image in the American Mind* (New York: Oxford University Press, 1960), 355–60, 368–74.

    For an example of a historical explanation of American values in the nineteenth century that utilized the primacy of the concept of equality, see Henry Steele Commager, *The American Mind: An Interpretation of American Thought and Character since the 1880s* (New Haven: Yale University Press, 1950), chap. 1. Commager barely mentioned the concept of liberty and believed that the overemphasis on liberty in the nineteenth century schools and popular culture would be seen by later generations as "naive" (38–39, 40).

    Arthur M. Schlesinger Jr., *The Vital Center: The Politics of Freedom* (Boston: Houghton Mifflin, 1949) argued that the historical basis of American liberalism in its post–New Deal–World War II mode encompassed the equality and justice of civil rights and civil liberties at home and the protection of freedom by anticommunism abroad. He extolled "the techniques of freedom" but referred to "liberty" only vaguely (compare 192, 209, and 256).

    The locus classicus of the conservative misuse of the concept of liberty in the opinion of New Deal liberals and historians was Barry Goldwater's statement in 1964: "I would remind you that extremism in the defense of liberty is no vice. And . . . that moderation in the pursuit of justice is no virtue." Barry Goldwater, "I Accept Your Nomination," in *Voices of Crisis: Vital Speeches on Contemporary Issues*, ed. Floyd W. Matson (New York: Odyssey Press, 1967), 125.

    For the radical turn in American historiography, see the essays in "A Roundtable: What Has Changed and Not Changed in American Historical Practice?," *Journal of American History* 76 (September 1989): 393–488.

The statement about interpretations of American history refers to the use of such terms as "racism," "sexism," or "statism" not simply as *a* factor in historical analysis, but as *the* factor or the *predominant* characteristic in historical interpretation. For a critique of monocausal and hegemonic interpretations, see note 27 below.

3   Steven L. Lawson, "Freedom Then, Freedom Now: The Historiography of the Civil Rights Movement," *American Historical Review* 96 (April 1991): 456–71 (quotation on 464); Kim Lacy Rogers, "Oral History and the History of the Civil Rights Movement," *Journal of American History* 75 (September 1988): 567–76; and Betty Friedan, *The Feminine Mystique,* 1st paper ed. (New York: Dell Publishing Co., 1964), chap. 4 and 364 n. 3. For the women's liberation writers and anthology editors and their attitude toward history, see "Woman's Place," *Atlantic,* March 1970, 81–126; Robin Morgan, ed., *Sisterhood Is Powerful: An Anthology of Writings from the Women's Liberation Movement* (New York: Vintage Books, 1970); Cellestine Ware, *Woman Power: The Movement for Women's Liberation* (New York: Tower Publications, 1970); *Women: A Journal of Liberation,* Spring 1970, back cover; and Miriam Schneir, *Feminism: The Essential Historical Writings* (New York: Vintage Books, 1972).

4   David A. Aaker and George S. Day, *Consumerism: Search for the Consumer Interest* (New York: Free Press, 1971), xvii–xix, 2–5, 23–41; Ralph Nader, *Unsafe at Any Speed: The Designed-In Dangers of the American Automobile* (New York: Grossman Publishers, 1965), vii–xi, 233–53; "Ralph Nader Becomes an Organization," *Business Week,* 28 November 1970, 86–88; and Michael Pertschuk, *Revolt against Regulation: The Rise and Pause of the Consumer Movement* (Berkeley: University of California Press, 1982).

5   Ann Swidler, "Culture in Action: Symbols and Strategies," *American Sociological Review* 51 (April 1986): 273–86; Mary Douglas, ed., *Rules and Meanings: The Anthropology of Everyday Knowledge* (New York: Penguin Books, 1973), introduction; Robert N. Bellah, et al., *The Good Society* (New York: Alfred A. Knopf, 1991), introduction and appendix "Institutions in Sociology and Public Philosophy"; Pierre Bourdieu, "Rites as Acts of Institution," in *Honor and Grace in Anthropology,* eds. J. G. Peristiany and Julian Pitt-Rivers (Cambridge: Cambridge University Press, 1992), 79–90; and Stephen Macedo, *Liberal Virtues: Citizenship, Virtue, and Community in Liberal Constitutionalism* (Oxford: Clarendon Press, 1990).

6   Daniel T. Rodgers, *Contested Truths: Keywords in American Politics since Independence* (New York: Basic Books, 1987); James A. Monroe, *Democratic Wish: Popular Participation and the Limits of American Government* (New York: Basic Books, 1990), 10–11; William M. Reddy, *Money and Liberty in Modern Europe: A Critique of Historical Understanding* (Cambridge: Cambridge University Press, 1987), 60 (quotation); and Ronald Dworkin, "Justice for Clarence Thomas," *New York Review of Books,* 7 November 1991, 43.

7   Craig Calhoun, Marshall W. Meyer, and W. Richard Scott, eds., *Structures of Power and Constraint: Papers in Honor of Peter M. Blau* (Cambridge: Cambridge University Press, 1990), introduction and pt. 1, "Exchange, Power and Inequality"; R. W. Connell, *Gender and Power: Society, the Person and Sexual Politics* (Stanford: Stan-

ford University Press, 1987), 94–99; Jacquelyn Dowd Hall, "Partial Truths," *Signs* 14 (Summer 1989): 902–11; Howard P. Chudacoff, "Success and Security: The Meaning of Social Mobility in America," *Reviews in American History* 10 (December 1982): 101–12; and Richard Oestreicher, "Urban Working-Class Political Behavior and Theories of American Electoral Politics, 1870–1940," *Journal of American History* 74 (March 1988): 1257–86.

8 Michael McGerr, "Political Style and Women's Power, 1830–1930," *Journal of American History* 77 (December 1990): 864–85; and Doris Weatherford, *Foreign and Female: Immigrant Women in America, 1840–1930* (New York: Schocken Books, 1986), pts. 4–7.

9 Victor W. Turner and Edward M. Bruner, eds., *The Anthropology of Experience* (Urbana: University of Illinois Press, 1986), 5–12.

10 This model was worked out in 1965–67 and then tested cross-culturally in two works published in 1973 and 1983. See Ross Evans Paulson, *Radicalism and Reform: The Vrooman Family and American Social Thought, 1837–1937* (Lexington: University of Kentucky Press for the Organization of American Historians, 1968), *Women's Suffrage and Prohibition: A Comparative Study of Equality and Social Control* (Glenview: Scott, Foresman, 1973), and *Language, Science, and Action: Korzybski's General Semantics—A Study in Comparative Intellectual History* (Westport: Greenwood Press for the Council on Intercultural and Comparative Studies, 1983). In the 1967 version, I drew on Robert K. Merton, *Social Theory and Social Structure* (Glencoe: Free Press, 1957), 131–60. I now find this initial model of intellectual *categories* too rigid and static; rather, in the model proposed here, I am interested in intellectual/action *roles* that are more temporal, even temporary, and dynamic. The proposed model thus conflates Merton's model as follows:

Proposed Four-Part Response Model	Merton's Modes of Adaptation
1. Resignation: Life as Routine	Conformity
2. Ritual: Life as Periodic Withdrawal and Renewal (Turner's liminal-liminoid distinction)	Ritualism and Retreatism
3. Reform: Life as Response and Reordering of Institutions and Values	Innovation
4. Radicalism: Life as Revolutionary Protest and Reconstruction of Society and Values	Rebellion

Furthermore, I agree with Robert Wuthnow that daily patterns of behavior that help to *maintain* social order should be called "routines," not "rituals" as Merton did. I follow Victor Turner's admonition that the term "ritual" should be used for those special patterns of behavior with expressive, intentional, and dramaturgical aspects that help to articulate the *meaning* of the social order. See Robert Wuthnow, *Meaning and Moral Order: Explorations in Cultural Analysis* (Berkeley: University of California Press, 1987), chap. 4 (criticism of Merton is on 98); Victor W. Turner, *Dramas, Fields, and Metaphors: Symbolic Action in Human Society* (Ithaca: Cornell University Press, 1974), chap. 6 (especially 251); and Edward M. Bruner, "Experience and Its Expressions," in *Anthropology of Experience,* ed. Turner and

Bruner, 7, 9–10. For a critique of some of these assumptions, see David I. Kertzer, *Ritual, Politics, and Power* (New Haven: Yale University Press, 1988), chaps. 1, 5, 6; and Donald Weber, "From Limen to Border: A Meditation on the Legacy of Victor Turner for American Cultural Studies," *American Quarterly* 47 (September 1995): 525–36.

11 James B. Gardner and George R. Adams, eds., *Ordinary People and Everyday Life: Perspectives on the New Social History* (Nashville: American Association of State and Local History, 1983). Note that "daily routines" implies some sense of compulsion, what we must do or are expected to do, and acquiescence to the status quo; periodic "ritual," on the other hand, implies a sense of conviction, what we choose to do, and implies some resistance to the status quo, however sporadic or temporary. Note, also, that "acquiescence" implies some conscious acceptance of the status quo and its public justifications whereas "quiescence" implies residual resistance to the status quo and its official values and the potential for rebellion under changed circumstances. Cf. John Gaventa, *Power and Powerlessness: Quiescence and Rebellion in an Appalachian Valley* (Urbana: University of Illinois Press, 1982), introduction and chaps. 3, 5.

12 Stanley J. Tambiah, *Culture, Thought, and Social Action: An Anthropological Perspective* (Cambridge: Harvard University Press, 1985), 1–4; Kathleen M. Ashley, ed., *Victor Turner and the Construction of Cultural Criticism: Between Literature and Anthropology* (Bloomington: Indiana University Press, 1990), xvi–xx; and Mary Jo Deegan, *American Ritual Dramas: Social Rules and Cultural Meanings* (Westport: Greenwood Press, 1989), 9 (quotation). I do not agree with Deegan's concept of a core *code* (Deegan, *American Ritual Dramas*, 20). I find this hegemonic concept too dependent on current media to have much use for historical explanation in earlier time periods.

13 Ronald L. Grimes, "Victor Turner's Definition, Theory, and Sense of Ritual," in *Turner and the Construction of Cultural Criticism*, ed. Ashley, 144–45; and Deegan, *American Ritual Dramas*, 10–11.

14 Mark C. Carnes, *Secret Ritual and Manhood in Victorian America* (New Haven: Yale University Press, 1989), 6–13, 74–80, 126, and epilogue; May Ann Clawson, *Constructing Brotherhood: Class, Gender, and Fraternalism* (Princeton: Princeton University Press, 1989); Karen J. Blair, *The Clubwoman as Feminist: True Womanhood Redefined, 1868–1914* (New York: Holms and Meier, 1980); Theodora Penny Martin, *The Sound of Our Own Voices: Women's Study Clubs, 1860–1910* (Boston: Beacon Press, 1987); and Estelle B. Freedman, "Separatism as Strategy: Female Institution Building and American Feminism, 1870–1930," in *Women and Power in American History: A Reader*, ed. Kathryn Kish Sklar and Thomas Dublin (Englewood Cliffs: Prentice Hall, 1991), 2:10–24.

15 Arthur E. Bestor, *Backwoods Utopias* (Philadelphia: University of Pennsylvania Press, 1950); Michael Barkun, *Crucible of the Millennium* (Syracuse: Syracuse University Press, 1986); Spencer Klaw, *Without Sin: The Life and Death of the Oneida Community* (New York: Penguin U.S.A., 1993); and Edward K. Spann, *Brotherly Tomorrows: Movements for a Cooperative Society in America, 1820–1920* (New York: Columbia University Press, 1989). The concepts of "liminal," "liminoid," and "marginal" activities will also account for some of the historical phe-

nomena mentioned in T. J. Jackson Lears, *No Place of Grace: Antimodernism and the Transformation of American Culture* (New York: Pantheon Books, 1981); Linda Kerber, "Separate Spheres, Female Worlds, Woman's Place: The Rhetoric of Women's History," *Journal of American History* 75 (June 1988): 32–36; and Günter H. Lenz, "Symbolic Space, Communal Rituals, and the Surreality of the Urban Ghetto: Harlem in Black Literature from the 1920s to the 1960s," *Callaloo: Journal of Afro-American and African Arts and Letters* 11 (Spring 1988): 309–45.

16   Robert H. Walker, ed., *The Reform Spirit in America: A Documentation of the Pattern of Reform in the American Republic* (New York: G. P. Putnam's Sons, 1976); Robert H. Walker, *Reform in America: The Continuing Frontier* (Lexington: University Press of Kentucky, 1985); and Walter Nugent, "The Agelessness of Reform," *Reviews in American History* 15 (June 1987): 185–90.

17   Steven Kesselman, *The Modernization of American Reform: Structures and Perceptions* (New York: Garland Publishing Co., 1979), 1–5, 8–9, 13–14; Arthur M. Schlesinger Jr., *The Crisis of Confidence: Ideas, Power and Violence in America* (New York: Bantham Books, 1969), 44–45, 53, 73, and *The Cycles of American History* (Boston: Houghton Mifflin, 1986), 27–31; and Louise L. Stevenson, *The Victorian Homefront: American Thought and Culture, 1860–1880* (New York: Twayne Publishers, 1991), chaps. 1–5.

18   Aileen S. Kraditor, *The Radical Persuasion, 1890–1917: Aspects of the Intellectual History and the Historiography of Three American Radical Organizations* (Baton Rouge: Louisiana State University Press, 1981); Peter L. Berger and Richard J. Neuhaus, *Movement and Revolution: On American Radicalism* (New York: Doubleday Anchor Books, 1970); William A. Gamson, *A Study of Social Protest* (Homewood, Ill.: Dorsey Press, 1975); and Seweryn Bialer, "On the Meaning, Sources, and Carriers of Radicalism in Contemporary Industrialized Societies: Introductory Remarks," in *Radicalism in the Contemporary Age*, vol. 1, *Sources of Contemporary Radicalism*, ed. Seweryn Bialer and Sophia Sluzar (Boulder: Westview Press, 1977), 3–30 (particularly 7).

Should religious communitarians be included among the radicals or among the ritualists as defined by the four-part response model? If religious communitarians are not "open" to temporary members but rather are "closed," and if they *do not* see themselves as a model *to be emulated by others* in the larger society, then their embodiment of alternate core values does function as a radical response in reference to the larger society rather than as a retreat and renewal response. If, on the other hand, the community is open and seeks to act as a temporary space for renewal, it would function as ritualistic.

The case of a Trappist monastery will illustrate differences between a ritual withdrawal and a radical response to society's perceived problems. Those who choose to live *permanently* within the discipline of the order, and who are marginal to the dynamics of the larger society, would fall in the broadly conceived "liminal" category (or what Turner also called "outsiderhood"). They choose not to be a part of the larger society and represent a radical response to its crisis of values. The individual who *temporarily* participates in a retreat at the monastery, would experience the community as "liminoid" and might experience a *renewal* of values through ritual participation. See the comments in Frank Lentricchia, "En Route to

Retreat: Making It to Mepkin Abbey," *Harper's*, January 1992, 68–78; and Donald Weber, "From Limen to Border," 529–30.

19   Chantal Mouffe, "Preface: Democratic Politics Today," in *Dimensions of Radical Democracy: Pluralism, Citizenship, Community*, ed. Chantal Mouffe (London: Verso, 1992), 1–2.

20   Ibid., 4 (quotation). The phrase "radically new" institutional arrangements I draw from Bradley Levinson of the anthropology program at Augustana College in his critical response to an early draft of this introduction.

21   On the role of "vision" in the posttotalitarian movement in history, see Václav Havel, "The Power of the Powerless," in *Václav Havel: Living in Truth*, ed. Jan Vladislav (London: Faber and Faber, 1990), 36–122.

22   The concepts of social languages and key words are adapted (with modifications) from Daniel T. Rodgers, "In Search of Progressivism," *Reviews in American History* 10 (December 1982): 113–32; and Rodgers, *Contested Truths*, introduction and chaps. 3–4.

23   On the role of conventions in communication and rhetorical strategies, see Kenneth Cmiel, *Democratic Eloquence: The Fight over Popular Speech in Nineteenth-Century America* (Berkeley: University of California Press, 1990), chaps. 1–3; Karlyn Kohrs Campbell, *Women Public Speakers in the United States, 1800–1925* (Westport: Greenwood Press, 1993), introduction; Hazel Dicken-Garcia, *Journalistic Standards in the Nineteenth Century* (Madison: University of Wisconsin Press, 1989), 206–22; Estelle C. Jelinek, *The Tradition of Women's Autobiography: From Antiquity to the Present* (Boston: Twayne Publishers, 1986), chaps. 6–8; Robert C. Holub, *Reception Theory: A Critical Introduction* (London: Methuen, 1984), chap. 4; Dominick LaCapra, *History and Criticism* (Ithaca: Cornell University Press, 1985), chap. 1; and Thomas W. Benson, ed., *American Rhetoric: Content and Criticism* (Carbondale: Southern Illinois University Press, 1989), chaps. 1, 8.

24   For some aspects of these methodological issues among historians, see David Harlan, "Intellectual History and the Return of Literature," *American Historical Review* 94 (June 1989): 581–609; Alan Megill, "Recounting the Past: 'Description,' Explanation, and Narrative in Historiography," *American Historical Review* 94 (June 1989): 627–53; Joyce Appleby, "One Good Turn Deserves Another: Moving beyond the Linguistic," *American Historical Review* 94 (December 1989): 1326–32; Mark Bevir, "The Errors of Linguistic Contextualism," *History and Theory* 31, no. 3 (1992): 276–98; Brian Stock, *Listening for the Text: On the Uses of the Past* (Baltimore: Johns Hopkins University Press, 1990), chaps. 1, 7–8; and Mark Poster, *Critical Theory and Poststructuralism: In Search of a Context* (Ithaca: Cornell University Press, 1989), introduction and chaps. 1, 7–8; Saul Cornell, "Splitting the Difference: Textualism, Contextualism, and Post-Modern History," *American Studies* 36 (Spring 1995): 57–80. For limitations of linguistics-influenced theories as applied to post–Civil War America, see Nell Irvin Painter, "Thinking about the Languages of Money and Race," *American Historical Review* 99 (April 1994): 396–404.

25   William A. Craigie and James R. Hulbert, eds., *A Dictionary of American English on Historical Principles* (Chicago: University of Chicago Press, 1942–44), vol. 3, "radical," and vol. 4, "ultra"; Harry R. Warfel, ed., *The Letters of Noah Webster* (New York: Library Publishers, 1953), 477, 482, 504; and Eric Foner, *Free*

Soil, Free Labor, Free Men: The Ideology of the Republican Party before the Civil War (New York: Oxford University Press, 1970), 86. For an example of the use of "ultra" and "radical" as adjectives in the 1850s, see Carol Lasser and Marlene Deahl Merrill, eds., *Friends and Sisters: Letters between Lucy Stone and Antoinette Brown Blackwell, 1846–1893* (Urbana: University of Illinois Press, 1987), 72; and Leslie Wheeler, ed., *Loving Warriors: Selected Letters of Lucy Stone and Henry B. Blackwell, 1853 to 1893* (New York: Dial Press, 1981), 48, 54–55, 77. For the developments in the 1860s, see David Donald, *Charles Sumner and the Rights of Man* (New York: Alfred A. Knopf, 1970), 139, 157; Leroy P. Graf and Ralph W. Haskins, eds., *The Papers of Andrew Johnson* (Knoxville: University of Tennessee Press, 1983), 4:xxxi, 239–44, 260 n. 85, and 6:646, 670, 757; and Eric McKitrick, *Andrew Johnson and Reconstruction* (Chicago: University of Chicago Press, 1960), 55.

26   Nancy F. Cott, *The Grounding of Modern Feminism* (New Haven: Yale University Press, 1987). On the methodological foundations of women's history, see Nancy F. Cott, "What's in a Name? The Limits of 'Social Feminism'; or, Expanding the Vocabulary of Women's History," *Journal of American History* 76 (December 1989): 809–29; Kerber, "Separate Spheres, Female Worlds, Woman's Place," 9–39; and Louise L. Stevenson, "Women's Intellectual History: A New Direction," *Intellectual History Newsletter* 15 (1993): 32–38.

27   For the critique of historical methodologies that focus on single determinate factors or that see human freedom as limited by the power of hegemonic elites, see Leon Fink, "The New Labor History and the Powers of Historical Pessimism: Consensus, Hegemony, and the Case of the Knights of Labor," *Journal of American History* 75 (June 1988): 115–36; T. J. Jackson Lears, "The Concept of Cultural Hegemony: Problems and Possibilities," *American Historical Review* 90 (June 1985): 567–93; John P. Diggins, "Comrades and Citizens: New Methodologies in American Historiography," *American Historical Review* 90 (June 1985): 614–38, "The Misuses of Gramsci," *Journal of American History* 75 (June 1988): 141–45, and "Power, Freedom, and the Failure of Theory," *Harper's,* January 1992, 15–19; and Fred Weinstein, *History and Theory: After the Fall* (Chicago: University of Chicago Press, 1990), 30.

Part 1: Old Languages and New Realities

1   Abraham Lincoln, *The Collected Works of Abraham Lincoln,* ed. Roy P. Basler (New Brunswick, N.J.: Rutgers University Press, 1953), 7: 301–2.

2   For the pre–Civil War meaning of liberty and equality, see Michael Kammen, *Spheres of Liberty: Changing Perceptions of Liberty in American Culture* (Madison: University of Wisconsin Press, 1986); David Hacket Fischer, *Albion's Seed: Four British Folkways in America* (New York: Oxford University Press, 1989); Oscar Handlin and Lillian Handlin, *Liberty in Expansion, 1760–1850* (New York: Harper and Row, 1989); Robert H. Webking, *The American Revolution and the Politics of Liberty* (Baton Rouge: Louisiana State University Press, 1988); John Phillip Reid, *The Concept of Liberty in the Age of the American Revolution* (Chicago: University of Chicago Press, 1988); Joyce Appleby, *Capitalism and a New Social Order: The Republican Vision of the 1790s* (New York: New York University Press, 1984);

Jack P. Greene, *Imperatives, Behaviors, and Identities: Essays in Early American Cultural History* (Charlottesville: University Press of Virginia, 1992); James M. McPherson, *Abraham Lincoln and the Second American Revolution* (New York: Oxford University Press, 1990), chap. 3; and Celeste Michelle Condit and John Louis Lucaites, *Crafting Equality: America's Anglo-African Word* (Chicago: University of Chicago Press, 1993).

1   Presidential Reconstruction and the Meaning of Liberty, Equality, and Justice, 1865–1866

1   Dan T. Carter, *When the War Was Over: The Failure of Self-Reconstruction in the South, 1865–1867* (Baton Rouge: Louisiana State University Press, 1985), 86.

2   Isa. 61:1–2 King James Version.

Vice President Andrew Johnson alluded to Isaiah's prophecy on 12 April 1864. *The Papers of Andrew Johnson*, ed. Leroy P. Graff and Ralph W. Haskins (Knoxville: University of Tennessee Press, 1983), 6:671.

3   Eric Foner, *Reconstruction: America's Unfinished Revolution, 1863–1877* (New York: Harper and Row, 1988), chaps. 1, 3–4. See also Douglas L. Colbert, "Liberating the Thirteenth Amendment," *Harvard Civil Rights-Civil Liberties Law Review* 30 (Winter 1995): 1–55.

The Thirteenth Amendment also recognized that liberty could be lost temporarily "as punishment for crimes whereof the parties shall have been duly convicted." This language was drafted by Senator Lyman Trumbull of Illinois and was based on the Northwest Ordinance of 1787. See Ralph J. Roske, *His Own Counsel: The Life and Times of Lyman Trumbull* (Reno: University of Nevada Press, 1979), 106–7.

4   In order to answer the question "Who were the Radical Republicans?" historians have applied a number of techniques borrowed from the behavioral sciences. See Allan G. Bogue, "Bloc and Party in the United States Senate: 1861–1863," *Civil War History* 13 (September 1967): 235–36; Glen M. Linden " 'Radicals' and Economic Policies: The Senate, 1861–1873," *Journal of Southern History* 32 (1977): 189–99; Edward L. Gambill, "Who Were the Senate Radicals?" *Civil War History* 11 (September 1965): 237–44; and Allan G. Bogue, *The Ernest Men: Republicans of the Civil War Senate* (Ithaca: Cornell University Press, 1981).

For the transition of terminology from "ultra" as a religious term to "radical" as a political term, see William A. Craigie and James R. Hulbert, eds., *A Dictionary of American English on Historical Principles* (Chicago: University of Chicago Press, 1942–44), vols. 3 and 4; Eric Foner, *Free Soil, Free Labor, Free Men: The Ideology of the Republican Party before the Civil War* (New York: Oxford University Press, 1960), 86; Carol Lasser and Marlene Deahl Merrill, eds., *Friends and Sisters: Letters between Lucy Stone and Antoinette Brown Blackwell, 1846–1893* (Urbana: University of Illinois Press, 1987), 72; Leslie Wheeler, ed., *Loving Warriors: Selected Letters of Lucy Stone and Henry B. Blackwell, 1853 to 1893* (New York: Dial Press, 1981), 48, 54–55, 77; and Eric McKitrick, *Andrew Johnson and Reconstruction* (Chicago: University of Chicago Press, 1960), 55.

I have used the term Radical Republicans in the narrow historical sense as designating that faction of congressional Republicans who pushed for protection of the civil rights of freedmen and white Unionists and who were willing to reconstruct southern and federal legal institutions to achieve this end.

5   For the psychological meaning of liberty as self-willed consent, see Louisa May Alcott, *Moods*, ed. Sarah Elbert (New Brunswick, N.J.: Rutgers University Press, 1991), 6–7.

Significantly, Sarah Elbert noted in her introduction that when Alcott came to revise the novel in 1881–82, the opening chapter in which the definition of consensual liberty appeared was cut from the manuscript. Between the first published version of *Moods* (1864) and the 1882 revised edition, Elbert noted, was Alcott's own psychosexual maturation. There were also losses and additions to the Alcott family, to their circle of old friends, and to Alcott's coterie of women writers, artists, and reformers of both sexes. An additional historical fact was the changing meaning of the term liberty in the debate over women's rights in the 1870s and 1880s as shall be shown later in this book.

6   Daniel Walker Howe, "The Evangelical Movement and Political Culture in the North during the Second Party System," *Journal of American History* 77 (March 1991): 1216–39; Foner, *Free Soil, Free Labor, Free Men*, chaps. 1, 3, 9; Earl J. Hess, *Liberty, Virtue, and Progress: Northerners and Their War for the Union* (New York: New York University Press, 1988); and Victor B. Howard, *Religion and the Radical Republican Movement, 1860–1870* (Lexington: University Press of Kentucky, 1990), chap. 7.

7   The free-labor ideology thus approximated that belief in "ordered liberty" outlined in Joyce Appleby, *Capitalism and a New Social Order: The Republican Vision of the 1790s* (New York: New York University Press, 1984), and Michael Kammen, *Spheres of Liberty: Changing Perceptions of Liberty in American Culture* (Madison: University of Wisconsin Press, 1986). For a critical review of the concept of classical republicanism as used by some recent historians, see Daniel T. Rodgers, "Republicanism: The Career of a Concept," *Journal of American History* 79 (June 1992): 11–38.

8   Here the Republicans confronted the ambiguity of the past. Thomas Jefferson had enshrined equality in the American political tradition in the Declaration of Independence. These words could be read to mean that natural equality was the primary value and civil liberty a subordinate means. However, they could also be read to mean that natural rights rested on a prior equal status, a precondition for a social contract. Such a reading would put equality safely in the *past* as a premise, not in the future as a promise. Thomas Paine, in the same historic year of 1776, had introduced the notion of equality as a goal into the American political discourse in his pamphlet *Common Sense*, but many Americans in the nineteenth century were ambivalent about Paine and his ideas. As recent historical studies have made clear, the Revolutionary generation meant by equality primarily the condition of not being subject to the arbitrary will of another, security of property, and access to political power (or democracy). See Gordon S. Wood, "Americans and Revolutionaries," review of *Revolutions: Reflections on American Equality and Foreign Liberations*, by David Brion Davis, *New York Review of Books*, 17 September 1990, 32–35; Appleby, *Capitalism and a New Social Order*, 15; John Phillip

Reid, *The Concept of Liberty in the Age of the American Revolution* (Chicago: University of Chicago Press, 1988); Ian Dyck, ed., *Citizen of the World: Essays on Thomas Paine* (New York: St. Martin's Press, 1988); and Foner, *Reconstruction*, 230–39.

On the relationship of democracy and liberty in American thought, see Michael Kammen, *Sovereignty and Liberty: Constitutional Discourse in American Culture* (Madison: University of Wisconsin Press, 1988), and Daniel T. Rodgers, *Contested Truths: Keywords in American Politics since Independence* (New York: Basic Books, 1987), chaps. 3–4.

9   Mark Tushnet, "The Politics of Equality in Constitutional Law: Equal Protection Clause, Dr. Du Bois, and Charles Hamilton Houston," *Journal of American History* 74 (December 1987): 886 (quotation); Harold M. Hyman, ed., *Radical Republicans and Reconstruction, 1861–1870* (Indianapolis: Bobbs-Merrill, 1967), pt. 7; and Foner, *Reconstruction*, 230–39.

On the background of white fears of social equality and black attitudes, see Winthrop D. Jordan, *White over Black: American Attitudes toward the Negro, 1550–1812* (New York: W. W. Norton, 1977), and Celeste Michelle Condit and John Louis Lucaites, *Crafting Equality: America's Anglo-African Word* (Chicago: University of Chicago Press, 1993), 106–8, 110.

10 Morton Keller, "Power and Rights: Two Centuries of American Constitutionalism," *Journal of American History* 74 (December 1987): 683; Foner, *Reconstruction*, 18–34.

11 Mark E. Neely Jr., *The Fate of Liberty: Abraham Lincoln and Civil Liberties* (New York: Oxford University Press, 1991), chap. 1; C. Vann Woodward, "The Inner Civil War," review of *Mind and the American Civil War: A Meditation on Lost Causes*, by Lewis P. Simpson, and *The Creation of Confederate Nationalism: Ideology and Identity in the Civil War South*, by Drew Gilpin Faust, *New York Review of Books*, 15 March 1990, 39–41.

Neely used the term "civil liberties" in a general way that presumed current usage, although he was primarily concerned with the right of habeas corpus. The term "civil liberties" is currently defined as referring to "those freedoms or liberties found in the first ten amendments of the Constitution (Bill of Rights)" (Alex Wellek, ed., *The Encyclopedic Dictionary of American Government*, 4th ed. [Guilford, Conn.: Duskin Publishing Group, 1991], 45). Technically, the right of habeas corpus is under Article I, Section 9 of the Constitution, not the Bill of Rights (but may be regarded as implied by Amendment V's clause, "nor be deprived of life, liberty, or property, without due process of law").

Use of the term "civil liberties" in its current usage to describe events or actions in the Civil War Era, moreover, is somewhat anachronistic. *Webster's Dictionary*, unabridged ed. (Springfield, Mass.: George and Charles Merriam, 1859), did not record the plural form. Rather, it used the singular form: "*Civil liberty* is the liberty of man in a state of society, or natural liberty, so far only abridged and restrained, as is necessary and expedient for the safety and interest of the society, state, or nation. . . . *Civil liberty* is an exemption from the arbitrary will of others, which exemption is secured by established laws, which restrain every man from injuring or controlling another. Hence the restraints of law are essential to *civil liberty"* (661). Under "bill of rights," it noted: "In America, a bill or declaration of rights is prefexed to most of the constitutions of the several states" (122; cf. 956).

William A. Craigie and James R. Hulbert, eds., *A Dictionary of American English on Historical Principles* (Chicago: University of Chicago Press, 1938–44), in volume 1 did not record any entry for "civil liberties." They did note in volume 4 the use of "Bill of Rights" with three definitions: (a) "one of various formal declarations of privileges and immunities of American citizens"; (b) "the first ten amendments to the Constitution"; and (c) figurative "and in allusive context." An 1862 example of such figurative use of the term referred to grammar as "that vile infraction of the Bill of Rights and the liberties of the people" (4:1949).

As shall be shown in chapters 10 and 13 of this book, the current meaning of the term "civil liberties" did not come into vogue until World War I.

12 Mark Wahlgren Summers, *The Press Gang: Newspapers and Politics, 1865–1878* (Chapel Hill: University of North Carolina Press, 1994), 27 (quotation); Alexander Saxton, *The Rise and Fall of the White Republic: Class Politics and Mass Culture in Nineteenth-Century America* (New York: Verso Books, 1990), chap. 6; Edward L. Gambill, *Conservative Ordeal: Northern Democrats and Reconstruction* (Ames: Iowa State University Press, 1981); Joel Silbey, *A Respectable Minority: The Democratic Party in the Civil War Era, 1860–1868* (New York: W. W. Norton, 1977), chaps. 8–10; and Michael O'Brien, *Rethinking the South: Essays in Intellectual History* (Baltimore: Johns Hopkins University Press, 1988), 116.

13 Condit and Lucaites, *Crafting Equality,* 101–15 (quotations on 108 and 109).

14 "Wade-Davis Bill" and Abraham Lincoln, "Veto Message on Wade-Davis Bill," in *Radical Republicans and Reconstruction,* ed. Hyman, 125–28, 134–36.

The Wade-Davis Bill would have relied on a majority of loyalist, that is Unionist, whites to reconstitute their states on a free-labor basis. It also had specific protections for freedmen and disqualifications for former Confederate office holders or anyone "who [had] voluntarily borne arms against the United States." For the test, see ibid., 128–34.

The terminology of "radicalism" and "conservatism," as political terms is found in George W. Julian's speech on 7 February 1865, reprinted in ibid., 162–70.

15 Kevin G. Harvey, "Andrew Johnson, Reconstruction, and Congressional Republicans: A Predestined Failure" (Senior history paper, Augustana College, May 1991).

16 Hans Trefausee, *Andrew Johnson: A Biography* (New York: W. W. Norton, 1989), chaps. 1–9; *Papers of Andrew Johnson,* 6:156 (quotation); and David Warren Bowen, *Andrew Johnson and the Negro* (Knoxville: University of Tennessee Press, 1989), chaps. 1–4.

17 Andrew Johnson, "Proclamation," in *Radical Republicans and Reconstruction,* ed. Hyman, 249–56 (quotation on 250).

18 Rendigs Fels, *American Business Cycles, 1865–1879* (Chapel Hill: University of North Carolina Press, 1959); Irwin Unger, *The Greenback Era: A Social and Political History of American Finance, 1865–1879* (Princeton: Princeton University Press, 1964), chaps. 1–4; and Milton Friedman and Anna Jacobson Schwartz, *A Monetary History of the United States, 1867–1960* (Princeton: Princeton University Press, 1963), chap. 2.

19   Elizur Wright, "Suffrage for the Blacks Sound Political Economy," in *Radical Republicans and Reconstruction*, ed. Hyman, 178 (quotation); Foner, *Reconstruction*, 224.

20   Carter, *When the War Was Over*, 86, 93–94 (quotation).

21   Frederick Douglass, "What the Black Man Wants" (April 1865), in *Radical Republicans and Reconstruction*, ed. Hyman, 171 (quotation).

22   William S. McFeely, *Frederick Douglass* (New York: W. W. Norton, 1991), 241 (letter of May 1865 quotation); Douglass, "What the Black Man Wants," in *Radical Republicans and Reconstruction*, ed. Hyman, 175. The diversity of free-black opinion *prior* to the Civil War is outlined in Wilson Jeremiah Moses, *The Golden Age of Black Nationalism, 1850–1925* (New York: Oxford University Press, 1978), chap. 2.

23   Foner, *Reconstruction*, 88–93, 102–6 (quotation on 103), 110–119.

24   Carter, *When the War Was Over*, 104–5, chap. 4; James L. Roark, *Masters without Slaves: Southern Planters in the Civil War and Reconstruction* (New York: W. W. Norton, 1977), chaps. 4–5; Foner, *Reconstruction*, chaps. 4–5; and James Oakes, *Slavery and Freedom: An Interpretation of the Old South* (New York: Alfred A. Knopf, 1990), 76–79.

25   *Congressional Globe*, 39th Cong., 1st sess., pt. 1, 498 (Trumbull's remarks); Civil Rights Act, 9 April 1866, sec. 1, reprinted in *Radical Republicans and Reconstruction*, ed. Hyman, 310.

26   Civil Rights Act, 9 April 1866, sec. 2–3, reprinted in *Radical Republicans and Reconstruction*, ed. Hyman, 310–12; Robert J. Kaczorowski, "To Begin the Nation Anew: Congress, Citizenship, and Civil Rights after the Civil War," *American Historical Review* 92 (February 1987): 48–58; Tushnet, "Politics of Equality in Constitutional Law," 886; Roske, *His Own Counsel*, 122. For the background on legal presuppositions in the Civil Rights Act of 1866, see Rowland Berthoff, "Conventional Mentality: Free Blacks, Women, and Business Corporations as Unequal Persons, 1820–1870," *Journal of American History* 76 (December 1989): 753–84.

27   U.S. Constitution, amend. 14; Foner, *Reconstruction*, 260. For the background and interpretation of the amendment, see Erving E. Beauregard, "Female Influence on the Authorship of the Fourteenth Amendment," *Journal of Unconventional History* 2 (1991): 51–68, and *Bingham of the Hills: Politician and Diplomat Extraordinary* (New York: Peter Lang, 1989), chap. 5; William E. Nelson, *The Fourteenth Amendment: From Political Principle to Judicial Doctrine* (Cambridge: Harvard University Press, 1988); Charles A. Lofgren, *The Plessy Case: A Legal-Historical Interpretation* (New York: Oxford University Press, 1987), chap. 4; and David A. J. Richards, *Conscience and the Constitution: History, Theory, and Law of the Reconstruction Amendments* (Princeton: Princeton University Press, 1993), chap. 4.

28   Fels, *American Business Cycles*; Unger, *The Greenback Era*, 44–61; and Foner, *Reconstruction*, 260, 264, 266–72. Foner noted that while *Ex Parte Milligan* had been decided in April 1866, the full text of the opinion was not released until December 1866, by which time Congress had reassembled.

   For the background on *Ex Parte Milligan*, see David P. Currie, *The Constitution in the Supreme Court: The First Hundred Years, 1789–1888* (Chicago: University of Chicago Press, 1985), chap. 9, pt. 1; Neely, *The Fate of Liberty*, 35–36, 175–79.

29   Thadeus Stevens, "Speech, 3 January 1867," reprinted in *Radical Republicans and Reconstruction*, ed. Hyman, 368–76; McFeely, *Frederick Douglass*, 255.

2   From Congressional Reconstruction to the Civil Rights Cases of 1883

1   The Reconstruction Act of 2 March 1867 and supplement of 23 March 1867 as reprinted in Harold M. Hyman, ed., *The Radical Republicans and Reconstruction, 1861–1870* (Indianapolis: Bobbs-Merrill, 1967), 379–88; Eric Foner, *Reconstruction: America's Unfinished Revolution, 1863–1877* (New York: Harper and Row, 1988), 333–45; David P. Currie, *The Constitution in the Supreme Court: The First Hundred Years, 1789–1888* (Chicago: University of Chicago Press, 1985), chap. 9; and Frederick J. Blue, *Salmon P. Chase: A Life in Politics* (Kent: Kent State University Press, 1987), 271–72.

2   Foner, *Reconstruction*, 496; U.S. Constitution, amend. 15; Irwin Unger, *The Greenback Era: A Social and Political History of American Finance, 1865–1879* (Princeton: Princeton University Press, 1964), chaps. 3–4; and Richard Franklin Bensel, *Yankee Leviathan: The Origins of Central State Authority in America, 1859–1877* (Cambridge: Cambridge University Press, 1990), chap. 5.

3   William Lloyd Garrison, "Speech, 9 April 1870," reprinted in *Radical Republicans and Reconstruction*, ed. Hyman, 492–502 (quotations on 492–93 and 495; emphasis added); Foner, *Reconstruction*, 277–80 (quotation on 278); and Robert J. Kaczorowski, "To Begin the Nation Anew: Congress, Citizenship, and Civil Rights after the Civil War," *American Historical Review* 92 (February 1987): 45–68 (quotations on 53 and 47). For the counterargument, that the northern legal community was not willing to be as flexible constitutionally during congressional Reconstruction as it had been during the Civil War, see Charles W. McCurdy, "Legal Institutions, Constitutional Theory, and the Tragedy of Reconstruction," *Reviews in American History* 4 (June 1976): 203; and R. Kent Newmyer, "Harvard Law School, New England Legal Culture, and the Antebellum Origins of American Jurisprudence," *Journal of American History* 74 (December 1987): 814–35.

For the role of William Lloyd Garrison, see William E. Cain, ed., *William Lloyd Garrison and the Fight against Slavery: Selections from "The Liberator"* (Boston: Bedford Books of St. Martin's Press, 1995), 1–57.

4   Richard H. Abbott, *The Republican Party and the South, 1855–1877* (Chapel Hill: University of North Carolina Press, 1986), chaps. 3–4; Mark E. Neely Jr., *The Fate of Liberty: Abraham Lincoln and Civil Liberties* (New York: Oxford University Press, 1991), chap. 10 and epilogue; and Charles Fairman, *Mr. Justice Miller and the Supreme Court, 1862–1890* (Cambridge: Harvard University Press, 1939), chaps. 2, 6.

5   Victor B. Howard, *Religion and the Radical Republican Movement, 1860–1870* (Lexington: University Press of Kentucky, 1990), 1–5; Laurence Veysey, ed., *The Perfectionists: Radical Social Thought in the North, 1815–1860* (New York: John Wiley, 1973), pts. 1, 4; Daniel Walker Howe, "The Evangelical Movement and Political Culture in the North during the Second Party System," *Journal of American History* 77 (March 1991): 1216–39; Reverend Andrew Clark, "Sermon, 26 November 1868," in *Radical Republicans and Reconstruction*, ed. Hyman, 465–76; and Cain, *William Lloyd Garrison*, 50–55.

I disagree somewhat with Foner, *Reconstruction*, 230, who seems to impose an overly political and secular framework on the Radical Republicans' essentially sociopsychological and religious perspective. In their view, social "sins" (slavery, drinking, war, subordination of women, lack of education, and oppression of the poor) corrupted both the oppressor and the oppressed, disrupted the family, degraded the female, divided the community, and distorted the exercise of benevolence. Not just the political realm (the state) but the whole community (the society) needed to be purged of such "sin." For a view of where Foner fits into changing cycles of historical interpretation of the South, see C. Vann Woodward, "Unfinished Business," review of *Reconstruction: America's Unfinished Revolution, 1863–1877,* by Eric Foner, *New York Review of Books,* 12 May 1988, 22–27; and Michael O'Brien, *Rethinking the South: Essays in Intellectual History* (Baltimore: Johns Hopkins University Press, 1988), 120–21.

6   Mark C. Carnes, *Secret Ritual and Manhood in Victorian America* (New Haven: Yale University Press, 1989), 7–9; Mary Ann Clawson, *Constructing Brotherhood: Class, Gender, and Fraternalism* (Princeton: Princeton University Press, 1989), 123–24, 136–40; Wyn Craig Wade, *The Fiery Cross: The Ku Klux Klan in America* (New York: Simon and Schuster, 1987), chap. 1; and Lynn Dumenil, *Freemasonry and American Culture, 1880–1930* (Princeton: Princeton University Press, 1984).

That fraternal orders touched a variety of interests is evident in the following list of organizations established at this time:

1864–Knights of Pythias (social)
1865—Military Order of the Loyal Legion (Union war veterans)
1866—Grand Army of the Republic (Union war veterans)
1866—Ku Klux Klan (Confederate veterans)
1866—Benevolent and Protective Order of Elks (social and charitable)
1867—Order of the Patrons of Husbandry ("the Grange," a farmer's organization)
1868—Ancient Order of United Workmen (labor and insurance)
1869—Holy and Noble Order of the Knights of Labor (labor)

7   Loretta J. Williams, *Black Freemasonry and Middle-Class Realities* (Columbia: University of Missouri Press, 1980), 44–45.

8   Carnes, *Secret Ritual and Manhood,* 131 (quotation); Dumenil, *Freemasonry,* 73 (quotation).

9   Carnes, *Secret Ritual and Manhood,* 121–27 and chap. 5; Clawson, *Constructing Brotherhood,* 110 and 132; Dumenil, *Freemasonry,* 10–14, 30, 72–73, 91; Williams, *Black Freemasonry,* chap. 7. For the background of fraternity as a core value, see Wilson Carey McWilliams, *The Idea of Fraternity in America* (Berkeley: University of California Press, 1973), chaps. 4, 10, 14.

10 Michael Les Benedict, "The Problem of Constitutionalism and Constitutional Liberty in the Reconstruction South," in *An Uncertain Tradition: Constitutionalism and the History of the South,* ed. Kermit L. Hall and James W. Ely Jr. (Athens: University of Georgia Press, 1989), 223, 228. See also Stanley N. Katz, "The Strange Birth and Unlikely History of Constitutional Equality," *Journal of American History* 75 (December 1988): 747–62. Katz reminded students of history that,

while *individual* equality as a natural right existed in the Revolutionary tradition, such equality was not to be found *literally* in either the Constitution or the Bill of Rights. The adoption of the Civil Rights Act of 1866 and the Fourteenth Amendment put individual equality on a new foundation, according to Katz, but it was a narrow one. Therefore, the late-twentieth-century understanding of civil rights and of federal protections for them cannot be read back into the history of congressional Reconstruction without distorting it.

11   Foner, *Reconstruction*, 454–55, 504–5; Wade, *Fiery Cross*, chaps. 2–3. Confederate general Nathan Bedford Forrest, grand wizard of the Empire of the Ku Klux Klan, was opposed to its turn toward political violence and ordered it to disband in 1869; however, local units continued to operate.

12   Foner, *Reconstruction*, chaps. 10–11; Carl N. Degler, *In Search of Human Nature: The Decline and Revival of Darwinism in American Social Thought* (New York: Oxford University Press, 1991), chap. 1.

13   Currie, *The Constitution in the Supreme Court*, 342–51, 363 (quotation); Blue, *Salmon P. Chase*, 306–7; Mary K. Bonsteel Tachau, "Women, the South, and the Constitution," in *An Uncertain Tradition: Constitutionalism and the History of the South*, ed. Hall and Ely, 361–63; and Foner, *Reconstruction*, 529. The "privileges and immunities" of citizens enumerated by the justices included the following: (1) *protection* of life, liberty, person, and property (in the United States, on the high seas, and in foreign countries); (2) *access* to government (its offices, courts, facilities, treaty rights, and administrative functions); (3) *freedom of* movement and residence; (4) *freedom from* certain types of laws (ex post facto, bills of attainder, laws impairing the obligation of contracts); (5) *freedom to* peaceably assemble, petition, and have access to the writ of habeas corpus; and, (6) in general, *freedom to* pursue "happiness" within the general restraints of laws passed for the general welfare. Only Justice Stephen J. Field, in dissent, and Justice Joseph P. Bradley specified the rights of free labor and the right to choose or pursue a profession, vocation, or trade (subject only to those necessary restrictions equally applicable to others).

14   Foner, *Reconstruction*, 555–56; Kaczorowski, "To Begin the Nation Anew," 68 (quotation); and Currie, *The Constitution in the Supreme Court*, 393–98. Currie has noted that from 1867 to 1877 "there was no Southerner on the Court at all, and not a single Democrat was appointed after 1863 until" Lucius Q. C. Lamar in 1888. Responsibility for the interpretation of the Reconstruction amendments and civil rights laws rested primarily with Republican appointees. See Currie, *The Constitution in the Supreme Court*, 362 n. 5 (quotation).

15   Foner, *Reconstruction*, 575–85 (quotation on 577); C. Vann Woodward, *Reunion and Reaction*, 2d ed., rev. (Garden City: Doubleday Anchor, 1956), chaps. 9–10.

16   William Cohen, *At Freedom's Edge: Black Mobility and the Southern White Quest for Racial Control, 1861–1915* (Baton Rouge: Louisiana State University Press, 1991), chap. 7 (quotations on 169); and Kenneth Marvin Hamilton, *Black Towns and Profit: Promotion and Development in the Trans Appalachian West, 1877–1915* (Urbana: University of Illinois Press, 1991).

17   Currie, *The Constitution in the Supreme Court*, 396–402; Joseph P. Bradley, majority opinion in *Civil Rights* cases (1883), reprinted in *The Annals of America* (Chi-

cago: Encyclopaedia Britannica, 1968), 10:577–81 (quotation on 578), and John Marshall Harlan, dissenting opinion in *Civil Rights* cases (1883), 10:581–83; John Marshall Harlan, as quoted by Rayford W. Logan, *The Betrayal of the Negro: From Rutherford B. Hayes to Woodrow Wilson*, new enl. ed. (London: Collier-Macmillan, 1965), 117 (quotation); and Michael Kammen, *A Machine That Would Go of Itself: The Constitution in American Culture* (New York: Alfred A. Knopf, 1986), 116–24 (quotation on 119).

18   David W. Blight, " 'For Something beyond the Battlefield': Frederick Douglass and the Struggle for the Memory of the Civil War," *Journal of American History* 75 (March 1989): 1156–78, and Linnea M. Anderson, " 'Brothers All, Enemies None': Memory and the 50th Anniversary of the Battle of Gettysburg," (Master's seminar paper, New York University, 15 December 1992), 13–23. Anderson noted that "the desire to depoliticize the Civil War surfaced in memories of the conflict which negated issues of racial injustice and slavery as causes of the war and asserted the pure motives of both sides in the contest" (quotation on 21–22). I am indebted to Linnea M. Anderson for permission to utilize this essay.

19   Cohen, *At Freedom's Edge*, 20–22; Gerald David Jaynes, *Branches without Roots: Genesis of the Black Working Class in the American South, 1862–1882* (New York: Oxford University Press, 1986), chaps. 1, 9–12, 15. See also Maris A. Vinovskis, "Have Social Historians Lost the Civil War? Some Preliminary Demographic Speculations," *Journal of American History* 76 (June 1989): 34–58; Michael W. Fitzgerald, " 'To Give Our Votes to the Party': Black Political Agitation and Agricultural Change in Alabama, 1865–1870," *Journal of American History* 76 (September 1989): 489–505; Loren Schweninger, "Prosperous Blacks in the South, 1790–1880," *American Historical Review* 95 (February 1990): 31–56; and Steven Hahn, "Class and State in Postemancipation Societies: Southern Planters in Comparative Perspective," *American Historical Review* 95 (February 1990): 75–98.

Eric Foner, *Reconstruction*, provided a sophisticated analysis of the ambiguity of the transition from slave labor to free labor: "Thus began the forging of a new class structure to replace the shattered world of slavery—an economic transformation that would culminate, long after the end of Reconstruction, in the consolidation of a *rural proletariat* composed of the descendants of former slaves and white yeoman, and of a new owning class of planters and merchants, itself subordinate to Northern financiers and industrialists" (170, emphasis added). A minor caveat is in order. Could not the small-scale, dependent agriculture of land-bound white and black farmers be better described as the creation of a *rural peasantry* in keeping with recent historical and anthropological studies? See Ronald E. Seavoy, "Portraits of Twentieth-Century American Peasants: Subsistence Social Values Recorded in *All God's Dangers* and *Let Us Now Praise Famous Men*," *Agricultural History* 68 (Spring 1994): 199–218; Ronald Bailey, "The Other Side of Slavery: Black Labor, Cotton, and the Textile Industrialization of Great Britain and the United States," *Agricultural History* 68 (Spring 1994): 35–50; Robert McC. Netting, *Smallholders, Householders: Farm Families and the Ecology of Intensive Sustainable Agriculture* (Stanford: Stanford University Press, 1993), prologue (particularly 20); and E. J. Hobsbawn, "From Social History to the History of Society," in *Historical Studies Today*, ed. Felix Gilbert and Stephen R. Graubard (New York: W. W. Norton, 1972), 1–26 (particularly 17–18 on concepts of proletariat and peasantry).

20   C. Vann Woodward, *The Burden of Southern History* (New York: Vintage Books, 1961), chap. 5; and Guion Griffis Johnson, "The Ideology of White Supremacy," in *The South and the Sectional Image*, ed. Dewey W. Grantham Jr. (New York: Harper and Row, 1967), 56–78.

21   Jer. 8:20–22 King James Version.

3   Which Way for Women's Rights? 1868–1888

1   Linda Kerber, "Separate Spheres, Female Worlds, Woman's Place: The Rhetoric of Women's History," *Journal of American History* 75 (June 1988): 9–39; Daniel Walker Howe, ed., *Victorian America* (Philadelphia: University of Pennsylvania Press, 1976), chap. 1; Karen Lystra, *Searching the Heart: Women, Men, and Romantic Love in Nineteenth Century America* (New York: Oxford University Press, 1989); Karen J. Blair, *The Clubwoman as Feminist: True Womanhood Redefined, 1868–1914*, chap. 2; Theodora Penny Martin, *The Sound of Our Own Voices: Women's Study Clubs, 1860–1910* (Boston: Beacon Press, 1987), chap. 2; and Estelle Freedman, "Separatism as Strategy: Female Institution Building and American Feminism, 1870–1930," in *Women and Power in American History: A Reader*, ed. Kathryn Kish Sklar and Thomas Dublin (Englewood Cliffs: Prentice Hall, 1991), 2:10–24.

2   Lucy Stone to Antoinette Brown, 11 July 1855, in *Friends and Sisters: Letters between Lucy Stone and Antoinette Brown Blackwell, 1846–1893*, ed. Carol Lasser and Marlene Deahl Merrill (Urbana: University of Illinois Press, 1987), 144.

3   Lucy Stone, remark at 1855 National Woman's Rights Convention, quoted in Leslie Wheeler, ed., *Loving Warriors: Selected Letters of Lucy Stone and Henry B. Blackwell, 1853 to 1893* (New York: Dial Press, 1981), 142.

4   Nancy Grey Osterud, "Rural Women during the Civil War: New York's Nanticoke Valley, 1861–1865," *New York History* 62 (October 1990): 357–85; Anne Firor Scott, *The Southern Lady: From Pedestal to Politics, 1830–1930* (Chicago: University of Chicago Press, 1970), chap. 4; Drew Gilpin Faust, "Altars of Sacrifice: Confederate Women and the Narratives of War," *Journal of American History* 76 (March 1990): 1200–28; Jacqueline Jones, *Labor of Love, Labor of Sorrow: Black Women, Work, and the Family from Slavery to the Present* (New York: Basic Books, 1985), chap. 2; Kathleen C. Berkeley, " 'Colored Ladies Also Contributed': Black Women's Activities from Benevolence to Social Welfare, 1866–1896," in *Black Women in American History: From Colonial Times through the Nineteenth Century*, ed. Darlene Clark Hine (Brooklyn: Carlson Publishers, 1990), 1:61–83; Jacqueline Jones, "Encounters, Likely and Unlikely, between Black and Poor White Women in the Rural South, 1865–1940," *Georgia Historical Review* 76 (Summer 1992): 333–53; Carole Turbin, "And We Are Nothing But Women: Irish Working Women of Troy," in *Women and Power in American History*, ed. Sklar and Dublin, 2:25–39; David Montgomery, *Beyond Equality: Labor and Radical Republicans*,

1862–1872 (New York: Viking Books, 1967), 33; and Paula Giddings, *When and Where I Enter: The Impact of Black Women on Race and Sex in America* (New York: William Morrow, 1984), preface and chap. 2.

5   Ellen Carol DuBois, *Feminism and Suffrage: The Emergence of an Independent Women's Movement in America, 1848–1869* (Ithaca: Cornell University Press, 1978), chaps. 2–3; Israel Kugler, *From Ladies to Women: The Organized Struggle for Women's Rights in the Reconstruction Era* (Westport: Greenwood Press, 1987), chaps. 4–6; Kathleen Barry, *Susan B. Anthony: A Biography of a Singular Feminist* (New York: New York University Press, 1988), 180–83; and Sojourner Truth, "Keeping the Thing Going While Things Are Stirring," in *Feminism: The Essential Historical Writings,* edited by Miriam Schneir (New York: Vintage Books, 1972), 129–31.

6   Kugler, *From Ladies to Women,* chaps. 7–8 (quotation on 69); Barry, *Susan B. Anthony,* 185–86; Lasser and Merrill, *Friends and Sisters,* 166; and Mary H. Grant, *Private Woman, Public Person: An Account of the Life of Julia Ward Howe from 1819 to 1868* (Brooklyn: Carlson Publishing, 1994), chap. 12.

   The policy of limiting office in the NWSA to women did not last and was, in effect, breached in 1870. See Elizabeth Frost and Kathryn Cullen-DuPont, *Women's Suffrage in America: An Eyewitness History* (New York: Facts on File, 1992), 207.

7   Grant, *Private Woman, Public Person,* 199–201; Lucy Stone to E. C. Stanton, 19 October 1869, in *Loving Warriors,* ed. Wheeler, 229. Barry, *Susan B. Anthony,* 180, noted that the split between moderate reformers and radical feminists began as early as 1860 with Elizabeth Cady Stanton's resolutions on divorce. On the issue of cultural radicalism and Victorian norms, see Louise L. Stevenson, *The Victorian Homefront: American Thought and Culture, 1860–1880* (New York: Twayne Publishers, 1991), 152–54, 162–64.

8   Lois W. Banner, *Elizabeth Cady Stanton: A Radical for Woman's Rights* (Boston: Little, Brown, 1980), chaps. 4–5 (quotation on 88); Barry, *Susan B. Anthony,* chaps. 5, 8; DuBois, *Feminism and Suffrage,* 46–47; and William Leach, *True Love and Perfect Union: The Feminist Reform of Sex and Society* (New York: Basic Books, 1980), chap. 6.

9   For a woman novelist who wrestled with some of these problems, see Louisa May Alcott's *Work, A Story of Experience,* written and published during the period 1861–73. For background, see Margaret R. Higonnet, "Civil Wars and Sexual Territories," in *Arms and the Woman: War, Gender, and Literary Representation,* ed. Helen M. Cooper, Adrienne A. Munich, and Susan M. Squier (Chapel Hill: University of North Carolina Press, 1989), 87–89; and Gillian Brown, *Domestic Individualism: Imagining Self in Nineteenth-Century America* (Berkeley: University of California Press, 1990). On the role of black women's participation in "consensual" (informal, emotional) voting in the racial and Republican public sphere and "mass meetings" of the Reconstruction period (as contrasted with the formal, legal-rational "representative" franchise voting), see Elsa Barkley Brown, "Negotiating and Transforming the Public Sphere: African American Political Life in the Transition from Slavery to Freedom," *Public Culture* 7 (Fall 1994): 108–16. Brown's point is that to look only at the history of the pursuit of the independent

franchise (woman suffrage) is to obscure the role of black women in the interdependent communal consensus process during Reconstruction.

10 Barry, *Susan B. Anthony*, 200–201, 259–64; Dorothy Sterling, ed., *We Are Your Sisters: Black Women in the Nineteenth Century* (New York: W. W. Norton, 1984), 411–18; and Giddings, *When and Where I Enter*, 65–66.

11 Kugler, *From Ladies to Women*, chaps. 8, 12, 13; Diane Balser, *Sisterhood and Solidarity: Feminism and Labor in Modern Times* (Boston: South End Press, 1987), chap. 5; DuBois, *Feminism and Suffrage*, chaps. 4–6 (particularly 178–79); Barbara Hilkert Andolsen, *"Daughters of Jefferson, Daughters of Bootblacks": Racism and American Feminism* (Macon, Ga.: Mercer University Press, 1986), 1–11; and Darlene Clark Hine, ed., *Black Women in America: An Historical Encyclopedia* (Brooklyn: Carlson Publishing, 1993), 1314. On tensions between working-class women and middle-class women's rights advocates, see Amy Dru Stanley, "Conjugal Bonds and Wage Labor: Rights of Contract in the Age of Emancipation," *Journal of American History* 75 (September 1988): 471–500; and Ardis Cameron, *Radicals of the Worst Sort: Laboring Women in Lawrence, Massachusetts, 1860–1912* (Urbana: University of Illinois Press, 1993), 37–46.

12 Joan Hoff, *Law, Gender, and Injustice: A Legal History of American Women* (New York: New York University Press, 1991), 140–41, 143–45, 152–61, 164–74; Ellen Carol DuBois, "Outgrowing the Compact of the Fathers: Equal Rights, Woman Suffrage, and the United States Constitution, 1820–1878," *Journal of American History* 74 (December 1987): 844–61; Barry, *Susan B. Anthony*, 200–201, 259–64; and Ellen Carol DuBois, "Taking the Law into Our Own Hands: Bradwell, Minor, and Suffrage Militance in the 1870s," in *Visible Women: New Essays on American Activism*, ed. Nancy A. Hewitt and Suzanne Lebsock (Urbana: University of Illinois Press, 1993), 19–40.

13 Hine, *Black Women in America: An Historical Encyclopedia*, 1125; Jack S. Blocker Jr., *"Give to the Winds Thy Fears": The Women's Temperance Crusade, 1873–1874* (Westport: Greenwood Press, 1985); Ruth Bordin, *Frances Willard: A Biography* (Chapel Hill: University of North Carolina Press, 1986); Jack S. Blocker Jr., *American Temperance Movements: Cycles of Reform* (Boston: G. K. Hall, 1989), particularly the section on the third temperance cycle, 1860–92; and Perry R. Duis, *The Saloon: Public Drinking in Chicago and Boston, 1880–1920* (Urbana: University of Illinois Press, 1983).

14 Bordin, *Frances Willard*, chaps. 6–9; and Suzanne M. Marilley, "Frances Willard and the Feminism of Fear," *Feminist Studies* 19 (Spring 1993): 123–46.

15 Stanley, "Conjugal Bonds and Wage Labor," 471–500; and Jane Jerome Camhi, *Women against Women: American Anti-Suffragism, 1880–1920* (Brooklyn: Carlson Publishing, 1994), chaps. 1–2 and 78–79.

16 Joyce Carol Oates, *(Woman) Writer: Occasions and Opportunities* (New York: E. P. Dutton, 1988), 196. Oates' comment concerned Susan Warner's *Diana*, an 1877 novel in which a strong-willed, assertive heroine learns self-sacrificial conformity and obedience to cultural norms.

17 Blair, *The Clubwoman as Feminist*, chap. 3; Martin, *The Sound of Our Own Voices*, chap. 6; Mary Ann Clawson, *Constructing Brotherhood: Class, Gender, and Fraternalism* (Princeton: Princeton University Press, 1989), chap. 6 (quotation on 209–

10); Lynn Dumenil, *Freemasonry and American Culture, 1880–1930* (Princeton: Princeton University Press, 1984), 25–27; Mark C. Carnes, *Secret Ritual and Manhood in Victorian America* (New Haven: Yale University Press, 1989), 84–89; and Selia Evans, *Royal Neighbors of America . . . 100 Years of Helping Hands* (Rock Island, Ill.: Royal Neighbors of America, 1995), 4–8. Clawson's argument that male fraternal rituals represented a *revolt against* current gender roles and feminized cultural norms while female fraternal rituals *reinforced* current gender roles and masculine power relationships seems to me to undervalue, as historians of women's clubs have pointed out, the ability of women to use such fraternal activities to learn new skills, raise confidence, and subtly subvert current cultural boundaries.

18   Evelyn Brooks Higginbotham, *Righteous Discontent: The Women's Movement in the Black Baptist Church, 1880–1920* (Cambridge: Harvard University Press, 1993), chaps. 1–2 (quotations on 15 and 59); and Giddings, *When and Where I Enter*, chap. 4.

19   Hoff, *Law, Gender, and Injustice*, 178–79, 388–92 (quotations on 390 and 392). There were few mentions of the term liberty in the document. They put liberty primarily in the past as a natural right rather than in the future as a means to achieve expanded rights. Also, the notion of the "liberties of the whole people" was covertly an attack on male-oriented judicial power (see 391–92).

20   Stevenson, *The Victorian Homefront*, chaps. 6–7; and Michael McGerr, "Political Style and Women's Power, 1830–1930," *Journal of American History* 77 (December 1990): 864–85. McGerr interpreted the criticism of male civil service reformers by more traditionally oriented males as the result of the *convergence* of gender roles and the emergence of a common political style by middle-class liberal men and women. It is also possible to argue that there was a *divergence* of gender roles and the creation of *separate* political styles among the middle class genders. Thus, Susan B. Anthony was criticized for being too masculine in her agitational tactics and alienated some men within the middle class who had initially shared liberal values with women and who had endorsed some demands for women's rights. For example, Joseph Keppler, a German-American political cartoonist, turned against woman suffrage because of violations of gender norms by the suffragists. See Richard Samuel West, *Satire on Stone: The Political Cartoons of Joseph Keppler* (Urbana: University of Illinois Press, 1988), 52, 90–91, 178–79.

21   DuBois, "Outgrowing the Compact of the Fathers," 861–62 (quotation on 861); Ruth Bordin, "Woman's Mighty Realm of Philanthropy," in *Women and Power in American History*, ed. Sklar and Dublin, 2:41–43; Ross Evans Paulson, *Women's Suffrage and Prohibition: A Comparative Study of Equality and Social Control* (Glenview: Scott, Foresman, 1973), 118–19; Rosalind Urbach Moss, "The 'Girls' from Syracuse: Kansas Women in Politics, 1887–1890," in *Women, Families, and Communities: Readings in American History*, ed. Nancy A. Hewitt (Glenview: Scott, Foresman/Little Brown Higher Education, 1990), 2:27–35; and Lasser and Merrill, *Friends and Sisters*, 166.

22   David Montgomery, *The Fall of the House of Labor: The Workplace, the State, and American Labor Activism, 1865–1925* (New York: Cambridge University Press, 1987), 139–40, 147; Susan Levine, "The Transformation of a Laboring Com-

munity: Mechanization and Mobilization of Women Weavers," in *Women, Families, and Communities*, ed. Hewitt, 2:46; and Turbin, "And We Are Nothing But Women," 2:31. Turbin's statistical study of working women in Troy, New York, showed that 1 percent were wives living with their husbands, 17 percent were widows, and the vast majority were young, single women who lived with their families (statistics on 28).

23   Peggy Pascoe, *Relations of Rescue: The Search for Female Moral Authority in the American West, 1874–1929* (New York: Oxford University Press, 1990), xvi and chaps. 3–4; Lori D. Ginzberg, *Women and the Work of Benevolence: Morality, Politics, and Class in the Nineteenth-Century United States* (New Haven: Yale University Press, 1990), chap. 6; Nancy A. Hewitt, *Women's Activism and Social Change: Rochester, New York, 1822–1872* (Ithaca: Cornell University Press, 1984); and Barry, *Susan B. Anthony*, 265–66, 311.

24   Pascoe, *Relations of a Rescue*, chap. 2; Barry, *Susan B. Anthony*, 265–66, 311. See also Evelyn Brooks Higginbotham, "African-American Women's History and the Metalanguage of Race," in *We Specialize in the Wholly Impossible: A Reader in Black Women's History*, ed. Darlene Clark Hine, Wilma King, and Linda Reed (Brooklyn: Carlson Publishing, 1995), 3–24.

4   Business and Labor from the Panic of 1873 to the Depression of 1893: Reorganization, Regulation, and Community Response

1   Herbert Hovenkamp, *Enterprise and American Law, 1836–1937* (Cambridge: Harvard University Press, 1990), chap. 1.

Technically there were alternatives to the limited-liability corporation as a form of enterprise. Hovenkamp noted that New York and Louisiana law allowed limited-liability *partnerships* in which "silent partners" with limited-liability protection provided an "active partner" with capital, but he assumed the greater personal risk for his conduct. Maury Klein and Harvey A. Kantor also noted the existence of an unincorporated shareholder *company* based upon a written agreement among the shareholders who then hired the managers to run the company. Whereas the limited-liability corporation was created by a public charter, the unincorporated shareholder company was based on a private contract. Phillip Scranton also noted the prevalence of family-owned firms but acknowledged that "as yet . . . the study of family business is conceptually incoherent" because such ownership with its generational continuity and disparate scope could coexist with a variety of structures and techniques of management. Whatever its origins as a public means to accomplish a public purpose, Hovenkamp concluded that by the 1850s "the corporation became nothing more than a device for assembling large amounts of capital so it could be controlled efficiently by a few active managers." See Hovenkamp, *Enterprise and American Law*, 12–13 (quotation on 12); Maury Klein and Harvey A. Kantor, *Prisoners of Progress: American Industrial Cities, 1850–1920* (New York: Macmillan, 1976), 37; Jonathon Prude, *The Coming of Industrial Order: Town and Factory Life in Rural Massachusetts, 1810–1860* (Cambridge: Harvard University Press, 1983), preface and chaps. 5–6, 8–9; Phillip Scranton, "Small Business, Family Firms, and Batch Production: Three Axes for Development in

American Business History," *Business and Economic History,* 2d ser., 20 (1991): 99–106 (quotation on 102), *Figured Tapestry: Production, Markets, and Power in Philadelphia Textiles, 1885–1941* (Cambridge: Cambridge University Press, 1989), 2–7, and "Build a Firm, Start Another: The Bromleys and Family Firm Entrepreneurship in the Philadelphia Region," *Business History* 34 (October 1993): 115–19.

2   Lee Benson, *The Concept of Jacksonian Democracy: New York as a Test Case* (Princeton: Princeton University Press, 1961), chaps. 5, 11, 15; William E. Nelson, *The Roots of American Bureaucracy, 1830–1900* (Cambridge: Harvard University Press, 1982), chap. 1; Leon Fink, "Looking Backward: Reflections on Workers' Culture and Certain Conceptual Dilemmas within Labor History," in *Perspectives on American Labor History: The Problems of Synthesis,* ed. J. Carroll Moody and Alice Kessler-Harris (DeKalb: Northern Illinois University Press, 1990), 8–14; Sean Wilentz, "The Rise of the American Working Class, 1776–1877," in *Perspectives on American Labor History,* ed. Moody and Kessler-Harris, 91–106; and Kim Voss, *The Making of American Exceptionalism: The Knights of Labor and Class Formation in the Nineteenth Century* (Ithaca: Cornell University Press, 1993), 29 n. 22, 29–33, 33 n. 44, 42–43.

3   Richard Franklin Bensel, *Yankee Leviathan: The Origins of Central State Authority in America, 1859–1877* (Cambridge: Cambridge University Press, 1990), 64–78, 88–93, 148–61, 178–83; Morton Keller, *Affairs of State: Public Life in Late Nineteenth Century America* (Cambridge: Harvard University Press, 1977), 162–65; Alfred D. Chandler Jr., *The Visible Hand: The Managerial Revolution in American Business* (Cambridge: Harvard University Press, 1977), 72–80 (quotation on 79); and Shelton Stromquist, *A Generation of Boomers: The Pattern of Railroad Labor Conflict in Nineteenth-Century America* (Urbana: University of Illinois Press, 1987), 4.

4   Chandler, *The Visible Hand,* 167–71; Hovenkamp, *Enterprise and American Law,* chap. 12; and Ari Hoogenboom and Olive Hoogenboom, *A History of the ICC: From Panacea to Palliative* (New York: W. W. Norton, 1976), chap. 1. An example of how even an investor could be drawn into the logic of the system can be found in the career of Jay Gould. See Maury Klein, *The Life and Legend of Jay Gould* (Baltimore: Johns Hopkins University Press, 1986), 140–60.

5   Attempts to change the "rules of the game" of business in the 1860–70s, whether internally or externally, implicitly recognized that business relationships represented contested domains of power. Proposals for change frequently were responses to unprecedented situations. For example, on the reorganization of the Stock Exchange in 1869 and its subsequent self-regulation, see John Steele Gordon, *The Scarlet Woman of Wall Street: Jay Gould, Jim Fisk, Cornelius Vanderbilt, the Erie Railway Wars, and the Birth of Wall Street* (New York: Weidenfeld and Nicolson, 1988), 209–13.

6   "Farmers' Declaration of Independence, 4 July 1873," in *The Reform Spirit in America: A Documentation of the Pattern of Reform in the American Republic,* ed. Robert H. Walker (New York: G. P. Putnam's Sons, 1976), 100, 102 (quotations).

7   Steven Skowronek, *Building a New American State: The Expansion of National Administrative Capacities, 1877–1920* (Cambridge: Cambridge University Press, 1982), 125–27, 139–40; and Hoogenboom and Hoogenboom, *History of the ICC,* 5.

Historical analysis of the role of government in the regulation of business in the period 1865–1900 has changed dramatically in the past four decades. In brief, government, or "the state," was once dealt with as a *dependent* variable, a natural response to, or effect of, inevitable economic change. More recently, "the state," has been dealt with as a cause, an *independent* variable, a deliberate attempt to restructure economic relationships by the use of political power related to the interests of hegemonic or bureaucratic elites. Whereas the earlier studies emphasized the administrative, regulatory, or welfare *aspects of the state,* the more recent studies emphasized the administrative, regulatory, or welfare *state* and its comprehensive activities. See, for example, Fritz Morstein Marx, *The Administrative State: An Introduction to Bureaucracy* (Chicago: University of Chicago Press, 1957), chap. 1; James E. Anderson, *The Emergence of the Modern Regulatory State* (Washington, D.C.: Public Affairs Press, 1962), ix, 7–11 and chap. 2; Keller, *Affairs of State,* chaps. 1–3; Nelson, *Roots of American Bureaucracy,* chap. 5; Skowronek, *Building a New American State,* chaps. 1, 5; William R. Brock, *Investigation and Responsibility: Public Responsibility in the United States, 1865–1900* (Cambridge: Cambridge University Press, 1984), chaps. 1–3; Bensel, *Yankee Leviathan,* chap. 1; and Theda Skocpol, "Bringing the State Back In: Strategies of Analysis in Current Research," in *Bringing the State Back In,* ed. Peter Evans, Dietrich Rueschemeyer, and Theda Skocpol (Cambridge: Cambridge University Press, 1985), chap. 1.

8   William Greenleaf, *American Economic Development since 1860* (Columbia: University of South Carolina Press, 1968), 100 (quotation). Hovenkamp has pointed out that the classical economic model of self-regulation by competition did not describe the current reality of the railroads and that some economists and experts realized this in the 1870s; however, an alternative economic model to explain the situation did not fully emerge until the 1880s. Hovenkamp, *Enterprises and American Law,* chaps. 11–12 (particularly 139–41).

9   William Gillette, *Retreat from Reconstruction* (Baton Rouge: Louisiana State University Press, 1979), 186–90 and chap. 10; Jerome Mushkat, *The Reconstruction of the New York Democracy, 1861–1874* (Rutherford, N.J.: Fairleigh Dickinson University Press, 1981), chap. 8; Brock, *Investigation and Responsibility,* chap. 7 (state railroad commissions); Skowronek, *Building a New American State,* 126, 139–40 (historiography of Granger laws); and David P. Currie, *The Constitution in the Supreme Court: The First Hundred Years, 1789–1888* (Chicago: University of Chicago Press, 1985), 370–73 (*Granger* cases).

For an example of a Democratic railroad executive who "was opposed to monopoly and thought that regulation of public utilities was necessary" but who, nevertheless, supported regional dominance by one railroad and "opposed 'interference' from other corporations," see George M. Jenks, "Franklin Benjamin Gowen," *Encyclopedia of American Business History and Biography: Railroads in the Nineteenth Century,* ed. Robert L. Frey (New York: Facts on File, 1988), 148–51 (quotation on 150).

10   George H. Miller, *Railroads and the Granger Laws* (Madison: University of Wisconsin Press, 1971), 185 (quotation).

Charles Frances Adams Jr., an early advocate of railroad regulation, noted another aspect of the language used to describe corporate behavior: "[Corporate dominance] is a new power, for which our language contains no name. We know what aristocracy, autocracy, democracy are; but we have no word to express government by moneyed corporation." Charles Francis Adams Jr., *Chapters of Erie and Other Essays* (New York: Henry Holt, 1886), 98, quoted in Stromquist, *A Generation of Boomers*, 15.

11   The "yes—but" character of the Supreme Court's decision has created a complicated historical evaluation of the *Granger* cases depending on whether one emphasizes the recognition of state regulation or the recognition of corporate judicial rights. See, for example, Miller, *Railroads and the Granger Laws*, for an example of the former interpretation, and Richard C. Cortner, *The Iron Horse and the Constitution: The Railroads and the Transformation of the Fourteenth Amendment* (Westport: Greenwood Press, 1993), for the latter interpretation.

David Dehnel, a constitutional expert, has criticized George Miller's interpretation of the Granger laws and the subsequent behavior of the Supreme Court. "An examination of all the relevant cases," he noted, "shows that the [Supreme) Court did not adhere dogmatically to either a localist or a pro-big business position. [Rather] . . . following the Civil War realignment the Court became relatively more active in protecting interstate business from hostile local legislation." David Dehnel, "The Policy Agenda of the Supreme Court in Three Partisan Eras," (Ph.D. diss., University of Minnesota, 1988), chap. 3 (quotation on 40).

12   Sean Wilentz, "Rise of the American Working Class," 129–30; Patricia T. Davis, *End of the Line: Alexander J. Cassatt and the Pennsylvania Railroad* (New York: Neale Watson Academic Publications, 1978), chaps. 5–6; and Stromquist, *A Generation of Boomers*, chaps. 1, 4.

13   Stromquist, *A Generation of Boomers*, 147–87, 245–47, 246 (quotation).

14   Leon Fink, "The New Labor History and the Powers of Historical Pessimism: Consensus, Hegemony, and the Case of the Knights of Labor," *Journal of American History* 75 (June 1988): 116–18, 122–25, 129; Stromquist, *A Generation of Boomers*, 186 (quotation); Voss, *The Making of American Exceptionalism*, 75–86; Wilentz, "Rise of the American Working Class," 127–29; and Bruce C. Nelson, *Beyond the Martyrs: A Social History of Chicago's Anarchists, 1870–1900* (New Brunswick: Rutgers and University Press, 1988), chap. 8.

My interpretation of the Knights of Labor as primarily a ritual withdrawal and renewal response takes into account its origins as a fraternal lodge, its labor republican ideology with roots in the 1830s, and the emphasis on preserving the values of the past, particularly the core values of liberty as autonomy or independence and equality. Voss, on the other hand, argues that the Knights were "a radical organization that challenged the status quo, but it was not a revolutionary association." Voss defined radicalism more in terms of means than ends and tacitly equated "alternative" with radical. Voss also downplayed the "producerism" in Knights' rhetoric and stressed "mutualism" instead. See Voss, *The Making of American Exceptionalism*, 80–87, 86 n. 49, 88–89 (quotation).

For a critique of the methodological assumptions underlying the historical analysis of working-class culture, see Leon Fink, "Looking Backwards," 5–29. For the attempt by anarchists to influence the Knights of Labor in the 1880s, see Ross

Evans Paulson, *Radicalism and Reform: The Vrooman Family and American Social Thought, 1837–1937* (Lexington: University of Kentucky Press for the Organization of American Historians, 1968), 42–53.

15 Skowronek, *Building a New American State*, 140–50 (quotations on 141 and 145); Mushkat, *Reconstruction of the New York Democracy*, 19–21; Hoogenboom and Hoogenboom, *History of the ICC*, 5, 8, 17; Scott C. James, "A Party System Perspective on the Interstate Commerce Act of 1887: The Democracy, Electoral College Competition, and the Politics of Coalition Maintenance," *Studies in American Political Development* 6 (Spring 1992): 163–200 (quotation on 191); and Shelby M. Cullom, *Fifty Years of Public Service*, 2d ed. (Chicago: A. C. McClurg, 1911), chap. 21. On the *Wabash v. Illinois* case, see Currie, *The Constitution in the Supreme Court*, 412–15.

16 Skowronek, *Building a New American State*, 150–54 (quotation on 150); Brock, *Investigation and Responsibility*, 233–42; and Hoogenboom and Hoogenboom, *History of the ICC*, 17–29.

   Intellectually the choice before the ICC commissioners was whether to follow the "logic of the market" or the "logic of the system." If they favored the competitive market, they could either adhere to the antimonopoly tradition and try to limit the size and number of the competing units or they could follow the regulatory tradition and police the terms and conditions of competition. On the other hand, if they favored the systems approach, they could either sanction pools (voluntary cooperation), allow expanded trunk lines (coordinated operation), or encourage mergers (consolidation).

17 Hovenkamp, *Enterprise and American Law*, 43–48 (quotation on 43).

18 Chandler, *The Visible Hand*, 167; William E. Forbath, *Law and the Shaping of the American Labor Movement* (Cambridge: Harvard University Press, 1991), chaps. 2–3; and Walter Licht, *Working for the Railroad: The Organization of Work in the Nineteenth Century* (Princeton: Princeton University Press, 1983), chap. 3.

   The notion that interregional, integrated railroad systems were inevitable was challenged by Gerald Berk, *Alternate Tracks: The Constitution of American Industrial Order, 1865–1917* (Baltimore: Johns Hopkins University Press, 1994). He argued that the decisions were essentially political rather than economic. For criticism of Berk's theory, see the review by Mark Wahlgren Summers in *American Historical Review* 100 (October 1995): 1307–8.

19 Scranton, "Small Business, Family Firms, and Batch Production," 100–104, *Figured Tapestry*, 7–8, 12–13, and "Diversity in Diversity: Flexible Production and American Industrialization, 1880–1930," *Business History Review* 65 (Spring 1991): 27–48; Stromquist, *A Generation of Boomers*, 6 (quotation); and Bruce Laurie and Mark Schmitz, "Manufacturing and Productivity: The Making of an Industrial Base," in *Philadelphia: Work, Space, Family, and Group Experience in the Nineteenth Century: Essays toward an Interdisciplinary History of the City*, ed. Theodore Hershberg (New York: Oxford University Press, 1981), 43–66.

20 Chandler, *The Visible Hand*, 315 (quotation); and Scranton, "Diversity in Diversity," 49–61.

21 Chandler, *The Visible Hand*, 320–25.

22   Martin J. Sklar, *The Corporate Reconstruction of American Capitalism, 1890–1916: The Market, the Law, and Politics* (New York: Cambridge University Press, 1988), 101–4 (quotation on 104, emphasis added).

23   Ibid., 106.

24   Hovenkamp, *Enterprise and American Law,* chap. 20; Richard E. Welch Jr., *George Frisbie Hoar and the Half-Breed Republicans* (Cambridge: Harvard University Press, 1971), 164–67, 165 n. 30; and Sklar, *Corporate Reconstruction of American Capitalism,* 105–17. Democrat John H. Reagan of Texas had introduced an ostensibly more stringent bill reflecting western interests, but it lost out to the revised version of the Sherman Act. Hovenkamp, *Enterprise and American Law,* chap. 20. Hovenkamp's thesis was that the Sherman Act combined the common law doctrine of restraint of trade with what he called neoclassical political economy. It also changed the definition of "coercion," which now included "the loss of market opportunities that competition would have afforded" (283). He regarded this as a revolutionary innovation that changed *unenforceable* common law contracts or combinations in restraint of trade into *illegal* acts by corporations that would be subject to prosecution.

25   Chandler, *Visible Hand,* 330; Sklar, *Corporate Reconstruction of American Capitalism,* chap. 2.

26   Oliver Zunz, *Making America Corporate, 1870–1920* (Chicago: University of Chicago Press, 1990), emphasizes how the modern corporate culture was created by generations of middle-rank executives, clerks, and skilled workers. Even the gendered division of labor that characterized the corporate environment could be found to be a product of negotiated class interests rather than the product of elite hegemony or male domination. The corporate culture was created in part by, rather than simply imposed upon, skilled workers and their children and generations of educated mid-rank executives. See also Louis Galambos, "The Triumph of Oligopoly," in *American Economic Development in Historical Perspective,* ed. Thomas Weiss and Donald Schaefer (Stanford: Stanford University Press, 1994), 241–53. Galambos provides a sophisticated synthesis of economic theory and the new business history to explain the transition from the highly competitive mode of the 1870s to near monopoly in the 1880s–90s and the subsequent predominance of the oligopolistic model.

5   Civil Rights, 1883–1898: High Hopes; Failed Promises

1   Bryan S. Turner, ed., *Citizenship and Social Theory* (London: Sage Publications, 1993).

2   Charles J. McClain, *In Search of Equality: The Chinese Struggle against Discrimination in Nineteenth-Century America* (Berkeley: University of California Press, 1994), chaps. 1, 2 (quotations on 75), 6 (particularly 150–60) and 8 (quotation on 192); Ronald Takaki, *Strangers from a Different Shore: A History of Asian Americans* (New York: Penguin Books U.S.A., 1989), chap. 3. For an interpretation of the origins of Chinese exclusion, see Ronald Takaki, *Iron Cages: Race and Culture in Nineteenth Century America* (New York: Oxford University Press, 1990), chap. 10.

3   Lucy Salyer, "Captives of Law: Judicial Enforcement of the Chinese Exclusion Laws, 1891–1905," *Journal of American History* 76 (June 1989): 91–117 (quotation on 97).

For the status of Chinese women in immigration, see "Memorial of the Chinese Six Companies to U. S. Grant, President of the U.S.A. [1876]," in *To Serve the Devil: A Documentary Analysis of America's Racial History,* vol. 2, *Colonials and Sojourners,* ed. Paul Jacobs, Saul Landau, and Eve Pell (New York: Vintage Books, 1971), 132–37; Judy Yung, *Unbound Feet: A Social History of Chinese Women in San Francisco* (Berkeley: University of California Press, 1995), chap. 1; and Peggy Pascoe, "Gender Systems in Conflict: The Marriages of Mission-Educated Chinese American Women, 1847–1939," in *Unequal Sisters: A Multicultural Reader in U.S. Women's History,* ed. Ellen Carol DuBois and Vicki L. Ruiz (New York: Routledge, 1990), 123–40.

4   McClain, *In Search of Equality,* 280–82, "Captives of Law," 102–12. For background, see Christian G. Fritz, *Federal Justice in California: The Court of Ogden Hoffman, 1851–1891* (Lincoln: University of Nebraska Press, 1991).

5   Brian W. Dippie, *The Vanishing American: White Attitudes and U.S. Indian Policy* (Middletown: Wesleyan University Press, 1982), 171–72; Valerie Sherer Mathes, "Helen Hunt Jackson as Power Broker," in *Between Indian and White Worlds: The Cultural Broker,* ed. Margaret Connell Szasz (Norman: University of Oklahoma Press, 1994), 144–46; and Frederick E. Hoxie, *A Final Promise: The Campaign to Assimilate the Indians, 1880–1920* (Lincoln: University of Nebraska Press, 1984), 75 (quotation from *Elk v. Wilkins*). During the 1886 Senate debate on the Dawes Act, Senator Maxey of Texas moved to strike the citizenship clause and cited the Chinese Exclusion Acts as precedent. The amendment was rejected. Senators Hoar and Dawes of Massachusetts had argued for immediate citizenship upon receipt of an allotment in keeping with the Fourteenth Amendment, but other senators disagreed, and the twenty-five-year trust period remained in the final version.

For the legal and constitutional background of Native American status, see Alexandra Witkin, "To Silence a Drum: The Imposition of United States Citizenship on Native Peoples," *Historical Reflections/Reflexions Historiques* 21, no. 2 (1995): 353–83.

6   Hoxie, *A Final Promise,* 70–75, 154–55, 212–13; L. G. Moses, "Interpreting the Wild West, 1883–1914," in *Between Indian and White Worlds,* ed. Szasz, 158–78 (quotation on 163); and Witkin, "To Silence a Drum," 359–63. For the contradictions between policy goals and bureaucratic implementation of Indian policy, see Janet A. McDonnell, *The Dispossession of the American Indian, 1887–1934* (Bloomington: Indiana University Press, 1991); Donald F. Lindsey, *Indians at Hampton Institute, 1877–1923* (Urbana: University of Illinois, 1995), chaps. 2–5, 8; and Jerry E. Clark and Martha Ellen Webb, "Susette and Susan LaFlesche: Reformer and Missionary," in *Being and Becoming Indian: Biographical Studies of North American Frontiers,* ed. James A. Clifton (Chicago: Dorsey Press, 1989), 137–59. Clark and Webb note that Susan LaFlesche "as a tribal member [Omaha], . . . had an allotment of 160 acres near Bancroft [Iowa] and received government annuity payments, even while in school in the East" (152). The impact of the Dawes Act

or similar legislation on Native American women depended on a number of factors: gender systems (patriarchal/matriarchal, patrilineal/matrilineal), community roles (medicine woman, wife, teacher), agricultural systems, religion, and education.

7   Witkin, "To Silence a Drum," 355 (quotations). For the issue of cultural identity, see James A. Clifton, "Alternate Identities and Cultural Frontiers," in *Being and Becoming Indian*, ed. Clifton, 1–37; and Gretchen M. Bataille and Kathleen Mullen Sands, *American Indian Women: Telling Their Lives* (Lincoln: University of Nebraska Press, 1984), chaps. 1–2.

8   Emma Lou Thornbrough, *T. Thomas Fortune: Militant Journalist* (Chicago: University of Chicago Press, 1972), 106–7 (quotation).

9   Ibid., 109–17. A month after the Chicago convention a group of black politicians and office holders met in Washington, D.C., and organized a rival American Citizens Civil Rights Association. J. C. Price was present and secured resolutions calling for unity with the National Afro-American League, but little came of it. Thornbrough, *T. Thomas Fortune*, 117, 117 n. 19. For Ida Wells's support of the proposed National Afro-American League, see Mildred I. Thompson, *Ida B. Wells-Barnett: An Exploratory Study of an American Black Woman, 1893–1930* (Brooklyn: Carlson Publishing, 1990), 20.

I have been unable to identify the individual delegates to the 1890 convention. Ida Wells did not attend the founding convention of the National Afro-American League in 1890 but did participate in the 1891 more poorly attended national convention in Knoxville. She also attended the Rochester convention in 1898 when the League reorganized as the Afro-American Council and served as its secretary until 1902. Emma Lou Thornbrough, "The National Afro-American League, 1887–1908," *Journal of Southern History* 27 (February 1961): 500–501, 504 n. 23; and Thompson, *Ida B. Wells-Barnett*, 72–74.

10 Theodore R. Mitchell, *Political Education in the Southern Farmers' Alliance, 1887–1900* (Madison: University of Wisconsin Press, 1987), prologue (quotations on 4 and 5); and William Cohen, *At Freedom's Edge: Black Mobility and the Southern White Quest for Racial Control, 1861–1915* (Baton Rouge: Louisiana State University Press, 1991).

11 Philip S. Foner and Ronald L. Lewis, eds., *The Black Worker: A Documentary History from Colonial Times to the Present*, vol. 3, *The Black Worker during the Era of the Knights of Labor* (Philadelphia: Temple University Press, 1987), 287–90 (quotations on 289–90).

12 Mitchell, *Political Education in the Southern Farmers' Alliance*, 157–64, 206–7 (quotations).

13 Ibid., 156; Foner and Lewis, *The Black Worker*, 3:315; Cohen, *At Freedom's Edge*, 209–10; and Lawrence Goodwyn, *Democratic Promise: The Populist Movement in America* (New York: Oxford University Press, 1976), chaps. 10–11, and 559–60.

14 Thornbrough, *T. Thomas Fortune*, 122; and August Meier, *Negro Thought in America, 1880–1915* (Ann Arbor: University of Michigan Press, 1963), chaps. 3–4.

15 *The Booker T. Washington Papers*, ed. Louis R. Harlan (Urbana: University of Illinois Press, 1974), 3:209–10, 217–19.

A similar conference was held on 21 February 1893 with similar resolutions, but added a condemnation of lynching: "We believe that the many acts of lawlessness and the increased frequency of lynching are not only injurious to the cause of good morals but that they greatly retard the prosperity of the South by keeping out capital and checking immigration" (3:298).

16   Ibid., 579–81.

I have cited the manuscript version of the address. The slight variations between the manuscript and standard printed version are noted in the footnotes in Harlan's edition. The most significant variation for the interpretation offered here is that the famous finger/hand passage in the manuscript version reads, "in all that pertains to our mutual *interests*," while the standard printed version reads, "in all things essential to mutual *progress*." I have used the manuscript version as being closer to Washington's *private* values; the standard printed version was closer to his *public* persona. A reporter for the New York *World* reported the sentence as ending "in all things essential to *social* progress." See *Booker T. Washington Papers*, 4:9 (emphasis added).

17   John Brown Childs, *Leadership, Conflict, and Cooperation in Afro-American Social Thought* (Philadelphia: Temple University Press, 1989), 14–17, 20–30, 44–47; *Booker T. Washington Papers*, 4:186 (quotation); and V. P. Franklin, *Living Our Stories, Telling Our Truths: Autobiography and the Making of the African-American Intellectual Tradition* (New York: Scribner, 1995), 48–55 (on Alexander Crummell and the self-help movement prior to Washington and its criticism of him). For *Plessy v. Ferguson* (1896), see John E. Semonche, *Charting the Future: The Supreme Court Responds to a Changing Society, 1890–1920* (Westport: Greenwood Press, 1978), 83; Charles A. Lofgren, *The Plessy Case: A Legal-Historical Interpretation* (New York: Oxford University Press, 1987), chaps. 4, 7–8; and "Interpreting the Fourteenth Amendment: Approaches in *Slaughter-House* and *Plessy*," in *Bench Marks: Great Constitutional Controversies in the Supreme Court*, ed. Terry Eastland (Washington, D.C.: Ethics and Public Policy Center, 1995), 13–44.

18   Gerda Lerner, ed., *Black Women in White America: A Documentary History* (New York: Pantheon Books, 1972), 196–205; Thornbrough, *T. Thomas Fortune*, 121–25; and Thompson, *Ida B. Wells-Barnett*, chaps. 2–5 (quotation on 66), 7.

19   Lerner, *Black Women in White America*, 440–47; *Booker T. Washington Papers*, 4:327 n. 2; Dorothy Salem, *To Better Our World: Black Women in Organized Reform, 1890–1920* (Brooklyn: Carlson Publishing, 1990), chaps. 1, 2 (quotation on 29). For background see also Beverly Washington Jones, *Quest for Equality: The Life and Writings of Mary Eliza Church Terrell, 1863–1954* (Brooklyn: Carlson Publishing, 1990), chaps. 1, 2; Cynthia Neverdon-Morton, *Afro-American Women of the South and the Advancement of the Race, 1895–1925* (Knoxville: University of Tennessee Press, 1989), chap. 10; and Deborah Gray White, "The Cost of Club Work, the Price of Black Feminism," in *Visible Women: New Essays on American Activism*, ed. Nancy A. Hewitt and Suzanne Lebsock (Urbana: University of Illinois Press, 1993), 247–69.

20   Thornbrough, *T. Thomas Fortune*, 179–80 (quotation on 180); and *Booker T. Washington Papers*, 4:460 n. 2.

21   Thornbrough, *T. Thomas Fortune*, 181–87; Jones, *Quest for Equality*, 21; and Thompson, *Ida B. Wells-Barnett*, 72–80.

22 For the ways in which white culture interpreted Indian culture, see L. G. Moses, "Interpreting the Wild West, 1883–1914," in *Between Indian and White Worlds,* ed. Szasz, 158–78. For the sinophobia of the 1890s, see McClain, *In Search of Equality,* chap. 9.

23 *In the Matter of Jacobs* (1885), quoted in Lofgren, *The Plessy Case,* 90 (emphasis added).

24 Lofgren, *The Plessy Case,* 191, 195 (quotation). For the complicated nature of the background of the position enunciated by Justice Harlan, see Andrew Kull, *The Color-Blind Constitution* (Cambridge: Harvard University Press, 1992); Tinsley E. Yarbrough, *Judicial Enigma: The First Justice Harlan* (New York: Oxford University Press, 1995), 157–60, 227–29; and Loren Beth, *John Marshall Harlan: The Last Whig Justice* (Lexington: University Press of Kentucky, 1992).

6 Unity and Diversity in the Search for Women's Rights, 1888–1898

1 Carol Smith-Rosenberg, *Disorderly Conduct: Visions of Gender in Victorian America* (New York: Alfred A. Knopf, 1985), 28 (quotation), and chaps. 2, 7.

2 Ruth Bordin, *Frances Willard: A Biography* (Chapel Hill: University of North Carolina Press, 1986), chap. 9; Mari Jo Buhle, *Women and American Socialism, 1870–1920* (Urbana: University of Illinois Press, 1981), 80–81; and Edith Mayo, introduction to *How I Learned to Ride The Bicycle: Reflections of an Influential 19th Century Woman,* by Frances E. Willard (Sunnyvale, Calif.: Fair Oaks Publishing, 1991), 10 (quotation), 79 n. 2. For background on Willard and the World's WCTU, see Ross Evans Paulson, *Women's Suffrage and Prohibition: A Comparative Study of Equality and Social Control* (Glenview: Scott, Foresman, 1973), 113–21.

　　Frances Willard's biographer, Ruth Bordin, has pointed out that many women's rights advocates, including Willard, Julia Ward Howe, Mary Livermore, and Lucy Stone, "were attracted to statist ideologies [which relied on a powerful government] such as Bellamy nationalism because they satisfied their quest for equality and justice." Furthermore, Bellamy nationalism and Christian socialism promised nonviolent, cooperative (i.e., "feminine") means to achieve these essentially reformist goals (146). But such an interpretation—that Willard was willing to countenance "radical" means to achieve essentially "reformist" ends—assumes that her understanding of her society's core values—liberty, equality, and justice—was unchanged by the confrontation with Bellamy nationalism, Christian socialism, and the economic crises of the late 1880s and early 1890s.

3 Frances E. Willard, *Glimpses of Fifty Years: The Autobiography of an American Woman* (Chicago: H. J. Smith for the WCTU, 1889), 695–96 (quotations, emphasis added).

4 Ibid., 475 (quotations), 609–11. According to Willard, even though husband and wife were equal partners, because motherhood was the supreme social value, "the wife will have undoubted custody of herself [i.e., her body], and, as in all the lower ranges of the animal creation, she will determine the frequency" of pregnancy and birth (614).

5 Paulson, *Women's Suffrage and Prohibition,* 60–62; Bordin, *Frances Willard,* 145–48; and Willard, *Glimpses of Fifty Years,* 475 (quotation).

Bordin noted that "Willard must have read Bellamy's book soon after it was published because in late 1887 and early 1888 she was corresponding with him about a 'manifesto' of Nationalism to be published in the [WCTU] *Union Signal*" (146). Thus, Willard's *Glimpses,* whose dedication page was dated 3 January 1889, was written during the time when she was first reacting to his ideas. See also Buhle, *Women and American Socialism,* 64, 80–81. For Willard and socialism, see Bordin, *Frances Willard,* chap. 12. On Bellamy's utopianism, see Howard P. Segal, *Technological Utopianism in American Culture* (Chicago: University of Chicago Press, 1985), and Daniel H. Borus, introduction to *Looking Backward, 2000–1887,* by Edward Bellamy (Boston: Bedford Books of St. Martin's Press, 1995), 1–28.

6   Gerda Lerner, *Black Women in White America: A Documentary History* (New York: Pantheon Books, 1972), 447–50; Karen Blair, *The Clubwoman as Feminist: True Womanhood Redefined, 1868–1914* (New York: Holmes and Meier, 1980), chaps. 4, 6; Theodora Penny Martin, *The Sound of Our Own Voices: Women's Study Clubs, 1860–1910* (Boston: Beacon Press, 1987), chaps. 1–2, 8; and Kathryn Kish Sklar, "The Historical Foundations of Women's Power in the Creation of the American Welfare State, 1830–1930," in *Mothers of a New World: Maternalist Politics and the Origins of Welfare States,* ed. Seth Koven and Sonya Michel (New York: Routledge, 1993), 63–64.

7   Ishbel Ross, *Silhouette in Diamonds: The Life of Mrs. Potter Palmer* (New York: Harper and Row, 1960). The rituals of deference are usually treated negatively by historians as part of the means by which Victorian patriarchy maintained control over women. Also, psychologists concerned with women's consciousness see deference rituals as the internalization of restrictive self-concepts. However, there is also some evidence in the historical record that shows how some women used these rituals positively to expand and justify their public roles or to create a "feminine space" by ritual withdrawal and renewal geared to the female life cycle. See Smith-Rosenberg, *Disorderly Conduct,* 55–76, 182–96, 245–95; Jean E. Friedman, *The Enclosed Garden: Women and Community in the Evangelical South, 1830–1900* (Chapel Hill: University of North Carolina Press, 1985), 34–39, 110–21, 128–31; H. Elaine Lindgren, *Land in Her Own Name: Women as Homesteaders in North Dakota* (Fargo: North Dakota Institute for Regional Studies, 1991), chaps. 1, 5, 7–8; and Mary H. Blewett, *We Will Rise in Our Might: Workingwomen's Voices from Nineteenth Century New England* (Ithaca: Cornell University Press, 1991), chaps. 7, 9–11.

8   Jeanne Madeline Weimann, *The Fair Women* (Chicago: Academy Chicago, 1981), 253 (quotation); and Ida B. Wells, "The Reason Why: The Colored American Is Not in the World's Columbian Exposition," in Mildred I. Thompson, *Ida B. Wells-Barnett: An Exploratory Study of an American Black Woman, 1893–1930* (Brooklyn: Carlson Publishing, 1990), 188–223.

9   Weimann, *The Fair Women,* 253; Sklar, "Historical Foundations of Women's Power," 64 (quotations); and Stacy A. Cordery, "Women in Industrializing America," in *The Gilded Age: Essays on the Origins of Modern America,* ed. Charles W. Calhoun (Wilmington, Del.: Scholarly Resources, 1996), 111–36.

10   James J. Kenneally, "Women in the United States and Trade Unionism," in *The World of Women's Trade Unionism: Comparative Historical Essays,* ed. Norbert C. Soldon (Westport: Greenwood Press, 1985), 65–66 (quotations); Buhle, *Women*

and American Socialism, 71–73, 91–92; Joanne J. Meyerowitz, *Women Adrift: Independent Wage Earners in Chicago, 1880–1930* (Chicago: University of Chicago Press, 1988), introduction and chap. 5; Blewett, *We Will Rise in Our Might,* chap. 14; and Susan A. Glenn, *Daughters of the Shtetl: Life and Labor in the Immigrant Generation* (Ithaca: Cornell University Press, 1990), chaps. 3–4. For the historiography of the shift from the "old" labor history to the "new," see essays by Mari Jo Buhle and Alice Kessler-Harris in *Perspectives on American Labor History: The Problems of Synthesis,* ed. J. Carrol Moody and Alice Kessler-Harris (DeKalb: Northern Illinois University Press, 1990), 55–82, 217–34.

11   Smith-Rosenberg, *Disorderly Conduct,* 176 (quotation).

12   Mary Jo Deegan, *Jane Addams and the Men of the Chicago School, 1892–1918* (New Brunswick: Transaction Books, 1988), 40 (quotation); Allen F. Davis and Mary Lynn McCree, eds., *Eighty Years at Hull-House* (Chicago: Quadrangle Books, 1969), 25–26. All students of Jane Addams are eagerly waiting for the new biography by Victoria Brown of Grinnell College.

13   Jane Addams, "The Subjective Necessity of Social Settlements," in *The American Intellectual Tradition: A Sourcebook,* ed. David A. Hollinger and Charles Capper (New York: Oxford University Press, 1993), 2:162–63 (quotations).

14   Weimann, *The Fair Women,* 541.

15   Davis and McCree, *Eighty Years at Hull-House,* 22; see also Deegan, *Addams and the Men of the Chicago School,* 40.

16   Jane Addams, *Twenty Years at Hull-House* (New York: New American Library, Signet Classics, 1961), 51 (quotation). See also Allen F. Davis, *American Heroine: The Life and Legend of Jane Addams* (New York: Oxford University Press, 1973), 49; T. J. Jackson Lears, *No Place of Grace: Antimodernism and the Transformation of American Culture, 1880–1920* (New York: Pantheon Books, 1981), chaps. 4–5; Davis and McCree, *Eighty Years at Hull-House,* 7; Allen F. Davis, "Ellen Gates Starr," in *Notable American Women, 1607–1950,* ed. Edward T. James and Janet James (Cambridge: Belknap Press of Harvard, 1971), 351–53; and Robin Fleming, "Picturesque History and the Medieval in Nineteenth-Century America," *American Historical Review* 100 (October 1995): 1061–94.

17   Linda K. Kerber, "Separate Spheres, Female Worlds, Woman's Place: The Rhetoric of Women's History," *Journal of American History* 75 (June 1988): 32–38; Deegan, *Addams and the Men of the Chicago School,* chap. 9; and Sarah Deutsch, "Learning to Talk More Like a Man: Boston Women's Class-Bridging Organizations, 1870–1940," *American Historical Review* 97 (April 1992): 379–404.

18   Deegan, *Addams and the Men of the Chicago School,* 49; Allen F. Davis, *Spearhead for Reform: The Social Settlement and the Progressive Movement, 1890–1914* (New York: Oxford University Press, 1967), chaps. 1–2.

19   Weimann, *The Fair Women,* 495 (quotation); Kathleen Barry, *Susan B. Anthony: A Biography of a Singular Feminist* (New York: New York University Press, 1988), 312–114.

20   Barbara Hilkert Andolsen, *"Daughters of Jefferson, Daughters of Bootblacks": Racism and American Feminism* (Macon, Ga.: Mercer University Press, 1986), 12; and Marjorie Spruill Wheeler, *New Women of the New South: The Leaders of the*

Woman Suffrage Movement in the Southern States (New York: Oxford University Press, 1993), chaps. 1, 4.

21   Adele Logan Alexander, "How I Discovered My Grandmother . . . and the Truth about Black Women and the Suffrage Movement," in *Black Women in American History*, ed. Darlene Clark Hine (Brooklyn: Carlson Publishing, 1990), 1:15–23 (quotation on 19). According to Alexander, as late as 1897 Anthony refused to endorse the idea of a black woman addressing a NAWSA convention on behalf of black women in the South (21). On Wells-Barnett, see Thompson, *Ida B. Wells-Barnett*, chaps. 5–6.

22   Margaret Murray Washington to Ednah Cheney, 23 November 1896, in *The Booker T. Washington Papers*, ed. Louis R. Harlan (Urbana: University of Illinois Press, 1975), 4:237–38 (quotation), 540–41; Andolsen, *"Daughters of Jefferson, Daughters of Bootblacks,"* 12; Emma Lou Thornbrough, *T. Thomas Fortune: Militant Journalist* (Chicago: University of Chicago Press, 1972), 179; and Cynthia Neverdon-Morton, *Afro-American Women of the South and the Advancement of the Race, 1895–1925* (Knoxville: University of Tennessee Press, 1989), 192–93.

23   Elizabeth Cady Stanton, "The Solitude of Self," in *The American Intellectual Tradition: A Sourcebook*, ed. Hollinger and Capper, 2:49–53 (quotation on 49, emphasis added); Elisabeth Griffith, *In Her Own Right: The Life of Elizabeth Cady Stanton* (New York: Oxford University Press, 1984), chap. 11; Estelle C. Jelinek, *The Tradition of Women's Autobiography: From Antiquity to the Present* (Boston: Twayne Publishers, 1986), chap. 9; and Barry, *Susan B. Anthony*, 311 (quotation).

24   Carol Ruth Berkin, "Private Woman, Public Woman: The Contradiction of Charlotte Perkins Gilman," in *Critical Essays on Charlotte Perkins Gilman*, ed. Joanne B. Karpinski (New York: G. K. Hall, 1992), 17–42; Mary A. Hill, *Charlotte Perkins Gilman: The Making of a Radical Feminist* (Philadelphia: Temple University Press, 1980), 230–31, 259–63; and Polly Wynn Allen, *Building Domestic Liberty: Charlotte Perkins Gilman's Architectural Feminism* (Amherst: University of Massachusetts Press, 1988), 31, 44–45.

25   Charlotte Perkins Gilman, "Women and Economics," in *Feminism: The Essential Historical Writings*, ed. Miriam Schneir (New York: Vintage Books, 1972), 232–33 (quotation).

26   Allen, *Building Domestic Liberty*, 47; Buhle, *Women and American Socialism*, 91–93; Daniel H. Borus, introduction to *Looking Backward*, 18–21; Margaret S. Marsh, *Anarchist Women, 1870–1920* (Philadelphia: Temple University Press, 1981), chaps. 1–2; and Marian J. Morton, *Emma Goldman and the American Left: "Nowhere at Home"* (New York: Twayne Publishers, 1992), chap. 2. Roy Rosenzweig has pointed out that anarchists such as Emma Goldman were alienated not only from the encompassing American society but also from their immigrant communities: "Goldman's rejection of Jewish religious and marital traditions concerned Worcester [, Massachusetts,] Jews more than her attacks on capitalism and the state, because it was the cultural values and institutions of the ethnic community that provided the moral and social principles around which they organized their lives." Roy Rosenzweig, *Eight Hours for What We Will: Workers and Leisure in an Industrial City, 1870–1920* (Cambridge: Cambridge University Press, 1983),

11. In this sense, an anarchist woman such as Goldman was like Charlotte Perkins Gilman, "a free lance radical."

27   Ida B. Wells-Barnett, "The Negro's Case in Equity," reprinted in Thompson, *Ida B. Wells-Barnett*, 246.

7   Business and Labor in the 1890s: Regulation, Resistance, and Reorganization

1   William Letwin, *Law and Economic Policy in America: The Evolution of the Sherwin Antitrust Act* (Chicago: University of Chicago Press, 1965), chaps. 1–2; James Livingston, "The Social Analysis of Economic History and Theory: Conjectures on Late Nineteenth-Century American Development," *American Historical Review* 92 (February 1987): 72–87; Thomas K. McCraw, "Rethinking the Trust Question," in *Regulation in Perspective: Historical Essays*, ed. Thomas K. McCraw (Cambridge: Harvard University Press, 1981), 2–9; and Carol Wiesbrod, *The Boundaries of Utopia* (New York: Pantheon Books, 1980), introduction and chap. 2. The newness of the corporation and its changing status in American law was evident in a highly regarded legal text, Victor Morawetz, *A Treatise on the Law of Private Corporations Other than Charitable* (Boston: Little, Brown, 1882). Did an act "performed in a corporate capacity, without legislative permission," have legal validity? "This question has been much agitated in the courts during the last thirty or forty years," Morawetz noted, "and the decisions upon it are far from being in harmony; but [the federal courts] seem now to have arrived at a philosophical and reasonable solution to the difficulty." He explained that solution as follows: "An assumption of the privilege of acting in a corporate capacity does not involve an infringement of the rights of other persons. It neither interferes with their property, their personal liberty, nor their security. Hence there is no reason of immediate justice to others, why a number of individuals should not be permitted to form a corporation of their own free will, and without first obtaining permission from the legislature, just as they may form a partnership or enter into ordinary contracts with each other" (24).

2   Letwin, *Law and Economic Policy in America*, chaps. 4–5; Donald T. Pisani, "Promotion and Regulation: Constitutionalism and the American Economy," *Journal of American History* 74 (December 1987): 755–62; Thomas K. McCraw, *Prophets of Regulation: Charles Francis Adams, Louis D. Brandeis, James M. Landis, Alfred E. Kahn* (Cambridge: Harvard University Press, 1984), chaps. 1–2, and *Regulation in Perspective*, 1–55; and George H. Miller, *Railroads and the Granger Laws* (Madison: University of Wisconsin Press, 1971), 192–93.

3   John L. Thomas, *Alternative America: Henry George, Edward Bellamy, Henry Demarest Lloyd, and the Adversary Tradition* (Cambridge: Harvard University Press, 1983), 289–90; and Peter J. Frederick, *Knights of the Golden Rule: The Intellectual as Christian Social Reformer in the 1890s* (Lexington: University Press of Kentucky, 1976), 56–77.

4   Thomas, *Alternative America*, chap. 4, 7 and 242–52; Edward Bellamy, *Looking Backwards, 2000–1887*, ed. Daniel H. Borus (Boston: Bedford Books of St. Martin's Press, 1995); and Laurence Gronlund, *The Cooperative Commonwealth* (Cambridge: Harvard University Press, 1965).

5   Thomas, *Alternative America*, chap. 5; and Robert J. Rafalko, "Henry George's Labor Theory of Value: He Saw the Entrepreneurs and Workers as Employers of Capital and Land, and Not the Reverse," *American Journal of Economics and Sociology* 48 (July 1989): 311–20.

A close modern approximation of George's theory would be a college graduate who secures a job in a booming city and rents an apartment. If everytime this young professional received a pay raise or promotion, the landlord raised the rent, then the young worker would experience the frustration that George's generation felt over the behavior of land monopolizers in the Gilded Age.

6   Nick Salvatore, *Eugene V. Debs: Citizen and Socialist* (Urbana: University of Illinois Press, 1982), chaps. 1–4, and 103 (quotation).

7   Leon Fink, "The New Labor History and the Power of Historical Pessimism: Consensus, Hegemony, and the Case of the Knights of Labor," *Journal of American History* 75 (June 1988): 129–34; Stuart Bruce Kaufman, *Samuel Gompers and the Origins of the American Federation of Labor, 1848–1896* (Westport: Greenwood Press, 1973), chaps. 8–9; Gerald Emanuel Stearn, ed., *Gompers* (Englewood Cliffs: Prentice-Hall, 1971), 27 (quotation).

8   Frederick, *Knights of the Golden Rule*, 58–68 (quotation on 59); and Thomas, *Alternative America*, 317, 329.

9   Salvatore, *Eugene V. Debs*, chap. 5.

10   Ibid., 161–69.

11   Kaufman, *Samuel Gompers*, chaps. 10–11; Stearn, *Gompers*, 154–60 (quotations on 155 and 156); and Irwin Yellowitz, "Samuel Gompers: A Half-Century in Labor's Front Rank," *Monthly Labor Review* (July 1989): 30–32.

12   Steven J. Rosenstone, Roy L. Behr, and Edward H. Lazarus, *Third Parties in America: Citizen Response to Major Party Failure* (Princeton: Princeton University Press, 1984), 67–75.

13   Daniel Nelson, *Frederick W. Taylor and the Rise of Scientific Management* (Madison: University of Wisconsin Press, 1980), chaps. 2–3; Charles D. Wrege and Ronald G. Greenwood, *Frederick W. Taylor: The Father of Scientific Management: Myth and Reality* (Homewood: Business One Irwin, 1991), 17–39, 45–51.

14   Naomi R. Lamoreaux, *The Great Merger Movement in American Business, 1895–1904* (London: Cambridge University Press, 1985), 1–2 (quotations). Lamoreaux included in her list of mergers "only horizontal consolidations of at least *five* previously competing firms." See 1 n. 2.

15   Ibid., 12, 33, 87–97, 100–116; and Glenn Porter, "Industrialization and the Rise of Big Business," in *The Gilded Age: Essays on the Origins of Modern America*, ed. Charles W. Calhoun (Wilmington, Del.: Scholarly Resources, 1996), 15–18.

16   Lamoreaux, *The Great Merger Movement*, 139; Alfred D. Chandler, *The Visible Hand: The Managerial Revolution in American Business* (Cambridge: Harvard University Press, 1977), 333, 375; Louis Galambos, "The Triumph of Oligopoly," in *American Economic Development in Historical Perspective*, ed. Thomas Weiss and Donald Schaefer (Stanford University Press, 1994), 241–53; and Philip Scranton, "Diversity in Diversity: Flexible Production and American Industrialization, 1880–1930," *Business History Review* 65 (Spring 1991): 27–90.

17   Letwin, *Law and Economic Policy in America*, 161–81 (quotation on 165). See also

A. D. Neale and D. G. Goyder, *The Antitrust Laws of the United States: A Study of Competition Enforced by Law* (London: Cambridge University Press, 1980), 19, 26–27, 36, 71–72; Willard L. King, *Melville Weston Fuller: Chief Justice of the United States, 1888–1910* (Chicago: University of Chicago Press, 1967), chaps. 11–18; and Galambos, "Triumph of Oligopoly," 241–42. Had the government prosecutors emphasized the sugar trusts' commercial role as a seller of sugar across state lines, the case might have gone the other way (as Justice Harlan emphasized in his dissent).

18   Nelson, *Taylor and the Rise of Scientific Management*, 62–63.

19   Lamoreaux, *The Great Merger Movement*, 80–83; Nelson, *Taylor and the Rise of Scientific Management*, 63–69; and Alfred D. Chandler and Stephen Salsburg, *Pierre S. DuPont and the Making of the Modern Corporation* (New York: Harper and Row, 1971), 29–39.

20   For the concept of the three-sided struggle for power, see William M. Reddy, *Money and Liberty in Modern Europe: A Critique of Historical Understanding* (London: Cambridge University Press, 1987), chap. 2 (particularly 60). For the contrasting views of the corporation, see David F. Noble, *America by Design: Science, Technology, and the Rise of Corporate Capitalism* (New York: Oxford University Press, 1977); Oliver Zunz, *Making America Corporate, 1870–1920* (Chicago: University of Chicago Press, 1990); and David Thelen, *Paths of Resistance: Tradition and Dignity in Industrializing Missouri* (New York: Oxford University Press, 1986). For the critique of the concept of hegemony as applied to history, see the introduction to this book, particularly the sources in note 27.

Part 2: New Languages and Old Realities: An Introduction

1   Daniel T. Rodgers, "In Search of Progressivism," *Reviews in American History* 10 (December 1982): 113–32 (quotation on 123).

2   A social language is not the same concept as an ideology. An ideology is an interlocking set of principles that function both as a *description* of the world by creating the semantic categories to describe it and as a *prescription* for how one should act in the world. An ideology, then, not only tells you *what* to believe and provides answers in advance about *how to act* in given situations but also frames perceptions and tells you *what to see*, and more importantly, *what not to see* in the world. A social language, on the other hand, is a collection of *labels* to categorize experiences and an *implicit hierarchy* of values to apply in constantly changing situations. A social language is a loose set of *preferences* and lacks the hard logic of an ideology. An ideology "uses" people, so to speak, because it limits their perceptions and guides their actions while people "use" social languages as ad hoc intellectual orientations and as a set of guides for deciding what actions to take. These concepts are not, however, mutually exclusive. Social languages can *supplement* ideologies for the sake of communication or social languages can act as a *substitute* for an ideology. Social languages, in summary, provide the "what," the vocabulary for talking about core values in given situations; rhetorical strategies provide the "how," the techniques to communicate with an audience.

3   John Dewey, *Essays in Experimental Logic* (1916; reprint, New York: Dover Publications, 1953), 186.

4   Woodrow Wilson, *The Papers of Woodrow Wilson*, ed. Arthur S. Link (Princeton: Princeton University Press, 1976), 22:443.

8   Women's Rights, Feminism, and the Social Gospel, 1898–1912

1   Alice Kessler-Harris, *Out to Work: The History of Wage-Earning Women in the United States* (New York: Oxford University Press, 1982), chaps. 5–6; Oliver Zunz, *Making America Corporate, 1870–1920* (Chicago: University of Chicago Press, 1990), 116–21 and chap. 5; Annelise Orleck, *Common Sense and a Little Fire: Women and Working-Class Politics in the United States, 1900–1965* (Chapel Hill: University of North Carolina Press, 1995), prologue and chap. 1; Burton J. Bledstein, *The Culture of Professionalism: The Middle Class and the Development of Higher Education in America* (New York: W. W. Norton, 1976), 118–20; Nancy Woloch, *Women and the American Experience* (New York: Alfred A. Knopf, 1984), chap. 12; and Dorothy Salem, *To Better Our World: Black Women in Organized Reform, 1890–1920* (Brooklyn: Carlson Publishing, 1990), chap. 1.

2   Stacy A. Cordery, "Women in Industrializing America," in *The Gilded Age: Essays on the Origins of Modern America*, ed. Charles W. Calhoun (Wilmington, Del.: Scholarly Resources, 1996), 114; Ross Evans Paulson, *Women's Suffrage and Prohibition: A Comparative Study of Equality and Social Control* (Glenview: Scott, Foresman, 1973), 139–40, 157; Jacqueline Van Voris, *Carrie Chapman Catt: A Public Life* (New York: Feminist Press at the City University of New York, 1987), 59–130; Karen J. Blair, *The Clubwoman as Feminist: True Womanhood Redefined, 1868–1914* (New York: Holmes and Meier, 1980), chap. 6; Rheta Childe Dorr, "Clubs as Instruments of Reform," in *The American Woman: Who Was She?*, ed. Anne Firor Scott (Englewood Cliffs: Prentice-Hall, 1971), 105–6; Ann Firor Scott, *Natural Allies: Women's Associations in American History* (Urbana: University of Illinois Press, 1991), 130–31, 155, 162–63; Dorothy Salem, *To Better Our World*, chap. 2 (particularly 35, on Terrell's critics within the NACW); Beverly Washington Jones, *Quest for Equality: The Life and Writings of Mary Eliza Church Terrell, 1863–1954* (Brooklyn: Carlson Publishing, 1990), 21–32; and Stephanie J. Shaw, "Black Club Women and the Creation of the National Association of Colored Women," in *We Specialize in the Wholly Impossible: A Reader in Black Women's History*, ed. Darlene Clark Hine, Wilma King, and Linda Reed (Brooklyn: Carlson Publishing, 1995), 433–48. For the unique situations of Chinese American women and Latina women, see Judy Yung, "The Social Awakening of Chinese American Women as Reported in *Chung Sai Yat Po*, 1900–1911," in *Unequal Sisters: A Multicultural Reader in U.S. Women's History*, ed. Ellen Carol DuBois and Vicki L. Ruiz (New York: Routledge, 1990), 195–207; and Vicki Ruiz, "Dead Ends or Gold Mines? Using Missionary Records in Mexican-American Women's History," in *Latina Issues: Fragments of Historia (Ella) (Herstory)*, ed. Antoinette Sedillo López (New York: Garland Publishing, 1995), 55–78.

3   Ellen Carol DuBois, "Working Women, Class Relations, and Suffrage Militance: Harriet Stanton Blatch and the New York Woman Suffrage Movement, 1894–1909," *Journal of American History* 74 (June 1987): 34–58; Rosalind Rosenberg, *Divided Lives: American Women in the Twentieth Century* (New York: Hill and

Wang, 1992), 42–44; and Jane Jerome Camhi, *Women against Women: American Anti-Suffragism, 1880–1920* (Brooklyn: Carlson Publishing, 1994), 124.

Many social scientists and historians have noted the proliferation of organizations in the early twentieth century. While these organizations were somewhat narrow in foci, served a limited clientele, and lobbied for particular interests, they also articulated values and defined issues for a broader audience. All self-appointed activists lived in hope of reaching this circle of interested clientele and moving it, hence the term "social movement," to support actions that would be beneficial to the organization and its priorities.

The classic work, which initiated the scholarly interest in organizations, was Kenneth E. Boulding, *The Organizational Revolution: A Study in the Ethics of Economic Organization* (New York: Harper and Brothers, 1950). On the role of organizations in this period of women's history, see Scott, *Natural Allies,* chaps. 6–7; and Karen J. Blair, *The History of American Women's Voluntary Organizations, 1810–1960: A Guide to Sources* (Boston: G. H. Hall, 1989). On the theory of social movements, see Ron Eyerman and Andrew Jamison, *Social Movements: A Cognitive Approach* (University Park: Pennsylvania State University Press, 1991), chaps. 1–4; and Anthony Oberschall, *Social Movements: Ideologies, Interests, and Identities* (New Brunswick: Transaction Publishers, 1993), chaps. 1–2.

4   Kathryn Kish Sklar, "Hull House in the 1890s: A Community of Women Reformers," in *Women, Families, and Communities: Readings in American History,* ed. Nancy A. Hewitt (Glenview: Scott, Foresman/Little Brown Higher Education, 1989), 2:74–87; Theda Skocpol, *Protecting Soldiers and Mothers: The Political Origins of Social Policy in the United States* (Cambridge: Harvard University Press, 1992), 352–54 (quotation on 352); and Kathryn Kish Sklar, *Florence Kelley and the Nation's Work: The Rise of Women's Political Culture, 1830–1900* (New Haven: Yale University Press, 1995), 52–61, 82–90, 100–120, 167–77, 306–14.

Working-class women had their own traditions of consumer boycotts, particularly among Jewish immigrants from Eastern Europe. These activities operated at different social levels and to separate rhythms to those of the NCL. See Paula E. Hymn, "Immigrant Women, Community Networks, and Consumer Protest: The New York City Kosher Meat Boycott of 1902," in *Women, Families and Communities,* ed. Hewitt, 2:88–98; and Orleck, *Common Sense and a Little Fire,* 23–30.

5   Nancy F. Cott, *The Grounding of Modern Feminism* (New Haven: Yale University Press, 1987), chap. 1 (quotation on 3); and DuBois, "Working Women, Class Relations, and Suffrage Militance," 42.

6   Cott, *Grounding of Modern Feminism,* 30–35; Polly Wynn Allen, *Building Domestic Liberty: Charlotte Perkins Gilman's Architectural Feminism* (Amherst: University of Massachusetts Press, 1988), chaps. 3–5; Margaret S. Marsh, *Anarchist Women, 1870–1920* (Philadelphia: Temple University Press, 1981), 111–12; Virginia Gardner, *"Friend and Lover": The Life of Louise Bryant* (New York: Horizon Press, 1982); and Nancy F. Cott, "What's in a Name? The Limits of 'Social Feminism'; or, Expanding the Vocabulary of Women's History," *Journal of American History* 76 (December 1989): 809–29. Cott distinguishes between three different kinds of consciousness: (1) feminist or ideological consciousness derived from shared ideas,

(2) female consciousness derived from the acceptance of gender-based responsibilities, particularly maternal ones, and (3) communal consciousness derived from membership in a group (whether class, ethnic, racial, religion, national, or geographical). These distinctions have been used in the analysis of this chapter.

7 Seth Koven and Sonya Michel, eds., *Mothers of a New World: Maternalist Politics and the Origins of Welfare States* (New York: Routledge, 1993), 2, 4 (quotations); Skocpol, *Protecting Soldiers and Mothers,* 333–40, 352–54, 367–71, 382; and Salem, *To Better Our World,* chaps. 3–4.

8 Woloch, *Women and the American Experience,* 204–17; Skocpol, *Protecting Soldiers and Mothers,* 349–53; and Orleck, *Common Sense and a Little Fire,* chap. 2. Linda Gordon warns against drawing too sharp a line between feminism and maternalism in the matter of child protection. See Linda Gordon, "Family Violence, Feminism, and Social Control," in *Unequal Sisters: A Multicultural Reader in U.S. Women's History,* ed. DuBois and Ruiz, 141–56.

9 Thomas K. McCraw, *Prophets of Regulation: Charles Francis Adams, Louis D. Brandeis, James M. Landis, Alfred E. Kahn* (Cambridge: Harvard University Press, 1984), 87–88; Skocpol, *Protecting Soldiers and Mothers,* 369, 393–95 (quotation on 394); Herbert Hovenkamp, *Enterprise and American Law, 1836–1937* (Cambridge: Harvard University Press, 1990), 133; and Mary Cornelia Porter, "Lockner and Company: Revisionism Revisited," in *Liberty, Property, and Government: Constitutional Interpretation before the New Deal,* ed. Ellen Frankel Paul and Howard Dickman (Albany: State University of New York Press, 1989), 11–38 (particularly 19). According to Skocpol, "the only protective laws for male workers allowed to stand by the courts were statutes about public works employment, where the state was a party to the contract, and hours laws narrowly targeted on especially dangerous occupations, like mining, or on industries where there were compelling public safety concerns, such as the railroads" (369).

10 Michael Kimmel, *Manhood in America: A Cultural History* (New York: Free Press, 1996), chaps. 3–5; Mark C. Carnes, *Secret Ritual and Manhood in Victorian America* (New Haven: Yale University Press, 1989), chap. 5; Mary Ann Clawson, *Constructing Brotherhood: Class, Gender, and Fraternalism* (Princeton: Princeton University Press, 1989), 4–17; and David I. McLeod, *Building Character in the American Boy: The Boy Scouts, YMCA, and Their Forerunners, 1870–1920* (Madison: University of Wisconsin Press, 1983), chaps. 6–8, and 146–53.

Clawson estimated membership in the main fraternal orders at 4 million in 1900 out of a potential of 21.9 million males, or about 10 percent of the male population.

For fraternalism in the African American community in the same time period, see David M. Fahey, *The Black Lodge in White America: "True Reformer" Browne and His Economic Strategy* (Dayton: Wright State University Press, 1994), 5–12, 23–33.

11 Robert M. Crunden, *Ministers of Reform: The Progressives' Achievement in American Civilization, 1889–1920* (New York: Basic Books, 1982), chaps. 1–3 (quotation on 40); Ronald C. White Jr. and C. Howard Hopkins, *The Social Gospel: Religion and Reform in Changing America* (Philadelphia: Temple University Press, 1976), 167 n. 13 (on the use of term "social gospel") and chaps. 15, 17; Charles Howard Hopkins, *The Rise of the Social Gospel in American Protestantism, 1865–1915* (New

Haven: Yale University Press, 1940), chaps. 9–10, 17–18 (the Social Creed is reprinted on 316–17); Aaron I. Abell, *American Catholicism and Social Action: A Search for Social Justice, 1865–1950* (Garden City: Doubleday, 1960), 131–36, and chap. 5 (quotation from 1900 conference on 134); and Ronald C. White, *Liberty and Justice for All: Racial Reform and the Social Gospel, 1877–1925* (San Francisco: Harper and Row, 1990), chaps. 6, 8, 10.

12   Walter Rauschenbusch, *Christianity and the Social Crisis* (New York: Macmillan Company, 1907), 134–35 (emphasis added).

13   Ibid., 276–79; Walter Rauschenbusch, *Christianizing the Social Order* (New York: Macmillan, 1913), 131 (woman suffrage), 414–16 (protective legislation for women); and Kimmel, *Manhood in America*, 175–79.

14   Gail Bederman, " 'The Women Have Had Charge of the Church Work Long Enough': The Men and Religion Forward Movement of 1911–1912 and the Masculinization of Middle-Class Protestantism," *American Quarterly* 41 (September 1989): 432–65 (quotation on 438).

15   Ibid., 435–56 (quotation on 453); Carnes, *Secret Ritual and Manhood*, 153–56; Clawson, *Constructing Brotherhood*, 16–17; Lynn Dumenil, *Freemasonry and American Culture, 1880–1930* (Princeton: Princeton University Press, 1984), 89–91; and Jodi Vandenberg-Davis, "The Manly Pursuit of a Partnership between the Sexes: The Debate over YMCA Programs for Women and Girls, 1914–1933," *Journal of American History* 78 (March 1992): 1324–46. For an interpretation of similar developments in England, with implications for the American case, see Jeff Hearn, *Men in the Public Eye: Critical Studies on Men and Masculinity* (London: Routledge, 1992), chap. 6.

9   Regulation of Business: Progressivism, Socialism, and the Gospel of Efficiency, 1898–1912

1   The question of the origins of progressivism has elicited a variety of answers from historians. For example, Anne Firor Scott, *Natural Allies: Women's Associations in American History* (Urbana: University of Illinois Press, 1991), chaps. 6–7 pointed to "municipal housekeeping" and social justice activities of women's organizations in the 1880s as the beginning of progressivism. David P. Thelen, *The New Citizenship: Origins of Progressivism in Wisconsin, 1885–1900* (Columbia: University of Missouri Press, 1972), and *Paths of Resistance: Tradition and Dignity in Industrializing Missouri* (New York: Oxford University Press, 1986), called attention to the role of farmers, traditionalism, and the continuity with populism as well as the consumers revolt. Nell Irvin Painter, *Standing at Armageddon: The United States, 1877–1919* (New York: W. W. Norton, 1987), introduction and chap. 6, stressed the primary role of the working-class quest for justice and saw middle-class progressivism as a reaction *against* it. Jean B. Quant, *From the Small Town to the Great Community: The Social Thought of Progressive Intellectuals* (New Brunswick: Rutgers University Press, 1970), and Robert M. Crunden, *Ministers of Reform: The Progressives' Achievement in American Civilization, 1889–1920* (New York: Basic Books, 1982), emphasized the continuity of small-town values and religion on progressives.

This chapter will utilize insights from all these approaches but will focus on the middle-class, urban origins of one variety of progressivism. It will also utilize social language analysis to clarify the role of core values in order to compare them with trade unionist and socialist views.

2 Alan Dawley, *Struggles for Justice: Social Responsibility and the Liberal State* (Cambridge: Harvard University Press, 1991), chap. 1; and Joe Weber and Lou Fields, "Trust Scene," Columbia Gramophone Company, 1908, record number A 1855 (author's collection).

3 Richard L. McCormick, "The Discovery That Business Corrupts Politics: A Reappraisal of the Origins of Progressivism," *American Historical Review* 86 (April 1981): 247–74.

In 1904 the acerbic economist Thorstein Veblen published an evolutionary explanation of the rise of the corporation and its impact on society and the state: "Because of [the] settled habit of seeing all the conjunctures of life from the business point of view, in terms of profit and loss, the management of the affairs of the community at large falls by common consent into the hands of business men and is guided by business considerations. Hence modern politics is business politics, even apart from the sinister application of the phrase to what is invidiously called corrupt politics." Thorstein Veblen, *The Theory of Business Enterprise* (New York: Charles Scribner's Sons, 1904), 268–69.

The current version of this theory is called "corporate liberalism." R. Jeffrey Lustig has summarized it as follows: "Classical liberalism approached public order from the standpoint of individual liberty." But the economic changes from the 1870s to World War I shifted the basis to the corporation. Whereas current interpretations pit conservatism (pro-business and anti-state) against liberalism (anti-business and pro-state), progressivism, the form of corporate liberalism, "was pro-business *and* pro-state, dedicated to private profit *and* to regulatory reform." R. Jeffrey Lustig, *Corporate Liberalism: The Origins of Modern Political Theory, 1890–1920* (Berkeley: University of California Press, 1982), chap. 1 (quotations on 2 and 7). In terms of historical methodology, Lustig admitted that "though no direct casual link existed between events and ideas, the informing logic of the new theory turned out to parallel the logic of social relations in that world" (7). For criticism, see reviews by Hugh O'Neill, *Political Science Quarterly* 98 (Winter 1983–84): 732; and Stephen Skowronek, *American Historical Review* 88 (October 1988): 1083.

4 David P. Thelen, *Robert M. La Follette and the Insurgent Spirit* (Boston: Little, Brown, 1976), chap. 2 (quotation on 22).

5 Louis L. Gould, *The Presidency of Theodore Roosevelt* (Lawrence: University Press of Kansas, 1991), 147–56; Henry F. Pringle, *Theodore Roosevelt: A Biography* (New York: Harcourt, Brace, 1956), bk. 2, chaps. 1–3; and Theodore Roosevelt, "Resurrection of the Sherman Anti-Trust Law," in *The Writings of Theodore Roosevelt*, ed. William H. Harbaugh (Indianapolis: Bobbs-Merrill, 1967), 83–91.

6 Pringle, *Theodore Roosevelt*, 254.

7 Thelen, *Robert M. La Follette*, 55–57; Gould, *Presidency of Theodore Roosevelt*, 156–65; and Stephen Skowronek, *Building a New American State: The Expansion of National Administrative Capacities, 1877–1920* (Cambridge: Cambridge University Press, 1982), 255–58.

8   Martin J. Sklar, *The Corporate Reconstruction of American Capitalism, 1890–1916: The Market, the Law, and Politics* (New York: Cambridge University Press, 1988), chap. 4 (quotation on 282).

9   Skowronek, *Building a New American State*, 176, 263–65; Sklar, *The Corporate Reconstruction of American Capitalism*, 145–47, 286, 328; Herbert Hovenkamp, *Enterprise and American Law, 1836–1937* (Cambridge: Harvard University Press, 1991), chaps. 20–24; and Keith L. Bryant Jr., *Railroads in the Age of Regulation, 1900–1980: Encyclopedia of American Business History and Biography* (New York: Facts on File, 1988), 276. A commerce court was established but repealed by Congress in 1913.

10   Aileen S. Kraditor, *The Radical Persuasion, 1890–1917: Aspects of the Intellectual History and the Historiography of Three American Radical Organizations* (Baton Rouge: Louisiana State University Press, 1981), sec. 2; and Nick Salvatore, *Eugene V. Debs: Citizen and Socialist* (Urbana: University of Illinois Press, 1982), 231.

11   *The Writings and Speeches of Eugene V. Debs*, ed. Arthur M. Schlesinger Jr. (New York: Hermitage Press, 1948), 111 (quotation); Mari Jo Buhle, *Women and American Socialism, 1870–1920* (Urbana: University of Illinois Press, 1981), chaps. 3–4.

12   Salvatore, *Eugene V. Debs*, 221. Accurate membership figures for the SPA in 1908 are not available, but it was estimated that women constituted 10 percent to 15 percent in 1912. Buhle, *Women and American Socialism*, 160.

13   Melvin I. Urofsky, *Louis D. Brandeis and the Progressive Tradition* (Boston: Little, Brown, 1981), chaps. 2–3; and Thomas K. McCraw, *Prophets of Regulation: Charles Francis Adams, Louis D. Brandeis, James M. Landis, Alfred E. Kahn* (Cambridge: Harvard University Press, 1983), 91–92.

14   Daniel Nelson, *Frederick W. Taylor and the Rise of Scientific Management* (Madison: University of Wisconsin Press, 1980), chaps. 5–8; David Montgomery, *Workers' Control in America: Studies in the History of Work, Technology, and Labor Struggles* (Cambridge: Cambridge University Press, 1979), chap. 2; and Samuel Haber, *Efficiency and Uplift: Scientific Management in the Progressive Era, 1890–1920* (Chicago: University of Chicago Press, 1964), ix–x, 24–27.

15   Frederick Winslow Taylor, *The Principles of Scientific Management* (1911; reprint, New York: W. W. Norton, 1967), 5–8 (quotation on 5).

16   Skowronek, *Building a New American State*, 189–91; Pringle, *Theodore Roosevelt*, bk. 3, 370–72; Sklar, *Corporate Reconstruction of American Capitalism*, 364–67; and Roderick Nash, ed., *The American Environment: Readings in the History of Conservation* (Reading, Mass.: Addison-Wesley Publishing, 1968), pt. 2, "The Progressive Conservation Crusade."

17   On the corporation as the context for the adaptation of middle-class aspirations and values, see Oliver Zunz, *Making America Corporate, 1870–1920* (Chicago: University of Chicago Press, 1990), chaps. 1–4; David F. Noble, *America By Design: Science, Technology, and the Rise of Corporate Capitalism* (New York: Oxford University Press, 1977), chaps. 3–4; Peter Dobkin Hall, "Organization as Artifact: A Case Study of Technical Innovation and Management Reform, 1893–1906," in *The Mythmaking Frame of Mind: Social Imagination and American Culture*, ed. James Gilbert, Amy Gilman, Donald M. Scott, and Joan W. Scott (Belmont, Calif.: Wadsworth Publishing Company, 1993), 178–208.

18   Casey Nelson Blake, *Beloved Community: The Cultural Criticism of Randolph Bourne, Van Wyck Brooks, Waldo Frank, and Lewis Mumford* (Chapel Hill: University of North Carolina Press, 1990), 2–8, 78–87, 266, and 274; and Howard P. Segal, *Technological Utopianism in American Culture* (Chicago: University of Chicago Press, 1985), chaps. 1–3.

10   Civil Liberty and Civil Rights, 1898–1912

1   Alex Wellek, ed., *The Encyclopedic Dictionary of American Government*, 4th ed. (Guilford, Conn.: Duskin Publishing Group, 1991), 45, 47.

2   William Graham Sumner, *On Liberty, Society, and Politics: The Essential Essays of William Graham Sumner*, ed. Robert C. Bannister (Indianapolis: Liberty Fund, 1992), 206, 237–50; John W. Burgess, "Civil Liberty and Constitutional Law," *Political Science Quarterly* 19 (December 1904): 568–72; Daniel T. Rodgers, *Contested Truths: Key Words in American Politics since Independence* (New York: Basic Books, 1987), chaps. 5–6; Frank J. Goodnow, *The American Conception of Liberty and Government* (Providence, R.I.: Standard Publishing Company, 1916), 9–31; and Stephen Skowronek, *Building a New American State: The Expansion of National Administrative Capacities, 1877–1920* (Cambridge: Cambridge University Press, 1982), 41–45, and chap. 3.

The argument in this chapter about the concept of "civil liberty" as a political legal status is not meant to say that there was no judicial concern for the Bill of Rights during the period 1898 to 1917. Rather, it is that the semantic content of the phrase "civil liberty" in the late nineteenth and early twentieth centuries is not identical to the semantic content of the current phrase "civil liberties." As shall be shown in chapter 13, the modern meaning of "civil liberties" did not emerge until World War I and its aftermath.

3   Oliver Wendell Holmes Jr., "The Theory of Legal Interpretation" (1899), quoted in Morton White, *Social Thought in America: The Revolt against Formalism* (Boston: Beacon Press, 1957), 61, and "The Path of the Law" (1897), in *The Mind and Faith of Justice Holmes: His Speeches, Essays, Letters, and Judicial Opinions*, ed. Max Lerner (Boston: Little, Brown, 1943), 71–89; John P. Diggins, *The Promise of Pragmatism: Modernism and the Crisis of Knowledge and Authority* (Chicago: University of Chicago Press, 1994), 217–22; White, *Social Thought in America*, chaps. 1–5, 8; and R. Jeffrey Lustig, *Corporate Liberalism: The Origins of Modern American Political Theory, 1890–1920* (Berkeley: University of California Press, 1982), chap. 5.

There is a difference in methodological approach between that of a legal scholar and that of an intellectual historian when dealing with an issue such as the meaning of "civil rights" and "civil liberties." In brief, legal scholars ask, "What does the term mean *now?*" They are interested in the past only to the extent that selected portions of it (key cases) have shaped this current understanding as legal precedents. On the other hand, intellectual historians ask, "What did the term mean *then?*" They are interested in the present only to the extent that selected portions of it have shaped the language necessary to communicate about the past with a present audience. Also, intellectual historians see public values as playing a larger role in the events under scrutiny than legal scholars who tend to focus more on procedures, priorities, and personalities within the judicial system. It is, in short, the difference between legal discourse and public discourse.

See also Robert E. Park, "How Lawyers Read the Constitution: An Introductory Bibliography," *American Studies International* 26 (April 1988): 2–34; and David A. J. Richards, *Toleration and the Constitution* (New York: Oxford University Press, 1986), pt. 1.

4   James Bryce, *The Hindrances to Good Citizenship* (New Haven: Yale University Press, 1909); Herbert Croly, *The Promise of American Life* (1909; reprint, Indianapolis: Bobbs-Merrill, 1965), 198–201; Carl N. Degler, *In Search of Human Nature: The Decline and Revival of Darwinism in American Social Thought* (New York: Oxford University Press, 1991), chaps. 1–2; and William H. Harbaugh, introduction to *The Writings of Theodore Roosevelt*, ed. William H. Harbaugh (Indianapolis: Bobbs-Merrill, 1967), xvii–xxxviii.

5   W. E. B. Du Bois, "Two Negro Conventions," in *Writings of W. E. B. Du Bois in Periodicals Edited by Others*, ed. Herbert Aptheker (New York: Kraus-Thomson Organization, 1982), 1:60 (quotation).

6   Ibid., 61. For the Hose incident, see *The Autobiography of W. E. B. Du Bois: A Soliloquy on Viewing My Life from the Last Decade of Its First Century* (New York: International Publishers, 1968), 222.

7   Mary Church Terrell, "The Duty of the National Association of Colored Women to the Race" (1899), reprinted in *Quest for Equality: The Life and Writings of Mary Eliza Church Terrell, 1863–1954*, ed. Beverly Washington Jones (Brooklyn: Carlson Publishing, 1990), 139–50 (quotations on 140, 141, 144, 145, and 149).

8   John Brown Childs, *Leadership, Conflict, and Cooperation in Afro-American Social Thought* (Philadelphia: Temple University Press, 1989), chap. 2; Evelyn Brooks Higginbotham, *Righteous Discontent: The Women's Movement in the Black Baptist Church, 1880–1920* (Cambridge: Harvard University Press, 1994), 14–17 and chap. 2; and Deborah Gray White, "The Cost of Club Work, the Price of Black Feminism," in *Visible Women: New Essays on American Activism*, ed. Nancy A. Hewitt and Suzanne Lebsock (Urbana: University of Illinois Press, 1993), 247–69.

9   W. E. B. Du Bois, "Southern Workman," May 1900, *Writings of W. E. B. Du Bois in Periodicals*, ed. Aptheker, 1:69.

10   W. E. B. Du Bois, remarks to Pan African Congress, July 1900, quoted in David Levering Lewis, *W. E. B. Du Bois: Biography of a Race, 1868–1919* (New York: Henry Holt, 1993), 251.

11   W. E. B. Du Bois, *The Souls of Black Folks*, reprinted in *Writings of W. E. B. Du Bois*, ed. Nathan I. Higgins (New York: Literary Classics of the United States, 1986), 359–547.

12   Ibid. (quotation on 437); and Ida Wells-Barnett, "Booker T. Washington and His Critics," reprinted in *Ida B. Wells-Barnett: An Exploratory Study of An American Black Woman, 1893–1930*, by Mildred I. Thompson (Brooklyn: Carlson Publishing, 1990), 255–60 (quotation on 259).

13   W. E. B. Du Bois, "Credo," quoted in Lewis, *W. E. B. Du Bois*, 312–13 (quotation on 313).

14   "Constitution and By-Laws of the Niagara Movement as Adopted July 12 and 13, 1905, at Buffalo, N.Y.," in *Pamphlets and Leaflets by W. E. B. Du Bois*, ed. Herbert Aptheker (White Plains, N.Y.: Kraus-Thomson Organizations, 1986), 59–62 (quotation on 59); Lewis, *W. E. B. Du Bois*, 315–22; and Childs, *Leadership, Conflict, and Cooperation*, 17–20. For the relationship between Theodore Roosevelt, Booker T. Washington, and African American civil rights, see Thomas G. Dyer, *Theodore Roosevelt and the Idea of Race* (Baton Rouge: Louisiana State University Press, 1980); William B. Gatewood Jr., *Theodore Roosevelt and the Art of Controversy* (Baton Rouge: Louisiana State University Press, 1970), chap. 2; and Ann J. Lane, *The Brownsville Affair: National Crisis and Black Reaction* (Port Washington, N.Y.: Kennikat Press, 1971).

15   *The Correspondence of W. E. B. Du Bois*, ed. Herbert Aptheker (Amherst: University of Massachusetts Press, 1973), 1:113; and W. E. B. Du Bois, "The Niagara Movement" (1906), in *The Oxford W. E. B. Du Bois Reader*, ed. Eric J. Sundquist (New York: Oxford University Press, 1996), 373–76.

16   Charles Flint Kellogg, NAACP: *A History of the National Association for the Advancement of Colored People*, vol. 1, *1909–1920* (Baltimore: Johns Hopkins University Press, 1967), chaps. 1–3, 5; Aldon D. Morris, *The Origins of the Civil Rights Movement: Black Community Organizing for Change* (New York: Free Press, 1984), 15, quoted in Kristin Bumiller, *The Civil Rights Society* (Baltimore: Johns Hopkins University Press, 1988), 56. See also Gilbert Osofsky, "Progressivism and the Negro: New York, 1900–1915," *American Quarterly* 16 (Summer 1964): 153–68; Jacqueline A. Rouse, "Atlanta's African-American Women's Attack on Segregation 1900–1920," in *Gender, Class, Race, and Reform in the Progressive Era*, ed. Noralee Frankel and Nancy S. Dye (Lexington: University Press of Kentucky, 1991), 10–23; and Dorothy Salem, *To Better Our World: Black Women in Organized Reform, 1890–1920* (Brooklyn: Carlson Publishing, 1990), chaps. 5–6. The National League on Urban Conditions Among Negroes was also organized in 1910–1911. The focus in this book on the NAACP is for continuity and clarity of values and is not meant to deny the role of other groups. See Jesse Thomas Moore Jr., *A Search for Equality: The National Urban League, 1910–1961* (University Park: Pennsylvania State University Press, 1981), chaps. 1–3.

17   William B. Hixson Jr., "Moorfield Storey and the Struggle for Equality," in *American Law and the Constitutional Order: Historical Perspectives*, ed. Lawrence M. Friedman and Harry N. Scheibler (Cambridge: Harvard University Press, 1978), 331–42 (quotation on 337). For the peonage issue, see N. Gordon Carper, "Slavery Revisited: Peonage in the South," *Phylon* 37 (March 1976): 85–99.

18   *Correspondence of W. E. B. Du Bois*, 1:188–89, 191, 194, 206–7; and Lewis, *W. E. B. Du Bois*, chap. 14. See especially Du Bois's letter of 11 March 1907 in *Correspondence of W. E. B. Du Bois*, 1:125.

19   Roger Daniels, *Asian America: Chinese and Japanese in the United States since 1850* (Seattle: University of Washington Press, 1988), chap. 4 (quotation from Phelan on 112); Sucheng Chan, *Asian Americans: An Interpretive History* (Boston: Twayne Publishers, 1991), 35–42 and chap. 3; and Robert Eugene Cushman, *Leading Constitutional Decisions*, 3d ed. (New York: F. S. Crofts, 1933), 277–83 (*Insular*

cases 1901–3). I have used this book, first published in 1925, and its explanation of the *Insular* cases as being closer in language and spirit to the issue of civil liberty and civil rights than later books.

20 Daniels, *Asian America,* 119–22, 138–40; Chan, *Asian Americans,* 55; and John Whiteclay Chambers II, *The Tyranny of Change: America in the Progressive Era, 1890–1920,* 2d ed. (New York: St. Martin's Press, 1992), 146 n.
    Daniels noted that the Gentlemen's Agreement "was 'sold' to Californians as tantamount to exclusion. It was not. Under its terms Japanese American population would more than double in less than twenty years" (126). For the larger context of Asian immigration, see Sucheng Chan, "European and Asian Immigration into the United States in Comparative Perspective, 1820s to 1920s," in *Immigration Reconsidered: History, Sociology, and Politics,* ed. Virginia Yans-McLaughlin (New York: Oxford University Press, 1990), 37–78.

21 Alexandra Witkin, "To Silence a Drum: The Imposition of United States Citizenship on Native Peoples," *Historical Reflections/Reflexions Historiques* 21, no. 2 (1995): 359.

22 Francis Paul Prucha, *Indian Policy in the United States: Historical Essays* (Lincoln: University of Nebraska Press, 1981), chap. 16 (quotations on 254–55); Brian W. Dippie, *The Vanishing American: White Attitudes and U.S. Indian Policy* (Middletown: Wesleyan University Press, 1982), 193. On Native American civil rights in this period, see Frederick E. Hoxie, *A Final Promise: The Campaign to Assimilate the Indians, 1880–1920* (Lincoln: University of Nebraska Press, 1984), chap. 7 and app. 3; and Witkin, "To Silence a Drum," 376–79.

23 Thomas Archdeacon, *Becoming American: An Ethnic History* (New York: Free Press, 1983), chap. 15; Gwendolyn Mink, *Old Labor and New Immigrants in American Political Development: Union, Party, and State, 1875–1920* (Ithaca: Cornell University Press, 1986), 165–66; and essays in Virginia Yans-McLaughlin, *Immigration Reconsidered: History, Sociology, and Politics* (New York: Oxford University Press, 1990).

24 Chambers, *Tyranny of Change,* 146 n–47; Daniels, *Asian America,* 118–19; Chan, "European and Asian Immigration into the United States," 48–52; David J. Hellwig, "Afro-American Reactions to the Japanese and the Anti-Japanese Movement, 1906–1924," *Phylon* 38 (March 1977): 93–104; Chan, *Asian Americans,* chap. 5; Ross Evans Paulson, *Radicalism and Reform: The Vrooman Family and American Social Thought, 1837–1937* (Lexington: University of Kentucky Press for the Organization of American Historians, 1968), 42–45; and H. Wayne Morgan, ed. *American Socialism, 1900–1960* (Englewood Cliffs: Prentice-Hall, 1964), 71–78.

25 Elisabeth Lasch-Quinn, *Black Neighbors: Race and the Limits of Reform in the American Settlement House Movement, 1890–1945* (Chapel Hill: University of North Carolina Press, 1993), chap. 1; Robert A. Slayton, *Back of the Yards: The Making of a Local Democracy* (Chicago: University of Chicago Press, 1986), chaps. 5, 8; Croly, *Promise of American Life,* 400–408; and Casey Nelson Blake, *Beloved Community: The Cultural Criticism of Randolph Bourne, Van Wyck Brooks, Waldo Frank, and Lewis Mumford* (Chapel Hill: University of North Carolina Press, 1990), introduction and chaps. 1, 3.

11   Progressivism and Power: Lobbying and Institutional Change, 1912–1916

1   Bernard Bailyn et al., *The Great Republic: A History of the American People,* 2d ed. (Lexington: D. C. Heath and Co., 1981), 2:677–78, 698 (quotations).

2   Michael E. McGerr, *The Decline of Popular Politics: The American North, 1865–1928* (New York: Oxford University Press, 1986), 177, 185–86, 205–6.

3   John F. Reynolds, *Testing Democracy: Electoral Behavior and Progressive Reform in New Jersey, 1880–1920* (Chapel Hill: University of North Carolina Press, 1988), chap. 5 and conclusion.

4   McGerr, *Decline of Popular Politics,* 155–62; Ross Evans Paulson, *Women's Suffrage and Prohibition: A Comparative Study of Equality and Social Control* (Glenview: Scott, Foresman and Co., 1973), 157–58; Nancy F. Cott, "What's in a Name? The Limits of 'Social Feminism'; or, Expanding the Vocabulary of Women's History," *Journal of American History* 76 (December 1989): 809–29; Charles Flint Kellogg, NAACP: *A History of the National Association for the Advancement of Colored People,* vol. 1, *1909–1920* (Baltimore: Johns Hopkins University Press, 1967), 142–45, 226; David Glassberg, "History and the Public: Legacies of the Progressive Era," *Journal of American History* 73 (March 1987): 957–80; and James A. Miller and Donald Yacovone, "Birth of a Nation," in *Encyclopedia of African-American Culture and History,* ed. Jack Salzman et al. (New York: Simon and Schuster Macmillan, 1996), 1:323–24, 961.

5   Melvin I. Urofsky, *Louis D. Brandeis and the Progressive Tradition* (Boston: Little, Brown, 1981), 77.

6   Ibid., 78–79; Louis D. Brandeis, *Other People's Money and How the Bankers Use It* (Boston: Bedford Books of St. Martin's Press, 1995), pt. 2.

7   Thomas K. McCraw, *Prophets of Regulation: Charles Francis Adams, Louis D. Brandeis, James M. Landis, Alfred E. Kahn* (Cambridge: Harvard University Press, 1984), chap. 3.

8   Martin J. Sklar, *The Corporate Reconstruction of American Capitalism, 1890–1916* (Cambridge: Cambridge University Press, 1988), 413.

9   Urofsky, *Louis D. Brandeis,* 72.
    I disagree with Urofsky's contention that Brandeis's role in the Federal Reserve debate was to convince Wilson of the *economic* correctness of Bryan's view (78). Brandeis's constant references to what the American people would accept and the public stance of the Wilson administration, which in Brandeis's view represented "the people" or public interest as opposed to the "desires of the financiers and of big business" or private interest, amounted essentially to *political* advice.

10   McCraw, *Prophets of Regulation,* 118; and Stephen Skowronek, *Building a New American State: The Expansion of National Administrative Capacities, 1877–1920* (Cambridge: Cambridge University Press, 1982), 167–76.

11   McCraw, *Prophets of Regulation,* 123.

12   Ibid., 125; and William Letwin, *Law and Economic Policy in America: The Evolution of the Sherman Antitrust Act* (Chicago: University of Chicago Press, 1965), 270–78.

13   Sklar, *Corporate Reconstruction of American Capitalism,* 331 (quotation); and Wil-

liam E. Forbath, *Law and the Shaping of the American Labor Movement* (Cambridge: Harvard University Press, 1991), 147–58.

14   John Milton Cooper Jr., *The Warrior and the Priest: Woodrow Wilson and Theodore Roosevelt* (Cambridge: Harvard University Press, 1983), 210 (quotation); and David Levering Lewis, *W. E. B. Du Bois: Biography of a Race, 1868–1919* (New York: Henry Holt, 1993), chaps. 15–16.

15   Arthur S. Link, *Wilson: The New Freedom* (Princeton: Princeton University Press, 1956), 224–48, 251–52.

16   Kellogg, *NAACP,* chap. 8 (particularly the analysis of Wilson's views on 168–69); Nancy J. Weiss, "The Negro and the New Freedom: Fighting Wilsonian Segregation," *Political Science Quarterly* 84 (March 1969): 61–79; and Lewis, *W. E. B. Du Bois,* chap. 17. On 5 July 1913 a writer in the *Literary Digest* commented somewhat complacently on the judicial demise of the Civil Rights Act of 1875 in the Supreme Court's decision in 1883 and the implications of that decision for a current case involving private discrimination. The Fourteenth Amendment, the author noted, bound only state acts and "was no guarantee against infringement of a citizen's civil rights by fellow citizens." See "Finish of the Civil Rights Act," *Literary Digest,* 5 July 1913, 8.

17   John A. Thompson, *Reformers and War: American Progressive Publicists and the First World War* (Cambridge: Cambridge University Press, 1987), 112: Steven M. Buechler, *Women's Movements in the United States* (New Brunswick: Rutgers University Press, 1990), 56; Jacqueline Van Voris, *Carrie Chapman Catt: A Public Life* (New York: Feminist Press at the City University of New York, 1987), chap. 4; and Link, *Wilson,* 255–59.

John Milton Cooper Jr., in his comparison of Theodore Roosevelt and Woodrow Wilson, noted that on the issue of woman suffrage "neither man felt strongly about the issue, regarding it as entirely a matter of expediency." Cooper, *Warrior and the Priest,* 210.

18   Woodrow Wilson, quoted in Van Voris, *Carrie Chapman Catt,* 135–36.

19   Van Voris, *Carrie Chapman Catt,* 137; Jane Jerome Camhi, *Women against Women: American Anti-Suffragism, 1880–1920* (Brooklyn: Carlson Publishing, 1994), 127–29; and Nick Salvatore, *Eugene V. Debs: Citizen and Socialist* (Urbana: University of Illinois Press, 1982), chap. 9.

20   Robert B. Westbrook, *John Dewey and American Democracy* (Ithaca: Cornell University Press, 1991), 43, 165–66, 194; D. Steven Blum, *Walter Lippman: Cosmopolitanism in the Century of Total War* (Ithaca: Cornell University Press, 1984), chap. 1; and John Patrick Diggins, *The Promise of Pragmatism: Modernism and the Crisis of Knowledge and Authority* (Chicago: University of Chicago Press, 1994), 205–12.

Westbrook clarified the meaning of equality of opportunity in Dewey's thought, the role of his concept of effective freedom (or instrumental freedom), and the fraternal or communitarian basis of much of his educational thought; but he also showed how isolated or ineffective Dewey was in terms of reaching a broad public audience until he joined the *New Republic* in 1914.

21   W. E. B. Du Bois, "The Immediate Program of the American Negro," reprinted in *Civil Rights and African Americans: A Documentary History,* ed. Albert P. Blaustein

and Robert L. Zangrando (Evanston: Northwestern University Press, 1968), 325–28 (quotation on 325–26).

22   Rayford W. Logan, *The Betrayal of the Negro: From Rutherford B. Hayes to Woodrow Wilson*, new enl. ed. (London: Collier-Macmillan, 1965), 363–69; "Voting Rights and the Grandfather Clause (1915)," in *Civil Rights and African Americans*, ed. Blaustein and Zangrando, 328–33.

As to the assumption that equality was guaranteed by the link between citizenship and equal rights, a comparison with the status of Native Americans is instructive. Historian Frederick E. Hoxie has pointed out that the Supreme Court, in the case of *United States v. Nice* (1916), "held that since guardianship and citizenship were compatible, the government's general responsibility to protect [Native Americans] continued after the granting of the franchise." Such matters as education, land tenure, resale of individual allotments of tribal land, prohibitions on the sale of liquor, restricted criminal proceedings, and even the exercise of the right to vote were thus subject to state and federal regulation under the doctrine of guardianship for such supposedly "uncivilized," "backward," or "childlike" peoples. Whereas the Supreme Court decision in *Plessy v. Ferguson* (1896) upholding Jim Crow segregation had maintained the legal fiction that African Americans were "*separate but equal*," the doctrine in *United States v. Nice* said, in effect, that Native Americans were "*assimilated but not equal*." Frederick E. Hoxie, *A Final Promise: The Campaign to Assimilate the Indians, 1880–1920* (Lincoln: University of Nebraska Press, 1984), 213–30 (quotation on 224).

Not all Native Americans disagreed with the rationale of the doctrine of guardianship, but they wanted assimilation on their own terms. See the discussion of "Indian Progressives" and the 1911 Society of American Indians in Brian W. Dippie, *The Vanishing American: White Attitudes and U.S. Indian Policy* (Middletown: Wesleyan University Press, 1982), 265–67.

23   Aileen S. Kraditor, *The Ideas of the Woman Suffrage Movement, 1890–1912* (New York: Columbia University Press, 1965), chap. 3; Rosalyn Terborg-Penn, "Discontented Black Feminists: Prelude and Postscript to the Passage of the Nineteenth Amendment," in *We Specialize in the Wholly Impossible: A Reader in Black Women's History*, ed. Darlene Clark Hine, Wilma King, and Linda Reed (Brooklyn: Carlson Publishing, 1995), 487–504; Marjorie Spruill Wheeler, *New Women of the New South: The Leaders of the Woman Suffrage Movement in the Southern States* (New York: Oxford University Press, 1993), chap. 4; Bettina Friedl, *On to Victory: Propaganda Plays of the Woman Suffrage Movement* (Boston: Northeastern University Press, 1987), 143–362 (see particularly the 1912 photograph on 200); and Annelise Orleck, *Common Sense and a Little Fire: Women and Working-Class Politics in the United States, 1900–1965* (Chapel Hill: University of North Carolina Press, 1995), chaps. 2–3.

24   David Montgomery, *Workers' Control in America: Studies in the History of Work, Technology, and Labor Struggles* (Cambridge: Cambridge University Press, 1979), 134; Salvatore, *Eugene V. Debs*, chap. 9; and Sklar, *Corporate Reconstruction of American Capitalism*, 422–30. On the past-oriented legal language of trade union leaders, see Forbath, *Law and the Shaping of the American Labor Movement*, 128–36.

12 Progressivism and Power: The Impact of Wartime Mobilization and the Gospel of Efficiency, 1916–1920

1 Eugene Nelson White, *The Regulation and Reform of the American Banking System, 1900–1929* (Princeton: Princeton University Press, 1983), chap. 3; Clay J. Anderson, *A Half-Century of Federal Reserve Policymaking, 1914–1964* (Philadelphia: Federal Reserve Bank of Philadelphia, 1965), chap. 1; Milton Friedman and Anna Jacobson Schwartz, *A Monetary History of the United States, 1867–1960* (Princeton: Princeton University Press, 1963), 189–221; and David P. Thelen, *Robert M. La Follette and the Insurgent Spirit* (Boston: Little, Brown, 1976), chap. 7.
   Eugene Nelson White pointed out that the Federal Reserve Board, on the assumption that the success of the Federal Reserve System required membership by *all* banks, was "wooing" the state-chartered banks and attempting to reassure the federally chartered national banks during the period 1914–1917. Thus, the Federal Reserve leadership was in no mood to evoke antimonopoly rhetoric or policies (134–35). Furthermore, Brandeis, one of the leading antimonopoly critics of the banking system, had been nominated to the Supreme Court by Wilson in January 1916. His confirmation in June 1916 had removed him from the ranks of the antimonopoly advisors to the president.

2 Henry Lee Higginson to Woodrow Wilson, 13 November 1917, Robert Goodwyn Rhett to Woodrow Wilson, 15 November 1917, and Diary of Josephus Daniels, 27 November 1917, reprinted in *The Papers of Woodrow Wilson*, ed. Arthur S. Link (Princeton: Princeton University Press, 1984), 45:44–45, 61–62 and 65, 147 (quotations).

3 Thomas K. McCraw, *Prophets of Regulation: Charles Francis Adams, Louis D. Brandeis, James M. Landis, and Alfred E. Kahn* (Cambridge: Harvard University Press, 1984), 147; and John A. Thompson, *Reformers and War: American Progressive Publicists and the First World War* (Cambridge: Cambridge University Press, 1987), 103–6, 108–11, 139–41.

4 Robert Lansing to Woodrow Wilson, enclosure from AFL, 25 October 1917, reprinted in *Papers of Woodrow Wilson*, ed. Link, 44:483–84; and Thompson, *Reformers and War*, 181–82.

5 Woodrow Wilson, Address to the American Federation of Labor, 12 November 1917, reprinted in *Papers of Woodrow Wilson*, ed. Link, 45:14–15 (quotation).

6 David Montgomery, *Workers' Control in America: Studies in the History of Work, Technology, and Labor Struggles* (Cambridge: Cambridge University Press, 1979), 98–99 and chap. 5.

7 Thompson, *Reformers and War*, 212–20; Ross Evans Paulson, *Radicalism and Reform: The Vrooman Family and American Social Thought, 1837–1937* (Lexington: University of Kentucky Press for the Organization of American Historians, 1968), 216–27, 228–38; Robert D. Cuff, *The War Industries Board: Business-Government Relations during World War I* (Baltimore: Johns Hopkins University Press, 1973); and David M. Kennedy, *Over Here: The First World War and American Society* (New York: Oxford University Press, 1980), chaps. 1–2.

8 Nell Irvin Painter, *Standing at Armageddon: The United States, 1877–1919* (New York: W. W. Norton, 1987), chaps. 11–12; and Dana Frank, "Housewives, Social-

ists, and the Politics of Food: The 1917 New York Cost-of-Living Protests," in *Women and Power in American History: A Reader*, ed. Kathryn Kish Sklar and Thomas Dublin (Englewood Cliffs: Prentice Hall, 1991), 2:101–14.

9   J. Stanley Lemons, *The Woman Citizen: Social Feminism in the 1920s* (Urbana: University of Illinois Press, 1973), chap. 1 (quotation on 21); Alice Kessler-Harris, *Out to Work: A History of Wage-Earning Women in the United States* (New York: Oxford University Press, 1982), chap. 7; Dorothy Salem, *To Better Our World: Black Women in Organized Reform, 1890–1920* (Brooklyn: Carlson Publishing, 1990), chap. 7; and William J. Breen, "Black Women and the Great War: Mobilization and Reform in the South," in *Black Women in American History: The Twentieth Century*, ed. Darlene Clark Hine (Brooklyn: Carlson Publishing, 1990), 2:133–40.

10   Anne Firor Scott, *Natural Allies: Women's Associations in American History* (Urbana: University of Illinois Press, 1991), 170–71; Karen J. Blair, *The History of American Women's Voluntary Organizations, 1810–1960: A Guide to Sources* (Boston: G. K. Hall, 1989); and Kennedy, *Over Here*, 284–87.

11   Alan Dawley, *Struggles for Justice: Social Responsibility and the Liberal State* (Cambridge: Harvard University Press, 1991), 203–10.

12   Lemons, *The Woman Citizen*, chap. 1; Christine A. Lunardini, *From Equal Suffrage to Equal Rights: Alice Paul and the National Woman's Party, 1910–1928* (New York: New York University Press, 1986), chaps. 7–8; Jacqueline VanVoris, *Carrie Chapman Catt: A Public Life* (New York: Feminist Press at the City University of New York, 1987), pt. 4; Rosalyn Terborg-Penn, "Discontented Black Feminists: Prelude and Postscript to the Passage of the Nineteenth Amendment," in *Women and Power in American History: A Reader*, ed. Kathryn Kish Sklar and Thomas Dublin (Englewood Cliffs: Prentice Hall, 1991), 2:132–45: and Jane Jerome Camhi, *Women against Women: American Anti-Suffragism, 1880–1920* (Brooklyn: Carlson Publishing, 1994), 126–43.

13   Louise M. Young, *In the Public Interest: The League of Women Voters, 1920–1970* (Westport: Greenwood Press, 1989), 21, 33–37.

14   Lunardini, *From Equal Suffrage to Equal Rights*, 156–57 (quotation); Nancy F. Cott, *The Grounding of Modern Feminism* (New Haven: Yale University Press, 1987), chap. 2.

15   Henri Florette, *Black Migration: Movement North, 1900–1920* (Garden City: Anchor Press, 1975), chaps. 2–3; Joe William Trotter Jr., *Black Milwaukee: The Making of an Industrial Proletariat, 1915–1945* (Urbana: University of Illinois Press, 1985), chaps. 1–3; Alferdteen Harrison, ed., *Black Exodus: The Great Migration from the American South* (Jackson: University of Mississippi, 1991); Malaika Adero, ed., *Up South: Stories, Studies, and Letters of This Century's Black Migrations* (New York: New Press, 1993), xv–xx, 1–18; E. David Cronon, *Black Moses: The Story of Marcus Garvey and the Universal Negro Improvement Association*, 2d ed. (Madison: University of Wisconsin Press, 1969), 23; and George E. Haynes, *The Trend of the Races* (New York: Council of Women for Home Missions and Missionary Education Movement of the United States and Canada, 1922), 113–35.

16   Mark Ellis, " 'Closing Ranks' and 'Seeking Honors': W. E. B. Du Bois in World War I," *Journal of American History* 79 (June 1992): 96–124; Herbert Aptheker,

ed., *The Correspondence of W. E. B. Du Bois* (Amherst: University of Massachusetts Press, 1973), 1:223–29 (the editorial is erroneously dated July 1917 on 227); David Levering Lewis, *W. E. B. Du Bois: Biography of a Race, 1868–1919* (New York: Henry Holt, 1993), 555–57, 560, 578; and Charles Flint Kellogg, *NAACP: A History of the National Association for the Advancement of Colored People*, vol. 1, *1909–1920* (Baltimore: Johns Hopkins University Press, 1967), 135.

17   Cronon, *Black Moses*, 44, 46; John Brown Childs, *Leadership, Conflict, and Cooperation in Afro-American Social Thought* (Philadelphia: Temple University Press, 1989), 115–22; Paula F. Pfeffer, *A. Philip Randolph, Pioneer of the Civil Rights Movement* (Baton Rouge: Louisiana State University Press, 1990), 13–17; and Mark D. Mathews, " 'Our Women and What They Think,' Amy Jacques Garvey and *The Negro World*," in *Black Women in American History: The Twentieth Century*, ed. Darlene Clark Hine (Brooklyn: Carlson Publishing, 1990), 3:866–77. Garvey's combination of radical values and appeals to racial pride was not confined to Harlem. See Emory J. Tolbert, *The U.N.I.A. and Black Los Angeles: Ideology and Community in the American Garvey Movement* (Los Angeles: University of California, 1980), 96–98.

18   Pfeffer, *A. Philip Randolph*, 11–12; Childs, *Leadership, Conflict, and Cooperation*, 49–69; Jervis Anderson, "Early Voice: Pt. 1. From Florida to Harlem [A. Philip Randolph biography]," *New Yorker*, 2 December 1972, 100 (quotation), and *A. Philip Randolph: A Biographical Portrait* (New York: Harcourt Brace Jovanovich, 1972), 98.

19   W. E. B. Du Bois, "Jim Crow" (January 1919), reprinted in *Writings of W. E. B. Du Bois*, ed. Nathan I. Huggins (New York: Literary Classics of the United States, 1986), 1177–78 (quotation on 1178).

20   W. E. B. Du Bois, "Returning Soldiers," quoted in Lewis, *W. E. B. Du Bois*, 578.

21   Cronon, *Black Moses*, 23–25, 32; Joseph Boskin, *Urban Racial Violence in the Twentieth Century* (Beverly Hills: Glencoe Press, 1969), 30–37; and Lewis, *W. E. B. Du Bois*, 537–39. For the background of Chicago, see James R. Barrett, *Work and Community in the Jungle: Chicago's Packinghouse Workers, 1894–1922* (Urbana: University of Illinois Press, 1987); James R. Grossman, *Land of Hope: Chicago, Black Southerners, and the Great Migration* (Chicago: University of Chicago Press, 1989); Louise Carroll Wade, *Chicago's Pride: The Stockyards, Packingtown, and Environs in the Nineteenth Century* (Urbana: University of Illinois Press, 1987); and Robert A. Slayton, *Back of the Yards: The Making of a Local Democracy* (Chicago: University of Chicago Press, 1986).

13   From Civil Liberty to Civil Liberties, 1914–1928

1   See *Reader's Guide to Periodical Literature* (Minneapolis: H. W. Wilson, Co., 1900–1904, 1905–1909, 1922–1924, 1925–1928); Upton Sinclair, "Protecting Our Liberties," *Nation*, 4 July 1923, 9–10; and Oswald Garrison Villard, "New Fight for Old Liberties," *Harper's*, September 1925, 440–47 [emphasis added to the titles].

It is a principle of library science that every classification system is a reflection of the current cultural assumptions, a "map" of the "mental universe" of the people who develop and use the classification system. The *Reader's Guide to Peri-*

odical Literature began in 1901 in Minneapolis, where Linda D. Reed, a cataloger for the Minneapolis Public Library, began to index twenty magazines for small libraries and women's reading clubs. In 1903 it merged with the Cumulative Index of Cleveland. Harriet Gross, editor, and Marion E. Potter, librarian, made suggestions as to subject headings. "Preface," *Reader's Guide to Periodical Literature* (Minneapolis: H. W. Wilson Co., 1905), I: vii–viii. I am indebted to my wife, Avis Nelson Paulson, a reference librarian, for this insight into library science and its implications for intellectual history methodology.

2   Raymond B. Fosdick, "Liberty in America," *Outlook,* 2 February 1916, 282–85 (quotation on 285).

3   Samuel Walker, *In Defense of American Liberties: A History of the ACLU* (New York: Oxford University Press, 1990), chap. 1; Paul L. Murphy, *World War I and the Origin of Civil Liberties in the United States* (New York: W. W. Norton, 1979), 39–40, 64–66 (quotation from Baldwin on 9, compare with 154 n. 35); and H. B. Alexander, "Limits of Tolerance," *Dial,* 11 October 1917, 326–29 (quotation on 326).

For the British influence on the American thinkers, see Arthur Marwick, *Britain in the Century of Total War: War, Peace, and Social Change, 1900–1967* (Boston: Little, Brown, 1968), 102; Sir Norman Angell, *Why Freedom Matters,* 2d ed. (London: National Council for Civil Liberties, 1917; reprinted in the United States by the National Civil Liberties Bureau, 1918); and Peggy Lamson, *Roger Baldwin: Founder of the American Civil Liberties Union* (Boston: Houghton Mifflin, 1976), 71–72. The impact of the war can be seen in the following quotation from Columbia University's president warning pacifist professors that they would be fired if they opposed official American policy: "So long as national policies were in debate, we gave complete freedom, as is our want and becomes a university, freedom of assembly, freedom of speech, and freedom of publication to all members of the University. . . . Wrongheadedness and folly we might deplore, but we are bound to tolerate. *So soon, however, as the nation spoke by the Congress and by the President, declaring that it would volunteer as one man for the protection and defense of civil liberty and self-government, conditions sharply changed.* What had been tolerated before became intolerable now. What had been wrongheadedness was now sedition, what had been folly was now treason." Dr. Nicholas Murray Butler, president of Columbia University, "Statement on Firing Pacifist Professors, 6 June 1917," *Columbia Alumni News* 9 (5 October 1917): 31 (emphasis added). I am indebted to Linnea Anderson, assistant director, Columbia University Archives, for a copy of this statement from the Columbiana Collection.

4   Paul A. Carter, *The Decline and Revival of the Social Gospel: Social and Political Liberalism in American Protestant Churches, 1920–1940* (Ithaca: Cornell University Press, 1954), chap. 3; Ross Evans Paulson, *Women's Suffrage and Prohibition: A Comparative Study of Equality and Social Control* (Glenview: Scott, Foresman, 1973), 157–68 (quotations on 157 and 161); William Howard Taft, "Is Prohibition a Blow at Personal Liberty?" *Ladies Home Journal,* 31 May 1919, 31, 78 (quotation on 78); and Kate Holladay Claghorn, *The Immigrant's Day in Court* (New York: Harper and Brothers, 1923; reprint, Arno Press, 1969), chap. 9.

5   Nick Salvatore, *Eugene V. Debs: Citizen and Socialist* (Urbana: University of Illinois

Press, 1982), 280–81, 285, 286 (quotation), 292 (quotation), 297, 299; and Marian J. Morton, *Emma Goldman and the American Left: "Nowhere at Home"* (New York: Twayne Publishers, 1992), 69. The government dropped the *Stokes* cases in 1921.

6   "Civil Liberty Dead," *Nation*, 14 September 1918, 282 (quotation); and "Liberty after the War," *Independent*, 21 September 1918, 374–75 (quotation on 375).

7   Oliver Wendell Holmes Jr., comments on *Schenk v. U.S.* (1919), in *The Mind and Faith of Justice Holmes: His Speeches, Essays, Letters, and Judicial Opinions*, ed. Max Lerner (Boston: Little, Brown, 1943), 296–97 (emphasis added).

8   Oliver Wendell Holmes Jr., comments on *Debs v. U.S.* (1919), in *Mind and Faith of Justice Holmes*, ed. Lerner, 303; and Walker, *In Defense of American Liberties*, 26–27.

9   Robert K. Murray, *Red Scare: A Study of National Hysteria, 1919–1920* (1955; reprint, New York: McGraw-Hill, 1964), chaps. 4–5 and 7.

10 Ibid., 166–67 (quotation).

11 Salvatore, *Eugene V. Debs*, 318–19; and Murray, *Red Scare*, 51–53 (quotation on 53).

12 Thomas A. Rumer, *The American Legion: An Official History, 1919–1989* (New York: M. Evans and Co., 1990), 24–29 (quotation on 25–26, emphasis added).

13 Alice Edgerton, "Individual Liberty in America," *Nation*, 11 October 1919, 494–95 (quotations).

14 Walter Lippmann, "The Basic Problem of Democracy: Part 1. What Modern Liberty Means," *Atlantic*, November 1919, 616–67 (quotations on 616 and 627, emphasis added). The ideas in the *Atlantic* articles became part of Lippmann's book *Liberty and the News* (New York: Harcourt, Brace and Howe, 1920), especially chap. 3. For Lippmann's situation in 1919, see D. Steven Blum, *Walter Lippmann: Cosmopolitanism in the Century of Total War* (Ithaca: Cornell University Press, 1984), 49–57.

15 Richara Roberts, "The Restoration of Civil Liberty," *Survey*, 15 November 1919, 109–10 (quotations).

16 Murray, *Red Scare*, 207, 213, 226–238 (quotation on 234); Morton, *Emma Goldman and the American Left*, 100.

17 Walker, *In Defense of American Liberties*, 40–47, 52 (quotation); "Are American Liberties Worth Saving? Letters from New York Lawyers," *Nation*, 17 April 1920, 506–8 (quotation); and Lamson, *Roger Baldwin*, chaps. 6, 10.

18 Murray, *Red Scare*, 242–46, 255; Walker, *In Defense of American Liberties*, 52–56; and Lamson, *Roger Baldwin*, chap. 11.

19 John Corbin, "Liberty above Equality," *North American Review* 212 (December 1920): 741–53 (quotation on 753); Gwendolyn Mink, *Old Labor and New Immigrants in American Political Development: Union, Party, and State, 1875–1920* (Ithaca: Cornell University Press, 1986), 256; Robert A. Wilson and Bill Hosokawa, *East to America: A History of the Japanese in the United States* (New York: William Morrow, 1980), 126–28; David P. Currie, *The Constitution in the Supreme Court: The Second Century, 1888–1986* (Chicago: University of Chicago Press, 1990), 138, 146–47 n. 60 (quotation); Sandra L. Cadwalader and Vine Deloria Jr., *The Aggressions of Civilization: Federal Indian Policy since the 1880s* (Philadelphia:

Temple University Press, 1985), 117; and Vine Deloria Jr., *American Indian Policy in the Twentieth Century* (Norman: University of Oklahoma Press, 1985), chap. 5.

20 Walter Lippmann, *Public Opinion* (1922), 196, quoted in John Patrick Diggins, *The Promise of Pragmatism: Modernism and the Crisis of Knowledge and Authority* (Chicago: University of Chicago Press, 1994), 334 (emphasis added) and chap. 8; "The Liberty Above All Others," *Nation*, 4 July 1923, 4 (quotation); William E. Borah, "Free Speech: The Vital Issue," *Nation*, 4 July 1923, 8; and Sinclair, "Protecting Our Liberties," 9–10. See also Lamson, *Roger Baldwin*, chaps. 10, 12.

21 Walker, *In Defense of American Liberties*, 63–64, 79–80 (quotation); and Currie, *The Constitution in the Supreme Court: The Second Century*, 154–60 (quotation on 155 n. 116, compare with Walker on Sanford). In recognition of the ACLU's influence in public discourse, the *Reader's Guide to Periodical Literature* added a category heading, "American Civil Liberties Union" in 1925.

22 Walter Lippmann, *The Phantom Public* (New York: Macmillan, 1927), 104–5.

14 Limits to Change in the New Era, 1920–1924

1 Josephus Daniels to Woodrow Wilson, 30 November 1917; William Gibbs McAdoo to Woodrow Wilson, 6 December 1917 and 15 December 1917; Frederic C. Howe to Woodrow Wilson, 15 December 1917; Woodrow Wilson to Joseph Tumulty, 18 December 1917; Diary of Colonel House, 18 December 1917 and 30 December 1917; and Woodrow Wilson to William Gibbs McAdoo, 31 December 1917, in *The Papers of Woodrow Wilson*, ed. Arthur S. Link (Princeton: Princeton University Press, 1984), 45: 170–71, 225–28, 304–6, 309–11, 318, 324–26, 398, 401.

2 Robert K. Murray, *Red Scare: A Study of National Hysteria, 1919–1920* (1955; reprint, New York: McGraw-Hill, 1964), 110–14, 117–19 (quotation on 119).

3 Ibid., 269; David Montgomery, *Workers' Control in America: Studies in the History of Work, Technology, and Labor Struggles* (Cambridge: Cambridge University Press, 1979), chaps. 4–5; and Jervis Anderson, *A. Philip Randolph: A Biographical Portrait* (New York: Harcourt Brace Jovanovich, 1972), 153–66.

4 Nick Salvatore, *Eugene V. Debs: Citizen and Socialist* (Urbana: University of Illinois Press, 1982), 323–25 (quotation on 323); Eugene V. Debs's reflection on the 1920 nomination is in *Writings and Speeches of Eugene V. Debs*, ed. Arthur M. Schlesinger Jr. (New York: Hermitage Press, 1948), 465; and Mari Jo Buhle, *Women and American Socialism, 1870–1920* (Urbana: University of Illinois Press, 1981), 239–41, 313, 318–21.

5 William J. Barber, *From New Era to New Deal: Herbert Hoover, the Economists, and American Economic Policy, 1921–1933* (Cambridge: Cambridge University Press, 1985); Ellis W. Hawley, ed., *Herbert Hoover as Secretary of Commerce: Studies in New Era Thought and Practice* (Iowa City: University of Iowa Press, 1981); and Joan Hoff Wilson, *Herbert Hoover: Forgotten Progressive* (Boston: Little, Brown, 1975).

6 Barber, *From New Era to New Deal*, 7–8 (quotation); Ellis W. Hawley, "Herbert Hoover and Economic Stabilization, 1921–22," in *Herbert Hoover as Secretary of Commerce*, ed. Ellis W. Hawley (Iowa City: University of Iowa Press, 1981), 43–79.

7   Barber, *From New Era to New Deal*, 10–12 (quotation on 11); and Hawley, "Hoover and Economic Stabilization," 61–64 (quotation on 62).

8   Thomas K. McCraw, *Prophets of Regulation: Charles Francis Adams, Louis D. Brandeis, James M. Landis, Alfred E. Kahn* (Cambridge: Harvard University Press, 1984), 116; and Barber, *From New Era to New Deal*, 199 n. 7 (quotation).

9   Harlan F. Stone, majority opinion in *Maple Flooring Manufacturer's Association* case (1925), as quoted in McCraw, *Prophets of Regulation*, 146.

10 McCraw, *Prophets of Regulation*, 15–27, 57–59; Melvin P. Leffler, "Herbert Hoover, the 'New Era', and American Foreign Policy, 1921–29," in *Herbert Hoover as Secretary of Commerce*, ed. Hawley, 155–56; and Milton Friedman and Anna Jacobson Schwartz, *A Monetary History of the United States, 1867–1960* (Princeton: Princeton University Press, 1963), 230–39.

11 Herbert Hoover, *American Individualism* (Garden City: Doubleday, Page and Co., 1922), 19, 42, 44, 54 (quotations); and Wilson, *Herbert Hoover*, 56 (quotation).

12 Jean B. Quant, *From the Small Town to the Great Community: The Social Thought of Progressive Intellectuals* (New Brunswick: Rutgers University Press, 1970); Robert M. Crunden, *Ministers of Reform: The Progressives' Achievement in American Civilization, 1889–1920* (New York: Basic Books, 1982); Robert B. Westbrook, *John Dewey and American Democracy* (Ithaca: Cornell University Press, 1991), 282 (quotation); and John P. Diggins, *The Promise of Pragmatism: Modernism and the Crisis of Knowledge and Authority* (Chicago: University of Chicago Press, 1994), chap. 6.

13 Rosalind Rosenberg, *Beyond Separate Spheres: Intellectual Roots of Modern Feminism* (New Haven: Yale University Press, 1982); Carl N. Degler, *In Search of Human Nature: The Decline and Revival of Darwinism in American Social Thought* (New York: Oxford University Press, 1991), chap. 5; Joan G. Zimmerman, "The Jurisprudence of Equality: The Women's Minimum Wage, the First Equal Rights Amendment, and *Adkins v. Children's Hospital*, 1905–1923," *Journal of American History*, 78 (June 1991): 188–225; Christine A. Lunardini, *From Equal Suffrage to Equal Rights: Alice Paul and the National Woman's Party, 1910–1928* (New York: New York University Press, 1986), 153–54, 164; and Theda Skocpol, *Protecting Soldiers and Mothers: The Political Origins of Social Policy in the United States* (Cambridge: Harvard University Press, 1992), 352–54, 368–70.

14 Louise M. Young, *In the Public Interest: The League of Women Voters, 1920–1970* (Westport: Greenwood Press, 1989), 45. A fourteenth point, a Woman's Bureau to be located in the Department of Labor, was passed by Congress in June 1920 and was consequently dropped from the list.

15 J. Stanley Lemons, *The Woman Citizen: Social Feminism in the 1920s* (Urbana: University of Illinois Press, 1973), 154; Molly Ladd-Taylor, " 'My Work Came Out of Agony and Grief': Mothers and the Making of the Sheppard-Towner Act," in *Mothers of a New World: Maternalist Politics and the Origins of Welfare States*, ed. Seth Koven and Sonya Michel (New York: Routledge, 1993), 321–28; and Skocpol, *Protecting Soldiers and Mothers*, 480–81.

16 Lemons, *The Woman Citizen*, 155–56.

17 Ladd-Taylor, "Mothers and the Making of the Sheppard-Towner Act," 325–28; and Skocpol, *Protecting Soldiers and Mothers*, 495–512.

18   Lemons, *The Woman Citizen,* 158, 167–69; Ladd-Taylor, "Mothers and the Making of the Sheppard-Towner Act," 328–29; Skocpol, *Protecting Soldiers and Mothers,* 500–501; and Cott, *Grounding of Modern Feminism,* 125–26.

19   Zimmerman, "The Jurisprudence of Equality," 195–202; Linda Gordon, "Social Insurance and Public Assistance: The Influence of Gender in Welfare Thought in the United States, 1890–1935," *American Historical Review* 97 (February 1992): 19–54; and Joseph M. Hawes, *The Children's Rights Movement: A History of Advocacy and Protection* (Boston: Twayne Publishers, 1991), chap. 4.

20   Zimmerman, "Jurisprudence of Equality," 202–17, 223; and Kathryn Kish Sklar, "Why Were Most Politically Active Women Opposed to the ERA in the 1920s?" in *Women and Power in American History: A Reader,* ed. Kathryn Kish Sklar and Thomas Dublin (Englewood Cliffs: Prentice Hall, 1991), 2:175–82.

21   Cott, *Grounding of Modern Feminism,* 76; Skocpol, *Protecting Soldiers and Mothers,* 515–24; William H. Chafe, *Women and Equality: Changing Patterns in American Culture* (New York: Oxford University Press, 1977), 34–42; and Rosalyn Terborg-Penn, "Discontented Black Feminists: Prelude and Postscript to the Passage of the Nineteenth Amendment," in *We Specialize in the Wholly Impossible: A Reader in Black Women's History,* ed. Darlene Clark Hine, Wilma King, and Linda Reed (Brooklyn: Carlson Publishing, 1995), 487–503 (quotation on 492).

15   Which Way for Civil Rights? Separation and Cooperation in the Jazz Age, 1920–1928

1   Wyn Craig Wade, *The Fiery Cross: The Ku Klux Klan in America* (New York: Simon and Schuster, 1987), chaps. 5–6; Robert L. Zangrando, *The NAACP Crusade against Lynching, 1905–1950* (Philadelphia: Temple University Press, 1980), 6, 38–39; Charles Flint Kellogg, *NAACP: A History of the National Association for the Advancement of Colored People,* vol. 1, *1909–1920* (Baltimore: Johns Hopkins University Press, 1967), 216–21, 232–35; and Richard C. Cortner, *A Mob Intent on Death: The NAACP and the Arkansas Riot Cases* (Middletown: Wesleyan University Press, 1988).

2   Robert A. Hill, ed., *The Marcus Garvey and Universal Negro Improvement Association Papers* (Berkeley: University of Chicago Press, 1983), 2:14 (quotation), 56, 58–60 n. 1. Rather than use the term "colored man," the *Chicago Defender* used the term "Race man." Taylor Branch, *Parting the Waters: America in the King Years, 1954–1963* (New York: Simon and Schuster, 1988), 45.

3   Hill, *Marcus Garvey and Universal Negro Improvement Association Papers,* 2:571–77 (quotations on 572, 573, 574, 576, 577). See also Marcus Garvey, "The Objective of the Universal Negro Improvement Association," in *Civil Rights and African Americans: A Documentary History,* ed. Albert P. Blaustein and Robert L. Zangrando (Evanston: Northwestern University Press, 1968), 343–46.

4   E. David Cronon, *Black Moses: The Story of Marcus Garvey and the Universal Negro Improvement Association,* 2d ed. (Madison: University of Wisconsin Press, 1969), chaps. 4–5; John Brown Childs, *Leadership, Conflict, and Cooperation in Afro-American Social Thought* (Philadelphia: Temple University Press, 1989), 115–22; and Wanda Hendricks, "Ida Bell Wells-Barnett (1862–1931)," in *Black Women*

in America: An Historical Encyclopedia, ed. Darlene Clark Hine (Brooklyn: Carlson Publishing, 1993), 2:1245. See also William Seraile, "Henrietta Vinton Davis and the Garvey Movement," in Black Women in American History: The Twentieth Century, ed. Darlene Clark Hine (Brooklyn: Carlson Publishing, 1990), 4:1073–91.

Historian Alan Dawley blamed FBI officials J. Edgar Hoover and William Burns for "political motives" in securing Garvey's indictment. See Alan Dawley, Struggles for Justice: Social Responsibility and the Liberal State (Cambridge: Harvard University Press, 1991), 274–75. The Marcus Garvey Papers record the behind-the-scenes opposition of some African American leaders. For background, see Hill, Marcus Garvey and Universal Negro Improvement Association Papers, 2:56–59, and 3:166, 361–62, 731–33; and William Pickens, Bursting Bonds: The Heir of Slaves and the Autobiography of a "New Negro," enl. ed., ed. William L. Andrews (Bloomington: Indiana University Press, 1991 [the autobiography was first published in 1923]).

5　David Burner, The Politics of Provincialism: The Democratic Party in Transition, 1918–1932 (New York: W. W. Norton, 1967), chap. 3 (quotation on 94).

6　Michael Kazin, "The Grass-Roots Right: New Histories of U.S. Conservatism in the Twentieth Century," American Historical Review 97 (February 1992): 136–55 (quotation on 140).

7　Ibid., 143 (quotation). See also Leonard J. Moore, Citizen Klansmen: The Ku Klux Klan in Indiana, 1921–1928 (Chapel Hill: University of North Carolina Press, 1991); Kathleen M. Blee, Women of the Klan: Racism and Gender in the 1920s (Berkeley: University of California Press, 1991), chaps. 1–2, 6; and William D. Jenkins, Steel Valley Klan: The Ku Klux Klan in Ohio's Mahoning Valley (Kent: Kent State University Press, 1990).

The interpretation of the Klan as a ritual withdrawal and renewal phenomenon (according to the model in the introduction of this book) is mine and not necessarily that of the authors noted above.

8　In what sense was Garvey's definition of rights in terms of racial identity to be judged as radical? American legislation and governmental action during the wartime mobilization and the postwar reconstruction era had increasingly defined individuals in terms of their membership in a group (racial, ethnic, religious, gender, class). Yet, as Herbert Hoover's efforts to reconcile his values with individualism or Alice Paul's reformulation of feminism in terms of individual legal rights show, the prevalent norms of public discourse in the early 1920s were still expressed in terms of individual rights. Individuals as citizens had rights; as members of groups they had responsibilities (conscription, taxation, etc.) or restrictions (immigration exclusion or quota limitation, etc.). However, in the 1920s some of these groups demanded respect by the government for their distinctive group characteristics. It is the transitional nature of the 1920s in this debate that makes the issue of Garvey's black nationalism and the Klan's ethnocentrism so difficult to evaluate historically. Garvey's total identification with his racial group as a basis for citizenship in a transgeographic "nation" was radical by official norms of individualism as the basis of citizenship in the 1920s.

On the individualistic basis of American core values and their changing meanings, see the essays in Richard O. Curry and Lawrence B. Goodheart, eds., *American Chameleon: Individualism in Trans-National Context* (Kent: Kent State University Press, 1991); Barry Alan Shain, *The Myth of American Individualism: The Protestant Origins of American Political Thought* (Princeton: Princeton University Press, 1994), chap. 4; and Ross Evans Paulson, "*Ubi Panis Ibi Patria*: Reflections on American Identity," *Word and World* 8 (Summer 1988): 219–25.

On the group basis of issues in the 1920s, see Lynn Dumenil, " 'The Insatiable Maw of Bureaucracy': Antistatism and Education Reform in the 1920s," *Journal of American History* 77 (September 1990): 499–524; April Schultz, "The Pride of the Race Has Been Touched: The 1925 Norse-American Immigration Centennial and Ethnic Identity," *Journal of American History* 77 (March 1990): 1265–95; and Alan Brinkley, "The Problem of American Conservatism," *American Historical Review* 99 (April 1994): 409–29.

9   Jacquelyn Dowd Hall, *Revolt against Chivalry: Jessie Daniel Ames and the Women's Campaign against Lynching* (New York: Columbia University Press, 1979), 62–77 (quotation on 63).

10   "The Colored Women's Statement to the Women's Missionary Council, American Missionary Association [1919]," in *Black Women in White America: A Documentary History*, ed. Gerda Lerner (New York: Random House, 1972), 461.

11   Ibid., 462–66. See also Cynthia Neverdon-Morton, *Afro-American Women of the South and the Advancement of the Race, 1895–1925* (Knoxville: University of Tennessee Press, 1989), chaps. 5–9; and Judith L. Stephens, "Anti-Lynch Plays by African American Women: Race, Gender, and Social Protest in America," *African American Review* 26 (Summer 1992): 329–39.

12   Zangrando, *NAACP Crusade against Lynching*, 43, 77; David Levering Lewis, *W. E. B. Du Bois: Biography of a Race, 1868–1919* (New York: Henry Holt, 1993), 552–53, 557–58, 578–79; Hall, *Revolt against Chivalry*, 77–80, 87–89, 94–98, 102–4; and Neverdon-Morton, *Afro-American Women of the South*, 207–18.

For the wartime origins of the Dyer Bill, see Mark Ellis, " 'Closing Ranks' and 'Seeking Honors': W. E. B. Du Bois in World War I," *Journal of American History* 79 (June 1992): 96–124.

13   Charlotte Hawkins Brown, "Speaking Up for the Race at Memphis, Tennessee, October 8, 1920" in *Black Women in White America: A Documentary History*, ed. Lerner, 467–72 (quotation on 469); and Neverdon-Morton, *Afro-American Women of the South*, 226–30.

14   Hall, *Revolt against Chivalry*, 94.

15   Ibid, 95–106. On the limits of social science language and racial assumptions on interracial communication, see Elisabeth Lasch-Quinn, *Black Neighbors: Race and the Limits of Reform in the American Settlement House Movement, 1890–1945* (Chapel Hill: University of North Carolina Press, 1993), chaps. 1, 4; Linda Gordon, "Black and White Visions of Welfare: Women's Welfare Activism, 1890–1945," *Journal of American History* 78 (September 1991): 559–90; and Anne Firor Scott, *Natural Allies: Women's Associations in American History* (Urbana: University of Illinois Press, 1991), 180–85.

16   Zangrando, NAACP *Crusade against Lynching*, 64–69, 77; Kellogg, NAACP, 244–45;
     Dorothy Salem, *To Better Our World: Black Women in Organized Reform, 1890–*
     1920 (Brooklyn: Carlson Publishing, 1990), 232–34; and Oliver Wendell Holmes
     Jr., comments on *Moore v. Dempsey*, in *Civil Rights and African Americans: A*
     Documentary History, ed. Blaustein and Zangrando, 341–42 (quotation on 342).
     Moorfield Storey, former president of the NAACP, has argued the case before the
     Supreme Court, thus linking the traditions of Charles Sumner and Frederick
     Douglass with the current situation.

17   Jervis Anderson, *A. Philip Randolph: A Biographical Portrait* (New York: Harcourt
     Brace Jovanovich, 1972), 153–66.

18   Ibid., 149–50; Paula F. Pfeffer, *A. Philip Randolph, Pioneer of the Civil Rights Move-*
     ment (Baton Rouge: Louisiana State University Press, 1990), 19–21.

19   Anderson, *A. Philip Randolph*, 208–9; Pfeffer, *A. Philip Randolph*, 22–25.

20   A. Philip Randolph to Milton Webster, July 1928, quoted in Anderson, *A. Philip*
     Randolph, 193–94.

21   Anderson, *A. Philip Randolph*, 181–209; Pfeffer, *A. Philip Randolph*, 23–27.

22   Wilson Record, *Race and Radicalism: The NAACP and the Communist Party in Con-*
     flict (Ithaca: Cornell University Press, 1964), chap. 2; and Pfeffer, *A. Philip Ran-*
     dolph, 26–27. See also Earl Ofari Hutchinson, *Blacks and Reds: Race and Class in*
     Conflict, 1919–1940 (East Lansing: Michigan State University Press, 1995).

23   Donald J. Lisio, *Hoover, Blacks, and Lily Whites: A Study of Southern Strategies*
     (Chapel Hill: University of North Carolina Press, 1985), 4.

24   Ibid., 4–12 (quotation on 12).

25   Joan Hoff Wilson, *Herbert Hoover: Forgotten Progressive* (Boston: Little, Brown,
     1975), 116–18; and Lisio, *Hoover, Blacks, and Lily Whites*, chaps. 10, 12, 22.

26   David P. Thelen, *Robert M. La Follette and the Insurgent Spirit* (Boston: Little,
     Brown, 1976), 187–88; David M. Kennedy, *Over Here: The First World War and*
     American Society (New York: Oxford University Press, 1980), 151–67, 246–47,
     287–95; Dawley, *Struggles for Justice*, 265–75; and Carl Degler, *In Search of Human*
     Nature: The Decline and Revival of Darwinism in American Social Thought (New
     York: Oxford University Press, 1991), chap. 7.

27   Nathan I. Huggins, *Harlem Renaissance* (New York: Oxford University Press,
     1973), 139–41 (quotation on 139); Harold Cruse, *The Crisis of the Negro Intellec-*
     tual (New York: William Morrow, 1967), chap. 1; David Levering Lewis, *When*
     Harlem was in Vogue (New York: Alfred A. Knopf, 1981), chaps. 1–2; James De
     Jongh, *Vicious Modernism: Black Harlem and the Literary Imagination* (New York:
     Cambridge University Press, 1990), chaps. 1–2; Celeste Michelle Condit and John
     Louis Lucaites, *Crafting Equality: America's Anglo-African Word* (Chicago: Univer-
     sity of Chicago Press, 1993), chap. 6; Günter H. Lenz, "Symbolic Space, Commu-
     nal Rituals, and the Surreality of the Urban Ghetto: Harlem in Black Literature
     from the 1920s to the 1960s," *Callaloo: Journal of Afro-American and African Arts*
     and Letters 11 (Spring 1988): 308–45; Cheryl A. Wall, *Women of the Harlem*
     Renaissance (Bloomington: Indiana University Press, 1995), chap. 1; and George
     Hutchinson, *The Harlem Renaissance in Black and White* (Cambridge: Harvard
     University Press, 1995), pt. 1.

16   Progressivism in Transition and on Trial, 1924–1932

1   David P. Thelen, *Robert M. La Follette and the Insurgent Spirit* (Boston: Little, Brown, 1976), 181–82; David Burner, *The Politics of Provincialism: The Democratic Party in Transition, 1918–1932* (New York: W. W. Norton, 1967), chap. 4.

2   Thelen, *Robert M. La Follette*, 181–86; and Burner, *Politics of Provincialism*, 136–37.

3   Robert La Follette, 3 February 1924, Progressive Party platform, and Robert La Follette to Robert P. Scripps, quoted in Thelen, *La Follette and the Insurgent Spirit*, 183, 187. For the tension between class and culture in the 1920s see Lynn Dumenil, "'The Insatiable Maw of Bureaucracy': Antistatism and Education Reform in the 1920s," *Journal of American History* 77 (September 1990): 499–524; Ira Katznelson, *City Trenches: Urban Politics and the Patterns of Class in the United States* (New York: Pantheon Books, 1981), 19; John S. Gilkeson Jr., *Middle Class Providence, 1820–1940* (Princeton: Princeton University Press, 1986), 2–11; and Reeve Vanneman and Lynn Weber Cannon, *The American Perception of Class* (Philadelphia: Temple University Press, 1987).

4   Thomas K. McCraw, *Prophets of Regulation: Charles Francis Adams, Louis D. Brandeis, James M. Landis, Alfred E. Kahn* (Cambridge: Harvard University Press, 1984), 144–47.

5   Robert M. La Follette, campaign speech, *New York Times*, 7 October 1924, reprinted in *La Follette*, ed. Robert S. Maxwell (Englewood Cliffs: Prentice Hall, 1969), 75 (emphasis added).

6   Robert La Follette, campaign speeches of 1924 in *La Follette*, ed. Maxwell, 73–87.

7   Thelen, *La Follette and the Insurgent Spirit*, 191 (quotation); Donald R. McCoy, *Calvin Coolidge: The Quiet President*, rev. ed. (Lawrence: University Press of Kansas, 1988), chap. 24; Burner, *Politics of Provincialism*, 136–37. Burner recorded La Follette's popular vote percentage as 17.2 percent, but Richard M. Seammon and Alice V. McGillivray, eds., *America at the Polls: A Handbook of American Presidential Election Statistics, 1968–1984* (Washington, D.C.: Elections Research Center, 1988) show 16.6 percent. See also Charles W. Eagles, "Congressional Voting in the 1920s: A Test of Urban-Rural Conflict," *Journal of American History* 76 (September 1989): 528–34; and Richard Oestreicher, "Urban Working-Class Political Behavior and Theories of American Electoral Politics, 1870–1940," *Journal of American History* 74 (March 1988): 1257–86.

8   Louise M. Young, *In the Public Interest: The League of Women Voters, 1920–1970* (Westport: Greenwood Press, 1989), 67–68 n. 5, 75–77; J. Stanley Lemons, *The Woman Citizen: Social Feminism in the 1920s* (Urbana: University of Illinois Press, 1973), chap. 8; and Joan G. Zimmerman, "The Jurisprudence of Equality: The Women's Minimum Wage, the First Equal Rights Amendment and *Adkins v. Children's Hospital, 1905–1923*," *Journal of American History* 78 (June 1991): 188–225.

9   McCoy, *Calvin Coolidge*, 258 (quotation); Thelen, *La Follette and the Insurgent Spirit*, 188–92; and Bruner, *Politics of Provincialism*, 117.

10   Robert B. Westbook, *John Dewey and American Democracy* (Ithaca: Cornell University Press, 1991), 284; Scott M. Gunther, *The American Flag, 1777–1924: Cul-*

tural Shifts from Creation to Codification (Rutherford, N.J.: Fairleigh Dickinson University Press, 1990); Dumenil, " 'Insatiable Maw of Bureaucracy,' " 506–8; and Alan Dawley, *Struggles for Justice: Social Responsibility and the Liberal State* (Cambridge: Harvard University Press, 1991), chap. 7.

11 McCoy, *Calvin Coolidge,* 256 (quotation); Michael Kazin and Steven J. Ross, "America's Labor Day: The Dilemma of a Workers' Celebration," *Journal of American History* 78 (March 1992): 1294–1323; Lemons, *The Woman Citizen,* 172–74; and Steven M. Buechler, *Women's Movements in the United States* (New Brunswick: Rutgers University Press, 1990), 210–11.

12 For background on the "family wage" issue, see Maurine Weiner Greenwald, "Working-Class Feminism and the Family Wage Ideal: The Seattle Debate on Married Women's Right to Work, 1914–1920," *Journal of American History* 76 (June 1989): 118–49; Leonore Davidoff and Belinda Westover, eds., *Our Work, Our Lives, Our Words* (New York: Barnes and Noble, 1986); and Ellis W. Hawley, *The Great War and the Search for a Modern Order: A History of the American People and Their Institutions, 1917–1933,* 2d ed. (New York: St. Martin's Press, 1992), chap. 9.

13 Willa Cather, "Nebraska: The End of the First Cycle," 5 September 1923, and H. L. Mencken, "H. L. Mencken," 5 December 1923, in *The Nation, 1865–1990: Selections from the Independent Magazine of Politics and Culture,* ed. Katrina Vanden Heuvel (New York: Thunder's Mouth Press, 1990), 49–53 (quotation by Cather on 51), 53–56 (quotation by Mencken on 54).

14 McCoy, *Calvin Coolidge,* chaps. 26, 28, 29, 30; James W. Davidson and Mark H. Lytle, *After the Fact: The Art of Historical Detection* (New York: Alfred A. Knopf, 1982), chap. 10 (Sacco and Vanzetti); Paul A. Carter, *The Decline and Revival of the Social Gospel: Social and Political Liberalism in American Protestant Churches, 1920–1940* (Ithaca: Cornell University Press, 1954), pt. 2 and chap. 10; Theda Skocpol, *Protecting Soldiers and Mothers: The Political Origins of Social Policy in the United States* (Cambridge: Harvard University Press, 1992), 512–14; Ruth Schwartz Cowan, "Two Washes in the Morning and a Bridge Party at Night: Consumer Culture and the American Housewife between the Wars," in *Women, Families, and Communities: Readings in American History,* ed. Nancy A. Hewitt (Glenview: Scott, Foresman/Little, Brown Higher Education, 1990), 2:152–66; Kathryn Kish Sklar, "Why Were Most Politically Active Women Opposed to the ERA in the 1920s?" in *Women and Power in American History: A Reader,* ed. Kathryn Kish Sklar and Thomas Dublin (Englewood Cliffs: Prentice Hall, 1991), 2:175–82; and Jacquelyn Dowd Hall, *Revolt against Chivalry: Jessie Daniel Ames and the Women's Campaign against Lynching* (New York: Columbia University Press, 1979).

15 Burner, *Politics of Provincialism,* chap. 7; Joan Hoff Wilson, *Herbert Hoover: Forgotten Progressive* (Boston: Little, Brown, 1975), 129 (quotation); Elisabeth Israels Perry, *Belle Moskowitz: Feminine Politics and the Exercise of Power in the Age of Alfred E. Smith* (New York: Oxford University Press, 1987), chap. 10; and Gilbert C. Fite, *George N. Peek and the Fight for Farm Parity* (Norman: University of Oklahoma Press, 1954), 203–20.

16 *The New Day: Campaign Speeches of Herbert Hoover* (Stanford: Stanford University Press, 1928), 40–41, 77–82, 162–63 (quotations), 196–98; Perry, *Belle Mosko-*

witz, 128–35, 151–54, 180–82; David R. Colburn, "Al Smith and the New York State Factory Investigating Commission, 1911–1915," in *Reform and Reformers in the Progressive Era*, ed. David R. Colburn and George E. Pozzetta (Westport: Greenwood Press, 1983), 25–45; Don S. Kirschner, *The Paradox of Professionalism: Reform and Public Service in Urban America, 1900–1940* (Westport: Greenwood Press, 1986), 72–74 and chap. 6; and Blanche Wiesen Cook, *Eleanor Roosevelt*, vol. 1, *1884–1933* (New York: Viking, 1992), chap. 14.

17   William J. Barber, *From New Era to New Deal: Herbert Hoover, the Economists, and American Economic Policy, 1921–1933* (Cambridge: Cambridge University Press, 1985), 118; and Tony Freyer, "Economic Liberty, Antitrust, and the Constitution, 1880–1925," in *Liberty, Property, and Government: Constitutional Interpretation before the New Deal*, ed. Ellen Frankel Paul and Howard Dickman (Albany: State University of New York Press, 1989), 187–215.

18   Lemons, *The Woman Citizen*, 230–31 (quotations).

19   Ibid., 133, 237, 243; Molly Ladd-Taylor, " 'My Work Came Out of Agony and Grief': Mothers and the Making of the Sheppard-Towner Act," in *Mothers of a New World: Maternalist Politics and the Origins of Welfare States*, ed. Seth Koven and Sonya Michel (New York: Routledge, 1993), 321–42; and Patricia M. Hummer, *The Decade of Elusive Promise: Professional Women in the United States, 1920–1930* (Ann Arbor: UMI Research Press, 1979).

20   Lisio, *Hoover, Blacks, and Lily Whites*, 256–57 (quotation).

21   Hall, *Revolt against Chivalry*, 108–27 (quotation on 127); Cynthia Neverdon-Morton, *Afro-American Women of the South and the Advancement of the Race, 1895–1925* (Knoxville: University of Tennessee Press, 1989), 225–26; Robert L. Zangrando, *The NAACP Crusade against Lynching, 1909–1950* (Philadelphia: Temple University Press, 1980), 6–7 and chap. 4; and Judith L. Stephens, "Anti-Lynch Plays by African American Women: Race, Gender, and Social Protest in America," *African American Review*, 26 (Summer 1992): 329–39.

22   Lisio, *Hoover, Blacks and Lily Whites*, 271 (quotation). In the 1932 presidential election it is estimated that 90 percent of the African American voters supported Franklin D. Roosevelt and other Democratic candidates. Gerald D. Nash, *The Crucial Era: The Great Depression and World War II, 1929–1945*, 2d ed. (New York: St. Martin's Press, 1992), 87.

23   Wilson, *Herbert Hoover*, chap. 5; and Albert U. Romasco, *The Poverty of Abundance: Hoover, the Nation, the Depression* (New York: Oxford University Press, 1965), chaps. 9, 11. Some of the new institutional means to deal with current problems that Hoover advocated were: (1) the Reconstruction Finance Corporation, which would provide credit to troubled banking and business institutions; (2) industry-wide codes, which would be included in the National Recovery Administration in the early New Deal; (3) the Glass-Steagal Act, which would help to revamp the Federal Reserve banking system on the eve of its crisis in 1933; and (4) public construction projects to stimulate employment that would also be used in the New Deal.

Bibliography

Aaker, David A., and George S. Day. *Consumerism: Search for the Consumer Interest.* New York: Free Press, 1971.

Abbott, Richard H. *The Republican Party and the South, 1855–1877.* Chapel Hill: University of North Carolina Press, 1986.

Abell, Aaron I. *American Catholicism and Social Action: A Search for Social Justice, 1865–1950.* Garden City: Doubleday, 1960.

Adams, Charles Francis, Jr. *Chapters of Erie and Other Essays.* New York: Henry Holt, 1886. Quoted in Shelton Stromquist, *A Generation of Boomers: The Pattern of Railroad Labor Conflict in Nineteenth-Century America* (Urbana: University of Illinois, 1987), 15.

Addams, Jane. "The Subjective Necessity of Social Settlements." In *The American Intellectual Tradition: A Sourcebook.* Vol. 2, *1865 to the Present,* edited by David A. Hollinger and Charles Capper. New York: Oxford University Press, 1993.

——. *Twenty Years at Hull-House.* New York: New American Library, Signet Classics, 1961.

Adero, Malaika, ed. *Up South: Stories, Studies, and Letters of This Century's Black Migrations.* New York: New Press, 1993.

Alcott, Louisa May. *Moods.* Edited by Sarah Elbert. New Brunswick: Rutgers University Press, 1991.

Alexander, Adele Logan. "How I Discovered My Grandmother . . . and the Truth about Black Women and the Suffrage Movement." In *Black Women in American History: From Colonial Times through the Nineteenth Century.* Vol. 1, edited by Darlene Clark Hine. Brooklyn: Carlson Publishing, 1990.

Alexander, H. B. "Limits of Tolerance." *Dial,* 11 October 1917, 326–29.

Allen, Polly Wynn. *Building Domestic Liberty: Charlotte Perkins Gilman's Architectural Feminism.* Amherst: University of Massachusetts Press, 1988.

Anderson, Clay J. *A Half-Century of Federal Reserve Policymaking, 1914–1964.* Philadelphia: Federal Reserve Bank of Philadelphia, 1965.

Anderson, James E. *The Emergence of the Modern Regulatory State.* Washington, D.C.: Public Affairs Press, 1962.

Anderson, Jervis. *A. Philip Randolph: A Biographical Portrait.* New York: Harcourt Brace Jovanovich, 1972.

——. "Early Voice: Pt. 1. From Florida to Harlem [A. Philip Randolph biography]." *New Yorker*, 2 December 1972, 60–120.

——. "Early Voice: Pt. 2. Reaching for the Moon." *New Yorker*, 9 December 1972, 48–106.

——. "Early Voice: Pt. 3. The March." *New Yorker*, 16 December 1972, 40–85.

Anderson, Linnea M. " 'Brothers All, Enemies None': Memory and the 50th Anniversary of the Battle of Gettysburg." Master's seminar paper, New York University, 15 December 1992.

Andolsen, Barbara Hilkert. *"Daughters of Jefferson, Daughters of Bootblacks": Racism and American Feminism*. Macon: Mercer University Press, 1986.

Angell, Sir Norman. *Why Freedom Matters*. 2d ed. London: National Council for Civil Liberties, 1917.

Appleby, Joyce. *Capitalism and a New Social Order: The Republican Vision of the 1790s*. New York: New York University Press, 1984.

——. "One Good Turn Deserves Another: Moving beyond the Linguistic." *American Historical Review* 94 (December 1989): 1326–32.

Aptheker, Herbert, ed. *The Correspondence of W. E. B. Du Bois*. Amherst: University of Massachusetts Press, 1973.

Archdeacon, Thomas. *Becoming American: An Ethnic History*. New York: Free Press, 1983.

"Are American Liberties Worth Saving? Letters from New York Lawyers." *Nation*, 17 April 1920, 506–8.

Ashley, Kathleen M., ed. *Victor Turner and the Construction of Cultural Criticism: Between Literature and Anthropology*. Bloomington: Indiana University Press, 1990.

Bailey, Ronald. "The Other Side of Slavery: Black Labor, Cotton, and the Textile Industrialization of Great Britain and the United States." *Agricultural History* 68 (Spring 1994): 35–50.

Bailyn, Bernard, et al. *The Great Republic: A History of the American People*. Vol. 2. 2d ed. Lexington: D. C. Heath and Co., 1981.

Balser, Diane. *Sisterhood and Solidarity: Feminism and Labor in Modern Times*. Boston: South End Press, 1987.

Banner, Lois W. *Elizabeth Cady Stanton: A Radical for Woman's Rights*. Boston: Little, Brown, 1980.

Barber, William J. *From New Era to New Deal: Herbert Hoover, the Economists, and American Economic Policy, 1921–1933*. Cambridge: Cambridge University Press, 1985.

Barkun, Michael. *Crucible of the Millennium*. Syracuse: Syracuse University Press, 1986.

Barrett, James R. *Work and Community in the Jungle: Chicago's Packinghouse Workers, 1894–1922*. Urbana: University of Illinois Press, 1987.

Barry, Kathleen. *Susan B. Anthony: A Biography of a Singular Feminist*. New York: New York University Press, 1988.

Bataille, Gretchen M., and Kathleen Mullen Sands. *American Indian Women: Telling Their Lives*. Lincoln: University of Nebraska Press, 1984.

Beauregard, Erving E. *Bingham of the Hills: Politician and Diplomat Extraordinary*. New York: Peter Lang, 1989.

——. "Female Influence on the Authorship of the Fourteenth Amendment." *Journal of Unconventional History* 2 (1991): 51–68.

Bederman, Gail. " 'The Women Have Had Charge of the Church Work Long Enough': The Men and Religion Forward Movement of 1911–1912 and the Masculinization of Middle-Class Protestantism." *American Quarterly* 41 (September 1989): 432–65.

Bellah, Robert N., et al. *The Good Society*. New York: Alfred A. Knopf, 1991.

Bellamy, Edward. *Looking Backward, 2000–1887*. Edited and with an introduction by Daniel H. Borus. Boston: Bedford Books of St. Martin's Press, 1995.

Benedict, Michael Les. "The Problem of Constitutionalism and Constitutional Liberty in the Reconstruction South." In *An Uncertain Tradition: Constitutionalism and the History of the South*, edited by Kermit L. Hall and James W. Ely Jr. Athens: University of Georgia Press, 1989.

Bensel, Richard Franklin. *Yankee Leviathan: The Origins of Central State Authority in America, 1859–1877*. Cambridge: Cambridge University Press, 1990.

Benson, Lee. *The Concept of Jacksonian Democracy: New York as a Test Case*. Princeton: Princeton University Press, 1961.

Benson, Thomas W., ed. *American Rhetoric: Context and Criticism*. Carbondale: Southern Illinois University Press, 1989.

Berger, Peter L., and Richard J. Neuhaus. *Movement and Revolution: On American Radicalism*. New York: Doubleday Anchor Books, 1970.

Berk, Gerald. *Alternate Tracks: The Constitution of American Industrial Order, 1865–1917*. Baltimore: Johns Hopkins University Press, 1994.

Berkeley, Kathleen C. " 'Colored Ladies Also Contributed': Black Women's Activities from Benevolence to Social Welfare, 1866–1896." In *Black Women in American History: From Colonial Times through the Nineteenth Century*. Vol. 1, edited by Darlene Clark Hine. Brooklyn: Carlson Publishers, 1990.

Berkin, Carol Ruth. "Private Woman, Public Woman: The Contradiction of Charlotte Perkins Gilman." In *Critical Essays on Charlotte Perkins Gilman*, edited by Jo-anne B. Karpinski. New York: G. K. Hall, 1992.

Berthoff, Rowland. "Conventional Mentality: Free Blacks, Women, and Business Corporations as Unequal Persons, 1820–1870." *Journal of American History* 76 (December 1989): 753–84.

Bestor, Arthur E. *Backwoods Utopias*. Philadelphia: University of Pennsylvania Press, 1950.

Beth, Loren. *John Marshall Harlan: The Last Whig Justice*. Lexington: University Press of Kentucky, 1992.

Bevir, Mark. "The Errors of Linguistic Contextualism." *History and Theory* 31, no. 3 (1992): 276–98.

Bialer, Seweryn. "On the Meaning, Sources, and Carriers of Radicalism in Contemporary Industrialized Societies: Introductory Remarks." In *Radicalism in the Contemporary Age*. Vol. 1, *Sources of Contemporary Radicalism*, edited by Seweryn Bialer and Sophia Sluzar. Boulder: Westview Press, 1977.

Blair, Karen J. *The Clubwoman as Feminist: True Womanhood Redefined, 1868–1914*. New York: Holms and Meier, 1980.

——. *The History of American Women's Voluntary Organizations, 1810–1960: A Guide to Sources.* Boston: G. K. Hall, 1989.

Blake, Casey Nelson. *Beloved Community: The Cultural Criticism of Randolph Bourne, Van Wyck Brooks, Waldo Frank, and Lewis Mumford.* Chapel Hill: University of North Carolina Press, 1990.

Blaustein, Albert P., and Robert L. Zángrando, eds. *Civil Rights and African Americans: A Documentary History.* Evanston: Northwestern University Press, 1991.

Bledstein, Burton J. *The Culture of Professionalism: The Middle Class and the Development of Higher Education in America.* New York: W. W. Norton, 1976.

Blee, Kathleen M. *Women of the Klan: Racism and Gender in the 1920s.* Berkeley: University of California Press, 1991.

Blewett, Mary H. *We Will Rise in Our Might: Workingwomen's Voices from Nineteenth Century New England.* Ithaca: Cornell University Press, 1991.

Blight, David W. " 'For Something beyond the Battlefield': Frederick Douglass and the Struggle for the Memory of the Civil War." *Journal of American History* 75 (March 1989): 1156–78.

Blocker, Jack S., Jr. *American Temperance Movements: Cycles of Reform.* Boston: G. K. Hall, 1989.

——. *"Give to the Winds Thy Fears": The Women's Temperance Crusade, 1873–1874.* Westport: Greenwood Press, 1985.

Blue, Frederick J. *Salmon P. Chase: A Life in Politics.* Kent: Kent State University Press, 1987.

Blum, D. Steven. *Walter Lippmann: Cosmopolitanism in the Century of Total War.* Ithaca: Cornell University Press, 1984.

Bogue, Allan G. "Bloc and Party in the United States Senate: 1861–1863." *Civil War History* 13 (September 1967): 221–41.

——. *The Ernest Men: Republicans of the Civil War Senate.* Ithaca: Cornell University Press, 1981.

Borah, William E. "Free Speech: The Vital Issue." *Nation,* 4 July 1923, 8.

Bordin, Ruth. *Frances Willard: A Biography.* Chapel Hill: University of North Carolina Press, 1986.

——. "Woman's Mighty Realm of Philanthropy." In *Women and Power in American History: A Reader.* Vol. 2, edited by Kathryn Kish Sklar and Thomas Dublin. Englewood Cliffs: Prentice Hall, 1991.

Borus, Daniel H. Introduction to *Looking Backward, 2000–1887,* by Edward Bellamy. Boston: Bedford Books of St. Martin's Press, 1995.

Boskin, Joseph. *Urban Racial Violence in the Twentieth Century.* Beverly Hills: Glencoe Press, 1969.

Boulding, Kenneth E. *The Organizational Revolution: A Study in the Ethics of Economic Organization.* New York: Harper and Brothers, 1950.

Bourdieu, Pierre. "Rites as Acts of Institution." In *Honor and Grace in Anthropology,* edited by J. G. Peristiany and Julian Pitt-Rivers. Cambridge: Cambridge University Press, 1992.

Bowen, David Warren. *Andrew Johnson and the Negro.* Knoxville: University of Tennessee Press, 1989.

Bradley Commission on History in Schools. *Building a History Curriculum: Guidelines for Teaching History in Schools.* Washington, D.C.: Educational Excellence Network, 1988.

Bradley, Joseph P. "Majority Opinion in *Civil Rights Cases* (1883)." In *Annals of America,* 10:577–81. Chicago: Encyclopaedia Britannica, 1968.

Brandeis, Louis D. *Other People's Money and How the Bankers Use It.* Boston: Bedford Books of St. Martin's Press, 1995.

Breen, William J. "Black Women and the Great War: Mobilization and Reform in the South." In *Black Women in American History: The Twentieth Century.* Vol. 2, edited by Darlene Clark Hine. Brooklyn: Carlson Publishing, 1990.

Brinkley, Alan. "The Problem of American Conservatism." *American Historical Review* 99 (April 1994): 409–29.

Brock, William R. *Investigation and Responsibility: Public Responsibility in the United States, 1865–1900.* Cambridge: Cambridge University Press, 1984.

Brown, Charlotte Hawkins. "Speaking Up for the Race at Memphis, Tennessee, October 8, 1920." In *Black Women in White America: A Documentary History,* edited by Gerda Lerner. New York: Random House, 1972.

Brown, Gillian. *Domestic Individualism: Imagining Self in Nineteenth-Century America.* Berkeley: University of California Press, 1990.

Bruner, Edward M. "Experience and Its Expressions." In *The Anthropology of Experience,* edited by Victor W. Turner and Edward M. Bruner. Urbana: University of Illinois Press, 1986.

Bryant, Keith L., Jr. *Railroads in the Age of Regulation, 1900–1980: Encyclopedia of American Business History and Biography.* New York: Facts on File, 1988.

Bryce, James. *The Hindrances to Good Citizenship.* New Haven: Yale University Press, 1909.

Buechler, Steven M. *Women's Movements in the United States.* New Brunswick: Rutgers University Press, 1990.

Buhle, Mari Jo. *Women and American Socialism, 1870–1920.* Urbana: University of Illinois Press, 1981.

Bumiller, Kristin. *The Civil Rights Society.* Baltimore: Johns Hopkins University Press, 1988.

Burgess, John W. "Civil Liberty and Constitutional Law." *Political Science Quarterly* 19 (December 1904): 568–72.

Burner, David. *The Politics of Provincialism: The Democratic Party in Transition, 1918–1932.* New York: W. W. Norton, 1967.

Butler, Nicholas Murray. "Statement on Firing Pacifist Professors, 6 June 1917." *Columbia Alumni News* 9 (5 October 1917): 31.

Cadwalader, Sandra L., and Vine Deloria Jr. *The Aggressions of Civilization: Federal Indian Policy since the 1880s.* Philadelphia: Temple University Press, 1985.

Cain, William E., ed. *William Lloyd Garrison and the Fight against Slavery: Selections from "The Liberator."* Boston: Bedford Books of St. Martin's Press, 1995.

Calhoun, Craig, Marshall W. Meyer, and W. Richard Scott, eds. *Structures of Power and Constraint: Papers in Honor of Peter M. Blau.* Cambridge: Cambridge University Press, 1990.

Cameron, Ardis. *Radicals of the Worst Sort: Laboring Women in Lawrence, Massachusetts, 1860–1912.* Urbana: University of Illinois Press, 1993.

Camhi, Jane Jerome. *Women against Women: American Anti-Suffragism, 1880–1920.* Brooklyn: Carlson Publishing, 1994.

Campbell, Karlyn Kohrs. *Women Public Speakers in the United States, 1800–1925.* Westport: Greenwood Press, 1993.

Carnes, Mark C. *Secret Ritual and Manhood in Victorian America.* New Haven: Yale University Press, 1989.

Carper, N. Gordon. "Slavery Revisited: Peonage in the South." *Phylon* 37 (March 1976): 85–99.

Carter, Dan T. *When the War Was Over: The Failure of Self-Reconstruction in the South, 1865–1867.* Baton Rouge: Louisiana State University Press, 1985.

Carter, Paul A. *The Decline and Revival of the Social Gospel: Social and Political Liberalism in American Protestant Churches, 1920–1940.* Ithaca: Cornell University Press, 1954.

Cather, Willa. "Nebraska: The End of the First Cycle." In *The Nation, 1865–1990: Selections from the Independent Magazine of Politics and Culture,* edited by Katrina Vanden Heuvel. New York: Thunder's Mouth Press, 1990.

Chafe, William H. *Women and Equality: Changing Patterns in American Culture.* New York: Oxford University Press, 1977.

Chambers, John Whiteclay, II. *The Tyranny of Change: America in the Progressive Era, 1890–1920.* 2d ed. New York: St. Martin's Press, 1992.

Chan, Sucheng. *Asian Americans: An Interpretative History.* Boston: Twayne Publishers, 1991.

——. "European and Asian Immigration into the United States in Comparative Perspective, 1820s to 1920s." In *Immigration Reconsidered: History, Sociology, and Politics,* edited by Virginia Yans-McLaughlin. New York: Oxford University Press, 1990.

Chandler, Alfred D., Jr. *The Visible Hand: The Managerial Revolution in American Business.* Cambridge: Harvard University Press, 1977.

Chandler, Alfred D., Jr., and Stephen Salsburg. *Pierre S. DuPont and the Making of the Modern Corporation.* New York: Harper and Row, 1971.

Childs, John Brown. *Leadership, Conflict, and Cooperation in Afro-American Social Thought.* Philadelphia: Temple University Press, 1989.

Chudacoff, Howard P. "Success and Security: The Meaning of Social Mobility in America." *Reviews in American History* 10 (December 1982): 101–12.

"Civil Liberty Dead." *Nation,* 14 September 1918, 282.

Claghorn, Kate Holladay. *The Immigrant's Day in Court.* New York: Harper and Brothers, 1923. Reprint, New York: Arno Press, 1969.

Clawson, Mary Ann. *Constructing Brotherhood: Class, Gender, and Fraternalism.* Princeton: Princeton University Press, 1989.

Clifton, James A. "Alternate Identities and Cultural Frontiers." In *Being and Becoming Indian: Biographical Studies in North American Frontiers,* edited by James A. Clifton. Chicago: Dorsey Press, 1989.

Cmiel, Kenneth. *Democratic Eloquence: The Fight over Popular Speech in Nineteenth-Century America.* Berkeley: University of California Press, 1990.

Cohen, William. *At Freedom's Edge: Black Mobility and the Southern White Quest for Racial Control, 1861–1915.* Baton Rouge: Louisiana State University Press, 1991.

Colbert, Douglas L. "Liberating the Thirteenth Amendment." *Harvard Civil Rights-Civil Liberties Law Review* 30 (Winter 1995): 1–55.

Colburn, David R. "Al Smith and the New York State Factory Investigating Commission, 1911–1915." In *Reform and Reformers in the Progressive Era*, edited by David R. Colburn and George E. Pozzetta. Westport: Greenwood Press, 1983.

"The Colored Women's Statement to the Women's Missionary Council, American Missionary Association [1919]." In *Black Women in White America: A Documentary History*, edited by Gerda Lerner. New York: Random House, 1972.

Commager, Henry Steele. *The American Mind: An Interpretation of American Thought and Character since the 1880s.* New Haven: Yale University Press, 1950.

Condit, Celeste Michelle, and John Louis Lucaites. *Crafting Equality: America's Anglo-African Word.* Chicago: University of Chicago Press, 1993.

Connell, R. W. *Gender and Power: Society, the Person, and Sexual Politics.* Stanford: Stanford University Press, 1987.

Cook, Blanche Wiesen. *Eleanor Roosevelt.* Vol. 1, *1884–1933.* New York: Viking, 1992.

Cooper, John Milton, Jr. *The Warrior and the Priest: Woodrow Wilson and Theodore Roosevelt.* Cambridge: Harvard University Press, 1983.

Corbin, John. "Liberty above Equality." *North American Review* 212 (December 1920): 741–53.

Cordery, Stacy A. "Women in Industrializing America." In *The Gilded Age: Essays on the Origins of Modern America*, edited by Charles W. Calhoun. Wilmington, Del.: Scholarly Resources, 1996.

Cornell, Saul. "Splitting the Difference: Textualism, Contextualism, and Post-Modern History." *American Studies* 36 (Spring 1995): 57–80.

Cortner, Richard C. *The Iron Horse and the Constitution: The Railroads and the Transformation of the Fourteenth Amendment.* Westport: Greenwood Press, 1993.

———. *A Mob Intent on Death: The NAACP and the Arkansas Riot Cases.* Middletown: Wesleyan University Press, 1988.

Cott, Nancy F. *The Grounding of Modern Feminism.* New Haven: Yale University Press, 1987.

———. "What's in a Name? The Limits of 'Social Feminism'; or, Expanding the Vocabulary of Women's History." *Journal of American History* 76 (December 1989): 809–29.

Cowan, Ruth Schwartz. "Two Washes in the Morning and a Bridge Party at Night: Consumer Culture and the American Housewife between the Wars." In *Women, Families, and Communities: Readings in American History.* Vol. 2, edited by Nancy A. Hewitt. Glenview: Scott, Foresman/Little, Brown Higher Education, 1990.

Craigie, William A., and James R. Hulbert, eds. *A Dictionary of American English on Historical Principles.* Vols. 3 and 4. Chicago: University of Chicago Press, 1942–44.

Croly, Herbert. *The Promise of American Life.* 1909. Reprint, Indianapolis: Bobbs-Merrill, 1965.

Cronon, E. David. *Black Moses: The Story of Marcus Garvey and the Universal Negro Improvement Association.* 2d ed. Madison: University of Wisconsin Press, 1969.

Crunden, Robert M. *Ministers of Reform: The Progressives' Achievement in American Civilization, 1889–1920.* New York: Basic Books, 1982.

Cruse, Harold. *The Crisis of the Negro Intellectual.* New York: William Morrow, 1967.

Cuff, Robert D. *The War Industries Board: Business-Government Relations during World War I*. Baltimore: Johns Hopkins University Press, 1973.

Cullom, Shelby M. *Fifty Years of Public Service*. 2d ed. Chicago: A. C. McClurg, 1911.

Currie, David P. *The Constitution in the Supreme Court: The First Hundred Years, 1789–1888*. Chicago: University of Chicago Press, 1985.

——. *The Constitution in the Supreme Court: The Second Century, 1888–1986*. Chicago: University of Chicago Press, 1990.

Curry, Richard O., and Lawrence B. Goodheart, eds. *American Chameleon: Individualism in Trans-National Context*. Kent: Kent State University Press, 1991.

Cushman, Robert Eugene. *Leading Constitutional Decisions*. 3d ed. New York: F. S. Crofts, 1933.

Daniels, Roger. *Asian America: Chinese and Japanese in the United States since 1850*. Seattle: University of Washington Press, 1988.

Davidoff, Leonore, and Belinda Westover, eds. *Our Work, Our Lives, Our Words*. New York: Barnes and Noble, 1986.

Davidson, James W., and Mark H. Lytle. *After the Fact: The Art of Historical Detection*. 1st ed. New York: Alfred A. Knopf, 1982.

Davis, Allen F. *American Heroine: The Life and Legend of Jane Addams*. New York: Oxford University Press, 1973.

——. "Ellen Gates Starr." In *Notable American Women, 1607–1950*, edited by Edward T. James and Janet James. Cambridge: Belknap Press of Harvard, 1971.

——. *Spearhead for Reform: The Social Settlement and the Progressive Movement, 1890–1914*. New York: Oxford University Press, 1967.

Davis, Allen F., and Mary Lynn McCree, eds. *Eighty Years at Hull-House*. Chicago: Quadrangle Books, 1969.

Davis, Patricia T. *End of the Line: Alexander J. Cassatt and the Pennsylvania Railroad*. New York: Neale Watson Academic Publications, 1978.

Dawley, Alan. *Struggles for Justice: Social Responsibility and the Liberal State*. Cambridge: Harvard University Press, 1991.

Debs, Eugene V. *The Writings and Speeches of Eugene V. Debs*. Edited by Arthur M. Schlesinger Jr. New York: Hermitage Press, 1948.

Deegan, Mary Jo. *American Ritual Dramas: Social Rules and Cultural Meanings*. Westport: Greenwood Press, 1989.

——. *Jane Addams and the Men of the Chicago School, 1892–1918*. New Brunswick: Transaction Books, 1988.

Degler, Carl N. *In Search of Human Nature: The Decline and Revival of Darwinism in American Social Thought*. New York: Oxford University Press, 1991.

Dehnel, David. "The Policy Agenda of the Supreme Court in Three Partisan Eras." Ph.D. diss., University of Minnesota, 1988.

De Jongh, James. *Vicious Modernism: Black Harlem and the Literary Imagination*. New York: Cambridge University Press, 1990.

Deloria, Vine, Jr., *American Indian Policy in the Twentieth Century*. Norman: University of Oklahoma Press, 1985.

Deutsch, Sarah. "Learning to Talk More Like a Man: Boston Women's Class-Bridging Organizations, 1870–1940." *American Historical Review* 97 (April 1992): 379–404.

Dicken-Garcia, Hazel. *Journalistic Standards in the Nineteenth Century.* Madison: University of Wisconsin Press, 1989.

Diggins, John P. "Comrades and Citizens: New Methodologies in American Historiography." *American Historical Review* 90 (June 1985): 614–38.

——. "The Misuses of Gramsci." *Journal of American History* 75 (June 1988): 141–45.

——. "Power, Freedom, and the Failure of Theory." *Harper's,* January 1992, 15–19.

——. *The Promise of Pragmatism: Modernism and the Crisis of Knowledge and Authority.* Chicago: University of Chicago Press, 1994.

Dippie, Brian W. *The Vanishing American: White Attitudes and U.S. Indian Policy.* Middletown: Wesleyan University Press, 1982.

Donald, David. *Charles Sumner and the Rights of Man.* New York: Alfred A. Knopf, 1970.

Dorr, Rheta Childe. "Clubs as Instruments of Reform." In *The American Woman: Who Was She?* edited by Anne Firor Scott. Englewood Cliffs: Prentice-Hall, 1971.

Douglas, Mary, ed. *Rules and Meanings: The Anthropology of Everyday Knowledge.* New York: Penguin Books, 1973.

Douglass, Frederick. "What the Black Man Wants." In *Radical Republicans and Reconstruction, 1861–1870,* edited by Harold M. Hyman. Indianapolis: Bobbs-Merrill, 1967.

DuBois, Ellen Carol. *Feminism and Suffrage: The Emergence of an Independent Women's Movement in America, 1848–1869.* Ithaca: Cornell University Press, 1978.

——. "Outgrowing the Compact of the Fathers: Equal Rights, Woman Suffrage, and the United States Constitution, 1820–1878." *Journal of American History* 74 (December 1987): 836–62.

——. "Taking the Law into Our Own Hands: Bradwell, Minor, and Suffrage Militance in the 1870s." In *Visible Women: New Essays on American Activism,* edited by Nancy A. Hewitt and Suzanne Lebsock. Urbana: University of Illinois Press, 1993.

——. "Working Women, Class Relations, and Suffrage Militance: Harriet Stanton Blatch and the New York Woman Suffrage Movement, 1894–1909." *Journal of American History* 74 (June 1987): 34–58.

Du Bois, W. E. B. *The Autobiography of W. E. B. Du Bois: A Soliloquy on Viewing My Life from the Last Decade of Its First Century.* New York: International Publishers, 1968.

——. "Constitution and By-Laws of the Niagara Movement as Adopted July 12 and 13, 1905, at Buffalo, N.Y." In *Pamphlets and Leaflets by W. E. B. Du Bois,* edited by Herbert Aptheker. White Plains, N.Y.: Kraus-Thomson Organization, 1986.

——. "The Immediate Program of the American Negro." Reprinted in *Civil Rights and African Americans: A Documentary History,* edited by Alfred P. Blaustein and Robert L. Zangrando. Evanston: Northwestern University Press, 1968.

——. "Jim Crow" (January 1919). Reprinted in *Writings of W. E. B. Du Bois,* edited by Nathan I. Huggins. New York: Literary Classics of the United States, 1986.

——. *The Oxford W. E. B. Du Bois Reader.* Edited by Eric J. Sundquist. New York: Oxford University Press, 1996.

——. *The Souls of Black Folk.* Reprinted in *Writings of W. E. B. Du Bois,* edited by Nathan I. Huggins. New York: Literary Classics of the United States, 1986.

——. "Two Negro Conventions." In *Writings of W. E. B. Du Bois in Periodicals Edited by Others*, Vol. 1, *1891–1909*, edited by Herbert Aptheker. Millwood, N.Y.: Kraus-Thomson Organization, 1982.

——. *Writings of W. E. B. Du Bois.* Edited by Nathan I. Huggins. New York: Literary Classics of the United States, 1986.

Duis, Perry R. *The Saloon: Public Drinking in Chicago and Boston, 1880–1920.* Urbana: University of Illinois Press, 1983.

Dumenil, Lynn. *Freemasonry and American Culture, 1880–1930.* Princeton: Princeton University Press, 1984.

——. " 'The Insatiable Maw of Bureaucracy': Antistatism and Education Reform in the 1920s." *Journal of American History* 77 (September 1990): 499–524.

Dworkin, Ronald. "Justice for Clarence Thomas." *New York Review of Books*, 7 November 1991, 41–45.

Dyck, Ian, ed. *Citizen of the World: Essays on Thomas Paine.* New York: St. Martin's Press, 1988.

Dyer, Thomas G. *Theodore Roosevelt and the Idea of Race.* Baton Rouge: Louisiana State University Press, 1980.

Eagles, Charles W. "Congressional Voting in the 1920s: A Test of Urban-Rural Conflict." *Journal of American History* 76 (September 1989): 528–34.

Edgerton, Alice. "Individual Liberty in America." *Nation*, 11 October 1919, 494–95.

Ellis, Mark. " 'Closing Ranks' and 'Seeking Honors': W. E. B. Du Bois in World War I." *Journal of American History* 79 (June 1992): 96–124.

Evans, Selia. *Royal Neighbors of America . . . 100 Years of Helping Hands.* Rock Island, Ill.: Royal Neighbors of America, 1995.

Eyerman, Ron, and Andrew Jamison. *Social Movements: A Cognitive Approach.* University Park: Pennsylvania State University Press, 1991.

Fahey, David M. *The Black Lodge in White America: "True Reformer" Browne and His Economic Strategy.* Dayton: Wright State University Press, 1994.

Fairman, Charles. *Mr. Justice Miller and the Supreme Court, 1862–1890.* Cambridge: Harvard University Press, 1939.

Faust, Drew Gilpin. "Altars of Sacrifice: Confederate Women and the Narratives of War." *Journal of American History* 76 (March 1990): 1200–28.

Fels, Rendigs. *American Business Cycles, 1865–1879.* Chapel Hill: University of North Carolina Press, 1959.

"Finish of the Civil Rights Act." *Literary Digest*, 5 July 1913, 8.

Fink, Leon. "Looking Backward: Reflections on Workers' Culture and Certain Conceptual Dilemmas within Labor History." In *Perspectives on American Labor History: The Problems of Synthesis*, edited by J. Carroll Moody and Alice Kessler-Harris. DeKalb: Northern Illinois University Press, 1990.

——. "The New Labor History and the Powers of Historical Pessimism: Consensus, Hegemony, and the Case of the Knights of Labor." *Journal of American History* 75 (June 1988): 115–36.

Fischer, David Hacket. *Albion's Seed: Four British Folkways in America.* New York: Oxford University Press, 1989.

Fite, Gilbert C. *George N. Peek and the Fight for Farm Parity.* Norman: University of Oklahoma Press, 1954.

Fitzgerald, Michael W. " 'To Give Our Votes to the Party': Black Political Agitation and Agricultural Change in Alabama, 1865–1870." *Journal of American History* 76 (September 1989): 489–505.

Fleming, Robin. "Picturesque History and the Medieval in Nineteenth-Century America." *American Historical Review* 100 (October 1995): 1061–94.

Florette, Henri. *Black Migration: Movement North, 1900–1920.* Garden City: Anchor Press, 1975.

Foner, Eric. *Free Soil, Free Labor, Free Men: The Ideology of the Republican Party before the Civil War.* New York: Oxford University Press, 1970.

——. *Reconstruction: America's Unfinished Revolution, 1863–1877.* New York: Harper and Row, 1988.

Foner, Philip S., and Ronald L. Lewis, eds. *The Black Worker: A Documentary History from Colonial Times to the Present.* Vol. 3, *The Black Worker during the Era of the Knights of Labor.* Philadelphia: Temple University Press, 1987.

Forbath, William E. *Law and the Shaping of the American Labor Movement.* Cambridge: Harvard University Press, 1991.

Fosdick, Raymond B. "Liberty in America." *Outlook,* 2 February 1916, 282–85.

Frank, Dana. "Housewives, Socialists, and the Politics of Food: The 1917 New York Cost-of-Living Protests." In *Women and Power in American History: A Reader.* Vol. 2, edited by Kathryn Kish Sklar and Thomas Dublin. Englewood Cliffs: Prentice Hall, 1991.

Frederick, Peter J. *Knights of the Golden Rule: The Intellectual as Christian Social Reformer in the 1890s.* Lexington: University Press of Kentucky, 1976.

Freedman, Estelle B. "Separatism as Strategy: Female Institution Building and American Feminism, 1870–1930." In *Women and Power in American History: A Reader.* Vol. 2, edited by Kathryn Kish Sklar and Thomas Dublin. Englewood Cliffs: Prentice Hall, 1991.

Freyer, Tony. "Economic Liberty, Antitrust, and the Constitution, 1880–1925." In *Liberty, Property, and Government: Constitutional Interpretation before the New Deal,* edited by Ellen Frankel Paul and Howard Dickman. Albany: State University of New York Press, 1989.

Friedan, Betty. *The Feminine Mystique.* 1st paper ed. New York: Dell Publishing Co., 1964.

Friedl, Bettina, ed. *On to Victory: Propaganda Plays of the Woman Suffrage Movement.* Boston: Northeastern University Press, 1987.

Friedman, Jean E. *The Enclosed Garden: Women and Community in the Evangelical South, 1830–1900.* Chapel Hill: University of North Carolina Press, 1985.

Friedman, Milton, and Anna Jacobson Schwartz. *A Monetary History of the United States, 1867–1960.* Princeton: Princeton University Press, 1963.

Fritz, Christian G. *Federal Justice in California: The Court of Ogden Hoffman, 1851–1891.* Lincoln: University of Nebraska Press, 1991.

Frost, Elizabeth, and Kathryn Cullen-DuPont. *Women's Suffrage in America: An Eyewitness History.* New York: Facts on File, 1992.

Galambos, Louis. "The Triumph of Oligopoly." In *American Economic Development in Historical Perspective,* edited by Thomas Weiss and Donald Schaefer. Stanford: Stanford University Press, 1994.

Gambill, Edward L. *Conservative Ordeal: Northern Democrats and Reconstruction.* Ames: Iowa State University Press, 1981.

———. "Who Were the Senate Radicals?" *Civil War History* 11 (September 1965): 237–44.

Gamson, William A. *A Study of Social Protest.* Homewood, Ill.: Dorsey Press, 1975.

Gardner, James B., and George R. Adams, eds. *Ordinary People and Everyday Life: Perspectives on the New Social History.* Nashville: American Association of State and Local History, 1983.

Gardner, Virginia. *"Friend and Lover": The Life of Louise Bryant.* New York: Horizon Press, 1982.

Garvey, Marcus. "The Objective of the Universal Negro Improvement Association." In *Civil Rights and African Americans: A Documentary History,* edited by Alfred P. Blaustein and Robert L. Zangrando. Evanston: Northwestern University Press, 1968.

Gatewood, William B., Jr. *Theodore Roosevelt and the Art of Controversy.* Baton Rouge: Louisiana State University Press, 1970.

Gaventa, John. *Power and Powerlessness: Quiescence and Rebellion in an Appalachian Valley.* Urbana: University of Illinois Press, 1982.

Giddings, Paula. *When and Where I Enter: The Impact of Black Women on Race and Sex in America.* New York: William Morrow, 1984.

Gilkeson, John S., Jr. *Middle-Class Providence, 1820–1940.* Princeton: Princeton University Press, 1986.

Gillette, William. *Retreat from Reconstruction.* Baton Rouge: Louisiana State University Press, 1979.

Gilman, Charlotte Perkins. "Women and Economics." In *Feminism: The Essential Historical Writings,* edited by Miriam Schneir. New York: Vintage Books, 1972.

Ginzberg, Lori D. *Women and the Work of Benevolence: Morality, Politics, and Class in the Nineteenth-Century United States.* New Haven: Yale University Press, 1990.

Glassberg, David. "History and the Public: Legacies of the Progressive Era." *Journal of American History* 73 (March 1987): 957–80.

Glenn, Susan A. *Daughters of the Shtetl: Life and Labor in the Immigrant Generation.* Ithaca: Cornell University Press, 1990.

Goldwater, Barry. "I Accept Your Nomination." In *Voices of Crisis: Vital Speeches on Contemporary Issues,* edited by Floyd W. Matson. New York: Odyssey Press, 1967.

Goodnow, Frank J. *The American Conception of Liberty and Government.* Providence, R.I.: Standard Publishing Company, 1916.

Goodwyn, Lawrence. *Democratic Promise: The Populist Movement in America.* New York: Oxford University Press, 1976.

Gordon, John Steele. *The Scarlet Woman of Wall Street: Jay Gould, Jim Fisk, Cornelius Vanderbilt, the Erie Railway Wars, and the Birth of Wall Street.* New York: Weidenfeld and Nicolson, 1988.

Gordon, Linda. "Black and White Visions of Welfare: Women's Welfare Activism, 1890–1945." *Journal of American History* 78 (September 1991): 559–90.

———. "Social Insurance and Public Assistance: The Influence of Gender in Welfare Thought in the United States, 1890–1935." *American Historical Review* 97 (February 1992): 19–54.

Gould, Louis L. *The Presidency of Theodore Roosevelt.* Lawrence: University Press of Kansas, 1991.

Grant, Mary H. *Private Woman, Public Person: An Account of the Life of Julia Ward Howe from 1819 to 1868.* Brooklyn: Carlson Publishing, 1994.

Greene, Jack P. *Imperatives, Behaviors, and Identities: Essays in Early American Cultural History.* Charlottesville: University Press of Virginia, 1992.

Greenleaf, William. *American Economic Development since 1860.* Columbia: University of South Carolina Press, 1968.

Greenwald, Maurine Weiner. "Working-Class Feminism and the Family Wage Ideal: The Seattle Debate on Married Women's Right to Work, 1914–1920." *Journal of American History* 76 (June 1989):118–49.

Griffith, Elisabeth. *In Her Own Right: The Life of Elizabeth Cady Stanton.* New York: Oxford University Press, 1984.

Grimes, Ronald L. "Victor Turner's Definition, Theory, and Sense of Ritual." In *Victor Turner and the Construction of Cultural Criticism: Between Literature and Anthropology,* edited by Kathleen M. Ashley. Bloomington: Indiana University Press, 1990.

Gronlund, Laurence. *The Cooperative Commonwealth.* Cambridge: Harvard University Press, 1965.

Grossman, James R. *Land of Hope: Chicago, Black Southerners, and the Great Migration.* Chicago: University of Chicago Press, 1989.

Gunther, Scott M. *The American Flag, 1777–1924: Cultural Shifts from Creation to Codification.* Rutherford: Fairleigh Dickinson University Press, 1990.

Haaland, Bonnie. *Emma Goldman: Sexuality and the Impurity of the State.* Montréal: Black Rose Books, 1993.

Haber, Samuel. *Efficiency and Uplift: Scientific Management in the Progressive Era, 1890–1920.* Chicago: University of Illinois Press, 1964.

Hahn, Steven. "Class and State in Postemancipation Societies: Southern Planters in Comparative Perspective." *American Historical Review* 95 (February 1990): 75–98.

Hall, Jacquelyn Dowd. "Partial Truths." *Signs* 14 (Summer 1989): 902–11.

———. *Revolt against Chivalry: Jessie Daniel Ames and the Women's Campaign against Lynching.* New York: Columbia University Press, 1979.

Hall, Peter Dobkin. "Organization as Artifact: A Case Study of Technical Innovation and Management Reform, 1893–1906." In *The Mythmaking Frame of Mind: Social Imagination and American Culture,* edited by James Gilbert, Amy Gilman, Donald M. Scott, and Joan W. Scott. Belmont, Calif.: Wadsworth Publishing Company, 1993.

Hamilton, Kenneth Marvin. *Black Towns and Profit: Promotion and Development in the Trans Appalachian West, 1877–1915.* Urbana: University of Illinois Press, 1991.

Handlin, Oscar, and Lillian Handlin. *Liberty in Expansion, 1760–1850.* New York: Harper and Row, 1989.

Harlan, David. "Intellectual History and the Return of Literature." *American Historical Review* 94 (June 1989):581–609.

Harlan, John Marshall. "Dissenting Opinion in *Civil Rights Cases* (1883)." In *Annals of America,* 10:581–83. Chicago: Encyclopaedia Britannica, 1968.

Harrison, Alferdteen, ed. *Black Exodus: The Great Migration from the American South.* Jackson: University of Mississippi, 1991.

Harvey, Kevin G. "Andrew Johnson, Reconstruction and Congressional Republicans: A Predestined Failure." Senior history paper, Augustana College, May 1991.

Havel, Václav. "The Power of the Powerless." In *Václav Havel: Living in Truth*, edited by Jan Vladislav. London: Faber and Faber, 1989.

Hawes, Joseph M. *The Children's Rights Movement: A History of Advocacy and Protection.* Boston: Twayne Publishers, 1991.

Hawley, Ellis W. *The Great War and the Search for a Modern Order: A History of the American People and Their Institutions, 1917–1933.* 2d ed. New York: St. Martin's Press, 1992.

———. "Herbert Hoover and Economic Stabilization, 1921–22." In *Herbert Hoover as Secretary of Commerce,* edited by Ellis W. Hawley. Iowa City: University of Iowa Press, 1981.

———. ed. *Herbert Hoover as Secretary of Commerce: Studies in New Era Thought and Practice.* Iowa City: University of Iowa Press, 1981.

Haynes, George E. *The Trend of the Races.* New York: Council of Women for Home Missions and Missionary Education Movement of the United States and Canada, 1922.

Hearn, Jeff. *Men in the Public Eye: Critical Studies on Men and Masculinity.* London: Routledge, 1992.

Hellwig, David J. "Afro-American Reactions to the Japanese and the Anti-Japanese Movement, 1906–1924." *Phylon* 38 (March 1977): 93–104.

Hess, Earl J. *Liberty, Virtue, and Progress: Northerners and Their War for the Union.* New York: New York University Press, 1988.

Hewitt, Nancy A. *Women's Activism and Social Change: Rochester, New York, 1822–1872.* Ithaca: Cornell University Press, 1984.

Higginbotham, Evelyn Brooks. "African-American Women's History and the Metalanguage of Race." In *We Specialize in the Wholly Impossible: A Reader in Black Women's History,* edited by Darlene Clark Hine, Wilma King, and Linda Reed. Brooklyn: Carlson Publishing, 1995.

———. *Righteous Discontent: The Women's Movement in the Black Baptist Church, 1880–1920.* Cambridge: Harvard University Press, 1993.

Higonnet, Margaret R. "Civil Wars and Sexual Territories." In *Arms and the Woman: War, Gender, and Literary Representation,* edited by Helen M. Cooper, Adrienne A. Munich, and Susan M. Squier. Chapel Hill: University of North Carolina Press, 1989.

Hill, Mary A. *Charlotte Perkins Gilman: The Making of a Radical Feminist.* Philadelphia: Temple University Press, 1980.

Hill, Robert A., ed. *The Marcus Garvey and Universal Negro Improvement Association Papers.* Vols. 2 and 3. Berkeley: University of California Press, 1983–84.

Hixson, William B., Jr. "Moorfield Storey and the Struggle for Equality." In *American Law and the Constitutional Order: Historical Perspectives,* edited by Lawrence M. Friedman and Harry N. Scheibler. Cambridge: Harvard University Press, 1978.

Hobsbawn, E. J. "From Social History to the History of Society." In *Historical Studies Today,* edited by Felix Gilbert and Stephen R. Graubard. New York: W. W. Norton, 1972.

Hoff, Joan. *Law, Gender, and Injustice: A Legal History of American Women.* New York: New York University Press, 1991.

Holmes, Oliver Wendell, Jr. *The Mind and Faith of Justice Holmes: His Speeches, Essays, Letters, and Judicial Opinions,* edited by Max Lerner. Boston: Little, Brown, 1943.

——. "The Path of the Law." In *The Mind and Faith of Justice Holmes: His Speeches, Essays, Letters, and Judicial Opinions,* edited by Max Lerner. Boston: Little, Brown, 1943.

——. "The Theory of Legal Interpretation." Quoted in Morton White, *Social Thought in America: The Revolt against Formalism.* Boston: Beacon Press, 1957.

Holub, Robert C. *Reception Theory: A Critical Introduction.* London: Methuen, 1984.

Hoogenboom, Ari, and Olive Hoogenboom. *A History of the ICC: From Panacea to Palliative.* New York: W. W. Norton, 1976.

Hoover, Herbert. *American Individualism.* Garden City: Doubleday, Page and Co., 1922.

——. *The New Day: Campaign Speeches of Herbert Hoover.* Stanford: Stanford University Press, 1928.

Hopkins, Charles Howard. *The Rise of the Social Gospel in American Protestantism, 1865–1915.* New Haven: Yale University Press, 1940.

Hovenkamp, Herbert. *Enterprise and American Law, 1836–1937.* Cambridge: Harvard University Press, 1991.

Howard, Victor B. *Religion and the Radical Republican Movement, 1860–1870.* Lexington: University Press of Kentucky, 1990.

Howe, Daniel Walker. "The Evangelical Movement and Political Culture in the North during the Second Party System." *Journal of American History* 77 (March 1991): 1216–39.

——, ed. *Victorian America.* Philadelphia: University of Pennsylvania Press, 1976.

Hoxie, Frederick E. *A Final Promise: The Campaign to Assimilate the Indians, 1880–1920.* Lincoln: University of Nebraska Press, 1984.

Huggins, Nathan I. *Harlem Renaissance.* New York: Oxford University Press, 1973.

Hummer, Patricia M. *The Decade of Elusive Promise: Professional Women in the United States, 1920–1930.* Ann Arbor: UMI Research Press, 1979.

Hutchinson, Earl Ofari. *Blacks and Reds: Race and Class in Conflict, 1919–1940.* East Lansing: Michigan State University Press, 1995.

Hutchinson, George. *The Harlem Renaissance in Black and White.* Cambridge: Harvard University Press, 1995.

Hyman, Harold M., ed. *Radical Republicans and Reconstruction, 1861–1870.* Indianapolis: Bobbs-Merrill, 1967.

James, Scott C. "A Party System Perspective on the Interstate Commerce Act of 1887: The Democracy, Electoral College Competition, and the Politics of Coalition Maintenance." *Studies in American Political Development* 6 (Spring 1992): 163–200.

Jaynes, Gerald David. *Branches without Roots: Genesis of the Black Working Class in the American South, 1862–1882.* New York: Oxford University Press, 1986.

Jelinek, Estelle C. *The Tradition of Women's Autobiography: From Antiquity to the Present.* Boston: Twayne Publishers, 1986.

Jenkins, William D. *Steel Valley Klan: The Ku Klux Klan in Ohio's Mahoning Valley.* Kent: Kent State University Press, 1990.

Jenks, George M. "Franklin Benjamin Gowen." In *Encyclopedia of American Business History and Biography: Railroads in the Nineteenth Century,* edited by Robert L. Frey. New York: Facts on File, 1988.

Johnson, Andrew. *The Papers of Andrew Johnson.* Vols. 4 and 6. Edited by Leroy P. Graf and Ralph W. Haskins. Knoxville: University of Tennessee Press, 1976 and 1983.

Johnson, Guion Griffis. "The Ideology of White Supremacy." In *The South and the Sectional Image,* edited by Dewey W. Grantham Jr. New York: Harper and Row, 1967.

Jones, Beverly Washington. *Quest for Equality: The Life and Writings of Mary Eliza Church Terrell, 1863–1954.* Brooklyn: Carlson Publishing, 1990.

Jones, Jacqueline. "Encounters, Likely and Unlikely, between Black and Poor White Women in the Rural South, 1865–1940." *Georgia Historical Review* 76 (Summer 1992): 333–53.

———. *Labor of Love, Labor of Sorrow: Black Women, Work, and the Family from Slavery to the Present.* New York: Basic Books, 1985.

Jordan, Winthrop D. *White over Black: American Attitudes toward the Negro, 1550–1812.* New York: W. W. Norton, 1977.

Kaczorowski, Robert J. "To Begin the Nation Anew: Congress, Citizenship, and Civil Rights after the Civil War." *American Historical Review* 92 (February 1987): 45–68.

Kammen, Michael. *A Machine That Would Go of Itself: The Constitution in American Culture.* New York: Alfred A. Knopf, 1986.

———. *Sovereignty and Liberty: Constitutional Discourse in American Culture.* Madison: University of Wisconsin Press, 1988.

———. *Spheres of Liberty: Changing Perceptions of Liberty in American Culture.* Madison: University of Wisconsin Press, 1988.

Katz, Stanley N. "The Strange Birth and Unlikely History of Constitutional Equality." *Journal of American History* 75 (December 1988): 747–62.

Katznelson, Ira. *City Trenches: Urban Politics and the Patterns of Class in the United States.* New York: Pantheon Books, 1981.

Kaufman, Stuart Bruce. *Samuel Gompers and the Origins of the American Federation of Labor, 1848–1896.* Westport: Greenwood Press, 1973.

Kazin, Michael. "The Grass-Roots Right: New Histories of U.S. Conservatism in the Twentieth Century." *American Historical Review* 97 (February 1992): 136–55.

Kazin, Michael, and Steven J. Ross. "America's Labor Day: The Dilemma of a Workers' Celebration." *Journal of American History* 78 (March 1992): 1294–323.

Keller, Morton. *Affairs of State: Public Life in Late Nineteenth Century America.* Cambridge: Harvard University Press, 1977.

———. "Power and Rights: Two Centuries of American Constitutionalism." *Journal of American History* 74 (December 1987): 675–94.

Kellogg, Charles Flint. *NAACP: A History of the National Association for the Advancement of Colored People.* Vol. 1, *1909–1920.* Baltimore: Johns Hopkins University Press, 1967.

Kenneally, James J. "Women in the United States and Trade Unionism." In *The World of Women's Trade Unionism: Comparative Historical Essays,* edited by Norbert C. Soldon. Westport: Greenwood Press, 1985.

Kennedy, David M. *Over Here: The First World War and American Society.* New York: Oxford University Press, 1980.

Kerber, Linda. "Separate Spheres, Female Worlds, Woman's Place: The Rhetoric of Women's History." *Journal of American History* 75 (June 1988): 9–39.

Kertzer, David I. *Ritual, Politics, and Power.* New Haven: Yale University Press, 1988.

Kesselman, Steven. *The Modernization of American Reform: Structures and Perceptions.* New York: Garland Publishing Co., 1979.

Kessler-Harris, Alice. *Out to Work: The History of Wage-Earning Women in the United States.* New York: Oxford University Press, 1982.

Kimmel, Michael. *Manhood in America: A Cultural History.* New York: Free Press, 1996.

King, Willard L. *Melville Weston Fuller: Chief Justice of the United States, 1888–1910.* Chicago: University of Chicago Press, 1967.

Kirschner, Don S. *The Paradox of Professionalism: Reform and Public Service in Urban America, 1900–1940.* Westport: Greenwood Press, 1986.

Klaw, Spencer. *Without Sin: The Life and Death of the Oneida Community.* New York: Penguin U.S.A., 1993.

Klein, Maury. *The Life and Legend of Jay Gould.* Baltimore: Johns Hopkins University Press, 1986.

Klein, Maury, and Harvey A. Kantor. *Prisoners of Progress: American Industrial Cities, 1850–1920.* New York: Macmillan, 1976.

Koven, Seth, and Sonya Michel, eds. *Mothers of a New World: Maternalist Politics and the Origins of Welfare States.* New York: Routledge, 1993.

Kraditor, Aileen S. *The Ideas of the Woman Suffrage Movement, 1890–1912.* New York: Columbia University Press, 1965.

——. *The Radical Persuasion, 1890–1917: Aspects of the Intellectual History and the Historiography of Three American Radical Organizations.* Baton Rouge: Louisiana State University Press, 1981.

Kramer, Lloyd, Donald Reid, and William L. Barney, eds. *Learning History in America: Schools, Cultures, and Politics.* Minneapolis: University of Minnesota Press, 1994.

Kugler, Israel. *From Ladies to Women: The Organized Struggle for Women's Rights in the Reconstruction Era.* Westport: Greenwood Press, 1987.

Kull, Andrew. *The Color-Blind Constitution.* Cambridge: Harvard University Press, 1992.

LaCapra, Dominick. *History and Criticism.* Ithaca: Cornell University Press, 1985.

Ladd-Taylor, Molly. " 'My Work Came Out of Agony and Grief': Mothers and the Making of the Sheppard-Towner Act." In *Mothers of a New World: Maternalist Politics and the Origins of Welfare States,* edited by Seth Koven and Sonya Michel. New York: Routledge, 1993.

La Follette, Robert M. Campaign Speech, *New York Times,* 7 October 1924. Reprinted in *La Follette,* edited by Robert S. Maxwell. Englewood Cliffs: Prentice Hall, 1969.

Lamoreaux, Naomi R. *The Great Merger Movement in American Business, 1895–1904.* London: Cambridge University Press, 1985.

Lamson, Peggy. *Roger Baldwin: Founder of the American Civil Liberties Union.* Boston: Houghton Mifflin, 1976.

Lasch-Quinn, Elisabeth. *Black Neighbors: Race and the Limits of Reform in the American Settlement House Movement, 1890–1945.* Chapel Hill: University of North Carolina Press, 1993.

Lasser, Carol, and Marlene Deahl Merrill, eds. *Friends and Sisters: Letters between Lucy Stone and Antoinette Brown Blackwell, 1846–1893.* Urbana: University of Illinois Press, 1987.

Laurie, Bruce, and Mark Schmitz. "Manufacturing and Productivity: The Making of an Industrial Base." In *Philadelphia: Work, Space, Family, and Group Experience in the Nineteenth Century: Essays toward an Interdisciplinary History of the City,* edited by Theodore Hershberg. New York: Oxford University Press, 1981.

Lawson, Steven F. "Freedom Then, Freedom Now: The Historiography of the Civil Rights Movement." *American Historical Review* 96 (April 1991): 456–71.

Leach, William. *True Love and Perfect Union: The Feminist Reform of Sex and Society.* New York: Basic Books, 1980.

Lears, T. J. Jackson. "The Concept of Cultural Hegemony: Problems and Possibilities." *American Historical Review* 90 (June 1985): 567–93.

——. *No Place of Grace: Antimodernism and the Transformation of American Culture, 1880–1920.* New York: Pantheon Books, 1981.

Leffler, Melvin P. "Herbert Hoover, the 'New Era,' and American Foreign Policy, 1921–29." In *Herbert Hoover as Secretary of Commerce: Studies in New Era Thought and Practice,* edited by Ellis W. Hawley. Iowa City: University of Iowa Press, 1981.

Lemons, J. Stanley. *The Woman Citizen: Social Feminism in the 1920s.* Urbana: University of Illinois Press, 1973.

Lentricchia, Frank. "En Route to Retreat: Making It to Mepkin Abbey." *Harper's,* January 1992, 68–78.

Lenz, Günter H. "Symbolic Space, Communal Rituals, and the Surreality of the Urban Ghetto: Harlem in Black Literature from the 1920s to the 1960s." *Callaloo: Journal of Afro-American and African Arts and Letters* 11 (Spring 1988): 309–45.

Lerner, Gerda. *Black Women in White America: A Documentary History.* New York: Pantheon Books, 1972.

Letwin, William. *Law and Economic Policy in America: The Evolution of the Sherwin Antitrust Act.* Chicago: University of Chicago Press, 1965.

Levine, Susan. "The Transformation of a Laboring Community: Mechanization and Mobilization of Women Weavers." In *Women, Families, and Communities: Readings in American History.* Vol. 2, edited by Nancy A. Hewitt. Glenview: Scott, Foresman/Little Brown Higher Education, 1990.

Lewis, David Levering. *W. E. B. Du Bois: Biography of a Race, 1868–1919.* New York: Henry Holt, 1993.

——. *When Harlem Was in Vogue.* New York: Alfred A. Knopf, 1981.

"The Liberty above All Others." *Nation,* 4 July 1923, 4.

"Liberty after the War." *Independent,* 21 September 1918, 374–75.

Licht, Walter. *Working for the Railroad: The Organization of Work in the Nineteenth Century.* Princeton: Princeton University Press, 1983.

Lincoln, Abraham. *The Collected Works of Abraham Lincoln.* Edited by Roy P. Basler. New Brunswick: Rutgers University Press, 1953.

Linden, Glen M. " 'Radicals' and Economic Policies: The Senate, 1861–1873." *Journal of Southern History* 32 (1977): 189–99.

Lindgren, H. Elaine. *Land in Her Own Name: Women as Homesteaders in North Dakota.* Fargo: North Dakota Institute for Regional Studies, 1991.

Lindsey, Donald F. *Indians at Hampton Institute, 1877–1923*. Urbana: University of Illinois, 1995.

Link, Arthur S. *Wilson: The New Freedom*. Princeton: Princeton University Press, 1956.

Lippmann, Walter. "The Basic Problem of Democracy: Part 1. What Modern Liberty Means." *Atlantic*, November 1919, 616–67.

——. *Liberty and the News*. New York: Harcourt, Brace and Howe, 1920.

——. *The Phantom Public*. New York: Macmillan, 1927.

Lisio, Donald J. *Hoover, Blacks, and Lily Whites: A Study of Southern Strategies*. Chapel Hill: University of North Carolina Press, 1985.

Livingston, James. "The Social Analysis of Economic History and Theory: Conjectures on Late Nineteenth-Century American Development." *American Historical Review* 92 (February 1987): 69–95.

Lofgren, Charles A. "Interpreting the Fourteenth Amendment: Approaches in *Slaughter-House* and *Plessy*." In *Bench Marks: Great Constitutional Controversies in the Supreme Court*, edited by Terry Eastland. Washington, D.C.: Ethics and Public Policy Center, 1995.

——. *The Plessy Case: A Legal-Historical Interpretation*. New York: Oxford University Press, 1987.

Logan, Rayford W. *The Betrayal of the Negro: From Rutherford B. Hayes to Woodrow Wilson*. New enl. ed. London: Collier-Macmillan, 1965.

Lunardini, Christine A. *From Equal Suffrage to Equal Rights: Alice Paul and the National Woman's Party, 1910–1928*. New York: New York University Press, 1986.

Lustig, R. Jeffrey. *Corporate Liberalism: The Origins of Modern Political Theory, 1890–1920*. Berkeley: University of California Press, 1982.

Lystra, Karen. *Searching the Heart: Women, Men, and Romantic Love in Nineteenth Century America*. New York: Oxford University Press, 1989.

Mabee, Carleton, with Susan Mabee Newhouse. *Sojourner Truth: Slave, Prophet, Legend*. New York: New York University Press, 1993.

Macedo, Stephen. *Liberal Virtues: Citizenship, Virtue, and Community in Liberal Constitutionalism*. Oxford: Clarendon Press, 1990.

Marilley, Suzanne M. "Frances Willard and the Feminism of Fear." *Feminist Studies* 19 (Spring 1993): 123–46.

Marsh, Margaret S. *Anarchist Women, 1870–1920*. Philadelphia: Temple University Press, 1981.

Martin, Theodora Penny. *The Sound of Our Own Voices: Women's Study Clubs, 1860–1910*. Boston: Beacon Press, 1987.

Marwick, Arthur. *Britain in the Century of Total War: War, Peace, and Social Change, 1900–1967*. Boston: Little, Brown, 1968.

Marx, Fritz Morstein. *The Administrative State: An Introduction to Bureaucracy*. Chicago: University of Chicago Press, 1957.

Mathes, Valerie Sherer. "Helen Hunt Jackson as Power Broker." In *Between Indian and White Worlds: The Cultural Broker*, edited by Margaret Connell Szasz. Norman: University of Oklahoma Press, 1994.

Mathews, Mark D. " 'Our Women and What They Think,' Amy Jacques Garvey and *The Negro World*." In *Black Women in American History: The Twentieth Century*. Vol. 3, edited by Darlene Clark Hine. Brooklyn: Carlson Publishing, 1990.

Mayo, Edith. Introduction to *How I Learned to Ride the Bicycle: Reflections of an Influential 19th Century Woman,* by Frances B. Willard. Sunnyvale, Calif.: Fair Oaks Publishing, 1991.

McClain, Charles J. *In Search of Equality: The Chinese Struggle against Discrimination in Nineteenth-Century America.* Berkeley: University of California Press, 1994.

McCormick, Richard L. "The Discovery That Business Corrupts Politics: A Reappraisal of the Origins of Progressivism." *American Historical Review* 86 (April 1981): 247–74.

McCoy, Donald R. *Calvin Coolidge: The Quiet President.* Rev. ed. Lawrence: University Press of Kansas, 1988.

McCraw, Thomas K. *Prophets of Regulation: Charles Francis Adams, Louis D. Brandeis, James M. Landis, Alfred E. Kahn.* Cambridge: Harvard University Press, 1984.

——. "Rethinking the Trust Question." In *Regulation in Perspective: Historical Essays,* edited by Thomas K. McCraw. Cambridge: Harvard University Press, 1981.

McCurdy, Charles W. "Legal Institutions, Constitutional Theory, and the Tragedy of Reconstruction." *Reviews in American History* 4 (June 1976): 203–11.

McDonnell, Janet A. *The Dispossession of the American Indian, 1887–1934.* Bloomington: Indiana University Press, 1991.

McFeely, William S. *Frederick Douglass.* New York: W. W. Norton, 1991.

McGerr, Michael. "Political Style and Women's Power, 1830–1930." *Journal of American History* 77 (December 1990): 864–85.

——. *The Decline of Popular Politics: The American North, 1865–1928.* New York: Oxford University Press, 1986.

McKitrick, Eric. *Andrew Johnson and Reconstruction.* Chicago: University of Chicago Press, 1960.

McLeod, David I. *Building Character in the American Boy: The Boy Scouts, YMCA, and Their Forerunners, 1870–1920.* Madison: University of Wisconsin Press, 1983.

McPherson, James M. *Abraham Lincoln and the Second American Revolution.* New York: Oxford University Press, 1990.

McWilliams, Wilson Carey. *The Idea of Fraternity in America.* Berkeley: University of California Press, 1973.

Megill, Alan. "Recounting the Past: 'Description,' Explanation, and Narrative in Historiography." *American Historical Review* 94 (June 1989): 627–53.

Meier, August. *Negro Thought in America, 1880–1915.* Ann Arbor: University of Michigan Press, 1963.

Merton, Robert K. *Social Theory and Social Structure.* Glencoe: Free Press, 1957.

Meyerowitz, Joanne J. *Women Adrift: Independent Wage Earners in Chicago, 1880–1930.* Chicago: University of Chicago Press, 1988.

Miller, George H. *Railroads and the Granger Laws.* Madison: University of Wisconsin Press, 1971.

Miller, James A., and Donald Yacovone. "Birth of a Nation." In *Encyclopedia of African-American Culture and History.* Vol. 1, edited by Jack Salzman, et al. New York: Simon and Schuster Macmillan, 1996.

Mink, Gwendolyn. *Old Labor and New Immigrants in American Political Development: Union, Party, and State, 1875–1920.* Ithaca: Cornell University Press, 1986.

Mitchell, Theodore R. *Political Education in the Southern Farmers' Alliance, 1887–1900.* Madison: University of Wisconsin Press, 1987.

Monroe, James A. *Democratic Wish: Popular Participation and the Limits of American Government.* New York: Basic Books, 1990.

Montgomery, David. *Beyond Equality: Labor and Radical Republicans, 1862–1872.* New York: Viking Books, 1967.

——. *The Fall of the House of Labor: The Workplace, the State, and American Labor Activism, 1865–1925.* New York: Cambridge University Press, 1987.

——. *Workers' Control in America: Studies in the History of Work, Technology, and Labor Struggles.* Cambridge: Cambridge University Press, 1979.

Moody, J. Carrol, and Alice Kessler-Harris, eds. *Perspectives on American Labor History: The Problems of Synthesis.* DeKalb: Northern Illinois University Press, 1990.

Moore, Jesse Thomas, Jr. *A Search for Equality: The National Urban League, 1910–1961.* University Park: Pennsylvania State University Press, 1981.

Moore, Leonard J. *Citizen Klansmen: The Ku Klux Klan in Indiana, 1921–1928.* Chapel Hill: University of North Carolina Press, 1991.

Morawetz, Victor. *A Treatise on the Law of Private Corporations Other than Charitable.* Boston: Little, Brown, 1882.

Morgan, Robin, ed. *Sisterhood Is Powerful: An Anthology of Writings from the Women's Liberation Movement.* New York: Vintage Books, 1970.

Morris, Aldon D. *The Origins of the Civil Rights Movement: Black Communities Organizing for Change.* New York: Free Press, 1984. Quoted in Kristen Bumiller, *The Civil Rights Society* (Baltimore: Johns Hopkins University Press), 56.

Morton, Marian J. *Emma Goldman and the American Left: "Nowhere at Home."* New York: Twayne Publishers, 1992.

Moses, L. G. "Interpreting the Wild West, 1883–1914." In *Between Indian and White Worlds: The Cultural Broker,* edited by Margaret Connell Szasz. Norman: University of Oklahoma Press, 1994.

Moses, Wilson Jeremiah. "Domestic Feminism Conservatism, Sex Roles, and Black Women's Clubs, 1893–1896." In *Black Women in American History: From Colonial Times through the Nineteenth Century.* Vol. 3, edited by Darlene Clark Hine. Brooklyn: Carlson Publishing, 1990.

Moss, Rosalind Urbach. "The 'Girls' from Syracuse: Kansas Women in Politics, 1887–1890." In *Women, Families, and Communities: Readings in American History.* Vol. 2, edited by Nancy A. Hewitt. Glenview: Scott, Foresman/Little Brown Higher Education, 1990.

——. *The Golden Age of Black Nationalism, 1850–1925.* New York: Oxford University Press, 1978.

Mouffe, Chantal. "Preface: Democratic Politics Today." In *Dimensions of Radical Democracy: Pluralism, Citizenship, Community,* edited by Chantal Mouffe. London: Verso, 1992.

Murphy, Paul L. *World War I and the Origin of Civil Liberties in the United States.* New York: W. W. Norton, 1979.

Murray, Robert K. *Red Scare: A Study of National Hysteria, 1919–1920.* 1955. Reprint, New York: McGraw-Hill, 1964.

Mushkat, Jerome. *The Reconstruction of the New York Democracy, 1861–1874.* Rutherford, N.J.: Fairleigh Dickinson University Press, 1981.

Nader, Ralph. *Unsafe at Any Speed: The Designed-In Dangers of the American Automobile.* New York: Grossman Publishers, 1965.

Nash, Gerald D. *The Crucial Era: The Great Depression and World War II, 1929–1945.* 2d ed. New York: St. Martin's Press, 1992.

Nash, Roderick, ed. *The American Environment: Readings in the History of Conservation.* Reading, Mass.: Addison-Wesley Publishing, 1968.

Neale, A. D., and D. G. Goyder. *The Antitrust Laws of the United States: A Study of Competition Enforced by Law.* London: Cambridge University Press, 1980.

Neely, Mark E., Jr. *The Fate of Liberty: Abraham Lincoln and Civil Liberties.* New York: Oxford University Press, 1991.

Nelson, Bruce C. *Beyond the Martyrs: A Social History of Chicago's Anarchists, 1870–1900.* New Brunswick: Rutgers University Press, 1988.

Nelson, Daniel. *Frederick W. Taylor and the Rise of Scientific Management.* Madison: University of Wisconsin Press, 1980.

Nelson, William E. *The Fourteenth Amendment: From Political Principle to Judicial Doctrine.* Cambridge: Harvard University Press, 1988.

———. *The Roots of American Bureaucracy, 1830–1900.* Cambridge: Harvard University Press, 1982.

Netting, Robert McC. *Smallholders, Householders: Farm Families, and the Ecology of Intensive Sustainable Agriculture.* Stanford: Stanford University Press, 1993.

Neverdon-Morton, Cynthia. *Afro-American Women of the South and the Advancement of the Race, 1895–1925.* Knoxville: University of Tennessee Press, 1989.

Newmyer, R. Kent. "Harvard Law School, New England Legal Culture, and the Antebellum Origins of American Jurisprudence." *Journal of American History* 74 (December 1987): 814–35.

Noble, David F. *America by Design: Science, Technology, and the Rise of Corporate Capitalism.* New York: Oxford University Press, 1977.

Nugent, Walter. "The Agelessness of Reform." *Reviews in American History* 15 (June 1987): 185–90.

Oakes, James. *Slavery and Freedom: An Interpretation of the Old South.* New York: Alfred A. Knopf, 1990.

Oates, Joyce Carol. *(Woman) Writer: Occasions and Opportunities.* New York: E. P. Dutton, 1988.

Oberschall, Anthony. *Social Movements: Ideologies, Interests, and Identities.* New Brunswick: Transaction Publishers, 1993.

O'Brien, Michael. *Rethinking the South: Essays in Intellectual History.* Baltimore: Johns Hopkins University Press, 1988.

Oestreicher, Richard. "Urban Working-Class Political Behavior and Theories of American Electoral Politics, 1870–1940." *Journal of American History* 74 (March 1988): 1257–86.

O'Neill, Hugh. Review of *Corporate Liberalism: The Origins of Modern Political Theory, 1890–1920,* by R. Jeffrey Lustig. *Political Science Quarterly* 98 (Winter 1983–84): 732.

Orleck, Annelise. *Common Sense and a Little Fire: Women and Working-Class Politics in the United States, 1900–1965.* Chapel Hill: University of North Carolina Press, 1995.

Osofsky, Gilbert. "Progressivism and the Negro: New York, 1900–1915." *American Quarterly* 16 (Summer 1964): 153–68.

Osterud, Nancy Grey. "Rural Women during the Civil War: New York's Nanticoke Valley, 1861–1865." *New York History* 62 (October 1990): 357–85.

Painter, Neil Irvin. *Standing at Armageddon: The United States, 1877–1919.* New York: W. W. Norton, 1987.

——. "Thinking about the Languages of Money and Race." *American Historical Review* 99 (April 1994): 396–404.

Park, Robert E. "How Lawyers Read the Constitution: An Introductory Bibliography." *American Studies International* 26 (April 1988): 2–34.

Pascoe, Peggy. *Relations of Rescue: The Search for Female Moral Authority in the American West, 1874–1929.* New York: Oxford University Press, 1990.

Paulson, Ross Evans. *Language, Science, and Action: Korzybski's General Semantics—A Study in Comparative Intellectual History.* Westport: Greenwood Press for the Council on Intercultural and Comparative Studies, 1983.

——. *Radicalism and Reform: The Vrooman Family and American Social Thought, 1837–1937.* Lexington: University of Kentucky Press for the Organization of American Historians, 1968.

——. "*Ubi Panis Ibi Patria:* Reflections on American Identity." *Word and World* 8 (Summer 1988): 219–25.

——. *Women's Suffrage and Prohibition: A Comparative Study of Equality and Social Control.* Glenview: Scott, Foresman, 1973.

Perry, Elisabeth Israils. *Belle Moskowitz: Feminine Politics and the Exercise of Power in the Age of Alfred E. Smith.* New York: Oxford University Press, 1987.

Pertschuk, Michael. *Revolt against Revolution: The Rise and Pause of the Consumer Movement.* Berkeley: University of California Press, 1982.

Peterson, Merrill D. *The Jefferson Image in the American Mind.* New York: Oxford University Press, 1960.

Pfeffer, Paula F. *A. Philip Randolph, Pioneer of the Civil Rights Movement.* Baton Rouge: Louisiana State University Press, 1990.

Pickens, William. *Bursting Bonds: The Heir of Slaves and the Autobiography of a "New Negro."* Enlarged ed. Edited by William L. Andrews. Bloomington: Indiana University Press, 1991.

Pisani, Donald T. "Promotion and Regulation: Constitutionalism and the American Economy." *Journal of American History* 74 (December 1987): 740–68.

Porter, Glenn. "Industrialization and the Rise of Big Business." In *The Gilded Age: Essays on the Origins of Modern America,* edited by Charles W. Calhoun. Wilmington, Del.: Scholarly Resources, 1996.

Porter, Mary Cornelia. "Lockner and Company: Revisionism Revisited." In *Liberty, Property, and Government: Constitutional Interpretation before the New Deal,* edited by Ellen Frankel Paul and Howard Dickman. Albany: State University of New York Press, 1989.

Poster, Mark. *Critical Theory and Poststructuralism: In Search of a Context.* Ithaca: Cornell University Press, 1989.

Pringle, Henry F. *Theodore Roosevelt: A Biography.* New York: Harcourt, Brace, 1956.

Prucha, Francis Paul. *Indian Policy in the United States: Historical Essays.* Lincoln: University of Nebraska Press, 1981.

Prude, Johnathon. *The Coming of Industrial Order: Town and Factory Life in Rural Massachusetts, 1810–1860.* Cambridge: Harvard University Press, 1983.

Quant, Jean B. *From the Small Town to the Great Community: The Social Thought of Progressive Intellectuals.* New Brunswick: Rutgers University Press, 1970.

Rafalko, Robert J. "Henry George's Labor Theory of Value: He Saw the Entrepreneurs and Workers as Employers of Capital and Land, and Not the Reverse." *American Journal of Economics and Sociology* 48 (July 1989): 311–20.

"Ralph Nader Becomes an Organization." *Business Week,* 28 November 1970, 86–88.

Rauschenbusch, Walter. *Christianity and the Social Crisis.* New York: Macmillan, 1907.

——. *Christianizing the Social Order.* New York: Macmillan, 1913.

Reader's Guide to Periodical Literature. "Preface." Minneapolis: H. W. Wilson Co., 1905.

Record, Wilson. *Race and Radicalism: The NAACP and the Communist Party in Conflict.* Ithaca: Cornell University Press, 1964.

Reddy, William M. *Money and Liberty in Modern Europe: A Critique of Historical Understanding.* Cambridge: Cambridge University Press, 1987.

Reid, John Phillip. *The Concept of Liberty in the Age of the American Revolution.* Chicago: University of Chicago Press, 1988.

Reynolds, John F. *Testing Democracy: Electoral Behavior and Progressive Reform in New Jersey, 1880–1920.* Chapel Hill: University of North Carolina Press, 1988.

Richards, David A. J. *Conscience and the Constitution: History, Theory, and Law of the Reconstruction Amendments.* Princeton: Princeton University Press, 1993.

——. *Toleration and the Constitution.* New York: Oxford University Press, 1986.

Roark, James L. *Masters without Slaves: Southern Planters in the Civil War and Reconstruction.* New York: W. W. Norton, 1977.

Roberts, Richara. "The Restoration of Civil Liberty." *Survey,* 15 November 1919, 109–10.

Rodgers, Daniel T. *Contested Truths: Keywords in American Politics since Independence.* New York: Basic Books, 1987.

——. "In Search of Progressivism." *Reviews in American History* 10 (December 1982): 113–32.

——. "Republicanism: The Career of a Concept." *Journal of American History* 79 (June 1992): 11–38.

Rogers, Kim Lacy. "Oral History and the History of the Civil Rights Movement." *Journal of American History* 75 (September 1988): 567–76.

Romasco, Albert U. *The Poverty of Abundance: Hoover, the Nation, the Depression.* New York: Oxford University Press, 1965.

Roosevelt, Theodore. *The Writings of Theodore Roosevelt,* edited by William H. Harbaugh. Indianapolis: Bobbs-Merrill, 1967.

Rosenberg, Rosalind. *Beyond Separate Spheres: Intellectual Roots of Modern Feminism.* New Haven: Yale University Press, 1982.

——. *Divided Lives: American Women in the Twentieth Century.* New York: Hill and Wang, 1992.

Rosenstone, Steven J., Roy L. Behr, and Edward H. Lazarus. *Third Parties in America:*

Citizen Response to Major Party Failure. Princeton: Princeton University Press, 1984.

Rosenzweig, Roy. *Eight Hours for What We Will: Workers and Leisure in an Industrial City, 1870–1920.* Cambridge: Cambridge University Press, 1983.

Roske, Ralph J. *His Own Counsel: The Life and Times of Lyman Trumbull.* Reno: University of Nevada Press, 1979.

Ross, Ishbel. *Silhouette in Diamonds: The Life of Mrs. Potter Palmer.* New York: Harper and Row, 1960.

Rouse, Jacqueline A. "Atlanta's African-American Women's Attack on Segregation, 1900–1920." In *Gender, Class, Race, and Reform in the Progressive Era,* edited by Noralee Frankel and Nancy S. Dye. Lexington: University Press of Kentucky, 1991.

——. *Lugenia Burns Hope: Black Southern Reformer.* Athens: University of Georgia Press, 1989.

Rumer, Thomas A. *The American Legion: An Official History, 1919–1989.* New York: M. Evans and Co., 1990.

Salem, Dorothy. *To Better Our World: Black Women in Organized Reform, 1890–1920.* Brooklyn: Carlson Publishing, 1990.

Salvatore, Nick. *Eugene V. Debs: Citizen and Socialist.* Urbana: University of Illinois Press, 1982.

Salyer, Lucy. "Captives of Law: Judicial Enforcement of the Chinese Exclusion Laws, 1891–1905." *Journal of American History* 76 (June 1989): 91–117.

Saxton, Alexander. *The Rise and Fall of the White Republic: Class Politics and Mass Culture in Nineteenth-Century America.* New York: Verso Books, 1990.

Schlesinger, Arthur M., Jr. *The Crisis of Confidence: Ideas, Power and Violence in America.* New York: Bantham Books, 1969.

——. *The Cycles of American History.* Boston: Houghton Mifflin, 1986.

——. *The Vital Center: The Politics of Freedom.* Boston: Houghton Mifflin, 1949.

Schneir, Miriam. *Feminism: The Essential Historical Writings.* New York: Vintage Books, 1972.

Schultz, April. "The Pride of the Race Has Been Touched: The 1925 Norse-American Immigration Centennial and Ethnic Identity." *Journal of American History* 77 (March 1990): 1265–95.

Schweninger, Loren. "Prosperous Blacks in the South, 1790–1880." *American Historical Review* 95 (February 1990): 31–56.

Scott, Anne Firor. *Natural Allies: Women's Associations in American History.* Urbana: University of Illinois Press, 1991.

——. *The Southern Lady: From Pedestal to Politics, 1830–1930.* Chicago: University of Chicago Press, 1970.

Scranton, Phillip. "Build a Firm, Start Another: The Bromleys and Family Firm Entrepreneurship in the Philadelphia Region." *Business History* 34 (October 1993): 115–51.

——. "Diversity in Diversity: Flexible Production and American Industrialization, 1880–1930." *Business History Review* 65 (Spring 1991): 27–90.

——. *Figured Tapestry: Production, Markets, and Power in Philadelphia Textiles, 1885–1941.* Cambridge: Cambridge University Press, 1989.

——. "Small Business, Family Firms, and Batch Production: Three Axes for Development in American Business History." *Business and Economic History,* 2d ser., 20 (1991): 99–106.

Seammon, Richard M., and Alice V. McGillivray, eds. *America at the Polls: A Handbook of American Presidential Election Statistics, 1968–1984.* Washington, D.C.: Elections Research Center, 1988.

Seavoy, Ronald E. "Portraits of Twentieth-Century American Peasants: Subsistence Social Values Recorded in *All God's Dangers* and *Let Us Now Praise Famous Men."* *Agricultural History* 68 (Spring 1994): 199–218.

Segal, Howard P. *Technological Utopianism in American Culture.* Chicago: University of Chicago Press, 1985.

Semonche, John E. *Charting the Future: The Supreme Court Responds to a Changing Society, 1890–1920.* Westport: Greenwood Press, 1978.

Shain, Barry Alan. *The Myth of American Individualism: The Protestant Origins of American Political Thought.* Princeton: Princeton University Press, 1994.

Silbey, Joel. *A Respectable Minority: The Democratic Party in the Civil War Era, 1860–1868.* New York: W. W. Norton, 1977.

Sinclair, Upton. "Protecting Our Liberties." *Nation,* 4 July 1923, 9–10.

Sklar, Kathryn Kish. *Florence Kelley and the Nation's Work: The Rise of Women's Political Culture, 1830–1900.* New Haven: Yale University Press, 1995.

——. "The Historical Foundations of Women's Power in the Creation of the American Welfare State, 1830–1930." In *Mothers of a New World: Maternalist Politics and the Origins of Welfare States,* edited by Seth Koven and Sonya Michel. New York: Routledge, 1993.

——. "Hull House in the 1890s: A Community of Women Reformers." In *Women, Families, and Communities: Readings in American History.* Vol. 2, edited by Nancy A. Hewitt. Glenview: Scott, Foresman/Little Brown Higher Education, 1989.

——. "Why Were Most Politically Active Women Opposed to the ERA in the 1920s?" In *Women and Power in American History: A Reader,* edited by Kathryn Kish Sklar and Thomas Dublin. Englewood Cliffs: Prentice Hall, 1991.

Sklar, Martin J. *The Corporate Reconstruction of American Capitalism, 1890–1916: The Market, the Law, and Politics.* New York: Cambridge University Press, 1988.

Skocpol, Theda. "Bringing the State Back In: Strategies of Analysis in Recent Research." In *Bringing the State Back In,* edited by Peter Evans, Dietrich Rueschemeyer, and Theda Skocpol. Cambridge: Cambridge University Press, 1985.

——. *Protecting Soldiers and Mothers: The Political Origins of Social Policy in the United States.* Cambridge: Harvard University Press, 1992.

Skowronek, Stephen. *Building a New American State: The Expansion of National Administrative Capacities, 1877–1920.* Cambridge: Cambridge University Press, 1982.

——. Review of *Corporate Liberalism: The Origins of Modern Political Theory, 1890–1920,* by R. Jeffrey Lustig. *American Historical Review* 88 (October 1988): 1083.

Slayton, Robert A. *Back of the Yards: The Making of a Local Democracy.* Chicago: University of Chicago Press, 1986.

Smith-Rosenberg, Carol. *Disorderly Conduct: Visions of Gender in Victorian America.* New York: Alfred A. Knopf, 1985.

Spann, Edward K. *Brotherly Tomorrows: Movements for a Cooperative Society in America, 1820–1920.* New York: Columbia University Press, 1989.

Stanley, Amy Dru. "Conjugal Bonds and Wage Labor: Rights of Contract in the Age of Emancipation." *Journal of American History* 75 (September 1988): 471–500.

Stanton, Elizabeth Cady. "The Solitude of Self." In *The American Intellectual Tradition: A Sourcebook.* Vol. 2, *1865 to the Present,* edited by David A. Hollinger and Charles Capper. New York: Oxford University Press, 1993.

Stearn, Gerald Emanuel, ed. *Gompers.* Englewood Cliffs: Prentice-Hall, 1971.

Stephens, Judith L. "Anti-Lynch Plays by African American Women: Race, Gender, and Social Protest in America." *African American Review* 26 (Summer 1992): 329–39.

Sterling, Dorothy, ed. *We Are Your Sisters: Black Women in the Nineteenth Century.* New York: W. W. Norton, 1984.

Stevenson, Louise L. "Women's Intellectual History: A New Direction." *Intellectual History Newsletter* 15 (1993): 32–38.

———. *The Victorian Homefront: American Thought and Culture, 1860–1880.* New York: Twayne Publishers, 1991.

Stock, Brian. *Listening for the Text: On the Uses of the Past.* Baltimore: Johns Hopkins University Press, 1990.

Stone, Lucy. Letter to Antoinette Brown, 11 July 1855. In *Friends and Sisters: Letters between Lucy Stone and Antoinette Brown Blackwell, 1846–1893,* edited by Carol Lasser and Marlene Deahl Merrill. Urbana: University of Illinois Press, 1987.

———. Remarks to 1855 National Woman's Rights Convention. In *Loving Warriors: Selected Letters of Lucy Stone and Henry B. Blackwell, 1853 to 1893,* edited by Leslie Wheeler. New York: Dial Press, 1981.

Stromquist, Shelton. *A Generation of Boomers: The Pattern of Railroad Labor Conflict in Nineteenth-Century America.* Urbana: University of Illinois, 1987.

Summers, Mark Wahlgren. *The Press Gang: Newspapers and Politics, 1865–1878.* Chapel Hill: University of North Carolina Press, 1994.

———. Review of *Alternative Tracks: The Constitution of American Industrial Order, 1865–1917,* by Gerald Berk. *American Historical Review* 100 (October 1995): 1307–8.

Sumner, William Graham. *On Liberty, Society, and Politics: The Essential Essays of William Graham Sumner,* edited by Robert C. Bannister. Indianapolis: Liberty Fund, 1992.

Swidler, Ann. "Culture in Action: Symbols and Strategies." *American Sociological Review* 51 (April 1986): 273–86.

Tachau, Mary K. Bonsteel. "Women, the South, and the Constitution." In *An Uncertain Tradition: Constitutionalism and the History of the South,* edited by Kermit L. Hall and James W. Ely Jr. Athens: University of Georgia Press, 1989.

Taft, William Howard. "Is Prohibition a Blow at Personal Liberty?" *Ladies Home Journal,* 31 May 1919.

Takaki, Ronald. *Iron Cages: Race and Culture in Nineteenth Century America.* New York: Oxford University Press, 1990.

———. *Strangers from A Different Shore: A History of Asian Americans.* New York: Penguin Books U.S.A., 1989.

Tambiah, Stanley J. *Culture, Thought, and Social Action: An Anthropological Perspective.* Cambridge: Harvard University Press, 1985.

Taylor, Frederick Winslow. *The Principles of Scientific Movement*. 1911. Reprint, New York: W. W. Norton, 1967.

Terborg-Penn, Rosalyn. "Discontented Black Feminists: Prelude and Postscript to the Passage of the Nineteenth Amendment." In *We Specialize in the Wholly Impossible: A Reader in Black Women's History*, edited by Darlene Clark Hine, Wilma King, and Linda Reed. Brooklyn: Carlson Publishing, 1995.

——. "Discontented Black Feminists: Prelude and Postscript to the Passage of the Nineteenth Amendment." In *Women and Power in American History: A Reader*, edited by Kathryn Kish Sklar and Thomas Dublin. Englewood Cliffs: Prentice Hall, 1991.

Terrell, Mary Church. "The Duty of the National Association of Colored Women to the Race." Reprinted in *Quest for Equality: The Life and Writings of Mary Eliza Church Terrell, 1863–1954*, edited by Beverly Washington Jones. Brooklyn: Carlson Publishing, 1990.

Thelan, David P. *The New Citizenship: Origins of Progressivism in Wisconsin, 1885–1900*. Columbia: University of Missouri Press, 1972.

——. *Paths of Resistance: Tradition and Dignity in Industrializing Missouri*. New York: Oxford University Press, 1986.

——. *Robert M. La Follette and the Insurgent Spirit*. Boston: Little, Brown, 1976.

Thomas, John L. *Alternative America: Henry George, Edward Bellamy, Henry Demarest Lloyd, and the Adversary Tradition*. Cambridge: Harvard University Press, 1983.

Thompson, John A. *Reformers and War: American Progressive Publicists and the First World War*. Cambridge: Cambridge University Press, 1987.

Thompson, Mildred I. *Ida B. Wells-Barnett: An Exploratory Study of an American Black Woman, 1893–1930*. Brooklyn: Carlson Publishing, 1990.

Thornbrough, Emma Lou. *T. Thomas Fortune: Militant Journalist*. Chicago: University of Chicago Press, 1972.

Tolbert, Emory J. *The U.N.I.A. and Black Los Angeles: Ideology and Community in the American Garvey Movement*. Los Angeles: University of California, 1980.

Trefausee, Hans. *Andrew Johnson: A Biography*. New York: W. W. Norton, 1989.

Trotter, Joe William, Jr. *Black Milwaukee: The Making of an Industrial Proletariat, 1915–1945*. Urbana: University of Illinois Press, 1985.

Trumball, Lymon. "On Civil Rights." *Congressional Globe*, 39th Cong., 1st sess, 1866, pt. 1: 498.

Truth, Sojourner. "Keeping the Thing Going While Things Are Stirring." In *Feminism: The Essential Historical Writings*, edited by Miriam Schneir. New York: Vintage Books, 1972.

——. *Narrative of Sojourner Truth*. Edited and introduction by Margaret Washington. New York: Vintage Classics, 1993.

Turbin, Carole. "And We Are Nothing But Women: Irish Working Women of Troy." In *Women and Power in American History: A Reader*. Vol. 2, edited by Kathryn Kish Sklar and Thomas Dublin. Englewood Cliffs: Prentice Hall, 1991.

Turner, Bryan S., ed. *Citizenship and Social Theory*. London: Sage Publications, 1993.

Turner, Victor W. *Dramas, Fields, and Metaphors: Symbolic Action in Human Society*. Ithaca: Cornell University Press, 1974.

Turner, Victor W., and Edward M. Bruner, eds. *The Anthropology of Experience*. Urbana: University of Illinois Press, 1986.

Tushnet, Mark. "The Politics of Equality in Constitutional Law: Equal Protection Clause, Dr. Du Bois, and Charles Hamilton Houston." *Journal of American History* 74 (December 1987): 884–903.

Unger, Irwin. *The Greenback Era: A Social and Political History of American Finance, 1865–1879.* Princeton: Princeton University Press, 1964.

Urofsky, Melvin I. *Louis D. Brandeis and the Progressive Tradition.* Boston: Little, Brown, 1981.

Vandenberg-Davis, Jodi. "The Manly Pursuit of a Partnership between the Sexes: The Debate over YMCA Programs for Women and Girls, 1914–1933." *Journal of American History* 78 (March 1992): 1324–46.

Vanneman, Reeve, and Lynn Weber Cannon. *The American Perception of Class.* Philadelphia: Temple University Press, 1987.

Van Voris, Jacqueline. *Carrie Chapman Catt: A Public Life.* New York: Feminist Press at the City University of New York, 1987.

Veblen, Thorstein. *The Theory of Business Enterprise.* New York: Charles Scribner's Sons, 1904.

Veysey, Laurence, ed. *The Perfectionists: Radical Social Thought in the North, 1815–1860.* New York: John Wiley, 1973.

Villard, Oswald Garrison. "New Fight for Old Liberties." *Harper's,* September 1925, 440–47.

Vinovskis, Maris A. "Have Social Historians Lost the Civil War? Some Preliminary Demographic Speculations." *Journal of American History* 76 (June 1989): 34–58.

Voss, Kim. *The Making of American Exceptionalism: The Knights of Labor and Class Formation in the Nineteenth Century.* Ithaca: Cornell University Press, 1993.

Wade, Louise Carroll. *Chicago's Pride: The Stockyards, Packingtown, and Environs in the Nineteenth Century.* Urbana: University of Illinois Press, 1987.

Wade, Wyn Craig. *The Fiery Cross: The Ku Klux Klan in America.* New York: Simon and Schuster, 1987.

Walker, Robert H. *Reform in America: The Continuing Frontier.* Lexington: University Press of Kentucky, 1985.

——. *The Reform Spirit in America: A Documentation of the Pattern of Reform in the American Republic.* New York: G. P. Putnam's Sons, 1976.

Walker, Samuel. *In Defense of American Liberties: A History of the ACLU.* New York: Oxford University Press, 1990.

Wall, Cheryl A. *Women of the Harlem Renaissance.* Bloomington: Indiana University Press, 1995.

Ware, Cellestine. *Woman Power: The Movement for Women's Liberation.* New York: Tower Publications, 1970.

Washington, Booker T. *The Booker T. Washington Papers.* Vols. 3 and 4. Edited by Louis R. Harlan. Urbana: University of Illinois Press, 1974–75.

Washington, Margaret Murray. Letter to Ednah Cheney, 23 November 1896. In *The Booker T. Washington Papers,* edited by Louis R. Harlan, 4:237–38. Urbana: University of Illinois Press, 1975.

Weatherford, Doris. *Foreign and Female: Immigrant Women in America, 1840–1930.* New York: Schocken Books, 1986.

Weber, Donald. "From Limen to Border: A Meditation on the Legacy of Victor Turner for American Cultural Studies." *American Quarterly* 47 (September 1995): 525–36.

Weber, Joe, and Lou Fields. "Trust Scene." Columbia Gramophone Company, 1908. Record number A 1855.

Webking, Robert H. *The American Revolution and the Politics of Liberty.* Baton Rouge: Louisiana State University Press, 1988.

Webster, Noah. *The Letters of Noah Webster.* Edited by Harry R. Warfel. New York: Library Publishers, 1953.

Weimann, Jeanne Madeline. *The Fair Women.* Chicago: Academy Chicago, 1981.

Weinstein, Fred. *History and Theory: After the Fall.* Chicago: University of Chicago Press, 1990.

Weiss, Nancy J. "The Negro and the New Freedom: Fighting Wilsonian Segregation." *Political Science Quarterly* 84 (March 1969): 61–79.

Welch, Richard E., Jr. *George Frisbie Hoar and the Half-Breed Republicans.* Cambridge: Harvard University Press, 1971.

Welleck, Alex, ed. *The Encyclopedic Dictionary of American Government.* 4th ed. Guilford, Conn.: Duskin Publishing Group, 1991.

West, Richard Samuel. *Satire on Stone: The Political Cartoons of Joseph Keppler.* Urbana: University of Illinois Press, 1988.

Westbrook, Robert B. *John Dewey and American Democracy.* Ithaca: Cornell University Press, 1991.

Wheeler, Leslie, ed. *Loving Warriors: Selected Letters of Lucy Stone and Henry B. Blackwell, 1853 to 1893.* New York: Dial Press, 1981.

Wheeler, Marjorie Spruill. *New Women of the New South: The Leaders of the Woman Suffrage Movement in the Southern States.* New York: Oxford University Press, 1993.

White, Deborah Gray. "The Cost of Club Work, the Price of Black Feminism." In *Visible Women: New Essays on American Activitism,* edited by Nancy A. Hewitt and Suzanne Lebsock. Urbana: University of Illinois Press, 1993.

White, Eugene Nelson. *The Regulation and Reform of the American Banking System, 1900–1929.* Princeton: Princeton University Press, 1983.

White, Morton. *Social Thought in America: The Revolt against Formalism.* Boston: Beacon Press, 1957.

White, Ronald C., Jr., and C. Howard Hopkins. *The Social Gospel: Religion and Reform in Changing America.* Philadelphia: Temple University Press, 1976.

Wiesbrod, Carol. *The Boundaries of Utopia.* New York: Pantheon Books, 1980.

Wilentz, Sean. "The Rise of the American Working Class, 1776–1877." In *Perspectives on American Labor History: The Problems of Synthesis,* edited by J. Carroll Moody and Alice Kessler-Harris. DeKalb: Northern Illinois University Press, 1990.

Willard, Frances E. *Glimpses of Fifty Years: The Autobiography of an American Woman.* Chicago: H. J. Smith for the WCTU, 1889.

——. *How I Learned to Ride The Bicycle: Reflections of an Influential Nineteenth Century Woman,* introduction by Edith Mayo. Sunnyvale, Calif.: Fair Oaks Publishing, 1991.

Williams, Loretta J. *Black Freemasonry and Middle-Class Realities.* Columbia: University of Missouri Press, 1980.

Wilson, Joan Hoff. *Herbert Hoover: Forgotten Progressive*. Boston: Little, Brown, 1975.

Wilson, Robert A., and Bill Hosokawa. *East to America: A History of the Japanese in the United States*. New York: William Morrow, 1980.

Wilson, Woodrow. *The Papers of Woodrow Wilson*. Vols. 44 and 45, edited by Arthur S. Link. Princeton: Princeton University Press, 1983–84.

Witkin, Alexandra. "To Silence a Drum: The Imposition of United States Citizenship on Native Peoples." *Historical Reflections/Reflexions Historiques* 21, no. 2 (1995): 353–83.

Woloch, Nancy. *Women and the American Experience*. New York: Alfred A. Knopf, 1984.

"Woman's Place." *Atlantic*, March 1970, 81–126.

Women: A Journal of Liberation, Spring 1970.

Wood, Gordon S. "Americans and Revolutionaries." Review of *Revolutions: Reflections on American Equality and Foreign Liberations*, by David Brion Davis. *New York Review of Books*, 17 September 1990, 32–35.

Woodward, C. Vann. *The Burden of Southern History*. New York: Vintage Books, 1961.

——. "The Inner Civil War." Review of *Mind and the American Civil War: A Meditation on Lost Causes*, by Lewis P. Simpson, and *The Creation of Confederate Nationalism: Ideology and Identity in the Civil War South*, by Drew Gilpin Faust. *New York Review of Books*, 15 March 1990, 39–41.

——. *Reunion and Reaction*. 2d ed., rev. Garden City: Doubleday Anchor, 1956.

——. "Unfinished Business." Review of *Reconstruction: America's Unfinished Revolution, 1863–1877*, by Eric Foner. *New York Review of Books*, 12 May 1988, 22–27.

Wrege, Charles D., and Ronald G. Greenwood. *Frederick W. Taylor: The Father of Scientific Management: Myth and Reality*. Homewood: Business One Irwin, 1991.

Wright, Elizur. "Suffrage for the Blacks Sound Political Economy." In *Radical Republicans and Reconstruction, 1861–1870*, edited by Harold M. Hyman. Indianapolis: Bobbs-Merrill, 1967.

Wuthnow, Robert. *Meaning and Moral Order: Explorations in Cultural Analysis*. Berkeley: University of California Press, 1987.

Yarbrough, Tinsley E. *Judicial Enigma: The First Justice Harlan*. New York: Oxford University Press, 1995.

Yans-McLaughlin, Virginia, ed. *Immigration Reconsidered: History, Sociology, and Politics*. New York: Oxford University Press, 1990.

Yellowitz, Irwin. "Samuel Gompers: A Half-Century in Labor's Front Rank." *Monthly Labor Review* (July 1989): 27–33.

Young, Louise M. *In the Public Interest: The League of Women Voters, 1920–1970*. Westport: Greenwood Press, 1989.

Zangrando, Robert L. *The NAACP Crusade against Lynching, 1909–1950*. Philadelphia: Temple University Press, 1980.

Zimmerman, Joan G. "The Jurisprudence of Equality: The Women's Minimum Wage, the First Equal Rights Amendment, and *Adkins v. Children's Hospital*, 1905–1923." *Journal of American History* 78 (June 1991): 188–225.

Zunz, Oliver. *Making America Corporate, 1870–1920*. Chicago: University of Chicago Press, 1990.

Index

Ross Evans Paulson is Professor of History Emeritus at Augustana College and author of *Language, Science, and Action: Korzybski's General Semantics; Women's Suffrage and Prohibition;* and *Radicalism and Reform: The Vrooman Family and American Social Thought, 1837–1937.*

Library of Congress Cataloging-in-Publication Data

Paulson, Ross Evans.
Liberty, equality, and justice : civil rights, women's rights, and the regulation of business, 1865–1932 / Ross E. Paulson. p. cm.
Includes bibliographical references and index.
ISBN 0-8223-1982-9 (cloth : alk. paper). — ISBN 0-8223-1991-8 (paper : alk. paper)
1. Civil rights—United States—History. 2. Industrial policy—United States—History. 3. Social values—United States—History. 4. United States—Social conditions—1865–1918. 5. United States—Social conditions—1918–1932. I. Title.
JC599.U5P38 1997
323'.0973'09034—dc21
96-53409 CIP